RESEARCH METHODS FOR BUSINESS:
A Skill-Building Approach

RESEARCH METHODS FOR BUSINESS:
A Skill-Building Approach

SECOND EDITION

UMA SEKARAN
Southern Illinois University at Carbondale

JOHN WILEY & SONS, INC.
New York   Chichester   Brisbane   Toronto   Singapore

Acquisitions Editor	Timothy Kent
Marketing Manager	Carolyn Henderson
Production Manager	Linda Muriello
Interior Design	Laura Ierardi
Cover Design	Laura Nichols
Production Supervisor	Micheline Frederick
Manufacturing Manager	Lorraine Fumoso
Copy Editor	Deborah Herbert
Illustration Coordinator	Sigmund Malinowski

Recognizing the importance of preserving what has been written, it is a policy of John Wiley & Sons, Inc. to have books of enduring value published in the United States printed on acid-free paper, and we exert our best efforts to that end.

Copyright © 1984, 1992, by John Wiley & Sons, Inc.

All rights reserved. Published simultaneously in Canada.

Reproduction or translation of any part of
this work beyond that permitted by Sections
107 and 108 of the 1976 United States Copyright
Act without the permission of the copyright
owner is unlawful. Requests for permission
or further information should be addressed to
the Permissions Department, John Wiley & Sons.

Library of Congress Cataloging in Publication Data:

Sekaran, Uma.
    Research methods for business : a skill-building approach / Uma
Sekaran. — 2nd ed.

        p.   cm.
    Includes bibliographical references and index.

    ISBN 0-471-61889-6
    1. Business—Research—Methodology.   I. Title.
HD30.4.S435   1992
650'.072—dc20   91-38872
                                                            CIP

Printed in the United States of America

10 9 8 7 6 5 4 3 2

To
Saroj, Bob, and Sudha
With Fond Love

PREFACE

The first edition of *Research Methods for Managers: A Skill-Building Approach* was received enthusiastically by students and professors alike, who were pleased that they had a book on the subject that was simple, clear, and practical. The expressed desire of many of the professors was that the second edition of the book should be geared to help *all* business students. In response, this current edition endeavors to offer a framework for conducting research in a systematic manner in all areas of business—management, marketing, accounting, and finance. Theoretical conceptualizations that chart the connections among the various factors operating in any given situation are integral to all business research and so are the basic principles of sampling, data collection, data analysis, and report writing. This revision is aimed at helping students understand the ways in which systematic research can be conducted to describe, explain, and predict phenomena of interest pertaining to various aspects of business.

Though researchers in accounting and finance generally tend to use data that are readily available, many of the researchers in finance, financial accounting, managerial accounting, and auditing draw on behavioral science research knowledge for their investigations. The methodologies used in behavioral accounting research, for instance, would be no different from those discussed in this book. Thus, a wide range of students in business can benefit from what they learn here.

The adopters of the first edition stated that the strength of the book was the clear and forthright manner in which concepts were explained and discussed. I have continued to keep the explanations simple in the current edition as well. I have also added a variety of business examples so that the conduct and application of research in business becomes clear. Further, the current edition includes additional chapters, together with the following, which were not a part of the first edition: (1) appendices expanding on several themes, (2) tables and expert-systems oriented decision models for research design choices, (3) updates on computer-based field data collection, (4) a refresher on statistics, (5) guidelines for oral presentations of research reports, and (6) specimens of research reports addressing different levels of problem solving. The appendices offer guidance in utilizing the facilities available for conducting research (Chapter 2), provide additional information for advanced students at the Master's level (Chapter 5), and also point out sources for some measures in management and marketing (Chapter 6).

The first edition contained eight chapters, which have now been expanded to eleven chapters. A full chapter has now been devoted to discussing the basic research design issues. The original Unit 5 on "Measurement of Variables and Data Collection Methods," has now been split into two separate chapters, one devoted primarily to measurement and the other to data collection (Chapters 6 and 7). A new chapter on statistical terms and tests has also been added to jog students' memory on statistics.

The approach of this edition, as of the first, is to help students to develop practical knowledge and skills to understand and carry out research projects. Toward this end, exercises and projects have been developed. Interpretation of data analysis has been discussed in detail, using actual computer outputs based on a business research project.

This book will be primarily useful for undergraduate and Master's students. It will also serve well as a basic supplement for doctoral students, who can quickly refresh and update their previous knowledge, or catch up on research knowledge easily, if they have had no prior exposure to research methods.

I wish to express my special appreciation to Dr. Larry Peters of Texas Christian University who helped me to tighten up the first edition in terms of preciseness. Several reviewers have helped me immensely with their critical comments and suggestions for improvement. In particular, I would like to acknowledge the inputs of Peter Allan, Pace University; Hubert S. Feild, Auburn University, Alabama; Robert Folger, Tulane University; William King, Fort Hays State University; K. Galen Kroeck, Florida International University; Meryl Louis, Boston University; James Nolan, Siena College; Richard Nordstrom, California State University, Fresno; Pamela S. Schindler, Wittenberg University; and Robert Siedman, New Hampshire College. I am also grateful to my colleague, Dr. Suresh Tadisina, who has been very helpful in clarifying certain statistical issues.

The search for updates on microcomputer technology for data collection and data analysis was undertaken by two of our then doctoral students, Ms. Bee Yew and Ms. Sandra Jeanquart. My heartfelt thanks to them both. Ms. Joy Peluchette,* then a doctoral candidate in the Management Department at SIUC, offered her comments from a student's perspective, which added to the clarity of what was being written. My deep appreciation to her for her help. Finally, Ms. Marinita Timban at John Wiley provided several press clippings, many of which came in handy in citing examples of business problems. My sincere thanks to Marinita Timban!

Revising an existing book is far more challenging and time consuming than writing the original version. I expect that students and professors alike will enjoy this revised edition.

Uma Sekaran

*Sandra Jeanquart and Joy Peluchette both now have doctoral degrees.

CONTENTS

CHAPTER 1

INTRODUCTION TO RESEARCH

TOPICS DISCUSSED

DEFINITION OF RESEARCH

APPLIED AND BASIC RESEARCH

WHY MANAGERS SHOULD KNOW ABOUT RESEARCH

SCIENTIFIC INVESTIGATION AND THE HALLMARKS OF SCIENCE
- Purposiveness
- Rigor
- Testability
- Replicability
- Precision and Confidence
- Objectivity
- Generalizability
- Parsimony

LIMITATIONS TO SCIENTIFIC RESEARCH IN MANAGEMENT

THE BUILDING BLOCKS OF SCIENCE AND THE HYPOTHETICO-DEDUCTIVE METHOD OF RESEARCH

THE SEVEN STEPS OF THE HYPOTHETICO-DEDUCTIVE METHOD
- Observation
- Preliminary Information Gathering
- Theory Formulation
- Hypothesizing
- Further Scientific Data Collection
- Data Analysis
- Deduction

MANAGERS AND THE CONSULTANT-RESEARCHER
- The Manager–Researcher Relationship
- Internal versus External Researchers and Consultants

CHAPTER OBJECTIVES

After completing Chapter 1 you should be able to:

1. Describe what research is and how it is defined.

2. Distinguish between applied and basic research, giving examples and discussing why they would fall into one or the other of the two categories.

3. Explain what is meant by scientific investigation, giving examples of nonscientific and scientific investigations, and fully explain the six hallmarks of science.

4. Briefly explain why research in the organizational behavior and management areas cannot be completely scientific.

5. Describe the building blocks of science.

6. Discuss the seven steps in the hypothetico-deductive method, using an example of your own.

7. Explain why managers should know about research.

8. Explain what managers should and should not do in order to interact most effectively with researchers.

9. Identify and fully discuss specific situations in which a manager would be better off using an internal research team, and when an external research team would be more advisable, giving reasons for the decisions.

10. Discuss what research means to you after reading Chapter 1, and how you might use the research knowledge as a manager.

Consider the following statements that have appeared in print:

- In a frantic drive to keep up with foreign competition, U.S. companies are tying their R & D labs more closely to business units—and business plans—to speed up product development (*Business Week,* Innovation 1989, p. 60).

- Cooper (Chairman, Upjohn) has boosted research-and-development spending from 9.4% of sales to around 14%, well above the industry average. And he's spending heavily on marketing (*Business Week,* September 18, 1989, p. 65).

- Turning on the research switch. At any given time, the [Electric Power Research] institute is helping to finance about 1500 projects, overseen by a staff of about 350 technical experts (*The New York Times,* May 14, 1989, p. 6F).

- No doubt about it: The more you research the better you do (*Business Week,* Innovation 1989, p. 177).

- Businesses are beginning to develop a strategic monitoring program to identify and understand competitors' strengths, weaknesses, and overall business strategies. Any firm can establish a competitor-analysis system that provides management with essential information about the wide range of strategies that rivals are likely to pursue. *The key is knowing where to gather relevant information and how to combine separate pieces of data into a coherent profile of each competing operation* (*Small Business Reports,* January 1989, p. 21; emphasis added).
- Faced with declining jeanswear sales, gigantic VF Corp. decided to go mass with its flagship Lee brand. A classic mistake (*Forbes,* February 6, 1989, p. 41).
- • Holly Farms roasted chickens—consumers liked these fully cooked birds, but retailers balked at their short shelf life.
- • Home banking—Consumers weren't ready for this complicated "service" (both from *Wall Street Journal,* November 28, 1989, p. B1).

The foregoing messages forcefully communicate the importance of research for business and industry, as well as how vital it is to know how to do *good* research. Research is essential for understanding even the basic everyday phenomena that need to be handled in organizations. For example, read the following scenario.

The twenty-five-story building housing the Gigantic Multipurpose Company, overlooking the banks of the Mississippi River, is bristling with activity. Let us take a look at the events occurring in four specific offices of the building on the fifth, eleventh, sixteenth, and twenty-fifth floors.

The fifth-floor manager in charge of one of the departments seems puzzled, vexed, and somewhat angry. He had been to a management seminar in Los Angeles a year ago, where an "expert" told the attendees that one way of ensuring employee involvement and commitment is by enriching their work. With all good intentions, the manager redesigned the jobs, introducing more variety, challenge, feedback, and "whole" jobs rather than fragmented pieces of work, and within three months of the changes, employee absenteeism increased tenfold!

In the eleventh-floor office of Ms. Sandy Raj, the purchasing manager, the women managers are holding a caucus. The discussion is about a news item in the morning's paper that women at all levels were being paid at least 40 percent less than males for performing comparable jobs and requiring similar abilities and skills.

The monthly meeting sponsored by the company for executives' wives is in progress in the conference room on the sixteenth floor. Several housewives who are attending the meeting are smiling bemusedly when they hear the speaker mention that members of dual-career families have to rethink their priorities and plan their lives better, because the divorce rate in dual-career families is on the increase. Several of the housewives attending the meeting have been contemplating divorce and seeing marriage counselors.

The president of Gigantic, on the twenty-fifth floor, is vehemently refuting the statement made by the organizational consultant that the organizations of today are to blame for the increasing number of alcoholics in our society.

What is your reaction to the four events just described? If the fifth-floor manager was told by an expert that job enrichment would increase employee involvement and commitment, why is absenteeism on the increase? Is it true that women are actually paid at least 40 percent less than men for equal jobs when they have equal skills and abilities? Is the divorce rate really greater in dual-career families than in single-career families? Are today's organizations really responsible for the increase in alcoholism in the country?

How do we answer these questions? We really cannot do so until and unless we probe more deeply into these issues, obtain more concrete facts, and analyze the relevant data to see what they tell us about the problem situations and their rectification. In other words, if absenteeism, unjust reward systems, divorce, and alcoholism are problems of concern to us, we need to research these issues in order to find viable answers to the problems.

This book discusses research and how it can be conducted to obtain valid information that would help in solving management problems in organizational settings. We begin by describing and defining research.

WHAT IS RESEARCH?

Research can be described as a systematic and organized effort to investigate a specific problem that needs a solution. It is a series of steps designed and followed, with the goal of finding answers to the issues that are of concern to us in the work environment. This means that the first step in research is to know where the problem areas are in the organization, and to identify as clearly and specifically as possible the problems that need to be studied and rectified. Once the problem or problems that need attention are clearly defined, then steps can be taken to gather information, analyze the data, and delineate the factors that are associated with the problem. By taking the necessary corrective action, the problem could be solved.

This entire process by which we attempt to solve problems is called research. Thus, research involves a series of well-thought-out and carefully executed activities that will enable us to know how organizational problems can be solved or at least minimized. Research thus encompasses the processes of inquiry, investigation, examination, and experimentation. These processes have to be carried out systematically, diligently, critically, objectively, and logically. The expected end results would be to discover new facts that will help us to deal with the problem situation.

The difference between the sensitive observer who uses common sense to arrive at some analysis and make a decision in a given situation and the investigator who uses a scientific method is that the latter does a systematic inquiry into the matter and tries to describe, explain, or predict phenomena based on data carefully collected for the purpose.

We can now define research as an organized, systematic, data-based, critical, scientific inquiry or investigation into a specific problem, undertaken with the objective of finding answers or solutions to it. In essence, research provides the information that enables managers to make decisions to rectify problems. The information provided can be the result of a careful analysis of data gathered first-hand or of data that are already available (in the company, industry, archives, etc.). Data can be quantitative (as generally gathered through questionnaires) or they can be qualitative (as generated from interviews or from responses to open-ended questions in a questionnaire).

Research methods refer to the ways in which research studies are designed (discussed later in the book) and the procedures by which data are analyzed. In this book we will focus primarily on the survey methodology—that is, the research that is conducted by collecting data and analyzing them to come up with answers to various issues of interest to us.

BUSINESS RESEARCH

In business, research is usually primarily conducted to resolve problematic issues in, or interrelated among, the areas of accounting, finance, management, and marketing. In **Accounting,** budget control systems, practices, and procedures are frequently examined. Inventory costing methods, accelerated depreciation, time-series behavior of quarterly earnings, transfer pricing, cash recovery rates, and taxation methods are some of the other areas that are researched. In **Finance,** the operations of financial institutions, optimum financial ratios, mergers and acquisitions, leveraged buyouts, intercorporate financing, yields on mortgages, the behavior of the NYSE, and such, form the focus for investigation. Several areas for research in Finance and Accounting have been identified for many years (see, for instance, Abbott, 1966; Abdel-khalik and Ajinkya, 1979). **Management** research could encompass the study of employee attitudes and behaviors, human resources management, the impact of changing demographics on management practices, production operations management, strategy formulation, information systems, and the like. **Marketing** research could address issues pertaining to product image, advertising, sales promotion, distribution, packaging, pricing, after-sales service, consumer preferences, new product development, and the like. Needless to say, not only are the issues within each subarea related to many factors within that particular system, but they have also to be investigated in the context of the external environment facing the business. For example, economic, political, demographic, technological, competitive, and other relevant factors will impinge on some of the dynamics that operate in a firm. These have to be scrutinized carefully, as well, to assess their impact, if any, on the problem researched.

TYPES OF RESEARCH

Research can be undertaken for two different purposes. One is to solve a currently existing problem in the work setting; the other is to add or contribute to the general body of knowledge in a particular area of interest to the researcher. When research is done with the intention of applying the results of its findings to solving specific problems currently being experienced in the organization, it is called **applied research.** However, when research is being done chiefly to improve our understanding of certain problems that commonly occur in organizational settings, and how to solve them, the research is called **basic** or **fundamental research.** It is also known as **pure research.** The findings from such research contribute to the building of knowledge in the various management areas.

Applied Research

Most organizations are interested in applied research and will pay researchers and consultants to study a problem of concern to them in order to find solutions that can be implemented to rectify the problem situation. Let us examine two instances where applied research will help companies to make good decisions.

1. U.S. manufacturing companies are now faced with at least three alternative strategies to improve their productivity—to expend their efforts on constant continuous improvement, or to focus only on new product development, or to simultaneously pursue both (*Fortune,* April 23, 1990, pp. 121–122). Doubtless, each alternative has advantages and disadvantages. Manufacturing companies that are concerned about their productivity will now have to research into each of these strategies and see which one would best suit their own company, taking into account their capabilities, knowhow, resources, and so on.

2. Flour Corporation in Irvine, California, has a policy where some 3000 employees accumulate extra hours to earn alternate Fridays off during summer. Similarly, 500 workers squeeze extra hours during other workdays so as to quit at 1:00 P.M. on Fridays in Thom McAn Shoe Co, Worcester, Massachusetts (*Wall Street Journal,* July 3, 1990). These companies pursue such policies since they feel that "it makes the employees feel good about the company" while keeping the costs of production the same. Other companies of different sizes are now contemplating whether they should also pursue a similar policy. Such policies may or may not be useful to all companies based on the type of employees they have, employees' work and leisure time preferences, whether the realities of the business will allow early closure on Fridays or not, and so on. Here is a need for applied research for each of the companies to work out the cost–benefit analysis in terms of both financial and employee morale outcomes. Such research is necessary because, once these benefits are given, withdrawing them later will be as difficult as the Promus Company (formerly Holiday Corp.) is now finding (*Wall Street Journal,* July 3, 1990).

Basic or Fundamental Research

Most research and development departments in various industries, as well as many professors in colleges and universities, do basic or fundamental research, so that more knowledge is generated in particular areas of interest to the industries, organizations, and researchers. The aim here is not to apply the findings to solve an immediate problem at hand, but rather to understand more about certain phenomena and problems that occur in several organizations and industries, and how they can be solved. Such investigations lend themselves to being designed such that the solutions generated for a particular type of problem—say turnover—could be applied not only to one organization such as a specific manufacturing company, but to several types of organizations such as hospitals, financial institutions, or restaurants.

The main purpose of conducting basic research is to generate more knowledge and understanding of the phenomena that occur and to build theories based on the research results. Such theories subsequently become the foundation for further study of the phenomena. This process of building on existing knowledge is the genesis for theory building in the management area.

An example of basic research is General Electric Company's experimentation with different applications of electrical energy—their motto being, "We bring good things to life." Computer companies in the silicon valley are constantly engaged in generating knowledge about the different uses of microcomputers in industry that are useful to managers and technicians. University professors engage in basic research in an effort to understand and generate more knowledge about various aspects of the business, such as how to improve the effectiveness of information systems, integrate technology into the overall strategic objectives of an organization, assess the impact of logos, increase the productivity of clerical workers in service industries, monitor sexual harassment incidents at the workplace, increase the effectiveness of small businesses, evaluate alternative inventory valuation methods, change the institutional structure of the money and capital markets, and the like.

As illustrated, the main distinction between applied and basic business research is that the former is specifically aimed at solving a current problem, whereas the latter has the more general objective of generating knowledge and understanding of phenomena and problems that occur in various organizational settings. Despite this distinction, both types of research follow the same steps of systematic inquiry to arrive at solutions to problems. As current or prospective practicing managers in organizations, most of us would probably be directly or indirectly engaged in applied research. We would also want to keep abreast of new basic knowledge generated in the management area by reading the published research in management journals, some of which may be relevant and applicable to our own organization.

MANAGERS AND RESEARCH

Why Should Managers Know About Research?

You yourself may not be doing research, but managers often need to understand, predict, and control events that are dysfunctional to the organization. For example, a new product developed may not be "taking off," or a financial investment may not be "paying off" as anticipated. Such perplexing phenomena have to be **understood** and explained. Unless this is done, it will not be possible to **predict** what will happen to that product or the investment and how future catastrophic outcomes can be **controlled.** A grasp of research methods will help managers to understand, predict, and control their environment.

A second question that might be running through your mind is that you will probably be bringing in researchers to solve problems and you may not yourself be doing the research. Why then should your understanding research be necessary? The reasons for studying research are fairly clear when one starts to think about it. With the increasing complexity of modern organizations, and the uncertainty of the environment they face, managing organizational systems has become a job ridden with sporadic problems in the work setting. It would help if managers could sense, spot, and deal with problems *before* they become serious. Knowing about research and problem-solving processes helps managers to identify the problems and to find out more about the situation before the problems get out of control. Initial information gathering and analysis of the situation would solve most of the minor problems. However, if they do become serious enough to warrant hiring outside researchers or consultants, then the manager needs to know about the research processes, design, and interpretation of data so as to be an intelligent and knowledgeable consumer of the research findings presented, because the recommended solutions may or may not be appropriate for implementation.

Another reason professional managers of today need to know about research methods in management is so that they become more discriminating consumers of the information contained in the journals they read. Some journal articles are more scientific and objective than others. Even among the scientific articles, some are more appropriate for adaptation to particular organizations and situations than others. This is a function of the sampling design, the types of organizations studied, and other factors reported in the journal articles. Unless the manager is able to comprehend fully what the published empirical research really means, she or he is likely to err in incorporating some of the suggestions made in such publications. Moreover, researchers may have discovered a way to solve a problem presently faced by a manager. The manager who knows about this can implement it, probably with considerable cost savings.

There are several other reasons professional managers should be knowledgeable about research and research methods in business. First, such knowledge enhances the sensitivity of managers to the myriad of variables operating in a situation and reminds them frequently of the multicausality and multifinality of phenomena, thus avoiding inappropriate, simplistic notions of one variable "causing" another. Second, when managers understand the research reports on their organizations that are given to them by other professionals, they will be in a position to take intelligent, educated, calculated risks with known probabilities attached to the success or failure of their decisions. Research then becomes a useful decision-making tool rather than a mass of incomprehensible statistical information. Third, because managers become knowledgeable about scientific investigations, vested interests inside or outside the organization will not be allowed to prevail. For instance, an internal research group within the organization will not be able to distort information or to twist the findings if managers are aware of the biases that could creep into research and know how data are analyzed and interpreted. As an example, an internal research team might state that a particular unit to which it is partial for whatever reason has shown increased profits and hence should be allocated more resources to buy sophisticated equipment to further enhance its effectiveness. However, the increased profit could have been a one-time windfall phenomenon due to market conditions, which had nothing to do with the unit's operating efficiency. Thus, realizing the different ways in which data can be camouflaged will help the manager to make the right decision. Fourth, knowledge about research helps the manager to relate to, and share pertinent information with, the researcher or consultant hired for problem solving.

In sum, being knowledgeable about research and research methods helps professional managers to

1. Identify and solve small problems in the work setting.
2. Know how to discriminate good from bad research.
3. Appreciate and constantly remember the multiple influences and multiple effects of factors impinging on a situation.
4. Take calculated risks in decision making, knowing full well the probabilities attached to the different/possible outcomes.
5. Prevent possible vested interests from operating in a situation.
6. Relate to hired researchers and consultants more effectively.

SCIENTIFIC INVESTIGATION

Earlier we defined research as an organized, systematic, data-based, critical, scientific inquiry into a specific problem that needs a solution. It is necessary to understand what the term *scientific* means. Scientific research has the focused goal of problem solving and pursues a step-by-step logical, organized, and rigorous method to identify problems, gather data, analyze the data, and draw valid conclusions therefrom. Thus, scientific research is not based on hunches, experience, and intuition alone, but is purposive and rigorous. Because of the rigorous way in which it is done, scientific research enables others interested in researching and knowing about similar issues to do research in similar situations and come up with comparable findings. Scientific research also helps researchers to state their findings more accurately and with confidence. This helps apply the solutions to various other organizational settings experiencing similar problems. Furthermore, scientific investigation tends to be more objective than subjective, and it helps managers to highlight the most critical factors in the workplace that need specific attention so as to avoid, minimize, or solve problems.

The term "scientific research" applies to both basic and applied research. Applied research may or may not be generalizable to other organizations, owing to similarities or differences in such factors as size, nature of work, characteristics of the employees, and structure of the organization. Nevertheless, applied research also has to be an organized and systematic process where problems are carefully identified, data scientifically gathered and analyzed, and conclusions drawn in an objective manner.

Do organizations always follow the rigorous step-by-step process? No. Sometimes, the problem may be so simple that it does not call for elaborate research, and past experiences might offer the solution to the problem. In other cases, exigencies of time (where quick decisions have to be made), unwillingness to expend the resources needed for doing good research, lack of knowledge, and other factors might prompt businesses to try to solve problems based on past experience or hunches. However, the probability of making wrong decisions in such cases is high. Even such business "gurus" as Lee Iacocca concede making big mistakes due to errors of judgment (see *Wall Street Journal,* September 17, 1990, p. 1). *Business Week, Fortune,* and the *Wall Street Journal,* among other business periodicals and newspapers, feature articles about many organizations that face difficulties because of wrong decisions made based on hunches alone. The cover story of *Business Week*'s March 19, 1990 issue, which carries the legend, *The Failed Vision: Jim Robinson's big plans for American Express are not working,* is a case in point.

THE HALLMARKS OF SCIENTIFIC RESEARCH

The hallmarks or main distinguishing characteristics of scientific research can be listed as follows:

1. Purposiveness.
2. Rigor.
3. Testability.
4. Replicability.
5. Precision and Confidence.
6. Objectivity.
7. Generalizability.
8. Parsimony.

Each of these characteristics can be explained in the context of a concrete example. Let us consider the case of a researcher who is interested in investigating how employees' commitment to the organization can be increased. We can examine how the eight hallmarks of science apply to this investigation so that it can be called scientific.

Purposiveness

The researcher has started with a definite aim or purpose for the research. The focus is on increasing the commitment of employees to the organization, which will help the organization in many ways. An increase in employee commitment will mean less turnover, less absenteeism, and probably increased performance levels, all of which would definitely benefit the organization. The research thus has a purposive focus.

Rigor

A good theoretical base and a sound methodological design would add rigor to a purposive study. Rigor connotes carefulness, scrupulousness, and the degree of exactitude in research investigations. In our example case, let us say the researcher asks a few employees in the organization—say ten to twelve people—to outline what would increase their commitment to the organization. If, on the basis of these people's responses alone, the researcher reaches several conclusions on how employee commitment can be increased, the whole approach to the investigation would be unscientific. It would lack rigor because, to mention just a few reasons, (1) the conclusions would be incorrectly drawn because they would be based on the thoughts of a few employees whose opinions may not be representative of those of the entire workforce; (2) the way in which the questions were framed and asked could have introduced bias or incorrectness in the responses; and (3) there may be many other important influences on organizational commitment that this small sample of respondents did not or could not verbalize during the interviews, and the researcher would have failed to include them. Therefore, conclusions drawn from an investigation that lacks a good theoretical foundation, as evidenced by reason (3), and methodological sophistication, as evident from (1) and (2), would be unscientific. Rigorous research involves a good theory base and a carefully thought-out methodology. These factors enable the researcher to collect the right kinds of information from an appropriate sample with the minimum amount of bias, and they facilitate appropriate data analysis once the data have been gathered. The rest of the book addresses these theoretical and methodological issues. Rigor in research design also makes possible the achievement of the other six hallmarks of science that will now be discussed.

Testability

If, after talking to a random selection of employees in the organization and reading about the previous research done in the area of organizational commitment, the researcher develops certain hypotheses on how employee commitment to the organization can be enhanced, then these hypotheses can be tested by applying certain statistical tests to the data collected for the purpose. For instance, the researcher might hypothesize that those employees who perceive greater opportunities for participation in decision making would be more committed to the organization. This is a hypothesis that can be tested when the data are collected. The test would indicate whether the hypothesis is substantiated or not.

Scientific research thus lends itself to testing logically developed hypotheses to see whether or not the data support the educated conjectures or hypotheses that are developed after a careful study of the problem situation. Testability thus becomes another hallmark of scientific research.

Replicability

Let us suppose that our researcher concludes that participation in decision making is one of the most important factors that influences the commitment of employees to the organization. If the same kinds of findings emerge when data are collected from employees in other organizations, we would have more faith in the findings. In other words, the results of the tests of hypotheses should be supported again and again when the research is repeated in other similar circumstances. To the extent that this does happen (i.e., the results are *replicated* or repeated), we will have confidence in our research being scientific. In other words, our hypotheses would not have been supported merely by chance. Replicability is thus another hallmark of scientific research.

Precision and Confidence

In management research we seldom have the luxury of being able to draw "definitive" conclusions based on the results of our data analysis. This is because we are unable to study the universe of items, events, or population we are interested in and hence base our findings on a sample that we draw from the universe. The sample we study will, in all probability, not be reflecting the exact characteristics of the phenomenon we try to study (these difficulties are discussed in greater detail in a later chapter). Measurement errors and other problems are also bound to introduce biases or errors in our findings. However, we would like to design the research in such a manner that our findings are as close to "truth" (i.e., the true state of affairs in the universe) as possible and we can put some faith or confidence in our findings.

Precision refers to how close the findings, based on a sample, are to "reality." In other words, precision reflects the degree of exactitude of the results based on the sample, to the phenomena studied as they exist in the universe. For example, if I estimated that the number of production days lost during the year due to absenteeism will be between thirty and forty and if it so happens that the actual number of days lost was thirty-five, then I would have been more precise in my estimation than if I had indicated that the production days lost would be somewhere between twenty and fifty. You may recall the term *confidence interval* in statistics, which is what is referred to here as precision.

Confidence refers to the probability that our estimations are correct. That is, it is not merely enough to be precise, but it is also important that we can say that 95 percent of the time, we are going to find our results to be true and there is only a 5 percent chance of our being wrong. This is also known as confidence level, and some refer to it as accuracy.

The narrower the gap within which we can estimate the range of our predictions (i.e., the more precise our findings) and the greater the confidence we have in our research results, the more useful and scientific the findings become. In social science research, a 95 percent confidence level, which implies that there is only a 5 percent probability that our findings may not be correct, is conventionally accepted and is usually referred to as a significance level of .05 ($p \leq .05$). Thus, precision and confidence are important aspects of research and can be obtained only by appropriate, scientific sampling design. The more precision and confidence we aim for in our research, the more scientific the investigation, and the more useful the results.

Objectivity

The conclusions drawn through the interpretation of the results of our data analysis should be objective; that is, they should be based on the facts resulting from the actual data and not on our own subjective or emotional values. For instance, if we had a hypothesis that stated that greater participation in decision making will increase organizational commitment and it was *not* supported, then there is no point in the researcher continuing to argue that increasing the opportunities for employee participation would still help! Such an argument would be based, not on the factual, data-based research findings, but on the subjective opinion of the researcher. If this was the researcher's belief all along, then there was no need to do the research in the first place!

Much damage can be done in organizations by the implementation of non-data-based or misleading conclusions drawn from research. For example, if the hypothesis relating to organizational commitment in our example was not supported, considerable time and effort would be wasted in finding ways to create opportunities for employee participation in decision making, only to find later that employees still keep quitting, remain absent, and do not commit themselves to the organization. Likewise, if research shows that increasing the pay of the employees is not going to increase their job satisfaction, then implementing a revised increased pay system is only going to cost the company more money without attaining the end result that is hoped for. Such an exercise, then, becomes one of nonscientific interpretation and implementation of the research results.

The more objective the interpretation of the data, the more scientific the research investigation becomes. Though researchers might start with some initial subjective values and beliefs, their interpretation of the data should be stripped of personal values and biases. Objectivity is thus another hallmark of scientific investigation.

Generalizability

Generalizability refers to the scope of applicability of the research findings in one organizational setting to other settings. Obviously, the wider the range of applicability of the solutions generated by research, the more useful the research is to the users of such research knowledge. For instance, if a researcher's findings that participation in decision making enhances organizational commitment, is found to be true in a variety of manufacturing, industrial, and service organizations, and not merely in the one organization studied by the researcher, then the generalizability of the findings to other organizational settings is widened. The more generalizable the research, the greater its usefulness and value.

Of course not many research findings can be generalized to all other settings, situations, or organizations. For wider generalizability, the research sampling design has to be logically developed, and a number of other meticulous details in the data-collection methods need to be followed. However, a more elaborate sampling design, though it would increase the generalizability of the results, would also increase research costs. Most applied research is generally confined to research within the particular area where the problem arises, and the results, at best, are generalizable only to other identical situations and settings. Though such limited applicability does not decrease its scientific value (if the research is properly conducted), its generalizability gets restricted.

Parsimony

Simplicity in explaining the phenomena or problems that occur, and in the application of solutions to problems, is always preferred to complex research frameworks that consider an unmanageable number of factors. For instance, if the researcher can identify for the manager two or three specific variables in the work situation that, when changed, would raise the organizational commitment of the employees by 45 percent, that would be more useful and valuable to the manager than the researcher telling the manager that the organizational commitment could be increased by 48 percent by changing ten different variables in the organization. Such an unmanageable number of variables might well be totally beyond the manager's control. Therefore, the achievement of a meaningful and parsimonious, rather than an elaborate and cumbersome, model for our problem solution becomes a critical issue in research.

Economy in research models is achieved when we can build into our research framework a lesser number of variables that would explain the variance far more efficiently than a complex set of variables that would only marginally add to the variance explained. Parsimony can be introduced with a good understanding of the problem and the important factors that influence it. Such a good conceptual theoretical model can be realized through unstructured and structured interviews with people in the situation and a thorough literature review of the previous research work in the particular problem area.

In sum, scientific research encompasses the eight criteria just discussed. These criteria are discussed in more detail later in the book.

Some Obstacles to Conducting Scientific Research in the Management Area

In the management and behavioral areas it is not always possible to conduct investigations that are 100 percent scientific. This is primarily because of problems we are likely to encounter in the measurement and collection of data in the subjective areas of feelings, emotions, attitudes, and perceptions. These problems crop up whenever we attempt to quantify human behavior. We might also encounter difficulties in obtaining a representative sample, which would restrict the generalizability of the findings. Thus, it is not always possible to meet all the hallmarks of science completely. Comparability, consistency, and wide generalizability are often difficult to obtain in research. Still, to the extent that we can design our research to ensure purposiveness, rigor, and the maximum possible testability, replicability, generalizability, objectivity, parsimony, and precision and confidence, we will have endeavored to engage in scientific investigation. Several other possible limitations in research studies are discussed in subsequent chapters.

THE BUILDING BLOCKS OF SCIENCE IN RESEARCH

Research can be designed to test some specific hypothesized predictions. For instance, studies have been done to find if controlling aversive noise in the environment increases the performance of individuals in solving mental puzzles. Here, the researcher began with the theory that noise adversely affects mental problem solving. He then developed the hypothesis that if the noise is controlled, mental puzzles can be solved more quickly and correctly. He subsequently designed a research project to test this hypothesis. The results of the study helped the researcher to deduce or conclude that controlling the aversive noise did indeed help the participants to improve their performance on mental puzzles. This method of starting with a theoretical framework, formulating hypotheses, and logically deducing from the results of the study is known as the *hypothetico-deductive* method of conducting research.

Another method of doing research is the *inductive* method, which proceeds in the opposite direction inasmuch as the researcher begins with data in hand and generates hypotheses and a theory from the ground up (Glaser & Strauss, 1967; Selltiz, Wrightsman, & Cook, 1981). An example of this is a researcher having access to data on consumer reactions to various new products and trying to make sense of what all that could mean to new product development. She might develop some hypotheses and test them. Most of the participant-observer studies that we will discuss in Chapter 7 are inductive studies. Generally, however, both inductive and deductive methods are used to study phenomena.

The building blocks of scientific inquiry are depicted in Figure 1.1. The significance of these building blocks can be illustrated through an example.

Figure 1.1
The building blocks of science.

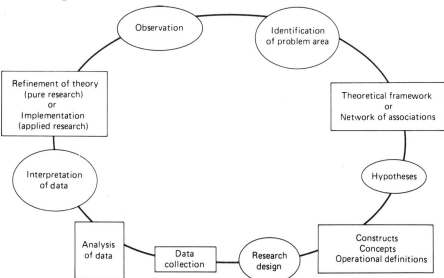

Example 1.1   A sales manager might *observe* that customers are perhaps not as pleased as they used to be. The manager may not be sure that this is really the case but may entertain some uneasy feelings regarding declining customer satisfaction. This process of *observation* or sensing of the phenomena around us is what gets most of the research started—whether it is applied or basic research. The next step for the manager is to determine if there is a real problem, and if so, how serious it is. This *problem identification* calls for some preliminary data gathering. The manager might talk casually to a few customers to find out how they feel about the products and customer service. During the course of these conversations the manager might find that the customers like the products but are upset because many of the items they need are frequently out of stock, and they perceive the salespersons as not being helpful. From discussions with some of the salespersons, the manager might realize that the factory does not supply the goods on time and promises delivery dates that it does not always keep. Salespersons might also indicate that they try to please and retain the customers by communicating the different delivery dates given to them by the factory.

Integration of the information obtained through the informal and formal interviewing process has helped the manager to determine that a problem does exist. It also helps the manager to formulate a conceptual model or *theoretical framework* of all the factors contributing to the problem. In this case, there is a network of connections among the following factors: delays by the factory in delivering goods; the notification of later delivery dates, which are not kept; the promises of the salespersons to the customers (in hopes of retaining them) that cannot be met—all of which contribute to customer dissatisfaction. From the theoretical framework, which is a meaningful integration of all the information gathered, several **hypotheses** can be generated and tested to determine if the data support the hypotheses. Concepts are then **operationally defined** so that they can be measured. A **research design** is set up to decide on, among other issues, how to **collect** further data, **analyze** and **interpret those data,** and, finally, to provide an answer to the problem. The process of drawing from logical analysis an inference that purports to be conclusive is called **deduction.** Thus, the building blocks of science provide the genesis for the hypothetico-deductive method of scientific research that is discussed in the following paragraphs.

THE HYPOTHETICO-DEDUCTIVE METHOD

The Seven-Step Process in the Hypothetico-Deductive Method

The seven steps involved in the hypothetico-deductive method of research are listed and discussed below.

1. Observation.
2. Preliminary information gathering.
3. Theory formulation.
4. Hypothesizing.

5. Further scientific data collection.

6. Data analysis.

7. Deduction.

Observation

Observation is the first stage, in which one senses that certain changes are occurring, or that some new behaviors, attitudes, and feelings are vaguely surfacing in one's environment, say the workplace. When the phenomena that are being observed are considered to be potentially important, one would proceed to the next step.

How does one observe phenomena and changes in the environment? The people-oriented manager is always sensitive to and aware of what is happening in and around the workplace. Changes in attitudes, behaviors, communication patterns and styles, and a score of other verbal and nonverbal cues can be readily picked up by managers who are sensitive to the various nuances. Irrespective of whether we are dealing with finance, accounting, marketing, or administrative matters, and no matter how sophisticated a machine system we might have installed, in the ultimate analysis, it is the people who achieve the goals and make things happen. Whether it is the installation of an effective Management Information System, manufacturing technology, distribution channel, strategic plan, cost accounting system, investment plan, or training scheme, it is only through the efforts of the employees that the goals are achieved. And, fortunately, the vast majority of people react and respond positively or negatively to various factors in the work environment, and knowingly or unwittingly transmit cues, which the manager can easily pick up. The manager may not be able to understand what exactly is happening, but he or she can definitely sense that things are not as they should be, when indeed there is a problem in the situation.

Preliminary Information Gathering

Preliminary information gathering involves the seeking of information to know more about what one observed. This could be done by talking informally to several people in the work setting or to clients, thus gathering information on what is happening and why. Through these unstructured interviews, one gets an idea or a "feel" for what is happening in the situation. Once the researcher increases her level of awareness of what is happening, she would then focus on the problem and the associated factors through further structured, formal interviews with the relevant groups. Additionally, by doing library research, the investigator would identify how such issues have been tackled in other situations. This information would give additional insights of possible factors operating in this particular situation that had not surfaced in previous interviews.

A mass of information would have been collected through the interviews and the library search. The next step is to make sense of the factors that have been identified in the information-gathering stage by piecing them together in some meaningful fashion.

Theory Formulation

Theory formulation, the next step, is an attempt to integrate the information logically so that the reason for the problem can be conceptualized. In this step the critical variables are examined as to their contribution or influence in explaining why the problem occurs and how it can be solved. The network of associations identified among the variables would then be theoretically woven together with justification as to why they might influence the problem. This process of theory formulation is discussed in greater detail in Chapter 3.

Hypothesizing

Hypothesizing is the next logical step after theory formulation. From the network of associations drawn among the variables, certain testable hypotheses or educated conjectures can be generated. For instance, at this point, one might hypothesize that if a sufficient number of items are stocked on shelves, customer dissatisfaction will be considerably reduced. This is a hypothesis that can be tested to determine if the statement would be supported.

Hypothesis testing is called **deductive** research. Sometimes, hypotheses that were not originally formulated do get generated through the process of **induction.** That is, after the data are obtained, some creative insights occur, and based on these, new hypotheses get generated. Generally, in research, hypotheses testing through deductive research and hypotheses generation through induction are both common. The Hawthorne experiments are a good example of this. In the relay assembly line many experiments were conducted that increased lighting and the like, based on the original hypothesis that these would account for increases in productivity. But later, when these hypotheses were disconfirmed, a new hypothesis was generated based on observed data. The mere fact that people were chosen for the study gave them a feeling of importance that increased their productivity whether or not lighting, heating, or anything else was increased or decreased; thus the coining of the term "the Hawthorne effect"!

Further Scientific Data Collection

After the development of the hypotheses, data with respect to each variable in the hypotheses need to be obtained. In other words, further scientific data collection is needed to test the hypotheses that are generated in the study. For instance, to test the hypothesis that stocking sufficient items will reduce customer dissatisfaction, one needs to measure the current level of customer satisfaction and collect further data on customer satisfaction levels whenever sufficient number of items are stocked and made readily available to the customers. Data on every variable in the theoretical framework from which hypotheses are generated would also be collected. These data then form the basis for further data analysis.

Data Analysis

In the data analysis step, the data gathered are statistically analyzed to see if the hypotheses that were generated have been supported. For instance, to see if stock levels influence customer satisfaction, one might want to do a correlational analysis and determine the relationship between the two factors. Similarly, other hypotheses could be tested through appropriate statistical analysis. Analyses of both quantitative and qualitative data can be done to determine if certain conjectures are substantiated. Qualitative data refer to information that is gathered in a narrative form through interviews and observations. For example, to test the theory that budgetary constraints adversely impact on managers' responses to their job, several interviews might be conducted with managers after budget restrictions are imposed. The responses obtained might be then organized to see the different categories under which they fall and the extent to which the same kinds of responses are articulated by the managers.

Deduction

Deduction is the process of arriving at conclusions by interpreting the meaning of the results of the data analysis. For instance, if it was found from the data analysis that increasing the stocks was positively correlated to (increased) customer satisfaction (say, .5), then one can deduce that if customer satisfaction is to be increased, the shelves have to be better stocked. Another inference from this data analysis is that stocking of shelves accounts for (or explains) 25 percent of the variance in customer satisfaction ($.5^2$).

Based on these deductions, the researcher would make recommendations on how the "customer dissatisfaction" problem could be solved.

In summary, there are seven steps involved in identifying and resolving a research issue. To make sure that the seven steps of the hypothetico-deductive method are properly understood, let us briefly review an example in an organizational setting and the activities that will be performed in the seven steps.

An Example of the Application of the Hypothetico-Deductive Method in Organizations

Observation

The Vice President in charge of Finance senses that the budgetary process is not working as well as it should. Managers seem to be overcautious, build excessive slack in their budgets, and all in all, seem to be acting defensively. In essence, the V.P. observes various phenomena and senses a problem.

Information Gathering Through Informal Interviews

The V.P. chats with a few of the managers and their subordinates. He finds that there is much anxiety among the managers in the system that the budgets for all departments are going to be slashed. There is also the perception that the new information system that was planned to be installed will deprive the managers of much of their original power and control. A general notion that the managers who have greater budgets will be evaluated more favorably also seems to prevail.

Gathering More Information Through Literature Survey

Amused by these findings, the V.P. started reading materials on effective budgetary processes and found that many factors, including the ones he discovered through the interviews, were instrumental in thwarting the idea of effective budgeting.

Formulating Theory About What is Happening

Piecing together the information obtained from the interviews and the literature, the manager develops a theory of possible factors that may be influencing ineffective budgeting practices. That is, he is developing a theoretical framework of the factors that could account for poor budgeting practices.

Hypothesizing

From the theory, the V.P. conjectures the relationships among the factors. For example, he hypothesizes that fear of budget cuts influenced the building of excessive slack in the budget.

Data Collection

In this phase, the manager collects data from the other managers anonymously, through a questionnaire, on various factors such as the extent of anxiety regarding perceived budget cuts, concern regarding the installation of the proposed information systems, and the like.

Data Analysis

The V.P. will then have the data analyzed to see if there were indeed significant correlations between each of the various factors and slack in the budget (i.e., he tests his hypotheses).

Deduction

If indeed significant correlations are found, on the basis of the results, the manager would deduce (or conclude) that misperceptions about budget cuts, purpose of information system, and so on, did indeed have an influence on the managers introducing excessive slack in their budgets. To solve the problem, the V.P. may then clarify the real situation to the managers and allay their fears.

Review of the Hypothetico-Deductive Method

In summary, the hypothetico-deductive method involves the seven steps of observation, preliminary data gathering, theory formulation, hypothesizing, scientific data collection, data analysis, and deduction. Other chapters in this book will be concerned with how scientific hypothetico-deductive research might be conducted in organizations. This information will be helpful to managers in solving problems while managing people, technology, strategy, operations, and situations.

Correlational versus Causal Relationships

Earlier, under Data Analysis, we introduced the term *correlation*. At this stage, it is important to note that there is a difference between causal and correlational investigations. **Correlational** studies simply identify the variables in a situation that **influence** a particular phenomenon of interest. For example, absenteeism (a phenomenon of interest to the manager) may be found to be influenced by such factors as noxiousness in the work environment, distance from home to the workplace, and the amount of overtime worked by the employees. In other words, all three of these factors have something to do with why employees may remain absent. **Causal** studies, on the other hand, try to trace the **cause–effect** relationships between two phenomena. For instance, absenteeism may be found to be caused, at least to a great extent, by the noxious fumes in the factory setting. Here, one feels that by somehow decreasing the noxiousness in the factory, absenteeism may be considerably lowered, since the toxicity of the fumes seems to cause people to remain absent. Even in carefully designed causal studies (discussed in Chapter 5) one cannot be absolutely sure that one variable, and that alone, causes another variable, because there are several other factors that might contaminate the cause–effect relationship. These are discussed more fully in Chapter 5.

Let us examine some other situations where correlational and causal effects might be distinguished. Excessive copying on the Xerox machine might **influence** its efficient operation, but does it always **cause** the machine to break down? Perhaps not. There might also be other factors that impact on its efficient operation such as the way it is handled, its age, wrong replacement parts, and the like. One could, on the other hand, be sure that severe disability would **cause** a highly motivated employee to take leave. In this case, we can be sure, because even if the employee can ill afford to take sick leave on half pay, he has no choice. The severity of his disability and that alone constrains him from coming to work. The differences between how causal and correlational studies are designed will be discussed later in the book, but for now, it is important to realize that the goals of tracing **correlations** as opposed to **causation** are different.

THE MANAGER AND THE CONSULTANT-RESEARCHER

Earlier in the chapter we discussed why it is important for the manager to know about research and research methods. The manager who senses a problem or is faced with one will seldom have the time to engage in a full-fledged scientific investigation, especially if the magnitude of the perceived or actual problem is big. The manager will then have to find a researcher who will act as a consultant and offer useful information and alternative courses of action. We will now briefly discuss how a manager might locate and select a researcher, what the manager-researcher relationship should ideally be, and the advantages and disadvantages of internal and external consultants.

How to Locate and Select a Researcher

Many organizational consulting firms are listed in telephone directories and can be used for consulting projects. If a broad indication about what needs to be researched is offered, the consulting firm will introduce the individuals who have expertise in that particular area. The credentials of these individuals are also usually presented or can be obtained by asking them. Other organizations who have used them can also be contacted to ascertain the effectiveness of the individuals and the reputation of the firm.

Many colleges of business also have professors who do organizational consulting work. Some of them have vast experience working with several organizations. These individuals can also be contacted and utilized if they have the time and would agree to do the study. In all cases, it is important to check the credentials of the individuals and/or the firm before hiring the researcher(s).

The Manager–Researcher Relationship

It often becomes necessary for managers to deal with researchers or consultants during the course of their career. Many academicians and research students engage in basic research, and modern organizations usually allow access to these researchers, asking only that a copy of the research project be made available to the organization. If the research has been done scientifically, then the results of the study would be beneficial to the manager, who would have obtained useful information without paying a cent in consulting fees. By being able to articulate the variables of concern to the researchers who come to do basic work, and by giving them useful insights, the manager thus stands to benefit a great deal. When the manager is knowledgeable about research, then the interactions between the manager and the researcher become more meaningful, purposeful, and beneficial to the organization and the researcher alike.

Quite frequently, organizations also hire outside research agencies to identify and solve problems for them. In such a case, the manager must not only interact effectively with the research team, but also must explicitly delineate the roles for the researchers and the management. He has to inform the researchers of the types of information that can be made available to them, and more importantly, what types of company records *cannot* be made available. Such records might include the personnel files of the employees, or certain trade secrets. Making these facts explicit at the very beginning can save a lot of frustration for both parties. Managers who are more knowledgeable about research can more easily decipher the types of information the researchers might require, and if certain documents cannot be made available, they can inform the research team at the outset. It is inefficient for the researchers to discover at a late stage that the company will not let them have certain information. If they know the constraints right from the beginning, the researchers might be able to identify alternate ways of tackling the problems and to formulate other testable hypotheses.

Beyond specifying the roles and constraints, the manager should also make sure that there is a congruence in the value systems of management and the consultants.

For example, the research team might very strongly believe and recommend that reducing the workforce and improving the work system is the ideal way to significantly cut down operating costs. Management's consistent philosophy, however, might be *not* to fire employees who render loyal service. Thus, there might be a clash of ideologies between management and the research team. Research knowledge will help managers to identify and explicitly state, ahead of time, the areas where value differences are likely to arise. Clarification of such issues offers the research team the opportunity to either accept the assignment or regret inability to undertake the project due to value differences. In either case, both the organization and the research team would be the better off for having discussed their value orientations, thus avoiding potential frustrations for both sides.

Exchange of information in a straightforward and forthright manner also helps to increase the rapport and trust levels between the two parties, which in turn motivates the two sides to interact effectively. Under these conditions, the researchers feel free to approach the management to seek assistance in making the research more purposeful. For instance, the research team is likely to request that management inform the employees of the purpose of the research and thus allay any fears they might have about the research.

To summarize, the manager should make sure while hiring researchers or consultants that

1. The roles and expectations of both parties are made explicit.
2. Relevant philosophies and value systems of the organization are made explicit and any special constraints are made known.
3. There is good rapport established with the researchers, and between the researchers and the employees in the organization, so that the latter will cooperate with the researchers.

Internal versus External Consultants and Researchers

Some organizations have their own consulting or research department, which might be called the management services department, the organization and methods department, the research and development department, or some other name. The people in this unit serve as internal consultants to subunits of the organization that face certain problems and seek help. Such a unit within the organization, if it exists, would be useful in several ways, and enlisting its help might be advantageous under some circumstances, but not in others. The manager often has to decide whether to use internal or external researchers or consultants. To make such a decision, the manager should become aware of the strengths and weaknesses of both, in order to weigh the advantages and disadvantages of using either, and thus come to a decision based on the needs of the situation. Some of the advantages and disadvantages of both the internal and external teams are now discussed.

Internal Consultants and Researchers

Advantages.   There are at least four advantages in engaging an internal team to do the research project:

1. The internal team would have a higher probability of being accepted more easily and quickly by the employees in the organization where research needs to be done.
2. They would require much less time to understand the structure, the philosophy and climate, and the functioning and work systems of the organization.
3. They would be available for implementing their recommendations after the research findings are accepted. This is very important because any "bugs" in the implementation of the recommendations could be removed with their help. They would also be available for evaluating the effectiveness of the changes, and for considering further changes when necessary.
4. The internal team might cost considerably less than an external team for the unit enlisting help in problem solving because they will need less time to grasp and understand the system. For problems that are relatively less complex, the internal team would be good.

Disadvantages.   There are also certain disadvantages to engaging internal research teams for purposes of problem solving. The three most critical ones are listed here.

1. Having been with the organization for a long time as internal consultants, the internal team may quite possibly fall into a stereotypical way of looking at the organization and its problems. This would inhibit any fresh ideas and perspectives that might be brought to the problem situation. This would definitely be a handicap where serious issues and complex problems are to be investigated.
2. There is scope for certain powerful coalitions in the organization to influence the internal team to conceal, distort, or falsely report certain facts. In other words, certain vested interests could prevail, especially where the issue is one of allocation of scarce resources.
3. There is also a possibility that even the most highly qualified internal research teams are not valued as "experts" by the staff and management, and hence their findings are not given the attention they deserve.

External Consultants and Researchers

The disadvantages of the internal research teams are the advantages of the external teams, and the former's advantages are the latter's disadvantages. However, the specific advantages and disadvantages of the external teams may be highlighted.

Advantages

1. The external team can draw on a wealth of experience from having worked with different types of organizations that have had the same or similar types of problems. This wide range of experience would enable them to think both divergently and convergently rather than coming to a solution immediately on the basis of the apparent facts in the situation. They would be able to think of several alternative ways of looking at the problem because of their extensive problem-solving experiences in various other situations. Having looked at the situation from several possible angles and viewpoints (divergently), they could then critically assess each of these, eliminate the less viable options and alternatives, and focus on selected feasible solutions (convergent thinking).

2. The external teams, especially those from established research and consulting firms, might have greater knowledge of current sophisticated problem-solving models through their periodic training programs, which may or may not be the case with the teams within the organization. Because knowledge obsolescence is a real threat in the consulting area, external research institutions ensure that their members are current on the latest innovations through organized training programs. The extent to which internal team members are kept abreast of the latest problem-solving techniques may vary considerably from organization to organization.

Disadvantages.   The major disadvantages in hiring an external research team are as follows:

1. The cost of hiring an external research team is usually high and is the main deterrent, unless the problems are very critical.

2. In addition to the considerable time required for the external team to understand the organization to be researched, they also are seldom welcomed or readily accepted by the employees in the organization. Therefore, eliciting employees' help and cooperation in the study is a little more difficult and time-consuming for the external researchers, when compared to the internal teams.

3. The external team also charges more money for assisting in the implementation and evaluation phases.

Given these advantages and disadvantages of both the internal and external teams, the manager needing research services has to weigh the pros and cons of engaging either, before making a decision.

If the problem is a complex one, or if there are likely to be vested interests, or if the very existence of the organization is imperiled because of one or more serious problems, it is probably advisable to engage external researchers despite the increased costs involved. However, if the problems that arise are fairly simple, if time is of the essence in solving moderately complex problems, or if there is a system-wide need to establish procedures and policies of a fairly routine nature, the internal team would probably be the better suited option.

Knowing about research methods and the comparative advantages and disadvantages of the external and internal teams helps managers to make decisions on how to approach problems and their solution.

Exhibit 1 below gives an idea of some commonly researched topical areas in business.

Exhibit 1: Some Commonly Researched Areas in Business

1. Employee behaviors such as performance, absenteeism, and turnover.
2. Employee attitudes such as job satisfaction, loyalty, and organizational commitment.
3. Supervisory performance, managerial leadership style, and performance appraisal systems.
4. Social and situational determinants of interview decisions.
5. Validation of performance appraisal systems.
6. Human resource management choices and organizational strategy.
7. Evaluations of assessment centers.
8. The dynamics of rating and rating errors in the judgment of human performance.
9. Strategy formulation and implementation.
10. Just-in-time systems, continuous-improvement strategies, and production efficiencies.
11. Organizational outcomes such as sales, market share, profits, growth, and effectiveness.
12. Distribution channels, advertising effectiveness, and effective test marketing strategies.
13. Brand loyalty, product life cycle, and product innovation.
14. Consumer complaints.
15. Location analysis.
16. Logo image.
17. Market feasibility studies, market testing.
18. Product positioning, product modification, new product development.
19. Cost of capital, valuation of firms, dividend policies, and investment decisions.
20. Portfolio investment, pricing models, future options.
21. Risk assessment, exchange rate fluctuations, and foreign investment.
22. Tax implications of reorganization of firms or acquisition of companies.
23. Qualified pension plans and cafeteria type of benefits for employees.
24. Deferred compensation plans.

---

25. Auditing practices.
26. Installing effective management information systems.
27. Use of expert systems in daily decision making.
28. Models of Executive Information Systems.
29. Mathematical models for assessing organizational effectiveness.
30. Advanced manufacturing technologies and information systems.
31. Designing career paths for dual-career couples.
32. Creative management of a diverse workforce.
33. Cultural differences and the dynamics of managing a multinational firm.
34. Alternative work patterns: Job sharing, flexitime, flexiplace, and part-time work.
35. Corporate culture and socialization processes.
36. Downsizing.
37. Participative management and performance effectiveness.
38. Gender differences in leadership styles.
39. Instrument development for assessing "true" gender differences.
40. Pollution emission and health of the workers.

SUMMARY

In this Chapter we have examined what research is, considered the two types of research, tried to understand scientific investigation, what the hypothetico-deductive method of research involves, why a manager should know about research, and the advantages and disadvantages of hiring internal and external teams of researchers or consultants.

We examine the research process in the next two chapters.

DISCUSSION QUESTIONS AND POINTS TO PONDER

1. Define research and explain the difference between applied and basic research.
2. Describe the hallmarks of scientific research.
3. What are the steps in hypothetico-deductive research? Explain them, using an example not in the book.
4. Why is it important for managers to know about research?
5. Why is the manager–researcher relationship important?

6. Describe a situation where it would be more advisable to use an external research team rather than an internal one.

7. One hears the word *research* being mentioned by several groups such as research organizations, college and university professors, doctoral students, graduate assistants working for faculty, graduate and undergraduate students doing their term papers, research departments in industries, newspaper reporters, journalists, lawyers, doctors, and several other professionals and non-professionals.

    In the light of what you have learned in this chapter, how would you rank the aforementioned groups of people in terms of the extent to which they might be doing "scientific" investigations in the areas of basic or applied research. Why?

8. If research in the management area cannot be 100 percent scientific, why bother to do it at all?

9. "Because basic research is not applied immediately to a problem, it is less valuable and useful than applied research." Comment on this statement.

10. "If managers learn how to do good research by taking a course such as this book gives, there would be no need to hire anybody to solve problems in organizations." How would you respond to this statement?

CHAPTER 2

THE RESEARCH PROCESS

Steps 1 to 3:
The Broad Problem Area
Preliminary Data
Gathering
Problem Definition

TOPICS DISCUSSED

THE BROAD PROBLEM AREA

PRELIMINARY DATA COLLECTION

SOME INFORMATION VITAL FOR RESEARCH
- Background Information on the Organization: Contextual Factors
- Structural Factors, Job Factors, Management Philosophy
- Perceptions, Attitudes, and Behavioral Responses

LITERATURE SURVEY
- Reasons for Literature Survey
- Conducting the Literature Survey
  - *Identifying the Relevant Sources*
  - *Extracting the Relevant Information*

WRITING UP THE LITERATURE SURVEY OR THE LITERATURE REVIEW

PROBLEM DEFINITION

IN THE APPENDIX:
- On-Line Data Bases
- Bibliographical Indexes
- Referencing in the APA Format
- Referencing and Quotation in the Literature Review Section
- Frequently Cited Business Journals

CHAPTER OBJECTIVES

After completing Chapter 2 you should be able to:

1. Identify the steps in the research process.
2. Identify problem areas that are likely to be studied in organizations.
3. Discuss how problem areas can be identified in work settings.
4. State research problems clearly and precisely.
5. Develop relevant and comprehensive bibliographies for any organizational research area.
6. Write a literature review on any given topic, documenting the references in the prescribed manner.
7. Apply all you have learned to a group project that might be assigned to you.

In this chapter we will examine ways to identify the variables that would be relevant in any specific problem situation. We will also see how a literature survey is done and how problems can be narrowed down and clearly defined.

THE RESEARCH PROCESS FOR APPLIED AND BASIC RESEARCH

In the previous chapter we discussed and illustrated through Figure 1.1 the foundation or the building blocks of science. For the sake of clarity, scientific inquiry in the hypothetico-deductive mode can be discussed as comprising two distinct aspects: the **process** of developing the conceptual framework and the hypotheses for testing, and the **design,** which involves the planning of the actual study dealing with such aspects as the location for the study, how to select the sample and collect the data, and how to analyze the data. Figure 2.1 captures the research process in the first five boxes. Boxes 6 and 7 embody the design aspects, which will be elaborated later in the book. Box 8 denotes the final deductions from the hypotheses testing. If all the hypotheses are substantiated and the research question is fully answered, we will be able to look at different ways of solving the problem. If, however, some hypotheses are not substantiated, or only partially supported, one goes back to examining the reasons for this. Note that the arrow is headed from box 8 to box 2 in Figure 2.1. It could go directly to box 3 or 4 or 5 as well.

Despite the fact that the research model is depicted and discussed in this book as if it were a step-by-step linear process, one has to bear in mind that it is not actually so in practice. For example, though the literature search and interviews might have been conducted before formulating the theoretical framework, one may have to go

Figure 2.1

The research process for basic and applied research.

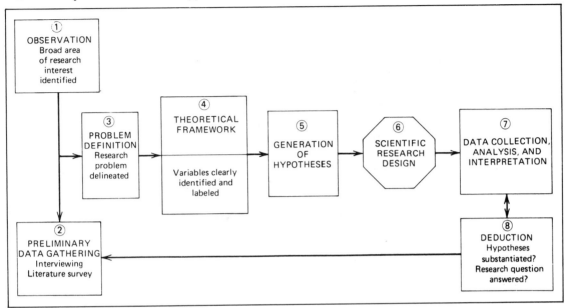

back and conduct more interviews and/or seek additional information in the literature to refine the theory through a clearer understanding. The research site, sample, measurement of the variables, and other design issues may also have to be simultaneously considered as one develops the problem, the theory, and the hypotheses.

Each of the components of the research model will be discussed in this book. This particular chapter will discuss steps 1 to 3 of Figure 2.1: (1) the broad problem area; (2) preliminary information gathering, especially through unstructured and structured interviews and literature survey; and (3) problem definition.

BROAD PROBLEM AREA

Identifying the broad problem area through the process of observing and focusing on the actual problem was discussed in Chapter 1. Recall that the broad problem area refers to the entire situation where one sees a possible need for research and problem solving. The specific issues that need to be researched within this situation may not be identified at this stage. Such issues might pertain to (1) problems currently existing in an organizational setting that need to be solved, (2) areas in the organization that a manager believes need to be improved, (3) a conceptual or theoretical issue that needs to be tightened up for the basic researcher to understand certain phenomena, and (4) some research questions that a basic researcher wants to answer empirically. Examples of each type can be provided taking the issue of sexual harassment, which is a problem that at least some organizations currently have to handle.

As an example of a problem **currently existing,** a situation might present itself where a manager might receive written complaints from women in some departments that they are not being "treated right" in the system. From the generalized nature of these complaints, the manager might know that he is facing a gender-related problem situation, but may not be able to pinpoint what exactly the problem is. That is, more investigation will be necessary before identifying the exact problems and attempting to resolve them. On the other hand, the following is an example of a situation **requiring improvement.** Supposing policies already exist regarding discrimination and sexual harassment, and legitimate complaints of discrimination continue to persist, then it is obvious that the policies are ambiguous and need improvement either in how they are formulated, in how they are understood, or in how they are enforced.

The example of a **conceptual issue that needs to be tightened** would be the basic researcher studying sexual harassment to define that concept in more precise and unambiguous terms. Currently, sexual harassment might only be broadly defined as:

> *Any unwelcome sexual advances, requests for sexual favors, and other verbal and physical conduct of a sexual nature.*

However, in practice, certain nonverbal or nonphysical attention, such as ogling, might also be unpalatable to some and could be termed "harassment." Thus, the researcher might want to come up with a more precise statement of what sexual harassment is and expand the definition of the term itself. Here is a clear case for a better understanding and definition of the concept itself. An example of a researcher wanting to find some **answers empirically** might be to explore the issue of perceived or actual sexual harassment and its impact on the consequences for the individuals (e.g., psychological stress) and organizations (poor performance) by gathering data and testing the relationships. Here is a situation where some specific answers to a research question are desired.

Examples of broad problem areas that a manager could observe in the workplace are as follows:

1. Training programs are perhaps not as effective as were anticipated.
2. The sales volume of a product is not picking up.
3. Minority groups are not making career progress in organizations.
4. The daily balancing of accounting ledgers is becoming a continuing concern.
5. The newly installed information system is not being used by the managers for whom it was primarily designed.
6. The introduction of flexible work hours has created more problems than it has solved in many companies.

7. The management of complex, multidepartmental projects is getting out of hand in a firm.

The broad problem area would be narrowed down to specific issues for investigation after some preliminary data are gathered by the researcher. This may take the form of interviews and library research.

PRELIMINARY DATA COLLECTION

Nature of Data to Be Collected

In Chapter 1 it was mentioned that unstructured interviews, structured interviews, and library research would help the researcher to define the problem more specifically and evolve a theory delineating possible variables that might influence the problem. The nature of information that would be needed by the researcher for the purpose could be broadly classified under three headings:

1. Background information of the organization—that is, the contextual factors.
2. Managerial philosophy, company policies, and other structural aspects.
3. Perceptions, attitudes, and behavioral responses of organizational members and client systems (if applicable).

Certain types of information such as the background details of the company can be obtained from available published records. Other types of written information such as company policies, procedures, and rules can be obtained from the organization's records and documents. Data gathered through such readily available sources are called *secondary data*. Some secondary sources of data are statistical bulletins, government publications, information published or unpublished and available from either within or outside the organization, databases available from previous research, and library records. Certain other types of information, such as the perceptions and attitudes of employees, are best obtained by talking to individuals, by observing events, people, and objects, or by administering questionnaires to individuals. Such data gathered for research from the actual situation where events occur are called *primary data*.

We will now see how the three broad types of information mentioned earlier can be gathered.

Background Information on the Organization

It is important for the researcher or the research team to know some background information about the company or organization to be studied before even conducting the first interview with the officials of the institution. Such background information might include, among other things, the following contextual factors, which may be obtained from various published sources such as trade publications, the

Census of Business and Industry, Directory of Corporations, several other business guides and services, and records available within the organization.

1. The origin and history of the company—when it was started, business it is in, rate of growth, ownership and control, and so on.
2. Size in terms of employees, or assets, or both.
3. Charter—purpose and ideology.
4. Location—regional, national, or other.
5. Resources—human and others.
6. Interdependent relationships with other institutions and the external environment.
7. Financial position during the last five to ten years, and other financial data.

Information gathered on the foregoing aspects will be useful in knowledgeably talking with the others in the company during the subsequent interviews and raising the appropriate issues that may be related to the problem. As an example, the problem of cash flow (which can be gleaned from the balance sheets) may be related to poor quality of raw materials purchased, resulting in a high rate of return of goods sold by the company. This issue can be tactfully investigated during the course of the discussions with the appropriate members in the system if this information is known. Or an industry analysis might reveal that some of the problems encountered are not unique to this company but are faced industrywide, such as competition from foreign producers (as currently being experienced in the auto industry). In such a case, more questions can be focused toward strategies developed by the company to increase sales in the face of foreign competition.

Information on Management Philosophy and Structural Factors

Information on management philosophy, company policies, structure, workflow, and the like, can be obtained by asking direct questions of the management. When questions are directed at several managers individually, it is quite possible that some information received might be conflicting and contradictory. Frequent occurrences of such contradictions might in themselves indicate problems such as poor communication or misperceptions of the organization's philosophy, goals, values, and so forth. These issues can be pursued by the researcher in subsequent interviews and might indicate the extent to which differences in perceptions exist in the organization.

Such information gathering would be particularly useful when new systems, processes, and procedures that have been established do not produce the desired results. The failure of many new technologies, well-meant benefit policies, strategic plans, or marketing or production practices is often due to misunderstandings and misperceptions of the motives of top administration rather than any inherent faults in the mechanisms themselves. Once the misperceptions are cleared, the problem might well disappear. Hence, it is useful to gauge the extent to which such problems exist, right at the start.

Questioning about managerial and company philosophy offers an excellent idea of the priorities and values of the company, as for example: (1) whether product quality is really important to the company or if only lip service is being paid to the concept; (2) whether the company has short-term or long-term goals; (3) whether controls are so tight that creativity is curbed, or they are so loose that nothing gets done, or if they are conducive to good performance; (4) whether this company always wants to play it safe or is a risk-taking venture; and (5) whether this is a people-oriented or solely profits-oriented organization.

Quite frequently, aspects of structure also influence the problem and need to be explored. Below are some of the structural factors.

1. Roles and positions in the organization and number of employees at each job level.
2. Extent of specialization.
3. Communication channels.
4. Control systems.
5. Coordination and span of control.
6. Reward systems.
7. Workflow systems and the like.

It is possible that the respondents' perceptions of the structural variables may not match the formal written structural policies and procedures of the organization. Where such is the case, these become relevant leads to follow during unstructured and structured interviews with various levels of employees in the organization.

Perceptions, Attitudes, and Behavioral Responses

Employee perceptions of the work and the work environment, and their attitudinal and behavioral responses can be tapped by talking to them, observing them, and seeking their responses through questionnaires. A general idea of people's perceptions of their work, the organizational climate, and other aspects of interest to the researcher can be obtained through both unstructured and structured interviews with the respondents. By establishing good rapport with the individuals and following the right questioning techniques—discussed in detail in Chapter 7—the researcher will be able to obtain useful information from the respondents. An understanding of the attitudinal and behavioral reactions of organizational members is often very helpful in arriving at a precise problem definition.

Attitudinal factors comprise people's beliefs about and reactions to the following:

1. Nature of the work.
2. Workflow interdependencies.
3. Superiors in the organization.
4. Participation in decision making.
5. Client systems.

6. Co-workers.

7. Rewards provided by the organization, such as pay and fringe benefits.

8. Opportunities for advancement in the organization.

9. Family environment and relationships.

10. Involvement in community, civic, and other social groups.

11. Views on taking time off the job.

Behavioral factors include actual work habits such as being industrious, extent of absenteeism, performance on the job, and the like.

The respondents could be encouraged at the interviewing stage to talk about their jobs, other work-related factors, non-work-related factors, and their attitudes, values, perceptions, and behaviors, some of which might influence the outcomes at the workplace. Talking to several people at various levels in the organization would give the interviewer a good idea of what is going on there. Detailed discussions on how the unstructured and structured interviews are to be conducted can be seen in Chapter 7, where data-collection methods are discussed.

At this stage a question might arise as to whether asking *all* this information on management philosophy, structure, and perceptions and attitudes is *always* necessary, how the materials will be utilized in the research project, and how much time one should expend in collecting such particulars. The answer to these questions is that there is no substitute for good judgment. Depending on the situation, the type of problem investigated, and the nature of some initial responses received, certain aspects may have to be explored in greater depth than others. For example, if the problem as identified by the manager is related to individuals' attitudes and behaviors, then the value system, the corporate culture, and employee perceptions may have to be delved into more than the structural aspects; on the other hand, if reorganization of the work layout is the subject for the study, then the workflow interdependencies and the coordination aspects will gain more attention. The main idea in gathering information on values, structures, and processes is that these might often reveal the root of the **real problem** rather than merely dealing with the **manifest symptoms.** These distinctions are elaborated later in this chapter. For now, as an illustration, many companies are introducing employee stock ownership plans (ESOP). Not all employees are necessarily excited about this. Rather than right away working toward making the package more attractive through cosmetic changes, talking to individuals might reveal that the employees perceive ESOP merely as a tool to deter takeovers and save taxes, with no true opportunities built in for employee involvement and participation. Understanding this as the main issue to be tackled helps the manager to attack the **real issues** (in this case, the concern and fear of the employees), rather than working on the surface **symptoms** (making cosmetic changes in the package to make it more attractive).

It is for this reason that talking to people at different levels, to understand what some of their concerns are, helps. Spending two or three days interviewing individuals at different levels in the system should generally suffice to get a grasp of the system and the culture of the organization.

Once the interviews are done, the next step for the researcher is to tabulate the various types of information that have been gathered during the interviews and determine if there is a pattern to the responses. For instance, it might be observed that some problems are frequently mentioned by employees at several levels in the organization. Certain factors such as insufficient lighting, untrained personnel, or inadequate tools may be brought out forcefully in the interviews by several workers. When the tabulation reveals that such variables have surfaced quite frequently, it gives the researcher some good ideas about how to proceed with the next step of surveying the literature to see how others have perceived such factors in other work settings and defined the problem before arriving at solutions. Because literature survey is one way of summarizing secondary data and is an important step in the research process for defining the research problem, we will now discuss it in some detail as one of the preliminary data-gathering tools.

Literature Survey

Literature survey is the documentation of a comprehensive review of the published and unpublished work from secondary sources of data in the areas of specific interest to the researcher. The library is a rich storage base for secondary data, and researchers usually spend several weeks, and sometimes months, going through books, journals, newspapers, magazines, conference proceedings, doctoral dissertations, master's theses, several government publications, and financial, marketing, and other reports, to find current information on their research topic.

The researcher is ready to begin the literature survey even as the information from the unstructured and structured interviews is being gathered. Reviewing the literature on the topic area at this time helps the researcher to focus the interviews more meaningfully on certain aspects that were found to be important in the published studies, even if these had not surfaced during the interviews.

Reasons for Literature Survey

The purpose of the literature review is to ensure that no important variable is ignored that has in the past been found repeatedly to have had an impact on the problem. It is possible that some of the critical variables are never brought out in the interviews, either because the employees cannot articulate them or are unaware of their impact, or because the variables seem so obvious to the interviewees that they are not specifically stated. *If there are variables that are not identified during the interviews, but that influence the problem critically, then doing research without considering them would be an exercise in futility.* In such a case, the true reason for the problem would remain unidentified even at the end of the research. To avoid such mishaps, the researcher needs to read all the important research work relating to the particular problem area.

The following example will help to highlight the importance of literature survey. In establishing employee selection procedures, a company might be doing the right things such as administering the appropriate tests to assess the applicants' analytical skills, judgment, leadership, motivation, oral and written communication skills, and the like. Yet, it might be consistently losing excellent MBAs hired as managers, within a year, despite being paid high salaries. The reasons for the turnover of MBAs may not be identified while conducting interviews with the recruiters. However, a review of the literature might indicate that when employees have unmet job expectations (that is, their original expectations of their role and responsibilities did not match actual experiences), they will have a tendency to leave the organization. Talking further to the company officials, it might be found that **realistic job previews** are never offered to the candidates when they are interviewed. This might explain why the candidates might experience frustrations on the job and leave after a while. This important factor significantly influencing the turnover of managerial employees may not have come to light but for the literature survey. If this variable is not included in the research investigation, the problem may not be solved at all!

A survey of the literature not only helps the researcher to include all the relevant variables in the research project, it also facilitates the creative integration of the information gathered from the structured and unstructured interviews with what is found in previous studies. In other words, it gives a good basic framework to proceed further with the investigation. A good literature survey thus provides the foundation for developing a comprehensive theoretical framework from which hypotheses can be developed for testing. The development of the theoretical framework and hypotheses is discussed in the next chapter.

A good literature survey thus ensures that:
1. Important variables that are likely to influence the problem situation are not left out of the study.
2. A clearer idea emerges as to what variables would be most important to consider (parsimony), why they would be considered important, and how they should be investigated to solve the problem. Thus, literature survey helps the development of the theoretical framework and hypotheses for testing.
3. Testability and replicability of the findings of the current research are enhanced.
4. The problem statement can be made with greater precision and clarity.
5. One does not run the risk of "reinventing the wheel," that is, wasting efforts on trying to rediscover something that is already known.
6. The problem investigated is perceived by the scientific community as relevant and of significance.

Conducting the Literature Survey

Based on the specific issues of concern to the manager and the factors identified during the interview process, a literature review needs to be done on these variables. The first step in this process involves identifying the various published and unpublished materials that are available on the topics of interest and gaining access to these. The second step is gathering the relevant information, and the third step is writing up the literature review. These are now discussed.

Identifying the Relevant Sources.   Previously, one had to go through several bibliographical indexes that are compiled periodically listing the journals, books, and other sources in which published work in the area of interest can be found. However, with modern technology, locating sources where the topics of interest have been published has become easy. Almost every library today has computer on-line systems to collect published information on various topics. These can be used to print out all the references that pertain to a given topic. Text databases such as the Source, Dialog, Bibliographic Retrieval Services (BRS), Dow Jones News Retrieval, and so on, made available by vendors can be accessed to obtain information about particular areas of interest. Laser disks or magnetic tapes containing the information needed on various topics are also available.

Basically, three forms of text databases are useful at this stage:

1. **Bibliographic database,** which displays only the bibliographic citations—i.e., the name of the author, the article, source of publication, year, volume, and page numbers.
2. **Abstract database,** which provides, in addition, an abstract or summary of the article.
3. **Full-text database,** which also provides a full text of the article. Thus, entire articles can be retrieved on-line, if necessary.

Some of these databases require familiarity with the vendor's protocals or syntax, but others like BRS's "Brkthru" and Dialog's "Business Connection" provide menu-driven software to access their databases.

Among the other on-line bibliographies available is the *Management Contents,* which provides current information (starting from 1974) on a variety of business and management topics for use in decision making and forecasting. The areas covered are accounting, marketing, operations research, organizational behavior, and public administration.

Business databases are also available for obtaining statistics—marketing, financial, and so on—and directories are organized by subject, title, geographic location, trade opportunities, foreign traders, industrial plants, and so on. Some of these on-line databases are listed in Section 1 of the appendix at the end of this chapter.

On-line searches provide a number of advantages. Besides saving enormous amounts of time, they are thorough in their review of references and focus on materials most central to the research effort. In addition, they are relatively inexpensive.

Bibliographical Indexes.   Bibliographical indexes, which list the articles published in periodicals, newspapers, books, and so on and are periodically updated, are also important sources of information easily accessible to the researcher. Some of these indexes are particularly useful to business students and are listed in Section 2 of the appendix at the end of this chapter. From these sources, a list of the published work in each subject area under the particular topic title can be easily obtained. Sometimes, these could supplement the on-line databases, if the latter are not up-to-date.

Extracting the Relevant Information

Accessing the on-line system and getting a printout of all the published information in the area of interest will provide a comprehensive bibliography on the subject, which will form the basis for the next step. Whereas the printout could sometimes include as many as a hundred or more listings, a glance at the titles of the articles or books will indicate which of these may be pertinent and which others are likely to be peripheral to the contemplated study. The abstract of such articles that seem to be relevant can then be obtained through the on-line system. This will give an idea of the articles that need to be looked into in depth. While reading these articles, detailed information on the problem that was researched, the design details of the study (such as the sample size and data collection methods), and the ultimate findings could be systematically noted. A format as per specimen below (Figure 2.2) might be very useful for the purpose. The advantage of having these sheets is that they would facilitate the writing up of the literature review with minimum disruption and maximum efficiency, rather than wading through a lot of journal articles that might have been Xeroxed. While reading the articles, it is possible that certain other factors are also found to be closely related to the problem at hand. For instance, while reading the articles on the effectiveness of Information Systems, the researcher might find that the size of the company has also been found to be an important factor. The researcher might then want to know more about how the size of organizations is categorized and measured by others and, hence, might want to read materials on organization size. All the articles considered relevant to the current study can be then listed as references using the appropriate referencing format which is discussed in Section 3 of the chapter appendix.

Writing Up the Literature Review

The documentation of the relevant studies citing the author and the year of the study is called literature review or literature survey. The literature survey is a clear and logical presentation of the research work done thus far in the area of investigation. As stated earlier, the purpose of literature survey is to identify and highlight the important variables, and to document the significant findings from earlier research that will serve as the foundation on which the subsequent theoretical framework for the current investigation can be based and the hypotheses developed. Such documentation is important to convince the reader that (1) the researcher is knowledgeable about the problem area and has done the preliminary homework that is necessary to conduct the research; and (2) the theoretical framework will be built on work already done and will add to the solid foundation of existing knowledge.

A point to note is that the literature survey should bring together all relevant information in a cogent and logical manner instead of presenting all the studies in chronological order with bits and pieces of uncoordinated information. A good literature survey also leads one logically into a good problem statement.

There are several accepted methods of citing references in the literature survey section and using quotations. The *Publications Manual of the American Psycholog-*

Figure 2.2
Specimen format for note taking.

Study on: <u>Absenteeism</u> Nath, E. (1945)
           (Topic)   Author/Year

Problem STT

What factors have the greatest influence on absenteeism?

Variables

Age, education, working conditions, marital status, type of job.

Sample

67 mine workers from the XYZ Mine Co., Illinois. Mean age = 35; all males.

Data Collection

All 67 employees were interviewed by three researchers within a period of 3 months inside the mine.

Data Analysis

Correlational and multiple-regression analysis used.

Results

Working conditions influenced absenteeism the most—especially toxic dust and explosions. None of the other variables was significantly related to absenteeism.

Conclusions

Chemicals that would absorb the toxic dust and mechanisms for explosion danger warnings should substantially reduce absenteeism.

Any Other Info/Comments

---

ical Association (1983) offers detailed information regarding citations, quotations, references, and so on, and is one of the accepted styles of referencing in the management area. Other formats include the Chicago *Manual of Style* (1969), and Turabian's *Manual for Writers* (1987). As earlier stated, details of the referencing style and quotations based on the APA Manual (1983) are offered in Section 3 of the appendix at the end of this chapter. Note also that Section 4 of the appendix lists some of the most frequently used journals in business research.

Example and Description of a Literature Survey

Let us take a *portion* of a literature review done by a scholar and examine how the activity has helped to (1) introduce the subject of study, (2) identify the research question, and (3) build on previous research to offer the basis to get to the next steps of theoretical framework and hypotheses development.

> *Organization theorists have defined organizational effectiveness (OE) in various ways. OE has been described in terms of objectives (Georgopolous & Tannenbaum, 1957), goals (Etzioni, 1960), efficiency (Katz & Kahn, 1966), resources acquisition (Yuchtman & Seashore, 1967), employee satisfaction (Cummings, 1977), and interdependence (Pfeffer, 1977). As Coulter (1979) remarked, there is little consensus on how to conceptualize, measure, or explain OE. This should, however, not come to us as a surprise since OE models are essentially value-based classification of the construct (the values being those of the researchers) and the potential number of models that can be generated by researchers is virtually limitless. Researchers are now moving away from a single model and are taking contingency approaches to conceptualizing OE (Cameron, 1981; Yetley, 1984). However, they are still limiting themselves to examining the impact of the dominant constituencies served, and the organization's life cycle on OE instead of taking a broader, more dynamic approach (Burke, 1990, p. 25).*

From the portion of the above extract, several insights can be gained. The literature review (1) introduces the subject of study (organizational effectiveness), (2) highlights the problem (that we do not have a good conceptual framework for understanding what OE is), and (3) summarizes the work so far done on the topic in a manner that convinces the reader that the researcher has indeed surveyed the work done in the area of OE and wants to contribute to the understanding of the concept, taking off on the earlier contingency approaches in a more creative way. The scholar has carefully paved the way for the next step, which is to develop a more viable and robust model of organizational effectiveness. This model will be logically developed integrating several streams of research done in other areas (such as cross-cultural management, sociology, etc.), which will be woven further into the literature review. Once the scholar has explicated the framework as to what constitutes OE and what the factors that influence OE are, the next step would be to develop testable hypotheses to see if the new model is indeed viable.

The literature survey thus provides the basis or foundation to develop a conceptual framework for looking at the problem in a more useful and/or creative way. This, in turn, helps to develop testable hypotheses that would substantiate or disprove our theory.

Examples of good literature survey can be found at the beginning of any article in the *Academy of Management Journal* and most other academic or practitioner-oriented journals. Specimens of a literature survey can also be found later in this book.

One important benefit derived from a well-written literature survey section is that the researcher would be able to delineate a logical, well-defined, and sharply focused problem for research investigation. This delineation or definition of the problem, which is the next step in the research process, is now discussed.

PROBLEM DEFINITION

After the interviews and the literature review, the researcher is in a position to narrow down the problem from its original broad base and define the issues of concern more clearly. It is critical that the focus for further research, or, in other words, the problem, be unambiguously identified and defined. No amount of good research can find solutions to the situation, if the critical issue or the problem to be studied is not clearly pinpointed.

A problem does not necessarily mean that something is seriously wrong with a current situation, which needs to be rectified immediately. A "problem" could simply indicate an interest in an issue where finding the right answers might help to improve an existing good situation. Thus, it is fruitful to **define a problem as any situation where a gap exists between the actual and the desired ideal state.** Basic researchers usually define their problems for investigation from this perspective. For instance, we would ideally like to see zero defects, low stocks of unsold goods, high share quotation in the stock market, and so on. These "problems" could then very well become the foci of research. Thus, problem definitions could encompass both existing problems in a current setting, as well as the quest for idealistic states in organizations. So we find some managers defining their problem as one of severe decline in productivity, or the company fast losing its market share, where the goal is to rectify the situation with a heightened sense of urgency. Other managers might define the "problem" as a situation in which there is considerable interest in attracting highly qualified engineers to the firm, or enhancing the quality of life for their employees.

In either case, one should know what exactly is the issue for which one is trying to seek answers. It is very important that **symptoms** of problems are not *defined* as the real problem. For instance, a manager might have tried to increase productivity by increasing the piece rate, but with little success. Here the real **problem** may be the low morale and motivation of employees who feel they are not being recognized as valuable contributors to the system and get no "praise" for the good work that they do. The low productivity may merely be a **symptom** of the deep-rooted morale and motivational problem. Under these conditions, a higher piece-rate will not improve productivity! Thus, finding the "right" answers to the "wrong" problem definitions will not help. It should be recognized that correct problem identification is as important as, if not more important than, finding the correct solutions.

Frequently, managers tend to describe the problem in terms of symptoms. Rather than accepting it as such, the researcher needs to identify the problem more accurately after talking to the employees and reviewing the literature, as discussed earlier. One way of determining that the problem rather than the symptom is being addressed is to ask the question (after gathering sufficient information through interviews and literature search), "Is this factor I have identified an **antecedent,** the real **problem,** or the **consequence?**" These terms can be discussed in the context of the earlier example of low productivity. The real issue or problem here is low morale and motivation. The consequence of the problem is low productivity. Note that the consequence (or effects) of low motivation can also manifest itself in absenteeism, sabotage, or any number of other ill-consequences for the firm. The real problem that needs to be addressed in this case, hence, is not productivity, but motivation. The antecedent of the problem (i.e., the contributing factor) in the given situation seems to be nonrecognition of the employees' contributions. Until such time as the employees are recognized for their work, their motivation and morale will not increase, nor will their productivity, as a consequence. Without addressing the central issue, if more money, or better equipment is provided to increase productivity the desired results will not ensue, because the right problem would not have been addressed.

Problem definition or problem statement, as it is also often called, is a clear, precise, and succinct statement of the question or issue that is to be investigated with the goal of finding an answer or solution. As mentioned earlier, problem definitions could pertain to (1) existing business problems where a manager is looking for a solution, (2) situations that may not be posing any problems at present but where the manager feels that things may be improved, (3) areas where some conceptual clarity is needed for better theory building, or (4) situations in which a researcher is trying to answer a research question empirically. The former two fall within the realm of applied research, and the latter two are basic research.

Examples of Well-Defined Problems

1. To what extent do the structure of the organization and type of information systems installed account for the variance in the perceived effectiveness of managerial decision making?

2. To what extent has the new advertising campaign been successful in creating the high-quality, customer-centered corporate image that it was intended to produce?

3. What is the influence of information on price and quality on consumers' evaluation of competing brands?

4. Does the income statement in the balance sheet elicit the same kinds of reader reactions toward the company as the cash flow statement?

5. Is the effect of participative budgeting on performance moderated by the control systems?

6. Does better automation lead to greater asset investment for dollar of output?

7. Does international expansion result in an increase in the firm's value?

8. What are the effects of downsizing on the long-range growth patterns of companies?

9. Can cultural differences account for the differences in the nature of hierarchical relationships between superiors and subordinates in Germany, India, Japan, Singapore, and the United States?

10. What are the components of "quality of life"?

SUMMARY

In this chapter, we learned about the first three steps in the research process: identification of the broad problem area to be researched, preliminary data gathering through interviews and literature survey, and problem definition. The appendix to this chapter offers information on on-line databases, bibliographical indexes, APA format for references, referencing previous studies and quoting original sources in the literature review section, and some of the most frequently cited business journals.

In the next chapter we will examine the next two steps in the research process: theoretical framework and hypotheses.

DISCUSSION QUESTIONS AND POINTS TO PONDER

1. How would you describe the research process?

2. Explain the preliminary data-collection methods.

3. Why is it important to gather information on the background of the organization?

4. Should a researcher *always* find information on the structural and job characteristics from those interviewed? Give reasons for your answer with examples.

5. How would you go about doing literature survey in the area of business ethics?

6. What is the purpose of literature survey?

7. Why is appropriate citation important? What are the consequences of not giving credit to the source from which materials are extracted?

8. "The problem definition stage is perhaps more critical in the research process than the problem solution stage." Discuss this statement.

9. Why should one get hung up on problem definition if one already knows the broad problem area to be studied?

10. Access the on-line system in your library and (a) generate a list of the references that relate to the performance of G.M. and (b) obtain the abstracts of these studies.

11. Access the on-line system and obtain a list of references that deal with product image.

12. Offer a clearly focused problem statement in the broad area of corporate culture.

13. After studying and extracting information from all the relevant work done previously, how does the researcher know which particular references, articles, and information should be given prominence in the literature survey?

PRACTICE PROJECT

Do the project assigned below, following the step-by-step process delineated therein:

1. Compile a bibliography on any one of the following topics, or any topic of interest to you from a business perspective: *(a) day care; (b) product development; (c) open-market operations; (d) information systems; (e) manufacturing technology; (f) assessment centers; (g) transfer pricing*

2. From this bibliography, select fifteen references that include books, periodicals, and newspaper items.

3. Based on these fifteen articles, write a literature review using different forms of citations as described in the appendix.

4. Formulate a problem statement.

APPENDIX FOR CHAPTER 2

Section 1
SOME OF THE ON-LINE DATABASES USEFUL FOR BUSINESS RESEARCH

1. **Dialog** offers bibliographies, corporate directories, technical reports, journal abstracts, and complete texts of several journals and newspaper items.

2. **Predicasts** provides business information from business magazines and newspapers, industry trade publications, company annual reports, and industry newsletters. International business, marketing and advertising, new product announcements, etc., are covered.

3. **ABI/INFORM** stresses decision sciences information and includes specific product and industry information.

4. **Disclosure II** offers extracts of reports filed with the U.S. Securities and Exchange Commission by publicly owned companies. Source of information for marketing intelligence, corporate planning and development, portfolio analysis, and legal and accounting research.

5. **ERIC** gives access to the *Psychological Abstracts* and the *Social Science Citation Index,* in addition to covering information from several federal agencies.

Additionally, **INFOTRAC** is a computerized index covering reviews of about 800 business-oriented periodicals.

Section 2
BIBLIOGRAPHICAL INDEXES

Materials for this section have been mostly culled from L. L. Byar's (1987) *Strategic Managment Planning and Implementation Concepts and Cases* (2nd ed.), New York: Harper & Row.

1. *Bibliographic Index: A Cumulative Bibliography of Bibliographies* is an index that lists, by subject, sources of bibliographies.

2. *Business Books in Print* indexes by author, title, and business subjects the books in print in the areas of finance, business, and economics.

3. *Business Periodicals Index* is a cumulative subject index covering 270 business periodicals.

4. *Management Information Guides* offers bibliographic references in many business areas.

5. *Personnel Management Abstracts* is an index of articles that deal with the management of people and organizational behavior.

6. *Psychological Abstracts* summarizes the literature in psychology, covering several hundred journals reports, monographs, and other scientific documents.

7. *Public Affairs Information Service Bulletin* has selective subject index of books, yearbooks, directories, government documents, pamphlets, and over a thousand periodicals relating to national and international economic and public affairs.

8. *Use of Management and Business Literature,* edited by K. D. C. Vernon, provides a bibliography of information on business and management. Includes British publications on business, corporate finance, management, accounting, organizational behavior, management and industrial relations, marketing, computers, and quantitative methods and production.

9. *Work Related Abstracts* contains abstracts of articles, dissertations, and books relating to labor, personnel, and organizational behavior.

FINANCIAL GUIDES AND SERVICES

1. *Business and Investment Service* analyzes production in basic industries, presents stock market trends and indexes, as well as earnings and prices of stocks in selected industries.

2. *Dun and Bradstreet Credit Service* collects, analyzes, and distributes credit information on manufacturers, wholesalers, and retailers. Includes information on the enterprise and offers a detailed statement of the methods of operation, financial statement analysis, management progress, and payment record.

3. *Moody's Bond Record* provides information on dividends declared, payment dates, ex-dividend rates, income bond interest payments, payments on bonds and default, stock split-ups, etc.

4. *Moody's Stock Survey* presents data on stocks, makes recommendations for purchase, sale, or exchange of individual stocks, and discusses industry trends and developments.

5. *Standard and Poor's Corporation Services* offers investment data weekly. They have several publications, one of which is *Standard & Poor's Register of Corporations, Directors, and Executives,* which has three volumes. Volume 1 is an alphabetical listing of over 45,000 U.S. and Canadian companies, volume 2 is a list of executives and directors with a brief about each, and volume 3 contains an index of companies by SIC number and by location.

REFERENCE GUIDES IN THE MARKETING AREA

1. *Topicator* is a classified guide to articles in advertising, communications and marketing periodicals.

2. *Standard Directory of Advertisers* is arranged by industry and gives the names of officers, products, advertising agency, media used, and a "Tradename List."

NEWSPAPER INDEXES OF CURRENT EVENTS

1. *New York Times Index,* published every two weeks, summarizes and classifies news alphabetically by subject, persons, and organizations. It is also accessible on-line.

2. *Wall Street Journal Index,* published monthly, gives complete report on current business. Grouped under "Corporate News" and "General News," the subject index of all articles that have appeared in the *Journal* is also given.

Note: Brown and Vasarhelyi's (1985) database of Accounting literature will be useful for researchers in the Accounting area. Ferris (1988) offers topical areas for Accounting research as well.

Section 3
APA FORMAT FOR REFERENCING THE ARTICLES RELEVANT TO THE STUDY

A *bibliography* is the listing of the work that is relevant to the main topic of research interest arranged in the alphabetical order of the last names of the authors. A *reference* list is a subset of the bibliography, which includes details of all the citations used in the literature survey and elsewhere in the paper, arranged again, in the alphabetical order of the last names of the authors. These listings enable the reader to access the original works cited, if there is a need to do so.

At least three modes of referencing are followed in business research. These are based on the *Manual of the American Psychological Association* (APA) format (1983), the Chicago *Manual* style (1969), and the Turabian style (1987). Each of these manuals specifies, with examples, how books, journals, newspapers, dissertations, and other materials are to be referenced in manuscripts.

Since the APA format is followed by many journals in the management area, we will highlight the distinctions in how books, journals, newspaper articles, dissertations, and so on, are referenced, using the Specimen Referencing format below. We will, in the later section, also briefly discuss how these references will be cited in the literature review section.

It is important that all the citations mentioned in the research report find a place in the references section at the end of the report.

Specimen Format for Referencing

	Item*
Aldag, R. J., & Brief, A. P. (1975). Impact of individual differences on employee affective responses to task characteristics. *Journal of Business Research, 3*(4), 311–322.	1
Alderfer, G. P. (1979). *Existence, relatedness and growth: Human needs in organizational settings.* New York: Free Press.	2
Anonymous (1990). Deeper than you think. *Ninjanka, 2,* p. 5	3
Doudna, C. (1985). Competition between couples: The dark side of success. *Glamour, 83*(3), 298, 299, 356–359, 363, 365.	4
Hackman, J. R., & Oldham, G. R. (1974). *The job diagnostic survey: An instrument for the diagnosis of jobs and the evaluation of job redesign projects* (Tech. Rep. No. 4). New Haven, Conn: Yale University, Department of Administrative Sciences.	5
Kidron, A. G. (1976). *Individual differences, job characteristics and commitment to the organizations.* Unpublished doctoral dissertation, Ohio State University, 1976.	6
Jeanquart, S. (1990, April). *Diversity in the workplace and superior-subordinate relationships.* Paper presented at the meeting of Cultural Diversity, San Jose, CA.	7
Peluchette, J. V. (1990). *Correlates of career success and satisfaction of professionals.* Unpublished manuscript, Southern Illinois University, Carbondale, Department of Management.	8
Sarachek, B. (1990). Chinese administrative thought. In S. B. Prasad (Ed.), *Advances in International Comparative Management: A research annual (5th volume)* (pp. 149–167). Greenwich, Conn.: Jai Press.	9
With GM pact ok, UAW bargainers move on to Ford. (1990, October 2). *Chicago Tribune,* p. 3.	10

	Item*
Yeshwant, M. (1987). Indian philosophy and religion. In S. Pennathur (Ed.), *Proceedings of the Fifth International Conference on Religion* (pp. 90–99). Madras, India.	11
Ziemba, S. (1990, October 2). JMB to sell majority stake in Wisconsin resort hotel. *Chicago Tribune,* p. 3.	12

*Numbers for discussion purposes only.

Nonprint Media

Film

Maas, J. B. (Producer), & Gluck, D. H. (Director). (1979). *Deeper into hypnosis* [film]. Englewood Cliffs, NJ: Prentice Hall.

Cassette Recording

Clark, K. B. (Speaker). (1976). *Problems of freedom and behavior modification* (Cassette Recording No. 7612). Washington, DC: American Psychological Association.

Discussion

First, note that the listing is in the alphabetical order of the last names of the first author. Where the name of the author is not available, the first letter of the article is used as the substitute for the author's name, as in item 10. Where the author has chosen to remain anonymous, this is so cited, as in item 3. The year of the publication is given in parenthesis immediately after the author.

Note that the journal title is underlined (italicized) where articles appear in journals (as in item 1) and book titles are underlined (as in item 2). Volume, issue, and page numbers are to be cited for journals and magazines (items 1 and 4). Discontinuous pages, as in item 4, are to be indicated. Note the differences in the referencing of Technical Reports (item 5), unpublished doctoral dissertation (item 6), and unpublished manuscripts (item 8). See the difference in how a paper presented at a meeting is referenced (item 7) as compared to a paper published in the *Proceedings* after it is presented (item 11). An article that is published as a chapter in an edited book is referenced under the name of the author who wrote the chapter with details of the edited book (item 9). Newspaper articles have the date after the year in parenthesis, as in items 10 and 12.

Occasionally, there may be a need to reference items available from non-print media such as films or cassettes. The last two items provide the format for these, which need to be placed in the alphabetical order in the reference list, if used. Complete details of these and other items that might not have been provided above can be found in the *Publications Manual of the American Psychological Association,* 3rd edition (1983).

Section 4
REFERENCING AND QUOTATION IN THE LITERATURE REVIEW SECTION

Cite all references in the body of the paper using the author–year method of citation; that is, the surname of the author(s) and the year of publication are given at the appropriate places. Examples of this are as follows:

a. Sekaran (1990) has shown . . .

b. In a recent study of dual-career families (Sekaran, 1990) . . .

c. In 1990, Sekaran compared dual-career and dual-earner families and found that . . .

As can be seen from the above, if the name of the author appears as part of the narrative as in the case of (a), the year of publication alone has to be cited in parenthesis. Note that in case (b), both the author and the year are cited in parenthesis, separated by a comma. If the year and the author are a part of the textual discussion as in (c) above, the use of parenthesis is not warranted.

Note also that within the same paragraph, you need not include the year after the first citation so long as the study cannot be confused with other studies cited in the article. An example of this is:

Gutek (1985) wrote a book titled *Sex and the Workplace.* Gutek found that. . . .

When a work is authored by two individuals, always cite both names every time the reference occurs in the text. When a work has more than two authors but fewer than six authors, cite all authors the first time the reference occurs, and subsequently include only the surname of the first author followed by "et al." as per the example below:

Sekaran, U., Martin, T., Trafton, R., and Osborn, R. N. (1980) found . . . (first citation)
Sekaran et al. (1980) found . . . (subsequent citations)

When a work is authored by six or more individuals, cite only the surname of the first author followed by et al. and the year for the first and subsequent citations.

Join the names in a multiple-author citation in running text by the word *and.* In parenthetical material, in tables, and in the reference list, join the names by an ampersand (&). Examples are given below.

a. . . . as Tucker and Snell (1989) pointed out . . .

b. . . . as has been pointed out (Tucker & Snell, 1989), . . .

When a work has no author, cite in text the first two or three words of the reference list entry. Use double quotation marks around the title of the article. For example, while referring to item 10 of the Bibliography on page 50, the text might read as follows:

While examining unions ("With GM pact," 1990) . . .

When a work's author is designated as "Anonymous," cite in text the word *Anonymous* followed by a comma and the date: (Anonymous, 1979). In the reference list, an anonymous work is alphabetized by the word *Anonymous.*

When the same author has several works published in the same year, cite them in the same order as they occur in the reference list, with the in-press citations coming last. For example:

Research on the mental health of dual-career family members (Sekaran, 1985a, 1985b, 1985c, 1990, in-press) indicates . . .

When more than one author has to be cited in the text, these should be in the alphabetical order of the first author's surname, and the citations should be separated by semicolons as per the illustration below:

In the job design literature (Aldag & Brief, 1976; Alderfer, 1972; Beatty, 1982; Jeanquart, 1990), . . .

Personal communication through letters, memos, telephone conversations, and the like, should be cited in the text only and not included in the reference list since these are not retrievable data. In the text, provide the initials as well as the surname of the communicator together with the date, as in the following example:

L. Peters (personal communication, June 15, 1990) feels . . .

In this section we have seen different modes of citation. We will next see how to use quotations.

QUOTATIONS IN TEXT

Quotations should be given exactly as they appear in the source. The original wording, punctuation, spelling, and italics must be preserved even if they are erroneous. The citation of the source of a direct quotation should always include the page number(s) as well as the reference.

Use double quotation marks for quotations in text. Use single quotation marks to identify the material that was enclosed in double quotation marks in the original source. If you want to emphasize certain words in a quotation, underline this and immediately after the underlined words, insert within brackets the words: *italics added.* Use three ellipsis points (. . .) to indicate that you have omitted material from the original source. See example that follows later.

If the quotation is of more than 40 words, set it in a free-standing style starting on a new line and indenting the left margin a further five spaces. Type the entire quotation double spaced on the new margin, indenting the first line of paragraphs five spaces from the new margin, as shown below.

In trying to differentiate dual-earner and dual-career families, Sekaran (1986) states:

> The distinction between dual-career and dual-earner families also gets blurred when spouses currently holding jobs are preparing themselves both educationally and technically to move up in their organizations. . . .
>
> Various terms are used to refer to dual-earner families: dual-worker families, two-paycheck families, dual-income families, two-job families, and so on. Spouses in dual-earner families may both hold jobs, or one of the partners may hold a job while the other pursues a career (p. 4).

If you intend publishing an article in which you have quoted extensively from a copyrighted work, it is important that you seek written permission from the owner of the copyright. Make sure that you also footnote the permission obtained with respect to the quoted material. Failing to do so may result in unpleasant consequences, including legal action taken through copyright protection laws.

Section 5
FREQUENTLY CITED BUSINESS JOURNALS

OB/OT AREA

Academy of Management Journal
Academy of Management Review
Administrative Science Quarterly
Advances in International Comparative Management
American Journal of Small Business
American Sociological Review
Behavioral Research Methods, Instruments, and Computers
Behavioral Science
Business and Society Review
Columbia Journal of World Business
Human Relations
International Journal of Management
Journal of Applied Behavioral Science

Journal of Applied Business Research
Journal of Applied Psychology
Journal of Applied Social Psychology
Journal of Business
Journal of Business Ethics
Journal of Business Research
Journal of Career Planning and Development
Journal of Communication
Journal of Conflict Resolution
Journal of International Business Studies
Journal of Management
Journal of Management Studies
Journal of Occupational Psychology
Journal of Organizational Behavior
Journal of Organizational Behavior Management
Journal of Small Business Management
Journal of Vocational Behavior
Organizational Behavior and Human Decision Processes
Organization Behavior Teaching Review
Sex Roles
Women in Business

OB/OT: PRACTITIONER

Academy of Management Executive
Business Horizons
California Management Review
Group and Organization Studies
Harvard Business Review
Organizational Dynamics
SAM Advanced Management Journal
Sloan Management Review
Supervision

PERSONNEL/HUMAN RESOURCES MANAGEMENT

Employee Benefits Journal
Employee Responsibilities & Rights Journal
Group and Organization Studies
Human Resource Planning
Human Resource Management
Human Resource Management Review
Industrial and Labor Relations Review
Journal of Applied Psychology

Journal of Human Resources
Journal of Human Resource Management
Personnel Administrator
Personnel Psychology
Psychological Bulletin

PERSONNEL: PRACTITIONER-ORIENTED

ASTD Journal
Compensation and Benefits Review
Human Resource Management
Human Resource Development Quarterly
Industrial and Labor Relations Review
Industrial Relations
Monthly Labor Review
Personnel
Personnel Journal
Public Personnel Management
Training
Training and Development Journal

STRATEGIC MANAGEMENT/POLICY

Advances in Strategic Management
International Labor Review
Journal of Business Strategy
Journal of Business Strategies
Journal of Business Venturing
Planning
Planning Review
Strategic Management Journal

STRATEGIC MANAGEMENT/POLICY: PRACTITIONER-ORIENTED

Business Horizons
Long Range Planning

PRODUCTION/OPERATIONS MANAGEMENT

Computer Integrated Manufacturing Review
International Journal of Operations and Production Management
International Journal of Production Research

International Journal of Project Management
Journal of Manufacturing Systems
Journal of Operations Management
Manufacturing and Operations Management
Operations Management Review
P/OM: An International Journal
Production and Inventory Management

POM: PRACTITIONER

Journal of Manufacturing
Industrial Engineering
Production and Inventory Management Review

MANAGEMENT SCIENCE/OPERATIONS RESEARCH

Asia Pacific Journal of Operations Research
Computers and Operations Research
Decision Sciences
European Journal of Operational Research
IIE Transactions
Interfaces
International Journal of Forecasting
International Journal of Project Management
Journal of Forecasting
Journal of Operational Research Society
Management Science
Mathematical and Computer Modeling
Mathematical Programming
Naval Research Logistics Quarterly
OMEGA
Operations Research
OPSEARCH
O.R. Letters
OR Spectrum
Socio-Economic Planning Sciences

MANAGEMENT INFORMATION SYSTEMS

Communications of the ACM
Computing Resources for the Professional
Computing Surveys
Data Base
Data Communications

Decision Sciences
Decision Support Systems
IBM Systems Journal
IEEE Expert
Information Age
Information and Management
Information Systems Management
Information Systems Research
Interfaces
International Journal of Computer Applications Technology
International Journal of Technology Management
Journal of Information Systems
Journal of Information Systems Management
Journal of Management Information Systems
Journal of Systems Management
MIS Quarterly
Neural Networks

MIS: PRACTITIONER

Business Communications Review
Computer World
Databased Advisor
Database Programming and Design
Datamation
Infoworld
Interface
MIS Week
Network World
PC World

RESEARCH AND DEVELOPMENT

Engineering Management International
IEEE Transaction in Engineering Management
International Journal of Technology Management
Research Policy
Research Management
Tecnovation

R&D: PRACTITIONER

Research Management

MARKETING

Advertising Age
Industrial Marketing Management
International Journal of Research in Marketing
Journal of Academy of Marketing Science
Journal of Advertising
Journal of Advertising Research
Journal of Business & Industrial Marketing
Journal of Consumer Research
Journal of Healthcare Marketing
Journal of International Marketing
Journal of Macromarketing
Journal of Marketing
Journal of Marketing Education
Journal of Marketing Research
Journal of Public Policy and Marketing
Journal of Retailing
Journal of Services Marketing
Marketing Science

MARKETING: PRACTITIONER

Direct Marketing
Journal of Business and Industrial Marketing
Journal of Consumer Marketing
Journal of Personal Selling and Sales Management
Journal of Services Marketing
Psychology and Marketing

ACCOUNTING

Accountancy
Accounting & Business Research
Accounting Historians Journal
Accounting, Organization and Society
Accounting Review
Auditing: A Journal of Theory and Practice
Behavioral Research in Accounting
International Journal of Accounting, Education & Research
Journal of Accountancy
Journal of Accounting and Economics
Journal of Accounting Research

Journal of Accounting, Auditing & Finance
Journal of Accounting and Public Policy
Journal of Accounting Literature
Journal of Real Estate Taxation
Journal of Taxation
Management Accounting Research
National Tax Journal
Woman CPA

ACCOUNTING: PRACTITIONER

Accounting Horizons
The CPA Journal
Journal of Accountancy
Management Accounting

FINANCE

Credit and Financial Management
Finance and Development
Financial Management
Financial Review
Journal of Accounting, Auditing and Finance
Journal of Banking and Finance
Journal of Business Finance and Accounting
Journal of Finance
Journal of Financial and Quantitative Analysis
Journal of Financial Economics
Journal of Financial Research
Journal of Financial Services Research
Journal of International Business
Journal of International Financial Markets Institutions and Money
Journal of Money, Credit and Banking
Midland Corporate Finance Journal
Review of Financial Studies

FINANCE: PRACTITIONER-ORIENTED

American Banker
Bankers Magazine
Economic Review of the FED

Financial Analysts Journal
Journal of Portfolio Management
Magazine of Bank Administration
Midland Corporate Financial Journal
Real Estate Finance

CHAPTER 3

THE RESEARCH PROCESS

Steps 4 and 5: Theoretical Framework Hypothesis Development

TOPICS DISCUSSED

THE NEED FOR A THEORETICAL FRAMEWORK

VARIABLES
- Dependent Variable
- Independent Variable
- Moderating Variable
- Intervening Variable

THE THEORETICAL FRAMEWORK AND ITS FIVE BASIC FEATURES

HYPOTHESIS DEVELOPMENT
- Definition
- If-Then Statements
- Directional and Nondirectional Hypotheses
- Null and Alternate Hypotheses

CHAPTER OBJECTIVES

After completing Chapter 3 you should be able to:

1. Identify and label variables associated with a given situation.
2. Trace and establish the links among the variables and evolve a theoretical framework.
3. Develop a set of hypotheses to be tested and state them in the null and the alternate.
4. Apply the learnings to a research project.

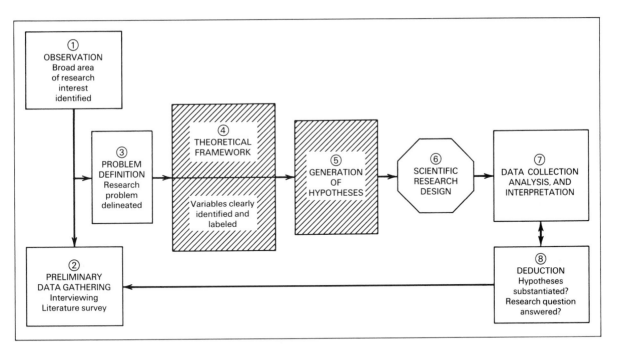

In the previous chapter, the focus was on learning how to narrow down and clearly define the research problem. We can now examine steps 4 and 5 in the research process model—the shaded portions in the figure above. Step 4 relates to evolving a theoretical framework, and step 5 is concerned with deriving testable hypotheses. In this chapter we will discuss both topics in some depth.

You will note, as you proceed in this chapter, that you are instructed to work out certain exercises organized at the end of the chapter. Doing these exercises at the time you are asked to, before reading further, will help you in becoming adept at formulating theoretical frameworks in a logical manner without getting confused.

THE NEED FOR A THEORETICAL FRAMEWORK

After conducting the interviews, completing a literature survey, and defining the problem, one is ready to develop a theoretical framework. A theoretical framework is a conceptual model of how one theorizes the relationships among the several factors that have been identified as important to the problem. This theory flows logically from the documentation of previous research in the problem area. Integrating one's logical beliefs with published research is pivotal in developing a scientific basis for investigating the research problem. In sum, the theoretical framework discusses the interrelationships among the variables that are deemed to be integral to the dynamics of the situation being investigated. Developing such a conceptual framework helps us to postulate and test certain relationships so as to improve our understanding of the dynamics of the situation.

From the theoretical framework, then, testable hypotheses can be developed to see whether the theory formulated is valid or not. The hypothesized relationships can thereafter be tested through appropriate statistical analyses. By being able to test and replicate the findings, we will also have more faith in the rigor of our research. Thus, the theoretical framework is the basis on which the entire research rests. Even if testable hypotheses are not necessarily generated (as in some applied research projects), developing a good theoretical framework is central to examining the problem under investigation.

Since the theoretical framework offers the conceptual foundation to proceed with the research, and since a theoretical framework is nothing other than identifying the network of relationships among the **variables** considered important to the study of any given problem situation, it is essential to understand what a variable means and what the different types of variables are.

VARIABLES

A variable is anything that can take on differing or varying values. The values can differ at various times for the same object or person, or the values can differ at the same time for different objects or persons. Examples of variables are exam scores, absenteeism, and motivation.

Example 3.1   *Exam score:* One's score on exams one, two, and three for a particular subject could be different (take on varying values), or the scores of different students for the same exam could be different. In both cases, the exam score has taken on different values and hence is a variable.

Example 3.2   *Absenteeism:* Today three class members may be absent, tomorrow five students may not show up in class; the day after, there may be no one absent. The value can thus theoretically range from "zero" to "all" being absent on the absenteeism variable.

Example 3.3   *Motivation:* The levels of motivation to learn among members in the class or in a work team might take on varying values ranging from "very low" to "very high." An individual's motivation to learn from different classes or in different work teams might also take on differing values. Now, how one *measures* the level of motivation is an entirely different matter. The factor called motivation has to be reduced from its level of abstraction and operationalized in a way that it becomes measurable. We will discuss this later, in Chapter 6.

Types of Variables

Four main types of variables are discussed in this chapter:

1. The dependent variable (also known as the criterion variable).
2. The independent variable (also known as the predictor variable).
3. The moderating variable.
4. The intervening variable.

Extraneous variables that confound cause → effect relationships are discussed in Chapter 5 on Experimental Design.

Dependent Variable

The dependent variable is the variable of primary interest to the researcher. The researcher's goal is to explain or predict the variability in the dependent variable. In other words, it is the main variable that lends itself as a viable issue for investigation. Through the analysis of the dependent variable (i.e., what variables influence it), it is possible to find answers or solutions to the problem. The researcher is interested in quantifying and measuring this variable, as well as the other variables that influence this variable.

Example 3.4   A manager is concerned that the sales of a new product introduced after market testing is not as high as he had expected. The dependent variable here is sales. Since the sales of the product can vary—can be low, medium, high—it is a variable; since sales is the main factor of interest to the manager, it is the dependent variable.

Example 3.5   A basic researcher is interested in investigating the extent to which organizational romances are either discouraged or frowned upon by corporate CEOs. Here the dependent variable is **attitude toward organizational romances.** The attitudes can vary from active discouragement to frowning to indifference to active encouragement.

Example 3.6   A personnel manager is concerned that the employees are not loyal to the organization and, in fact, switch their loyalties to other institutions. The dependent variable in this case would be *organizational loyalty.*

Here again, there is variance found in the levels of organizational loyalty in employees. The personnel manager might want to know what accounts for the variance in the loyalty of organizational members, so that he can control the variance. Suppose that he finds that high pay would keep members loyal to the organization and they will not leave the job for another position with another organization. Pay increases given to employees might then help control the variability, and people may stick to this organization.

It is possible to have more than one dependent variable in a study. For example, there is always a tension between quality and volume of output, between low-cost production and customer satisfaction, and so on. In such cases, the manager will be interested in knowing the factors that influence all the dependent variables of interest and how some of the factors might differ in regard to different dependent variables. These investigations may call for multivariate statistical analyses. Whereas multiple regression analysis is discussed later in this book, discussions of multivariate analyses are beyond the scope of this book.

Now respond to Exercises 3.1 and 3.2.

Independent Variable

An independent variable is one that influences the dependent variable in either a positive or a negative way. That is, when the independent variable is present, the dependent variable is also present, and with each unit of increase in the independent variable, there is an increase or decrease in the dependent variable also. In other words, the variance in the dependent variable is accounted for by the independent variable. To establish causal relationships, the independent variable is manipulated as described in Chapter 5 on Experimental Designs.

Example 3.7   Research studies indicate that successful new product development has an influence on the stock market price of the company. Here the development of a successful new product influences the stock market price and explains the variance in it. That is, the more successful the new product is believed to be, the higher will be the stock market price of that firm. Therefore, the **success of the new product** is the *independent variable,* and **stock market price** is the *dependent variable.* The degree of perceived success of the new product developed will explain the variance in the stock market price of the company. This relationship and the labeling of the variables is diagrammed in Figure 3.1.

Figure 3.1
Diagram showing the relationship between the independent variable (new product success) and the dependent variable (stock market price).

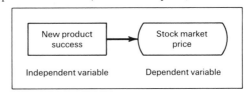

Figure 3.2
Diagram showing the relationship between the independent variable (managerial values) and the dependent variable (power distance).

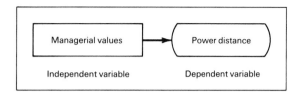

Example 3.8   Cross-cultural research indicates that managerial values govern the power distance between superiors and subordinates. Here, power distance (i.e., egalitarian interactions between the boss and the employee versus the high-power superior in interaction with the low-power subordinate) is the subject of interest and hence is the **dependent variable.** Managerial values, which explain the variance in power distance, is the **independent variable.** This relationship is diagrammed in Figure 3.2.

> **Now do Exercises 3.3 and 3.4.**

Moderating Variable

The moderating variable is one that has a strong contingent effect on the independent variable–dependent variable relationship. That is, the presence of a third variable (the moderating variable) modifies the originally expected relationship between the independent and the dependent variables. This becomes clear through the following examples.

Example 3.9   It has been found that there is a relationship between the number of books that five- and six-year-old children have access to at home and their reading abilities. That is, if five- and six-year-olds are provided with a lot of children's books, their reading skills and abilities will improve because the children have greater opportunities to read more books—an activity in which they are assisted by their parents—and hence read better. As a corollary, if children are reared in homes where there are no books, they will have no opportunities to cultivate the reading habit, and hence their reading skills and abilities will be deficient. It is thus argued that there is a relationship between the independent variable, *number of books,* and the dependent variable, *reading abilities,* which is diagrammed in Figure 3.3a.

Although this relationship can be said to hold true generally for all children, it is nevertheless contingent on the extent of literacy of the parents who facilitate the preschool children to learn to read at home. With totally illiterate parents, no

Figure 3.3a
Diagram showing the relationship between the independent variable (number of books) and the dependent variable (reading abilities).

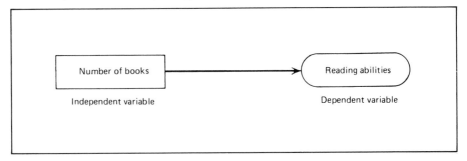

amount of books at home will help the child to develop reading skills and abilities! Thus *parents' literacy* moderates the relationship between the number of books and reading abilities. To put it differently, the relationship between the number of children's books at home and the reading abilities of five- and six-year-old children is contingent or dependent on the literacy of the parents. This influence of parents' literacy on the relationship between the independent and the dependent variable can be diagrammed as in Figure 3.3b.

As in the above case, whenever the relationship between the independent variable and the dependent variable becomes contingent or dependent on another variable, we say that the third variable has a moderating effect on the independent variable–dependent variable relationship. The variable that moderates the relationship is known as the moderating variable.

Figure 3.3b
Diagram of the relationship between the independent variable (number of books) and the dependent variable (reading abilities) as moderated by the moderating variable (parents' literacy).

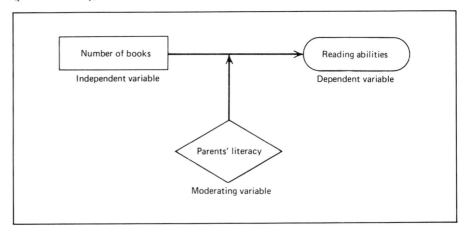

Figure 3.4
Diagram of the relationships among the three variables: workforce diversity, organizational effectiveness, and managerial expertise.

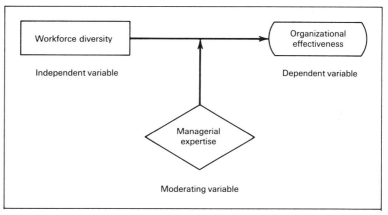

Example 3.10   Let us take another example of a moderating variable related to the organizational setting. An emerging theory is that the projected diverse workforce of the future (comprising different ethnic origins, races, and nationalities) will contribute more to organizational effectiveness because each group will bring its own special expertise and skills to the workplace. This synergy can be captured, however, only if managers know how to harness the special talents of the diverse work group.

In the above scenario, organizational effectiveness is the **dependent variable,** which is positively influenced by the diverse workforce, which is the **independent variable.** However, to harness the potential, managers must know how to encourage and coordinate the talents of the various groups to make things work. If not, the synergy will not be captured. In other words, the effective utilization of different talents, perspectives, and eclectic problem-solving capabilities to enhance organizational effectiveness is contingent upon the skill of the managers in acting as catalysts. This managerial expertise then becomes the **moderating variable.** These relationships can be depicted as in Figure 3.4.

The Distinction Between an Independent Variable and a Moderating Variable

At times, one could get confused as to when a variable is to be treated as an independent variable and when it would become a moderating variable. For instance, there may be two situations as follows:

Situation 1

A research study indicates that the better the quality of the training programs in an organization and the greater the growth needs of the employees, the greater their willingness to learn new ways of doing things.

Situation 2

Another research study indicates that the willingness of the employees to learn new ways of doing things is not influenced by the quality of the training programs offered by the organizations for *all* people. Only those who have high growth needs seem to be willing to learn to do new things through specialized training.

In the above two situations, we have the same three variables. In the first case, the training programs and growth need strength are the independent variables that influence employees' willingness to learn—the dependent variable. In the second case, however, the quality of the training program is the independent variable, and while the dependent variable remains the same, growth need strength becomes a moderating variable. In other words, only those who have high growth needs (i.e., the growth need is strong) will become more willing to learn to do new things when the quality of the training program is increased. Thus the relationship between the independent and dependent variables has now become contingent on the existence of a moderator.

The above illustration makes it clear that even though the variables used may be the same, the decision whether to label them dependent, independent, or moderating would depend on how they affect one another. The differences between the effects of the independent and the moderating variables could be visually depicted as in Figures 3.5a and b.

Now do Exercises 3.5 and 3.6.

Intervening Variable

An intervening variable is one that surfaces between the time the independent variables operate to influence the dependent variable and their impact on the dependent variable. There is thus a temporal quality or time dimension to the intervening variable. The intervening variable surfaces as a function of the independent variable(s) operating in any situation, and helps to conceptualize and explain the influence of the independent variable(s) on the dependent variable. The following example illustrates this point.

Example 3.11   In Example 3.10 where the **independent variable** workforce diversity influenced the **dependent variable** organizational effectiveness, an **intervening variable** that surfaces as a function of the diversity in the workforce is *creative synergy*. This creative synergy results from a multiethnic, multiracial, and multinational (i.e., diverse) workforce interacting and bringing together their multifaceted expertise in problem solving. This helps us to understand how organizational effectiveness can result from having diversity in the workforce. Note that creative synergy, the intervening variable, surfaces at time t_2 as a function of workforce diversity, which was in place at time t_1, to bring about organizational effectiveness in time t_3. The

Figure 3.5a
Illustration of the influence of independent variables on the dependent variable when no moderating variable operates in the situation.

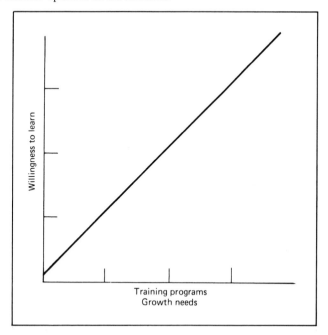

Figure 3.5b
Illustration of the influence of an independent variable on the dependent variable when a moderating variable is operating in the situation.

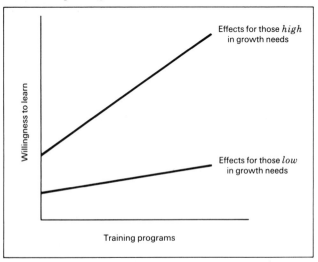

Figure 3.6
Diagram of the relationships among the independent, intervening, and dependent variables.

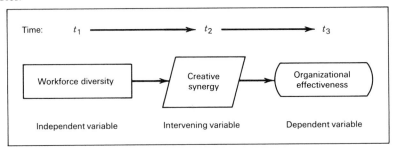

intervening variable of creative synergy helps us to conceptualize and understand how workforce diversity brings about organizational effectiveness. The dynamics of these relationships are illustrated in Figure 3.6.

Example 3.12   It would be interesting to see how the inclusion of the moderating variable *managerial expertise* in the foregoing example would change the model or affect the relationships. The new set of relationships that would emerge in the presence of the **moderator** can be depicted as in Figure 3.7. As can be seen therefrom, managerial expertise moderates the relationship between workforce diversity and creative synergy. In other words, creative synergy will not emerge from the multi-faceted problem-solving skills of the diverse workforce unless the manager is capable of harnessing that synergy by creatively coordinating the different skills. If the manager has no expertise to perform this role, then no matter how many

Figure 3.7
Diagram of the relationships among independent, intervening, moderating, and dependent variables.

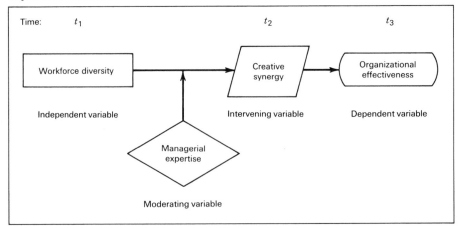

different problem-solving skills the diverse workforce has, synergy will just not surface. The organization might just remain static instead of functioning effectively.

It is now easy to see what the differences among an independent variable, intervening variable, and a moderating variable are. The **independent** variable helps to *explain* the variance in the dependent variable; the **intervening** variable *surfaces at time* t_2 as a function of the independent variable, which also helps us to conceptualize the relationship between the independent and dependent variables; and the **moderating** variable has a *contingent effect* on the relationship between two variables. To put it differently, while the independent variable explains the variance in the dependent variable, the intervening variable does not add to the variance already explained by the independent variable, whereas the moderating variable has an interaction effect with the independent variable in explaining the variance. That is, unless the moderating variable is present, the theorized relationship between the other two variables considered will not hold.

Whether a variable is an independent variable, a dependent variable, an intervening variable, or a moderating variable should be determined by a careful reading of the dynamics operating in any particular situation. For instance, a variable such as motivation to work could be a dependent variable, an independent variable, an intervening variable, or a moderating variable, depending on the theoretical model that is being advanced.

> **Now do Exercises 3.1, 3.8, and 3.9.**

THEORETICAL FRAMEWORK

Having examined the different kinds of variables that could operate in a situation and how the relationships among these can be established, it is now possible to see how we can develop conceptual models, or theoretical frameworks, for our research.

The theoretical framework is the foundation on which the entire research project is based. It is a logically developed, described, and elaborated network of associations among variables that have been identified through such processes as interviews, observations, and literature survey. These variables are deemed relevant to the problem situation. It becomes evident at this stage that to find good solutions to the problem, one should first identify the problem correctly and then identify variables that contribute to the problem. The importance of conducting good surveys and doing a thorough literature review now becomes clear. After the identification of the proper variables, the network of associations among the variables needs to be elaborated so that relevant hypotheses can be developed and subsequently tested. Based on the results of the tests of hypotheses (which would indicate whether or not the hypotheses have been supported), the extent to which the problem can be solved through the findings of the research becomes evident. The theoretical framework is thus an important step in the research process.

The relationship between the literature survey and the theoretical framework is that the literature survey provides a solid foundation for developing the theoretical framework. That is, the literature survey identifies the variables that might be important, as determined by previous research findings. This, in addition to other logical connections that can be conceptualized, forms the basis for the theoretical model. The theoretical framework elaborates the relationships among the variables, explains the theory underlying these relations, and describes the nature and direction of the relationships. Just as the literature survey sets the stage for the theoretical framework, a good theoretical framework, in turn, provides the logical base for developing testable hypotheses.

The Components of the Theoretical Framework

A good theoretical framework identifies and labels the important variables in the situation that are relevant to the problem defined. It logically describes the interconnections among these variables. The relationships among the independent variables, the dependent variables, and if applicable, the moderating and intervening variables are elaborated. If there are any moderating variables, it is important to explain how and what specific relationships they would moderate. An explanation of why they operate as moderators should also be presented. If there are any intervening variables, a discussion on how or why they are treated as intervening variables would be necessary. Any interrelationships among the independent variables themselves, or among the dependent variables themselves (in case there are two or more dependent variables of interest to the researcher), should also be clearly spelled out and adequately explained.

The elaborations in the theoretical framework thus address the issues of why or how we expect certain relationships to exist, and the nature and direction of the relationships among the variables of interest. A schematic diagram of the conceptual model described in the theoretical framework will also help the reader to visualize the theorized relationships.

It may be noted that we have used the terms *theoretical framework* and *model* interchangeably. There are differences of opinion as to what a model actually represents. Some describe models as simulations; others view a model as a representation of relationships between and among concepts. We use the term *model* in the latter sense as a conceptual scheme connecting concepts.

There are five basic features that should be incorporated in any theoretical framework.

1. The variables considered relevant to the study should be clearly identified and labeled in the discussions.
2. The discussions should state how two or more variables are related to each other. This should be done for the important relationships that are theorized to exist among the variables.

3. If the nature and direction of the relationships can be theorized on the basis of the findings from previous research, then there should be an indication in the discussions as to whether the relationships would be positive or negative.

4. There should be a clear explanation of why we would expect these relationships to exist. The arguments could be drawn from the previous research findings.

5. A schematic diagram of the theoretical framework should be given so that the reader can visualize the theorized relationships.

Let us see how these five features can be incorporated in a theoretical framework in a problem situation faced by Delta Airlines, as explained in Example 3.13.

Example 3.13   Very briefly, with airline deregulation, there were price wars among the various airlines, which tried to cut costs in different ways. In 1987, **Delta Airlines** faced charges of **air safety violations** when there were several near collisions midair and one accident resulting in 137 deaths. Four important factors that seemed to have influenced these are poor communication among the cockpit crew members themselves, poor coordination between ground staff and cockpit crew, minimal training given to the cockpit crew, and management philosophy that encouraged a decentralized structure. It would be nice to know if these factors did indeed contribute to the safety violations and if so, to what extent.

Developing a Theoretical Framework

Information Needed to Research the Problem in Example 3.13

The variable of primary interest to this research is **safety violations,** the variance in which is attempted to be explained by the four independent variables. At different times during the period from airline deregulation to the point when Delta was charged with safety violations, the number of incidents varied. Presuming that we can gain access to the records of (1) communications among cockpit crew members, (2) communication between cockpit crew and ground control, (3) training given to the various pilots, and (4) the extent to which decentralization operated in the system during each time period when the incidents occurred, we can research the issue using the following theoretical framework.

Theoretical Framework for Example 3.13

The dependent variable is safety violation, which is the variable of primary interest, the variance in which is attempted to be explained by the four independent variables of communication among crew members, communication between ground control and the cockpit crew, training received by the cockpit crew, and decentralization.

Figure 3.8
Schematic diagram of the theoretical framework in Example 3.13.

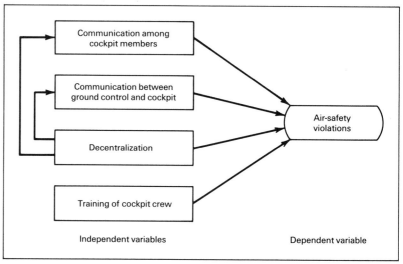

The less the communication among the crew members themselves, the greater the probability of air safety violations since there will be very little information shared among the members, as for example, the navigator and the pilot, when there are threats to safety. Each member will be doing his or her own thing and lose sight of the big picture. When ground crew do not give the right information at the right time, mishaps are bound to occur with aborted flights and collisions. Coordination between ground and cockpit crew is at the very heart of air safety. Thus, the less the coordination between ground control and cockpit crew, the greater the possibility of air-safety violations taking place. Both the above factors are exacerbated by the managerial philosophy of Delta Airlines, which emphasizes decentralization. While this philosophy might have worked before the deregulation of the airlines, when the number of flights was manageable, with deregulation and increased flights overall in midair with all airlines operating many more flights, centralized coordination and control assume great importance. Thus, the greater the degree of decentralization, the greater the scope for lower levels of communication both among in-flight staff and between ground staff and cockpit crew, and the greater the scope for air-safety violations. Also, when cockpit crew members are not trained well, they may not know what the safety standards are or how to handle emergency situations and avoid collisions. Thus, poor training also adds to the probability of increased safety violations. These relationships are diagrammed in Figure 3.8.

Note how the five basic features of the theoretical framework have been incorporated in the example.

1. Identification and labeling of the dependent and independent variables have been done in the theoretical framework.

2. The relationships among the variables were discussed, establishing that the four independent variables are related to the dependent variable, and that the independent variable decentralization is related to the other two independent variables, communication among the cockpit members and between ground control and the cockpit crew.

3. The nature and direction of the relationship of each independent variable with the dependent variable and the relationship of decentralization to the two independent variables mentioned in item 2 above were clearly stated. For example, it was indicated that the lower the training level of the cockpit crew, the greater the chances of air-safety violations. Thus, as the training is lowered, the hazard is increased, or conversely, the higher the training, the less likely the air-safety violations, indicating a negative relationship between the two variables. Such a negative relationship exists between each of the independent variables and the dependent variable. There is also a negative relationship between decentralization and communication among cockpit members (the more the decentralization, the less the communication) and decentralization and coordination (the more the decentralization, the less the coordination).

4. Why these relationships can be expected was explained through several logical statements, as for example describing why decentralization, which worked before deregulation, would not now work. More specifically, it was argued that:
   a. lower communication among cockpit crew would fail to alert the pilot about impending hazards;
   b. poor coordination between ground control and cockpit crew would be detrimental because such coordination is the very essence of safety;
   c. encouragement of decentralization would only reinforce poorer communication and coordination efforts;
   d. inadequate training of cockpit crew will fail to build survival skills.

5. The relationships among the variables have been schematically diagrammed (see Figure 3.8).

It would now be interesting to see if we can interject an **intervening** variable in the model. For example, we can say that lack of adequate training makes the pilots **nervous and diffident,** and this in turn explains why they are not able to confidently handle situations in midair when many aircraft are in flight. Nervousness and diffidence are a function of lack of training and help to explain why inadequate training would result in air-safety hazard. This scenario can be depicted as in Figure 3.9.

We can also substantially change the model by using poor training as a moderating variable as shown in Figure 3.10. Here, we are theorizing that poor communication, poor coordination, and decentralization are likely to result in air-safety violations only in such cases where the pilot in charge has had inadequate training. In other words, those who have had adequate training in deftly handling hazardous situations through simulated training sessions, and so forth, would not be handicapped by poor communication and coordination, and in cases where the aircraft is in charge of well-trained pilots, poor communication and coordination will not result in hazards to safety.

Figure 3.9
Schematic diagram of the theoretical framework including an intervening variable.

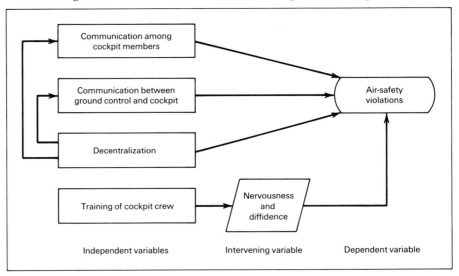

Figure 3.10
Schematic diagram of the theoretical framework including a moderating variable.

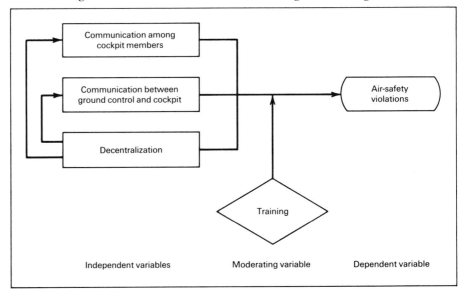

These examples illustrate that the same variable could be an independent, intervening, or moderating variable, depending on how we conceptualize our theoretical model.

Now do Exercises 3.10 and 3.11.

HYPOTHESES DEVELOPMENT

Once we have identified the important variables in a situation and established the relationships among them through logical reasoning in the theoretical framework, we are in a position to test whether the relationships that have been theorized do in fact hold true. By testing these relationships scientifically, through appropriate statistical analyses or through negative case analysis in qualitative research (described later in the chapter) we are able to obtain some reliable information on what kinds of relationships exist among the variables operating in the problem situation. The results of these tests offer us some clues as to what could be changed in the situation to solve the problem. Formulating such testable statements is called hypotheses development.

Definition of Hypothesis

An hypothesis is an educated guess about a problem's solution. It can be defined as a logically conjectured relationship between two or more variables expressed in the form of testable statements. These relationships are conjectured on the basis of the network of associations established in the theoretical framework formulated for the research study.

Example 3.14   Several testable statements or hypotheses can be drawn from the theoretical framework formulated in Example 3.13. One of them could be as follows:

If the pilots are given adequate training to handle midair crowded situations, air-safety violations will be reduced.

The above is a testable statement. By measuring the extent of training given to the various pilots and the number of safety violations committed by them over a period of time, we can statistically examine the relationship between these two variables to see if there is a significant negative correlation between the two. If we do find a significant negative correlation, then the hypothesis is substantiated; if a significant negative correlation is not found, then the hypotheses would not have been substantiated. By convention in the social sciences, to call a relationship "statistically significant," it should be possible to find the observed relationship **by chance** only five times out of a hundred. To put it differently, we should be confident that ninety-five times out of a hundred, the observed relationship will hold true.

We would of course expect our hypothesis to be substantiated through the data analysis, because it is a logically conjectured relationship. However, if the hypothesis is not substantiated, we would search for possible reasons for this. We might even suspect that some other important variable that has a contingent influence on the relationship between the two variables was ignored. After reviewing the literature, we might in fact discover that previous research has identified such a moderating variable. Thus we might discover, perhaps a little too late, that the theoretical framework missed an important moderating variable. Incidentally, a situation such as this sensitizes us to the fact that a thorough literature survey is essential to ensure adequately and appropriately developed theoretical frameworks. In other words, a good literature survey helps to develop a good theoretical framework, and a good theoretical framework enables us to develop good, testable hypotheses, where the conjectured relationships would hold.

Statement of Hypotheses: Formats

If-Then Statements

As already stated, a hypothesis is a testable statement of the relationship among variables. A hypothesis can also test whether there are differences between two groups (or among several groups) with respect to any variable or variables. To examine whether the conjectured relationships or differences exist or not, these hypotheses can be set either as propositions or in the form of **if-then** statements. The two formats can be seen in the following two examples.

Example 3.15   Employees who are more healthy will take sick leave less frequently.

Example 3.16   **If** employees are more healthy, **then,** they will take sick leave less frequently.

If, in stating the relationship between two variables or comparing two groups, terms such as "positive," "negative," "more than," "less than," and the like are used, then these hypotheses are **directional.** These are called directional hypotheses because they indicate the direction of the relationship between the variables (positive/negative) as in Example 3.17 below or postulate the nature of the difference between two groups on a variable (more than/less than) as in Example 3.18.

Example 3.17   The greater the stress experienced in the job, the lower the job satisfaction of employees.

Example 3.18   Women are more motivated than men.

On the other hand, **nondirectional** hypotheses are those that do postulate a relationship or difference, but offer no indication of the direction of these relationships or differences. In other words, though it may be conjectured that there would be a significant relationship between two variables, we may not be able to say whether the relationship would be positive or negative as in Example 3.19. Likewise, even if we can conjecture that there will be differences between two groups on a particular variable, we will not be able to say which group will be more and which less on that variable, as in Example 3.20.

Example 3.19   There is a relationship between age and job satisfaction.

Example 3.20   There is a difference between the work ethic values of American and Asian employees.

Nondirectional hypotheses could be formulated either because the relationships or differences have never been previously explored and hence there is no basis for indicating the direction, or because there have been conflicting findings in previous research studies on the variables. In some studies a positive relationship might have been found, while in others, a negative relationship might have been traced. Hence, the current researcher might only be able to hypothesize that there would be a significant relationship, but the direction may not be clear. In such cases, the hypotheses could be stated nondirectionally. Note that in Example 3.19 there is no clue as to whether age and job satisfaction are positively or negatively correlated, and in Example 3.20 we do not know whether the work ethic values are stronger in Americans or in Asians. However, in Example 3.19, it would have been possible to state that age and job satisfaction are positively correlated, since previous research has indicated such a relationship. Wherever the direction is known, it is better to indicate the direction for reasons that will shortly become clear.

Null and Alternate Hypotheses

The null hypothesis is a proposition that states a definitive, exact relationship between two variables. That is, it states that the population correlation between two variables is equal to zero or that the difference in the means of two groups in the population is equal to zero (or some **definite** number). In general, the null statement is expressed as no (**significant**) relationship between two variables or no (**significant**) difference between two groups, as we will see in the various examples in this chapter. The alternate hypothesis, which is the opposite of the null, is a statement expressing a relationship between two variables or indicating differences between groups.

To explain it further, in setting up the null hypothesis, we are stating that there is no difference between what we might find in the population characteristics (i.e., the total group we are interested in knowing something about) and the samples we are studying (i.e., a limited number representative of the total population or group that we have chosen to study). Since we do not know the true state of affairs in the population, all we can do is to make inferences about it on the basis of our sample. What we are implying through the null hypothesis is that any differences found between two sample groups or any relationships found between two variables based on our sample is simply due to random sampling fluctuations and not due to any "true" differences between the two population groups (say, men and women), or relationships between two variables. The null hypothesis is thus formulated so that it can be tested for possible rejection. If we reject the null hypothesis, then all permissible alternative hypotheses relating to the particular relationship tested could be supported. It is the theory that allows us to have faith in the alternative hypothesis that is generated in the particular research investigation. This is one more reason why the theoretical framework should be grounded in sound, defendable logic to start with. Otherwise, other researchers are likely to refute and postulate other defensible explanations through different alternative hypotheses.

The null hypothesis in respect to group differences stated in our Example 3.18 would be:

$$H_0: \mu_M = \mu_W$$

or

$$H_0: \mu_M - \mu_W = 0$$

where H_0 represents the term null hypothesis
μ_M is the mean motivational level of the men
μ_W is the mean motivational level of the women

The alternate for the above example would statistically be set as follows:

$$H_A: \mu_M < \mu_W$$

which is the same as

$$H_A: \mu_W > \mu_M$$

where H_A represents the term alternate hypothesis and μ_M and μ_W are the mean motivation levels of men and women, respectively. For the **nondirectional** hypothesis of mean group differences in work ethic values in Example 3.20, the null hypothesis would be:

$$H_0: \mu_{AM} = \mu_{AS}$$

or

$$H_0: \mu_{AM} - \mu_{AS} = 0$$

where H_0 represents the null hypothesis
μ_{AM} is the mean work ethic value of Americans
μ_{AS} is the mean work ethic value of Asians

The alternate hypothesis for the above example would statistically be set as:

$$H_A: \mu_{AM} \neq \mu_{AS}$$

where H_A represents the term alternate hypothesis and μ_{AM} and μ_{AS} are the mean work ethic values of Americans and Asians, respectively.

The null hypothesis for the relationship between the two variables in Example 3.17 would be

H_0: There is no relationship between stress experienced on the job and the job satisfaction of employees.

This would be statistically expressed by

$$H_0: \rho = 0$$

where ρ represents the correlation between stress and job satisfaction, in this case equal to 0 (i.e., no correlation).

The alternate hypotheses for the above null, which has been expressed directionally in Example 3.17, can be statistically expressed as

$$H_A: \rho < 0 \qquad \text{(The correlation is negative.)}$$

For example 3.19 which has been stated nondirectionally, while the null hypothesis would be statistically expressed as:

$$H_0: \rho = 0$$

the alternative hypothesis would be expressed as:

$$H_A: \rho \neq 0$$

Having thus formulated the null and alternate hypotheses, the appropriate statistical tests can then be conducted that would indicate whether or not support has been found for the alternate—that is, that there is a significant difference between groups or that there is a significant relationship between variables as hypothesized. When we find support for our alternate hypothesis, we can think of ways of solving the problem (e.g., by lowering stress levels through relaxation sessions during work hours, etc.).

You will recall that in Chapter 1 we briefly discussed why significance levels are important and stated that in social sciences $p \leq .05$ is an accepted level of significance. The null hypothesis is rejected if the results do not meet the $p \leq .05$ level of significance. When we state a directional hypothesis, all tests that meet the .05 level of confidence are accepted. However, if we state a nondirectional hypothesis, we are indicating that a relationship can be either positive or negative or that the difference between two groups can have a positive or negative value. Since we are not sure to which side of the normal curve our sample belongs, we have to subject the results to two-tailed tests of significance, which means that we can no longer be satisfied with a .05 level of significance, but the results have to be significant at the .025 level (.025 on each side of the normal curve ultimately amounts to .05). Thus, the results of nondirectionally stated alternate hypotheses should meet a more stringent significance level to be accepted.

Before concluding the discussion on hypotheses, it has to be restated that hypotheses generation and testing can be done both through the process of deduction (i.e., develop the model, formulate testable hypotheses, collect data, and then test the hypotheses that have been developed) and the process of induction (i.e., collect the data, formulate new hypotheses based on what is known from the data collected, and test them).

We discussed in Chapter 1 with the example of the Hawthorne experiments, how new hypotheses can be developed for testing after the data are collected and analyzed. That is, new hypotheses that were not originally thought of or which have been previously untested might be developed after data are collected. Creative insights might compel researchers to test a new hypothesis, which, if substantiated, would add new knowledge and help theory building. That is, it would enhance the value of the conceptual model or the theoretical framework, which will enable us to understand more completely and better, the dynamics operating in a situation. This is an important benefit, which accrues to the total body of knowledge in the area.

HYPOTHESES TESTING WITH QUALITATIVE RESEARCH: NEGATIVE CASE ANALYSIS

Hypotheses can also be tested through qualitative data. For example, let us say that a researcher has developed the theoretical framework after extensive interviews, that unethical practices by employees are a function of their being ignorant of what is right and wrong, or because of a need for more money, or because of the organization's indifference to such practices. To test the hypothesis that these three factors are the primary ones that influence unethical practices, the researcher will look for data that would disconfirm the hypothesis. When even a single case disconfirms the hypothesis, he will revise the theory. Let us say that the researcher finds that one individual deliberately engaged in accepting kickbacks (despite the fact that he was knowledgeable enough to differentiate between right and wrong, was not in need of money, and in his case he knew that the organization would not be indifferent to his behavior), simply because he wanted to "get back" at the system, which "would not listen to his advice." This new discovery through disconfirmation of his original hypothesis (known as the negative case method) enables the researcher to revise the theory and the hypothesis till such time as the theory becomes robust.

Now do Exercises 3.12 and 3.13.

We have thus far seen how a literature review is done, theoretical frameworks are formulated, and hypotheses are developed. Let us now illustrate this logical sequence through a mini example where a researcher wants to examine the organizational factors influencing women's progress to top management positions. The literature survey and the number of variables are deliberately kept small since the purpose is merely to show how a theoretical framework is developed from the literature survey, and how hypotheses are developed based on the theoretical framework.

Example 3.21   EXAMPLE OF LITERATURE REVIEW, THEORETICAL FRAMEWORK, AND HYPOTHESES DEVELOPMENT

Introduction

Despite the dramatic increase in the number of managerial women during the current decade, the number of women in top management positions continues to be very small and static, suggesting a glass ceiling effect that women currently face (Morrison, White, & VanVelsor, 1987). Given the projected demographics of the workplace, which forecasts that for every six or seven women entering the workforce in the future, there will be only three or so white males joining the labor market, it becomes important to examine the organizational factors that would facilitate the advancement of women to top executive positions as early as possible. This study is an effort to identify the organizational factors that currently impede women's progress to the top.

A Brief Literature Survey

It is often proposed that since women have only recently taken on careers and entered the managerial ranks, it will take more time to see them in top executive positions. However, many women in higher middle management positions feel that there are at least two major stumbling blocks to women's advancement: gender role stereotypes and inadequate access to critical information (Crosby, 1985; Welch, 1980).

Gender stereotypes, or sex-role stereotypes as they are also known, are societal beliefs that men are more suited for taking on leadership roles and positions of authority and power, whereas women are more suited to taking on nurturing and helping roles (Eagly, 1989; Kahn & Crosby, 1985). These beliefs influence the positions that are assigned to organizational members. Whereas capable men are given line positions and developed to take on higher responsibilities and executive positions in due course of time, capable women are assigned to staff positions and dead-end jobs. Without exposure to management of budgets and significant decision making, women are seldom groomed for top level positions.

Women are also excluded from the "old boys" network because of their gender. Information exchange, development of career strategies, clues regarding access to resources, and such important information vital to upward mobility are thus lost to women. While many other factors impinge on women's upward mobility, the two variables—sex-role stereotypes and being shut out from critical information—are particularly detrimental to women's advancement to senior level positions.

Theoretical Framework

The main variable of interest to the study is the dependent variable of advancement of women to top management positions. The two most important independent variables that influence the dependent variable are sex-role stereotyping and access to critical information. It should be noted that the two independent variables are also interrelated as explained below.

Sex-role stereotypes adversely impact on women's career progress. Since women are perceived as ineffective leaders but good nurturers, they are not assigned line positions in their early career but offered staff responsibilities. It is only in line positions that managers make significant decisions, control budgets, and interact with the higher bosses who have an impact on their future careers. These opportunities to learn, grow and develop on the job, and gain visibility in the system help managers to advance to top level positions. However, since women in staff positions do not gain these experiences or have the visibility to be identified as key people in the organization who have the potential to be successful top managers, their advancement to top level positions is never considered by the system and they are always overlooked. Thus, sex-role stereotypes hinder the progress of women to the top.

Being excluded from the networks where men informally interact in the golf course, pubs, and so on, also bars women from gaining access to key information and resources vital for their advancement. For example, much of the significant organizational changes and happenings are discussed informally among men outside of the work setting. Women are generally unaware of the most recent developments since they are not a part of the informal group that interacts and exchanges information away from the workplace. This is definitely a handicap. For example, knowing ahead of time that there is going to be a vacancy enables one to strategize to occupy that position by becoming a key contender, preparing to present the appropriate credentials to the right people at the right time, finding out more information relevant to the job interview, and paving the way for success. Thus, access to critical information is important for the progress of all, including women. When women do not have the critical information that is shared in informal networks, their chances of progress to top positions also get severely restricted.

Figure 3.11
Schematic diagram for Example 3.21.

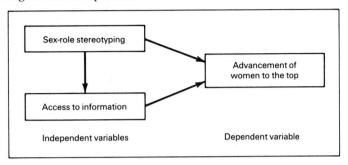

Gender-role stereotypes also hinders access to information. If women are not considered to be decision makers and leaders, but perceived merely as support personnel, they will not be apprised of critical information, since this would not be seen as a relevant thing to do. When both stereotyping and withholding of critical information are in operation, there is no way that women can reach the top. These relationships are schematically diagrammed in Figure 3.11.

In sum, both gender-role stereotypes and access to critical information significantly influence women's advancement to top level positions in organizations and explain the variance in it.

Hypotheses

1. The greater the extent of gender stereotyping in organizations, the fewer will be the number of women at the top.

2. Male managers will have more access to critical information than women managers in the same ranks.

3. There will be a significant positive correlation between access to information and chances for promotion to top level positions.

4. Sex-role stereotyping and access to critical information will be positively correlated.

5. Sex-role stereotyping and access to critical information will both significantly explain the variance in promotional opportunities for women to top level positions.

SUMMARY

In this chapter we examined the four types of variables: dependent, independent, moderating, and intervening. We also discussed how theoretical frameworks are developed and testable hypotheses are generated therefrom as they relate to both qualitative and quantitative research. In the next chapter we will examine the basic research design issues.

DISCUSSION QUESTIONS AND POINTS TO PONDER

1. "Because literature survey is a time-consuming exercise, a good, in-depth inter-view should suffice to develop a theoretical framework." Critique this statement.

2. There is an advantage to stating the hypothesis both in the null and in the alternate; it adds clarity to our thinking about what we are testing. Explain.

3. It is advantageous to develop a directional hypothesis whenever we are sure of the predicted direction. Why is this necessary?

PRACTICE PROJECT

For the topic you chose to work on for the project in the previous chapter, do the following:

1. Go through the bibliography you generated by accessing the computer once again.

2. Define a problem statement that, in your opinion, would be most useful for organizational researchers to investigate.

3. Write up a literature review using about twenty references that would seem to offer the greatest potential for developing a good theoretical framework.

4. Develop the theoretical framework applying the five basic features of it as discussed in the chapter.

5. Generate a set of testable hypotheses based on the theoretical framework, stat-ing them both in the null and in the alternate.

EXERCISES

Exercise 3.1   An applied researcher wants to increase the commitment of organizational mem-bers in a particular bank.
What would be the dependent variable in this case?

Exercise 3.2   A production manager is wondering why the workers in her department are reluc-tant to communicate with her.
What would be the dependent variable in this case?

Exercise 3.3   List the variables in this and the next exercise, individually, and label them as dependent or independent, giving brief reasons and explaining why they are so labeled. Diagram the relationships.

> A manager believes that good supervision and training will increase the production level of the workers.

Exercise 3.4

> A consultant is of the opinion that increasing the pay and fringe benefits, contrary to common belief, decreases job satisfaction instead of increasing it.

Exercise 3.5 List and label the variables in the following situation and explain and diagram the relationships among the variables.

> A manager finds that off-the-job classroom training has a great impact on the productivity of the employees in his department. However, he also observes that employees over fifty years of age do not seem to derive much benefit and do not improve from such training.

Exercise 3.6 List and label the variables in the following situation and explain and diagram the relationships among the variables.

> A visitor to a factory observes that the workers in the packing department have to interact with each other to get their jobs done. The more they interact, the more they seem to tend to stay after hours and go to the local pub together for a drink. However, the women packers, even though they interact with the others as much as the men, do not stay late and visit the pub after work hours.

Exercise 3.7 Make up three different situations in which motivation to work would be an independent variable, an intervening variable, and a moderating variable.

Exercise 3.8 List and label the variables in the following situation, explain the relationships among the variables, and diagram these.

> The multiple roles that members of dual-career families take impose considerable stress on them that, in turn, impairs the satisfactions they derive from their lives. The life satisfaction of those members who have a high self-concept, however, is not influenced by stress.

Exercise 3.9 List and label the variables in the following situation. Explain the relationships among the variables and diagram them. What might be the problem statement or problem definition for the situation?

> The manager of Haines Company observes that the morale of employees in her company is low. She thinks that if the working conditions, the pay scales,

and the vacation benefits of the employees are bettered, the morale will improve. She doubts, though, that increasing the pay scales is going to raise the morale of all employees. Her guess is that those who have good side incomes will just not be "turned on" by higher pay. However, those without side incomes will be happy with increased pay and their morale will improve.

Exercise 3.10   Develop a theoretical framework for the following situation after stating what the problem definition of the researcher would be in this case.

A family counselor, engaged in counseling married couples who are both professionals, is caught in a dilemma. He realizes that the focus of the counseling sessions should be on both family satisfaction and job satisfaction; however, he is not sure how job and family satisfactions can be integrated in the dual-career family. Husbands, who are the traditional breadwinners, seem to derive more job satisfaction as they get more involved in their jobs and also spend more discretionary time on job-related activities. This, however, does not seem to be true in the case of the wives, who perform the dual role of careerperson and homemaker. However, both husbands and wives seem to enjoy high levels of family satisfaction when they spend more time together at home and help each other in planning family-oriented activities.

Exercise 3.11   Define the problem and develop the theoretical framework for the following situation.

The probability of cancer victims successfully recovering under treatment was studied by a medical researcher in a hospital. She found three variables to be important for recovery.

- Quick and correct diagnosis by the doctor.
- The nurse's careful following of the doctor's instructions.
- Peace and quiet in the vicinity.

In a quiet atmosphere, the patient rested well and recovered sooner. Patients who were admitted in advanced stages of cancer did not respond to treatment even though the doctor's diagnosis was done immediately on arrival, the nurses did their best, and there was plenty of peace and quiet in the area.

Exercise 3.12   For the theoretical framework developed for the Haines Company in Exercise 3.9, develop five different null hypotheses and the alternate hypothesis for each null.

Exercise 3.13

A *production* manager is concerned about the low output levels of his employees. The articles that he read on job performance frequently mentioned four variables as important to job performance: skill required by job, rewards, motivation, and satisfaction. In several of the articles it was also indicated that only if the rewards were valent (attractive) to the recipients, did motivation, satisfaction, and job performance increase—not otherwise.

Given this situation, do the following

1. Define the problem.
2. Evolve a theoretical framework.
3. Develop at least six hypotheses.

CHAPTER 4

THE RESEARCH PROCESS

Step 6: Elements of Research Design

CHAPTER OBJECTIVES

After completing this chapter you should be able to:

1. Understand the different aspects relevant to designing a research study.

2. Identify the scope of a given study and the purposes for which the results will be used.

3. Decide on the type of investigation needed, the study setting, the extent of researcher interference that will be required, what should be the unit of analysis, and what should be the time horizon of the study.

4. Given different situations, decide what research designs would be most appropriate, and for what reason.

THE RESEARCH DESIGN

The Research Design, which involves a series of rational decision-making choices, was originally represented in a simplistic manner in boxes 6 and 7 in Figure 2.1, which is reproduced as Figure 4.1. The various issues involved in the research

Figure 4.1
The research process.

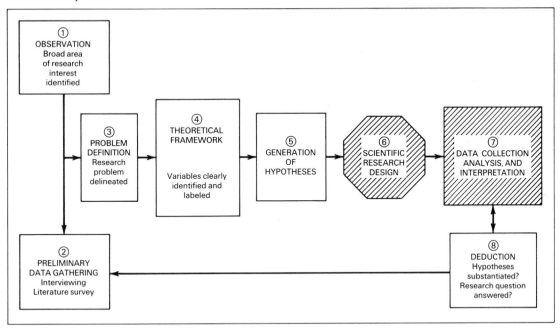

Figure 4.2
The research design.

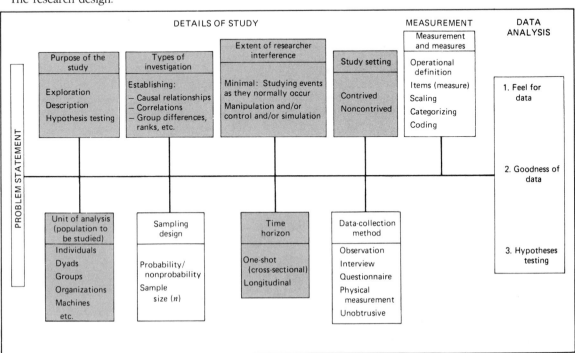

design will be discussed in this chapter and are now more comprehensively shown in Figure 4.2. As can be seen, the issues pertinent to research design relate to where the study will be conducted (i.e., the study setting), what type of a study it would be (type of investigation), the extent to which the researcher manipulates and controls the study (extent of researcher interference), the duration of the study (time horizon), and at what level the data will be analyzed (unit of analysis), as well as deciding what the sample would be (sampling design), how the data would be collected (data collection methods), how variables will be measured (measurement), and how they will be analyzed to test the hypotheses (data analysis).

As shown in Figure 4.2, each component of the research design offers several critical choice points. The extent of scientific rigor in a research study depends on how carefully the researcher has chosen the appropriate alternatives, taking into consideration the purpose for which the study is undertaken. For instance, if a critical decision to invest millions of dollars in a project is to be based on the results of a research investigation, then it goes without saying that much careful attention to details will be necessary to ensure that the study has maximum precision and confidence, which implies, as we will see later in the book, that close attention is paid to sampling, measurement, data collection, and so on. Contrast this to the research goal of generating a profile of managers in an organization to publish a newsletter. In this case, the rigor of the research design will not be anywhere near as critical as in the first case.

It is important to note that the more sophisticated and rigorous the research design becomes, the greater the time, costs, and other resources expended on the study are likely to be. Hence, it is relevant to ask the question at every decision point whether the benefits that result from a more sophisticated design to ensure accuracy, confidence, generalizability, and so on, are worth the investment of more resources.

In this chapter we will examine the most basic aspects of research design. Specifically, we will discuss the purpose of the study, the types of investigation, the extent of researcher interference, the study setting, the unit of analysis, and the time horizon of the study (the shaded parts in Figure 4.2). The other aspects of measurement, data-collection methods, sampling design, and data analysis will be discussed in subsequent chapters.

THE PURPOSE OF THE STUDY: EXPLORATORY, DESCRIPTIVE, HYPOTHESIS TESTING (ANALYTICAL AND PREDICTIVE)

Studies can be either exploratory in nature, or descriptive, and/or conducted to test hypotheses. The nature of the study depends on the stages of advancement of knowledge in the research area. The design decisions become more rigorous as we proceed from the exploratory stage, where we try to explore new areas of organizational research, to the descriptive stage, where we try to describe certain characteristics of the phenomena we are interested in knowing about, to the hypotheses-testing stage, where we examine whether or not the conjectured relationships have been substantiated and an answer to the research question obtained. We will now look at each of these in some detail.

Exploratory Study

An exploratory study is undertaken when we do not know much about the situation at hand, or when we have no information on how similar problems or research issues have been solved in the past. In such cases, extensive preliminary work needs to be done to gain familiarity with the phenomena in the situation, and to understand what is happening before we can develop a model and set up a rigorous design for complete investigation.

In essence, exploratory studies are done to better comprehend the nature of the problem since very few studies might have been conducted regarding the phenomena needed to be understood. Extensive interviews with many people might have to be undertaken to get a handle on the situation and the phenomena. Once a better understanding is obtained, more rigorous research can then proceed.

Some qualitative studies (as opposed to quantitative data gathered through questionnaires, etc.) using observational techniques or interviewing as a means of gathering data, are exploratory in nature. When the data reveal some pattern regarding the phenomena of interest, theories are developed and hypotheses formulated for subsequent testing. For example, Henry Mintzberg interviewed managers to explore the nature of managerial work. Based on the analysis of his interview data, he formulated theories of managerial roles, the nature and types of managerial activities, and so on. These are now being tested in different settings through both interview and questionnaire surveys.

Exploratory studies are thus important for obtaining a good grasp of the phenomena of interest and for advancing knowledge through good theory building. The following is an example where exploratory research would be necessary.

Example 4.1   The manager of a multinational corporation is curious to know if the work ethic values of employees working in the subsidiary in Pennathur would be different from those of Americans. There is very little information about Pennathur (besides that it is stated to be a small city in Southern India), and since there is a lot of controversy about what work ethic values mean to people in other cultures, the manager's curiosity can only be addressed by an exploratory study of the employees in Pennathur. Religion, political, economic, and social conditions, upbringing, cultural values, and so on, play a big part in how people view their work in different parts of the world. Here, since very little is known about work ethic values (and even if it is a viable concept for study!) in India, an exploratory study will have to be undertaken.

In the management and organizational behavior areas, many topics of interest and concern to management have been studied, and information is available in the library on these subject areas. Although there are very few exploratory studies currently undertaken in the management area, from time to time researchers do explore new grounds with the changing dynamics that occur at the workplace. Not long ago, for instance, research on these topics of women in management and dual-career families were explored. Because of the subsequent studies, research on these topics have now progressed beyond the exploratory stage.

The same is also true of research on quality of life. At one time, exploratory studies were undertaken to understand what the concept *quality of work life* meant. After extensive interviews with various groups of people, the concept was considered to encompass such factors as enriched jobs, healthy work environment, stress-free work relationships, job satisfaction, work role involvement, and other work-related factors. Current thinking is that the concept *quality of work life* is too narrow and limited to be useful for research and that the concept *quality of life* is more encompassing since work and nonwork cannot be viewed as two tightly compartmentalized aspects of an individual's life. Current research now takes both the work and nonwork factors (family, community, etc.) into consideration while examining *quality of life*. This stream of knowledge development would not have been possible without the initial exploratory studies.

Currently, exploratory studies about organizationally relevant differences in race, ethnic, and country origins are being undertaken so that good theories about managing a diverse work group can be evolved for the future. Such exploratory studies are necessary since we do not currently know if there are differences in communication styles, interpretation schemas, superior–subordinate relationship expectations, and the like. If conflict and stress in the system are to be reduced and productivity maintained and enhanced in the years to come, as the demographics of the workplace change, understanding the differences, learning to value the differences, and adopting new styles of management will become necessary.

It is important to note that doing a study for the first time in a particular organization does *not* make the research exploratory in nature; only when knowledge is scant and a deeper understanding is aimed at does the study become exploratory.

Descriptive Study

A descriptive study is undertaken in order to ascertain and to be able to describe the characteristics of variables in a situation. For instance, describing a class in terms of the percentage of members who are in their senior and junior years, sex composition, age groupings, number of semesters left for graduation, and number of business courses taken, would be descriptive in nature. Quite frequently, descriptive studies are undertaken in organizations in order to learn about and describe the characteristics of a group of employees, as for example, the age, educational level, job status, and length of service, of say, Hispanics, working in the system. Descriptive studies are also undertaken to understand the characteristics of organizations that follow common practices. For example, one might want to know and be able to describe the characteristics of the organizations that implement flexible manufacturing systems (FMS) or which have a certain debt-to-equity ratio.

The goal of a descriptive study, hence, is to describe relevant aspects of the phenomena of interest to the researcher from an individual, organizational, industry, or other perspective. In many cases, such information may be vital before even contemplating further steps, as for example: **Should the organization consider changing its practices?** If most firms in the industry follow *just-in-time* systems, for instance, maybe organization Z should also seriously consider the feasibility of this practice. Or if a descriptive study indicates the need to introduce flexible work hours for parents of children under three years of age, this may have to be seriously considered, and a further more focused study initiated.

Descriptive studies that present data in a meaningful form thus help to (1) understand the characteristics of a group in a situation of interest, (2) aid in thinking systematically about aspects in a given situation, (3) offer ideas for further probing and research, and/or (4) help make certain simple decisions (such as how many and what kinds of individuals should be transferred from one department to another).

Below are examples of situations warranting a descriptive study.

Example 4.2   A bank manager wants to have a profile of the individuals who have loan payments outstanding for six months and above. The profile that he would get will describe the defaulters in terms of their average age, earnings, type of occupation they are in, full-time/part-time employment status, and the like. This information might help him to ask for further information or make a decision right away on the types of individuals to whom he would not extend loans in the future.

Example 4.3   A CEO may be interested in having a description of organizations in her industry that follow the LIFO system. In this case, the description might be in terms of the age of the organizations, their location, their production levels, assets, sales, inventory levels, suppliers, and profits. Such information might help to compare the performance levels of specific types of companies, later.

Example 4.4   A marketing manager might want to develop a pricing, sales, distribution, and advertising strategy for her product. With this in mind, she might ask for information regarding the competitors with respect to the following:

1. The percentage who have prices higher and lower than the industry norm; a profile of the terms of sale; and the percentage of companies where prices are controlled regionally as opposed to those controlled from a central headquarters.

2. The percentage hiring in-house staff to handle sales and those who use independent agents.

3. Percentage of sales groups organized by product line, by accounts, and by region.
4. The types of distribution channels used and the percentage using each.
5. Percentage of competitors spending more advertising/promotion dollars than this firm and those spending less; a categorization of their target audiences, and the media form that is most frequently used.

Descriptive studies thus become essential in many situations. Whereas qualitative data obtained by interviewing individuals may help the understanding of phenomena at the exploratory stages of a study, more quantitative data in terms of frequencies, or mean and standard deviations, become necessary for descriptive studies. A report on the results of a descriptive study of the reaction of organizational members to the introduction of a cafeteria style of benefits, for instance, might look somewhat like this:

Whereas 30 percent of the employees were in favor of the concept of cafetaria style of benefits, at least 40 percent felt that it was totally unnecessary. Another 20 percent felt that it would be confusing to employees and give room for suspicion and distrust of the system. The balance 10 percent were indifferent to the idea.

More women than men were favorably inclined toward the idea (almost 2:1), and while parents with two or more children overwhelmingly desired this, employees without children were opposed to the introduction of cafeteria style of benefits.

Employees who are over 50 years of age and those who are below 23 do not seem to be in favor of this scheme. However, women between 25 and 45 (a total of 45 women) seem to desire it the most.

For all employees, the average preference indicated for cafetaria style of benefits was neither high nor low (a mean of 3 on a 5-point scale), but the dispersion was rather high, the standard deviation being 1.98. This indicates that there were some who indicated a strong preference for this style of benefits, while some were totally against it.

The average preference indicated by women between the ages of 30 and 45 with children was the highest (4.5 on a 5-point scale) with very little dispersion (the standard deviation for this group of 42 women was .38).

Hypotheses Testing

Studies that engage in hypotheses testing usually try to explain the nature of certain relationships, or establish the differences among groups or the independence of two or more factors in a situation. Examples of such studies are given below.

Example 4.5   A marketing manager would like to know if the sales of the company will increase if he doubles the advertising dollars. Here, the manager wants to know the nature of the relationship between advertising and sales that can be established by testing the hypothesis: *If advertising is increased, then sales will also go up.*

Example 4.6   Given people's tensions about whether or not to buy a gun in these days of crime in big cities and small, a marketing researcher might be interested in predicting the factors that would significantly account for the variance in individuals' decision to purchase guns. Here, the researcher would have theorized the factors that would influence people's decision to possess guns (through literature search and interviews) and then test his hypothesis that four specific variables will significantly account for the variance in people's intention to buy a gun. Here again, the researcher is interested in understanding and accounting for the variance in the dependent variable through hypothesis testing.

Example 4.7   The testing of a hypothesis such as: *More men than women are whistleblowers,* establishes the difference between two groups—men and women in regard to their whistleblowing behaviors.

Example 4.8   The independence between two variables that are qualitative in nature can also be established through hypothesis testing. Consider the hypothesis: *Working the night shift (as opposed to the day shift) is related to whether or not one is married.* A chi-square test of independence will easily provide the answer to this question.

As can be seen, in *hypotheses testing,* the research goes beyond merely describing the variables in a situation to understanding the relationships among factors of interest.

Review of the Purpose of the Study

It is not difficult to see that in exploratory studies, the researcher is basically interested in exploring the situational factors so as to get a grip on the characteristics of the phenomena of interest. The descriptive study is undertaken when the characteristics or the phenomena to be tapped in a situation are known to exist, and one wants to be able to describe them better. Hypothesis testing offers an enhanced understanding of the relationships that exist among variables. Hypothesis testing could also establish cause $\rightarrow$ effect relationships, as we will see in the next chapter. As discussed in the previous chapter, hypothesis testing can be done with both qualitative and quantitative data.

The methodological rigor increases as we move from a descriptive to a hypothesis-testing study, and with this, the costs of research also increase. As we will see later, increases in sample size, multiple methods of data collection, developing sophisticated measuring instruments, and the like, are expensive.

TYPE OF INVESTIGATION: CAUSAL VERSUS NONCAUSAL

A researcher should determine whether a causal or a noncausal study is needed to answer the research question. The former type of study is done when it is necessary to establish a definitive "cause → effect" relationship. However, if the researcher merely wants to identify the important factors "associated with" the problem, then a correlational study is called for. In the former case, the researcher is keen on delineating one or more factors that are undoubtedly *causing* the problem. In other words, the intention of the researcher conducting a causal study is to be able to state that variable X causes variable Y. So, when variable X is removed or altered in some way, the problem Y is solved. Quite often in organizations, though, it is not just one or two variables that **cause** a problem. Given the fact that most of the time there are multiple factors that influence one another and the problem in a chainlike fashion, the researcher might be more interested in identifying the crucial factors that are associated with the problem, rather than establishing a cause → effect relationship.

When the researcher wants to delineate the cause of a problem, then the study is called a **causal** study. When the researcher is interested in delineating the important variables that are associated with the problem, it is called a **correlational** study. It may be of interest to know that attempts are sometimes made to establish cause → effect relationships through certain types of correlational or regression analyses, such as cross-lagged correlations and path analysis (Billings & Wroten, 1978; Namboodiri, Carter, & Blalock, 1975). Whether a study is a causal or a correlational one thus depends on the type of research questions asked and how the problem is defined. The following example will illustrate the difference.

Example 4.9

A causal study question: Does smoking *cause* cancer?

A correlational study question: Are smoking, drinking, and chewing tobacco *associated* with cancer? If so, which of these contributes most to the variance in the dependent variable?

The answer to the first question will help determine whether people who do not smoke will not develop cancer. The latter situation recognizes that there are perhaps several other factors that influence cancer apart from the three identified, but do these three help to explain a significant amount of the variance in cancer? If they do, then which among the three variables examined is the one that has the greatest association with it, which is the next important, and which is the third? The answer to the correlational study would help us to determine the extent of risk people take of getting cancer by smoking, drinking, and chewing tobacco. The intention here is not to establish a **causal** connection between one factor and another, but merely to see if some relationship does exist among the variables investigated.

The distinction between causal and correlational studies can be made clear by the following two examples as well.

Example 4.10   The fear of an earthquake predicted recently in the New Madrid Fault zone was instrumental (i.e., **causal**) in an unprecedented number of house owners in the Midwest region obtaining earthquake insurance.

Example 4.11   Increases in property taxes, the recession, and the fear of a predicted earthquake considerably slowed down the business of real estate agents in the Midwest.

Note that Example 4.10 indicates a **causal** relationship between the earthquake prediction and earthquake insurance, whereas Example 4.11 indicates that several factors, including the predicted earthquake *influenced* (not caused) the real estate agents' business to slow down. This is a correlational study the goal of which is not to establish cause → effect relationships.

It is important to decide whether one is keen on detecting causal connections or simply wants to know all the factors that influence the variable of interest, since the study setting, the extent of researcher interference, and the time frame of the study (all of which are discussed later in this chapter), will be influenced by this decision.

If it is a causal study, then some variables may have to be manipulated and others controlled. If, in contrast, it is a correlational study, the study can be conducted in the natural setting where events occur without researchers interfering with the variables. However, it should be noted that it is possible to attempt the establishment of causal relationships without researcher interference with the natural flow of events by using special analytical techniques, or by collecting data at different points in time.

Sometimes, without conducting experimental studies, researchers try to get a handle on causal connections through certain statistical procedures such as path analysis. At least partly dependent on the researcher's choice is whether one wants to conduct a causal study interfering with the natural flow of events, or understand a causal relationship that might exist by resorting to special data analytic techniques, or is content with a correlational study. Causal studies using artificial settings (described later in this chapter) consume more time and other resources. Unless it is absolutely essential to establish a direct cause → effect relationship, such a study may not be necessary in organizational settings. However, there may be other cases where such a study might be necessary. For instance, there is currently a theory floating around (recently covered by CBS's *60 Minutes* as well) that the mercury that is added to the silver dental filling is linked directly to poisonous vapors that induce in some individuals arthritis, Alzheimer's disease, multiple sclerosis, and other ailments. The American Dental Association is vehemently disputing this theory. Current suppliers of materials for silver fillings also have a vested interest in refuting this theory. Here is a situation that calls for a well-developed causal study. Getting a representative sample of individuals who have had silver fillings, and removing the fillings in some while retaining the fillings in others, should indicate if problems are indeed caused by mercury and whether they can be overcome, say in six months' time—the time that some ex-arthritis and multiple sclerosis patients say it took before they found relief after removal of their filling. Unless such a study is done and a cause → effect relationship is either established or disproved, there will be continued anxiety among patients whose dentists recommend silver fillings. The FDA can also take no action until a causal relationship has been established. Here, the costs of the study may be well worth it to the marketers of mercury, especially if they are sure that the mercury vapors do not cause diseases.

EXTENT OF RESEARCHER INTERFERENCE WITH THE STUDY

The extent of researcher interference has a direct bearing on whether a causal or correlational study is undertaken. A correlational study is conducted in the natural environment of the organization with the researcher interfering minimally with the normal flow of events. For example, if a researcher wants to study the factors influencing training effectiveness, all that the individual has to do is to develop a theoretical framework and collect the relevant data and analyze them to come up with the findings. Though there is some disruption to the normal flow of events in the system as the researcher interviews employees and administers questionnaires, the researcher's interference in the system is minimal as compared to that exercised during causal studies.

In causal studies conducted to establish cause → effect relationships, the researcher tries to *manipulate* certain variables so as to study the effects of such manipulation on the dependent variable of interest. In other words, the researcher deliberately changes certain variables in the setting and interferes with the normal flow of events as they usually occur in the organization. As an example, a researcher might want to study the influence of lighting on worker performance, and hence manipulate the intensity of lighting in the work situation to varying degrees. Here, there is a good amount of researcher interference with the natural and normal setting. In other cases the researcher might even want to create an altogether new setting where the cause → effect relationships can be studied by manipulating certain variables and tightly *controlling* certain others. Thus there could be varying degrees of interference by the researcher in the manipulation and control of variables in the research study, either in the natural setting or in an artificial research setting.

Let us give examples of research with varying degrees of interference—minimal, a good amount, and a lot—in the normal flow of events usually occurring in organizational settings.

Example 4.12   A researcher wants to see the relationship between the perceived emotional support systems that exist in a hospital and the stresses experienced by the nursing staff. In other words, she wants to do a correlational study.

Here, the researcher will collect data from the nurses (perhaps through a questionnaire) as to how much emotional support they get in the hospital and to what extent they experience stress. (We will learn in a later chapter in the book how to measure these variables.) By correlating the two variables, the researcher will find the answer that is being sought.

In this case, beyond administering a questionnaire to the nurses, the researcher has not interfered with the normal flow of events in the hospital. In other words, researcher interference has been *minimal.*

Example 4.13   The same researcher is now no longer content with finding the correlation, but wants to firmly establish a causal connection. That is, having emotional support does indeed *cause* the nurses to experience less stress. If this can be established, then by offering emotional support, stress can definitely be reduced.

To test the cause → effect relationship, the researcher will measure the stress currently experienced by the nurses in three wards in the hospital, and then manipulate the variable of emotional support deliberately for various groups of nurses in the three wards for perhaps a week and measure the amount of stress at the end of that period. For one group, the researcher will ensure that there are a number of lab technicians, doctors, and even the hospital administrator helping and comforting the nurse when, say, patients are suffering too much distress in the ward. For a group of nurses in another ward, the researcher might make sure that only a moderate amount of emotional support is offered and only by the lab technicians. The third ward might operate without any emotional support.

If the experimenter's theory is correct, then the difference in the stress levels before and after the one-week period should be greatest for the nurses in the first ward, moderate for those in the second ward, with no difference for the nurses in the third ward.

Here we find that not only does the researcher collect data from nurses on their experienced stress at two different points in time (minimal interference), but has also "played with" or manipulated the normal flow of events by deliberately increasing and decreasing the amount of emotional support received by the nurses. Here, the researcher has interfered *more than minimally.*

Example 4.14   The above researcher, after doing the previous experiment, feels that the results may or may not be valid since other external factors might have influenced the stress levels experienced by the nurses. For example, during that experimental week, the nurses in one or more wards may not have encountered many stressful experiences. In addition, the differences found may be not due to the emotional support received, but because the stress level was low (there were no serious illnesses, deaths, etc., in that ward).

The researcher might now want to make sure that such extraneous factors that might affect the cause → effect relationship are controlled. So he may take three groups of medical students, put them in three different rooms, and confront all of them with the same stressful task. For example, he may ask them to describe the surgical procedures in the minutest detail in performing surgery on a patient who has not responded to chemotherapy. Although the task is the same for all, one group might get help from a doctor who voluntarily offers assistance and offers clarifications when students stumble. In the second group, a doctor might be around, but might offer help only if the group seeks it. In the third group, there is no doctor around and no help is available.

In this case, not only is the support manipulated, but even the setting in which this experiment is conducted is artificial inasmuch as the researcher has taken the subjects away from their normal working place and put them in a totally different setting. Here, the researcher has intervened *maximally* with the normal setting, the actors, and the task. In the next chapter, we will see why such changes are necessary to establish cause → effect relationships beyond doubt.

As seen, the extent of researcher interference would depend on whether the study is correlational or causal and also the extent to which causal relationships have to be established beyond the shadow of a doubt.

For many organizational problems, a causal study is seldom necessary. In any case, researcher interference through a change in the setting in which the causal study is conducted may seldom be called for.

STUDY SETTING: CONTRIVED AND NONCONTRIVED

As we have just seen, research can be done in the natural environment where events normally occur—that is, in noncontrived settings—or in artificial, contrived settings. Correlational studies are invariably conducted in noncontrived settings, whereas rigorous causal studies are done in contrived lab settings.

Correlational studies done in organizations are called **field studies.** Studies conducted to establish cause → effect relationships using the same natural environment in which employees normally function are called **field experiments.** Here, as we have seen earlier, the researcher does interfere with the natural flow of events inasmuch as the independent variable is manipulated. For example, a researcher wanting to study the effects of pay on performance would ask the president of the company to raise the salary of employees in one department, decrease the pay of employees in another department, but leave the pay of the employees in a third department as it currently is. The researcher is tampering with or manipulating the pay system to establish a cause → effect relationship between pay and performance, but the experiment is still conducted in the natural setting and hence is called a field experiment.

Experiments done to establish cause → effect relationships beyond the shadow of a doubt require the creation of an artificial, contrived environment in which all the extraneous factors are strictly controlled. Subjects are carefully chosen by the researcher to respond to certain manipulated stimuli. These are referred to as **lab experiments.** Let us give another example to understand the differences among a field study (a noncontrived setting with minimal researcher interference), a field experiment (noncontrived setting but with researcher interference to a moderate extent), and a lab experiment (a contrived setting with researcher interference to the maximum extent).

Example 4.15   FIELD STUDY

A bank manager wants to analyze the relationship between interest rates and bank deposit patterns of clients. She tries to correlate the balances in different kinds of savings, certificates of deposit, golden passbooks, and interest bearing checking accounts.

This is a field study where the bank manager has just taken the balances in various types of accounts and correlated them to the interest rates. Research here is done in a noncontrived setting with minimal interference with the normal flow of work.

Example 4.16   FIELD EXPERIMENT

A banker wants to detect the cause → effect relationship between interest rate and the savings inclinations of clients. He selects four branches within a 60-mile radius for the experiment. For one week only, he advertises the annual rate for new certificates of deposit received during that week in the following manner: the interest rate would be 9 percent in one branch, 8 percent in another, 10 percent in the third. In the fourth branch, the interest rate remained the same as before—7.5 percent. Within the week, he would be able to determine the effects, if any, of interest rates on deposit mobilisation.

This would be a **field experiment** since nothing but the interest rate is manipulated, with the events occurring in their normal and natural environment. Hopefully, all four branches chosen would be more or less the same in size, number of depositors, deposit patterns, and the like so that the interest–savings relationships are not contaminated by some third factor. But who knows, there could be some other factor that affects the findings. For example, in one area there may be more retirees who have settled down, and they may not have additional income that they could save despite the attraction of a good interest rate! The banker may not be aware of this fact while setting up his experiment!

Example 4.17   LAB EXPERIMENT

The banker in Example 4.14 wants to establish the causal connection between interest rates and savings beyond a doubt. Because of this he wants to create an artificial environment and trace the cause → effect relationship. He recruits forty students who are all business majors in their final year of study and are more or less of the same age. He splits them into four groups and gives each one of them chips that count for $1000 that they can dispose of in any manner and in any amounts they desire. The options are: gambling (with the possibility of doubling their money or losing it all), saving (with manipulated interest rates of 0, 10, 13, and 15 percent), helping a student friend to buy books that are desperately needed by the individual, and doing whatever else the subject wants.

Here, the banker has created an artificial condition and has manipulated the interest rates for savings. He has also chosen similar subjects in terms of their exposure to money matters (business students). If the banker finds that the students who are offered more interest are inclined to save more, with a significant difference of high magnitude in the tendencies to save between those who were offered no interest incentives and those who were, then he might be able to establish a cause → effect relationship between interest rate and savings tendencies.

In this lab experiment with the contrived setting, the researcher interference has been maximal—the setting is different, the independent variable has been manipulated, most outside nuisance factors have been controlled, and so on.

The experimental designs are discussed in detail in the next chapter. However, the above examples have shown us that it is important to decide the various design details before conducting the research study since one decision criterion might have impact on others. For example, if one wants to conduct an exploratory, descriptive, or a correlational hypothesis-testing study, then the necessity for the researcher to interfere with the normal flow of events in the organization will be minimal. However, if causal connections are to be established, then experimental designs need to be set up either in the organization where the events normally occur (the field experiment) or in an artificially created laboratory setting (the lab experiment).

In summary, we have thus far made a distinction among (1) *field studies,* where various factors are examined in the natural setting in which events normally occur, with minimal researcher interference, (2) *field experiments,* where cause → effect relationships are studied with some amount of researcher interference, but still within the natural setting where events normally occur, and (3) *lab experiments,* where the researcher explores cause → effect relationships exercising a high degree of control and also in an artificially created setting.

In the next chapter, we will see the advantages and disadvantages of using contrived and noncontrived settings for establishing cause → effect relationships. Depending on the degree to which establishing the cause → effect relationship *unequivocally* is important to a research project, as compared to its *generalizability,* a contrived or a noncontrived setting would be relevant for causal studies. Thus, the choice of the setting becomes an important issue in causal studies. As explained earlier, an artificial setting is rarely called for in business research.

UNIT OF ANALYSIS: INDIVIDUALS, DYADS, GROUPS, ORGANIZATIONS, CULTURES

The unit of analysis refers to the level of aggregation of the data during subsequent analysis. If, for instance, the problem statement focuses on how to raise the motivational levels of employees in general, then we are interested in individual employees in the organization and would like to know what we can do to raise their motivation. Here, obviously, the unit of analysis is the **individual.** We will be looking at the data gathered from each individual and treating each employee's response as an individual data source. If the researcher is interested in studying two-person interactions, then several two-person groups, also known as dyads, will become the unit of analysis. Analysis of husband–wife interactions in families and supervisor–immediate boss relationship in the workplace are good examples of **dyads** as the unit of analysis. However, if the problem statement is related to group effectiveness, then obviously the unit of analysis would be at the group level. In other words, even though we may gather relevant data from all individuals comprising, say, six groups, we would aggregate the individual data into group data so as to see the differences among the six **groups.** If we are comparing different departments in the organization, then the data analysis will be done at the departmental level—that is, the individuals in the department will be treated as one unit, and comparisons will be made treating the department as the unit of analysis.

Our research question will determine the unit of analysis in our study. For example, if we desire to study group decision-making patterns, we would probably be examining such aspects as group size, group structure, cohesiveness, and the like in trying to explain the variance in group decision making. Here, our main interest is not in studying individual decision making but group decision making, and we will be studying the dynamics that take place in several different groups and the factors that influence group decision making. Our unit of analysis will be **groups.**

As our research question addresses issues that move away from the individual to dyads, and to groups, organizations, and even nations, the unit of analysis would also likewise shift from individuals to dyads, groups, organizations, and nations. The characteristic of these "levels of analysis" is that the lower levels are subsumed within the higher levels. Thus, if we study buying behaviors, we can collect data from, say, sixty individuals, and analyze the data. If we want to study groups, we may need to study, say, six to ten groups or more and analyze the data gathered from studying the patterns in each of the groups, and so on. Since individuals do not have the same characteristics as groups (e.g., structure, cohesiveness) and groups do not have the same characteristics as individuals (e.g., IQs, stamina), the nature of the information collected, as well as how the data are analyzed, is integral to the unit of analysis.

Determining the unit of analysis based on our research question is thus an important aspect of the research design.

It is necessary to determine the unit of analysis even as we formulate the research question since the data collection methods, sample size, and even the variables included in the framework may sometimes be determined or guided by the level at which data will be aggregated at the time of analysis.

Let us examine some research scenarios that would call for different units of analysis.

Example 4.18 INDIVIDUALS AS THE UNIT OF ANALYSIS

A director wants to know how many managers are interested in having their secretaries trained in word processing and Lotus 123 on personal computers. Here, information on the matter will be collected from every manager and the data tabulated and presented to the director as to the number of managers who desire this training for their secretaries. The unit of analysis is at the individual level (each manager).

Example 4.19   DYADS AS THE UNIT OF ANALYSIS

Having read about the benefits of mentoring for employees, a personnel manager wants to first identify the number of employees in three departments of the organization who are in mentor–mentee relationships and then find out what the jointly perceived benefits of such a relationship are (i.e., by both the mentor and the mentee).

Here, once the mentor and mentee pairs are identified, the joint perceptions can be obtained by treating each pair as one unit. Hence, if the personnel manager wants data from a sample of ten pairs, he will have to deal with twenty individuals, a pair at a time. The information obtained from each pair will be a data point for subsequent analysis. Thus, the unit of analysis here is the dyad.

Example 4.20   GROUPS AS THE UNIT OF ANALYSIS

A manager wants to see the patterns of usage of the newly installed information system (IS) by the production, sales, and operations personnel. Here three groups of personnel are involved and information on the number of times the IS is used by each of the three groups, and other relevant information will be collected and analyzed. The final results will indicate the mean usage of the system per day or month for each group. The data will be analyzed on the basis of each group's patterns of usage.

Here the unit of analysis is the group. The usage of each member of the group will be totalled and the mean for the group will be calculated.

Example 4.21   DIVISIONS AS THE UNIT OF ANALYSIS

Proctor and Gamble wants to see which of its various divisions (soap, paper, oil, etc.) have made profits of over 12 percent during the current year. Here, the profits of each of the divisions will be examined and the information aggregated across the various geographical units of the division. Hence, the unit of analysis will be the division, at which level the data will be aggregated.

Example 4.22   INDUSTRY AS THE UNIT OF ANALYSIS

An employment survey specialist wants to see the proportion of the workforce employed by the health care, utilities, transportation, and manufacturing industries. In this case, the researcher has to aggregate the data relating to each of the subunits comprising each of the industries and report the proportions of the workforce employed at the industry level. The health care industry, for instance, includes hospitals, nursing homes, mobile units, small and large clinics, and other health-providing facilities. The data from these subunits will have to be aggregated to see how many employees are employed by the health care industry. Likewise, for each of the other industries, data will have to be aggregated at each industry level.

Example 4.23   COUNTRIES AS THE UNIT OF ANALYSIS

The chief accountant of a multinational corporation wants to know the profits made during the last five years by the subsidiaries in England, Germany, France, and Spain. It is possible that there are many regional offices of these subsidiaries in each of these countries. The profits of the various regional centers for each country have to be totalled and the profits for each country for the past five years have to be provided to the chief accountant. In other words, the data will now have to be aggregated at the country level.

As can be easily seen, the data collection and sampling processes become more cumbersome at higher levels of units of analysis (industry, country) than at the lower levels (individuals and dyads).

It is obvious that the unit of analysis has to be clearly identified as dictated by the research question. Sampling plan decisions will also be governed by the unit of analysis. For example, if I am interested in comparing two cultures, say India and the United States—where my unit of analysis is the country—my sample size will be only two, despite the fact that I will be gathering data from several hundred individuals from a variety of organizations in the different regions of each country, incurring huge costs. However, if my unit of analysis is individuals (say, I am interested in studying the buying patterns of customers in the southern part of the United States), I can perhaps collect data from a representative sample of a hundred individuals in that region and conduct my study with very low costs!

It is now easier to see why the unit of analysis should be given serious consideration even as the research question is being formulated and the research design planned.

TIME HORIZON: CROSS-SECTIONAL VERSUS LONGITUDINAL STUDIES

Cross-Sectional Studies

A study can be done in which data are gathered just once, perhaps over a period of days or weeks or months, in order to answer a research question. Such studies are called one-shot or cross-sectional studies.

Example 4.24   Data were collected from bank employees between April and June of last year to investigate a research question. Data with respect to this particular research have not been collected before from these banks, nor will they be collected again.

Example 4.25   After reading an article titled: "Wooing aging baby-boomers: Consumers 35 to 44 will soon be the nation's biggest spenders, so advertisers must learn how to appeal to this over-the-thrill crowd" (*Fortune,* February 1, 1988), an advertising agency did a survey of the apparel preferences of working women between the ages of 35 and 44. This is a one-shot or cross-sectional study, the results of which will offer some directions for advertisers to target this consumer group.

The purpose of both the studies in the two foregoing examples is to collect information that will be pertinent to find the answer to the research question as soon as the data are collected and analyzed. In Example 4.25, the research question was: What are the apparel preferences of working women between the ages of 35 and 44, so that advertising can be targeted toward their preferences? By analyzing the data collected through a survey, the answer to the research question can be found. Data collection at one point in time will suffice for this purpose.

Longitudinal Studies

In some cases, however, the researcher might want to study people or phenomena at several points in time in order to answer a research question. For instance, the researcher might want to study employees' behavior before and after there is a change in the top management so as to know the effects of the change on their behavior. Here, because data are gathered at two different points in time, it is not a cross-sectional or a one-shot study, but it is a study carried longitudinally across a period of time. Such studies are called longitudinal studies. That is, to answer the research question, data on the dependent variable have to be gathered at two or more points in time.

Example 4.26   "Slice: The fruit-juice soda was a hit at first, but is now losing its fizz" (*New York Times,* July 15, 1988, pp. D1 & D3). Pepsico officials feel that building a brand name takes years and there is no reason to panic. One would expect their marketing department to do a longitudinal study on the sales of the product year after year to see if the sales do pick up through time, even if slowly.

Example 4.27   "K Mart looks to new logo to signify broad changes" (*Wall Street Journal,* September 13, 1990). K Mart is dropping its red and turquoise signs in favor of a new logo to communicate the changes in its stylish goods and apparel, but it is also concerned that the new logo might alienate the shoppers. A longitudinal study obtaining customer perceptions of and reactions to the store now and a few months after the changes are introduced would offer a good idea as to whether customers' perceptions of the store are influenced positively, negatively, or remain unchanged by the new logo.

Since data are collected on the dependent variable at two different points in time, this will be a longitudinal study. Note, though, that any changes observed in customer reactions could be due to other factors, other than change in the logo (e.g., pricing, product mix, etc.).

Longitudinal studies often take more time and effort than cross-sectional studies. However, well-planned longitudinal studies could help to identify cause → effect relationships. For example, one could study the sales volume of a product before and after the introduction of an advertisement, and provided other environmental changes have not impacted on the results, one could attribute the increase in the sales volume, if any, to the advertisement. If there is no increase in sales, then, either the advertisement is ineffective or it will take a longer time to take effect.

Experimental designs invariably are longitudinal studies since data are collected both before and after a manipulation. Field studies could also be longitudinal. For example, a comparison of the data pertaining to the reactions of managers toward working women ten years ago and now will be a longitudinal field study. Most field studies conducted, however, are cross-sectional in nature because of the effort, time, and costs involved in collecting data over several time periods. Longitudinal studies will, of course, be necessary if a manager wants to keep track of certain factors over a period of time (sales; debt-equity ratio, etc.) to assess improvements or to detect possible causal connections (sales promotions and actual sales data; frequency of drug testing and reduction in drug usage, etc.). Though often expensive, longitudinal studies can offer some good insights.

Review of Elements of Research Design

This concludes the discussions on the basic design issues involving the type of investigation, purpose of the study, extent of researcher interference, study setting, the unit of analysis, and the time horizon. The researcher would determine the appropriate decisions to be made in the study design based on the problem definition, the research objectives, the extent of rigor desired, and costs. Sometimes, because of the time and costs involved, a researcher might be constrained to settle for less than what would be the "ideal" research design. For instance, the researcher might have to conduct a cross-sectional instead of a longitudinal study, choose a smaller rather than a larger sample size, do a field study rather than an experimental design, and so on, thus suboptimizing the research design decisions and settling for a lower level of scientific quality because of resource constraints. This trade-off between rigor and resources will be a deliberate and conscious decision made by the researcher based on the scope and reasons for the study and will have to be explicitly stated in any written report or presentation made by the researcher. Such compromises made also account for the reason why management studies are not entirely scientific, as discussed in Chapter 1.

A rigorous research design, which might involve higher costs, is essential if the results of the study are critical for making important decisions affecting the organization's survival and/or the well-being of the vast majority of the publics of the system, as was illustrated in the examples of the dental amalgam. It is best to think about the research design issues even as the theoretical framework is being developed. One has to be very clear about each aspect discussed in this chapter before embarking on data collection.

> ### Do Exercise 4.1.

SUMMARY

In this chapter we examined the basic research design issues and the choice points available to the researcher. We also discussed the circumstances in which each design decision will be appropriate.

In the next chapter we discuss how experimental designs are set up and the ways in which cause → effect relationships can be determined.

DISCUSSION QUESTIONS AND POINTS TO PONDER

1. What are the basic research design issues? Describe them in some detail.
2. Why are the basic design issues important to consider before conducting the study and even as early as at the time of formulating the research question?
3. Is a field study totally out of the question if one is trying to establish cause → effect relationships?
4. "An exploratory study is just as useful as a predictive study." Discuss this statement.
5. Why is the unit of analysis an integral part of the research design?
6. Discuss the interrelationships among noncontrived setting, the purpose of the study, type of investigation, researcher interference, and time horizon of study.
7. Below are two scenarios. For each, indicate how the researcher should proceed i.e. determine the following, giving reasons:
   a. The purpose of the study
   b. The type of investigation
   c. The extent of researcher interference
   d. The study setting
   e. The time horizon for the study
   f. The unit of analysis

Scenario A

Ms. Joyce Lynn, the owner of a small business (a women's dress boutique), has invited a consultant to tell her how she is different from similar small businesses within a sixty-mile radius with respect to her usage of the most modern computer technology, her sales volume, her profit margin, and the way she trains her staff.

Scenario B

Mr. Paul Hodge, the owner of several restaurants on the East Coast, is concerned about the wide differences in the profit margins of the various restaurants. He would like to try some incentive plans for increasing the efficiency levels of those restaurants that are lagging behind. But before he introduces this, he would like to be sure that the idea will work. He asks a researcher to help him with this issue.

EXERCISES

Exercise 4.1   A machine tool operator thinks that fumes emitted in the workshop are instrumental in the low efficiency of the operators. She would like to prove this to her supervisor through a research study.

1. Would this be a causal or a correlational study? Why?
2. Is this an exploratory, descriptive, or hypothesis-testing (analytical or predictive) study? Why?
3. What would be the study: field, lab experiment, or field experiment? Why?
4. What would be the unit of analysis? Why?
5. Would this be a cross-sectional or a longitudinal study? Why?

Exercise 4.2   Many are concerned about the operations of the infamous BCCI, the international banking institution. Government might desire to probe into the details and order an investigation. Would this investigation call for

1. A causal or correlational study? Why?
2. An exploratory, descriptive, or hypothesis-testing study? Why?
3. A field study or a lab study? Why?
4. A cross-sectional or longitudinal study? Why?

CHAPTER 5

EXPERIMENTAL DESIGNS

CHAPTER OBJECTIVES

After completing Chapter 5 you should be able to:

1. Distinguish between causal and correlational analysis.

2. Explain the difference between lab and field experiment.

3. Explain the following terms: nuisance variables, manipulation, experimental and control groups, treatment effect, matching, and randomization.

4. Discuss internal and external validity in experimental designs.

5. Discuss the seven possible threats to internal validity in experimental designs.

6. Describe the different types of experimental designs.

7. Discuss the Solomon four-group design and its implications for internal validity.

8. Apply what has been learned to class assignments and exams.

SCENARIO A

"It's not how much you pay CEOs—but HOW." Lindley Clark Jr. (*Wall Street Journal,* May 17, 1990, p. A18) feels that individual companies and the economy will be served better if executive contracts are written to make CEOs accountable for performance rather than the present compensation system of top executives being paid, virtually independent of their performance, making them permanent corporate fixtures.

Changing to the new mode is likely to irk the chiefs, but it is definitely worth a try if it does work. But how can we be sure that it would work?

SCENARIO B

"ABSENTEEISM: What companies are doing to curb it" (*INC,* May 1989, p. 122). This report indicated that companies used the following incentives to reduce absenteeism:

14%   give bonus days
39%   offer cash
39%   give out recognition awards
4%   give prizes
4%   pursue other strategies

Asked about the effectiveness of using incentives in reducing absenteeism,

22%   of the companies said they were very effective
66%   said they were somewhat effective
12%   said they were not at all effective

What does the above information tell us? How do we know what kinds of incentives **cause** people not to be absent? What particular incentive(s) did the 22% of companies that found their strategies to be "very effective" use? *Is there a direct causal connection between one or two specific incentives and absenteeism?*

The answers to the questions raised in Scenarios A and B might be found by using experimental designs in researching the issues.

In this chapter we will discuss experimental designs—both lab experiments and field experiments. Experimental designs are set up to study possible cause → effect relationships among variables. These are in contrast to correlational studies, which examine the relationships among variables without necessarily trying to establish which variable causes another. Correlational studies can be done as field studies (i.e., the phenomena can be studied as they occur in their natural environment), but causal studies usually have varying degrees of artificial constraints imposed on them, interrupting the natural sequence or flow of events as we discussed briefly in the last chapter. We will examine the various aspects of experimental designs in this chapter.

CAUSAL VERSUS CORRELATIONAL ANALYSIS

Sometimes managers may not be content with knowing what the correlates of a dependent variable of interest are. They may want to know which independent variable "causes" the dependent variable. For example, a manager might want to know what causes a decrease or drop in sales or which variable causes stress in employees, and so on. The manager in these cases is not content with knowing all the variables that are associated with the dependent variable, but wants to know which particular variable causes the dependent variable to vary. Knowing this, the manager could eliminate the variable in question so that its adverse consequences on the dependent variable would be removed or changed. In the foregoing scenario of executive compensation, will the stipulation of CEO's performance accountability in the contract **cause** better results for the company? If so, future company contracts can have this as a clause. However, one cannot rule out the possibility that if a company has made unprecedented profits after getting a new CEO with the new contract clause, that the huge profits are not due to (or at least not solely due to) the CEO's superior performance. A sudden surge in the demand for the goods sold by the company might have boosted sales and profits, which has no relationship to the CEO's direction of the company! Cause → effect relationships can be identified by studying the factors through experimental designs. That is, the causal variable is identified by studying the situation through experimental designs. Thus experimental designs help determine cause → effect relationships.

A correlational study is distinguished from an experimental design in that the former is concerned with identifying the important correlates that explain the variance in the dependent variable, and the study is conducted in the environment where events naturally occur without any artificial constraints being imposed in the setting. The latter, in contrast, helps to isolate the variable that causes the dependent variable, and the researcher does interfere with the natural flow of events to some degree. Setting up an experimental design thus calls for careful and well-thought-out strategies. Isolating a causal factor is difficult because we have to establish beyond the shadow of a doubt that variable X causes variable Y. That is, we are no longer content as in the correlational field studies, with making statements such as the following: variables X, D, and C covary with variable Y—that is, whenever these variables operate in a situation, we can expect that variable Y will also be varying along with increases or decreases in the extent to which variables X, D, and C vary. Instead, in a causal study we want to be able to say that if variable X is not present, then variable Y will not occur, no matter how many other factors may be present in the situation.

Also, in establishing a causal relationship, we have to be sure that variable X causes variable Y, and that there is no possibility that variable Y could or would cause variable X. The following example illustrates this. Suppose a doctor tells his patient, who is a heavy smoker, that she should stop smoking because her lungs are becoming affected by it. The patient might ask the doctor whether smoking is the cause for the deterioration in the lungs, and the doctor might say "yes". The patient might understandably get upset by this statement and argue with the doctor that it is not really smoking that is causing her lung condition, but it is the other way around. That is, she is smoking so much because her lungs are craving for a smoke and find relief through her smoking. In other words, the patient is saying, in her own words, that it is not smoking that causes the lung condition, but it is the lung condition itself that is causing her to smoke. Seeing how upset the patient is (she is now visibly trembling with anxiety) and not wanting to upset her any further during this particular visit, the doctor might say that he could not agree with the patient's logic, but at this stage he would only be willing to say that there is a connection between smoking and lung condition. What the doctor did was to change his argument from "smoking *causes* weak lungs," to "smoking and weak lungs are *associated* very strongly—that is, each influences the other and there could be reciprocal causation."

The dialogue between the doctor and the patient can be depicted as in Figure 5.1 through the direction of the arrows. If the doctor has to prove to the patient that smoking causes cancer, and it is not the weak lungs that cause people to smoke, the doctor will have to show that people with weak lungs do not always smoke, and that those who smoke have weak lungs.

To establish that variable X **causes** variable Y, *all three* of the following conditions should be met:

1. Both X and Y should covary [i.e., when one goes up, the other should also simultaneously go up (or down)].

2. X (the presumed causal factor) should precede Y. In other words, there should be a time order in which the two occur.

3. No other variable should possibly be causing the change in the dependent variable Y.

Figure 5.1

Distinction between Causal effects and Correlational influences.

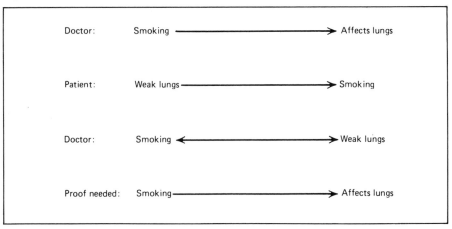

It can thus be seen that to establish causal relationships in an organizational setting, several variables that might covary with the dependent variable have to be controlled in order to allow us to say that variable X and variable X alone causes the dependent variable Y. Establishing this also implies that when variable X is eliminated, variable Y will also be eliminated. Useful as it is to know the cause → effect relationships, establishing them is not easy, because several other variables that covary with the dependent variable have to be controlled. It is not always possible in research on organizations where the events are allowed to occur and follow their natural sequence, to control several variables while manipulating the causal factor—that is, the one independent variable that is causing the dependent variable. It is, however, possible to first isolate the effects of a variable in a tightly controlled artificial setting (the lab setting), and after testing and establishing the cause → effect relationship under these tightly controlled conditions, see how generalizable these cause → effect relationships are to the natural settings (field setting).

Let us illustrate this with an example. Suppose a manager or a researcher believes that staffing the accounting department completely with personnel with M.Acc. (Master of Accountancy) degrees will increase its productivity; it is well nigh impossible to transfer all those without the M.Acc. degree currently in the department to other departments and recruit those with M.Acc. degrees to take their place, because this would disrupt the work of the entire organization—that is, many new people would have to be trained, work would slow down, employees would be upset, and so on. However, the hypothesis that M.Acc. degree would **cause** increases in productivity can be tested in an artificially created setting (i.e., not at the regular workplace) in which an accounting job can be given to three groups of people: those with a M.Acc. degree, those without a M.Acc. degree, and a mixed group of those with and without a M.Acc. degree (as is the case in the present work setting). If the first group performs exceedingly well, the second group poorly, and the third group somewhere in the middle, there will be evidence to indicate that the M.Acc. degree might indeed **cause** productivity to rise. If such evidence is found, then planned and systematic efforts can be made to slowly transfer those without the M.Acc. degree in the accounting department to other departments and recruit others with such a degree to this department. It is then possible to see to what extent productivity does, in fact, go up in the department because all the staff members do have an M.Acc. degree.

Experimental designs fall into two categories: experiments done in an artificial or contrived environment, known as **lab experiments,** and those done in the natural environment in which activities regularly take place, known as the **field experiment.**

THE LABORATORY (LAB) EXPERIMENT AND THE FIELD EXPERIMENT

The Lab Experiment

As stated earlier, when a cause → effect relationship is to be clearly established between an independent and a dependent variable of interest, then all other variables that might contaminate or confound the relationship have to be tightly controlled. In other words, the possible effects of other variables on the dependent variable have to be in some way accounted for, so that the actual causal effects of the investigated independent variable on the dependent variable can be determined. It is also necessary to manipulate the independent variable so that the extent of its causal effects can be established. The controls and manipulations are best done in an artificial setting called the laboratory, where the causal effects can be tested. When artificial controls and manipulations are introduced to establish cause → effect relationships, we have laboratory experimental designs, also known as lab experiments.

Because we are using the terms *control* and *manipulation,* let us examine what these concepts mean.

CONTROL

When we postulate cause → effect relationships between two variables X and Y, it is possible that some other factor, say A, might also influence the dependent variable Y. In this case, it will not be possible to determine the extent to which Y happened or varied only because of X and to what extent Y has been additionally influenced by the presence of the other factor A. For instance, a Human Resource Development manager might arrange for special training in a new word processing language to a set of newly recruited secretaries to prove to the V.P. (his boss) that such training would **cause** them to learn faster. However, some of the new secretaries might learn faster also because they have had previous experience with another word processing language. In this case, the manager cannot prove that the special training alone **caused** faster learning, since the previous experience with another word processing language is a contaminating factor. If the true effect of the training on learning is to be assessed, then the learners' previous experience with another language has to be controlled. This might be done by *not* including in the experiment those who already know some kind of word processing. This is what we mean by having to control for contaminating factors, and we will later see how this can be done.

MANIPULATION OF THE INDEPENDENT VARIABLE

In order to examine the causal effects of an independent variable on a dependent variable, certain manipulations need to be tried. Manipulation simply means that we *create* different levels of the independent variable to assess the impact on the dependent variable. For example, if we want to test the theory that deep knowledge of various manufacturing technologies is **caused** by the rotation of employees on the production line and being exposed to the various systems over a two-week period, then we can **manipulate** the independent variable, "rotation and exposure." That is, one group of production workers can be rotated and exposed to all the systems during a two-week period, one group of workers could be exposed and rotated partially during the two weeks (i.e., being exposed to only half of the manufacturing technologies), and the third group could continue to do what they are currently doing without any special rotation and exposure. By measuring the deep knowledge of these three groups both before and after the manipulation (also known as the "treatment"), it would be possible to assess the extent to which the treatment **caused** the effect, after controlling for the contaminating factors. If deep knowledge is indeed caused by rotation and exposure, the results would show that the third group had the lowest increase in deep knowledge, the second group had some significant increase, and the first group had the greatest gains!

Let us look at another example on how causal relationships are established by manipulating the independent variable. Let us say we want to test the effects of lighting on worker production levels among sewing machine operators. To establish cause → effect relationship, we must first measure the production levels of all the operators over a fifteen-day period with the usual amount of light they work with—say 60-watt bulbs. We might then want to split the group of fifty operators into five groups of ten members each, and while allowing one subgroup to work under the same conditions as before (60-watt electric bulbs) we might want to manipulate the intensity of the light for the other four subgroups, by making one group work with 80-watt bulbs, another with 90 watts, the third with 100 watts, and the fourth with 120 watts. After the different groups have worked with these varying degrees of light exposures for fifteen days, each group's total production for these fifteen days may be checked to see if the difference between the preexperimental production and the postexperimental production among the groups is directly proportional to the intensity of the light beams to which they have been exposed. If our hypothesis that more light increases the production levels is correct, then the subgroup that did not have any change in the lighting—called the control group—should have no increases in production; all the other groups should show increases in production levels; and the ones having more light should show greater increases than those who had lesser amounts of increased lighting.

In this case the independent variable, lighting, has been manipulated by exposing different groups to different degrees of changes in the lighting. This manipulation of the independent variable is also known as the *treatment,* and the results of the treatment are called *treatment effects.*

Let us illustrate how variable X can be both controlled and manipulated in the lab setting through Example 5.1.

Example 5.1   Let us say an entrepreneur—the owner of a toy shop—is rather disappointed with the number of imitation "Ninja turtles" (which are in great demand) produced by his workers, who are paid wages at an hourly rate. He might be wondering whether paying them piece rates would increase their production levels. However, before implementing the piece-rate system, he would want to know for sure that switching over to the new system will result in an increase in production.

In a case like this, the researcher might first want to test the causal relationships in a lab setting, and if the results are encouraging, the experiment might then be conducted in a field setting. For the lab experimental design, the researcher should first think of possible factors that might affect the production level of the workers, and then try to control these. Other than piece rates, previous job experience might influence rate of production because familiarity with the job makes it easy for people to increase their productivity levels; gender differences may affect productivity, especially if the jobs are very strenuous and require muscular strength; age may also influence the productivity of employees, and for some types of jobs, educational levels may be important, too. Let us say that for the type of production job in question, age, gender, and prior experience of the employees are the factors that would influence the production levels of the employees. The researcher needs to control these three variables. Let us see how this can be done.

Suppose the researcher is going to set up four groups of fifteen people each for the lab experimental design—one group is to be used as the control, and the other three to be subjected to three different pay manipulations. Now, the three variables can be controlled in two different ways—either by matching the groups or through randomization. These concepts should be explained before we proceed further.

CONTROLLING THE CONTAMINATING
OR "NUISANCE" VARIABLES

Matching Groups

One way of controlling for the contaminating or "nuisance" variables is to match the various groups by taking the confounding characteristics and deliberately spreading them across groups. For instance, if there are twenty women among the sixty members, then each group will be assigned five women, so that the effects of gender are distributed across the four groups. Likewise, age and experience factors can be matched across the four groups, such that each group has a similar mix of individuals in terms of gender, age, and experience. Because the suspected contaminating factors are matched across the groups, we can be comfortable in saying that variable X alone causes variable Y, if such is the finding after the experiment.

Randomization

Another way of controlling for the contaminating variables is to assign the sixty members randomly (i.e., with no predetermination) to the four groups. That is, every member would have a known and equal chance of being assigned to any of these four groups. For instance, we might throw the names of all the sixty members into a hat, and draw their names. The first fifteen names drawn may be assigned to the first group, the second fifteen names to the second group, and so on, or the first person drawn might be assigned to the first group, the second person drawn to the second group, and so on. Thus, in randomization, both the process by which individuals are drawn is random (i.e., everybody has a known and equal chance of being drawn) and the assignment of the individual to any particular group is also random (each individual could be assigned to any one of the groups set up). By thus randomly assigning members to the groups we would be distributing the confounding variables among the groups equally. That is, the variables of age, sex, and previous experience—the controlled variables—will have an equal probability of being distributed among the groups. The process of randomization would ideally ensure that each group is comparable to the other, and that the effects of age, sex, and previous experience are controlled. That is, each of the groups will have some members who have more experience mingled with those who have less or no experience. All groups will have members of different age and sex composition. Thus randomization would ensure that if these variables do indeed have a contributory or confounding effect, by distributing these confounding effects across groups, we have controlled their confounding effects. This is achieved because when we manipulate the independent variable of piece rates by having no piece-rate system at all for one group (control) and having different piece rates for the other three groups (experimental), we can determine the causal effects of the piece rates on production levels; any errors or biases caused by age, sex, and previous experience are now normally distributed (see explanation in next section) with equal probability among all four groups. Any causal effects found would be over and above the effects of the confounding variables.

To make it clear, let us illustrate this with some actual figures as in Table 5.1. Note that because the effects of experience, sex, and age have been controlled in all the groups by randomly assigning the members to the four groups, and the old hourly rate control group had no increase in the productivity rates, it can be safely concluded from the table that the percentage increases in production are a result of the piece-rate treatment effects. In other words, piece rates are the cause of the increase in the number of toys produced. We cannot now say that the cause → effect relations have been confounded by other "nuisance" variables, because they have been controlled through the process of randomly assigning members to the groups. Here, we have high **internal validity** or confidence in the cause → effect relationship.

Table 5.1
Cause → Effect Relationships after Randomization

Groups	Treatment	Treatment effect (% increase in production over pre–piece rate system)
Experimental group 1	$1.00 per piece	10
Experimental group 2	$1.50 per piece	15
Experimental group 3	$2.00 per piece	20
Control group (no treatment)	Old hourly rate	0

Advantages of Randomization

The difference between matching and randomization is that in the former case individuals are deliberately and consciously matched for the various controlled characteristics, whereas in the latter case we expect that the process of randomization will distribute the inequalities among the groups, based on the laws of normal distribution, and we need not be particularly concerned about any confounding factors. The normal distribution is represented by a bell-shaped curve (shown in Figure 5.2), which is useful for examining many phenomena that occur in the organizational context. When we examine characteristics such as abilities, talents, and the like, we presume that nearly 68 percent of the population falls within one

Figure 5.2
Normal distribution represented by the bell curve.

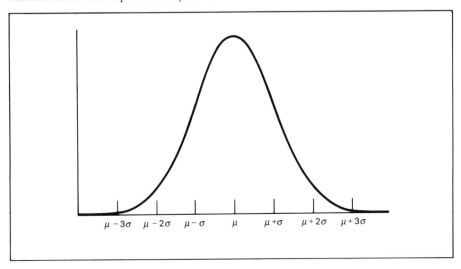

$\mu - 3\sigma$ $\mu - 2\sigma$ $\mu - \sigma$ μ $\mu + \sigma$ $\mu + 2\sigma$ $\mu + 3\sigma$

standard deviation (σ) of the mean (μ) (i.e., between $\mu - \sigma$ and $\mu + \sigma$), about 95 percent within two standard deviations ($\mu - 2\sigma$ and $\mu + 2\sigma$), and about 99 percent within three standard deviations ($\mu - 3\sigma$ and $\mu + 3\sigma$). In other words, individuals who are very high or very low in the characteristics we are interested in (i.e., those who are in the extreme left or right of the curve) are very small in numbers, but they nevertheless do exist. When we randomly assign members to the various groups, we expect that those who may be having very high or very low scores on a particular variable that might confound the cause → effect relationship are going to be spread among all the groups. To put it differently, we will be distributing the "normal" and the "abnormal" characteristics across all the groups.

Compared to randomization, matching might be less effective, since we may not know *all* the factors that could possibly contaminate the cause → effect relationship in any given situation, and hence fail to match some critical factors across all groups while conducting an experiment. Randomization, however, will take care of this, since all the known and unknown contaminating factors will be spread across all groups. Moreover, even if we know the confounding variables, we may not be able to find a match for all such variables. For instance, if gender is a confounding variable, and if there are only two women in a four-group experimental design, we will not be able to match all the groups with respect to gender. Randomization solves these dilemmas as well.

In sum, experimental designs involve controlling the contaminating variables through the process of either matching or randomization, and the manipulation of the treatment. Internal validity indicates the extent to which conclusions can be drawn about the causal effects of one variable on another. That is, internal validity addresses the question, "To what extent does the research design permit us to say that the independent variable A **causes** a change in the dependent variable B? As Kidder and Judd (1986) note, in research with high internal validity, we are relatively more able to argue that the relationship is causal, whereas in studies with low internal validity, causality cannot be inferred at all. In lab experiments where cause → effect relationships are substantiated, internal validity can be said to be high.

So far we have talked about establishing cause → effect relationships within the lab setting, which is an artificially created, controlled situation. You might yourself have been a subject taking part in one of the lab experiments conducted by the psychology or other departments on campus at some time. You might not have been told exactly what cause → effect relationships the experimenter was looking for, but if you have been a participant in any of the lab experiments, you probably would have been told what experiences you will encounter in the experiment and that you will be given a full account of the results at the end of the experiment, in addition to having your questions answered. You would have also been debriefed after the experiment was over. That is how lab experiments are usually done. Subjects are selected and assigned to different groups through a matching or randomization process; they are put into a lab (i.e., a controlled) setting; they are given some details and a task to perform; and some kind of questionnaire or other tests will be administered both before and after the task is completed. The results of these studies would indicate the cause → effect relationships under investigation.

ETHICAL ISSUES IN RESEARCH AND LAB EXPERIMENTS

It is appropriate at this juncture to briefly discuss a few of the many ethical issues involved in doing research, some of which are particularly relevant for conducting lab experiments. The following practices are considered unethical:

- Putting pressure on individuals to participate in research (through coercion, applying social pressure, etc.).
- Asking demeaning questions that diminish their self-respect.
- Deceiving subjects by deliberately misleading them as to the true purpose of the research.
- Exposing participants to physical or mental stress.
- Not allowing them to withdraw from the research when they want to.
- Using the research results to disadvantage the participants, or for purposes that the participants would not like.
- Withholding benefits from control groups.

The last item is somewhat controversial as to whether or not it should be an ethical dilemma, especially in organizational research. If three different incentives are offered for three experimental groups and none offered to the control group, it is a fact that the control group has participated in the experiment with absolutely no benefit. Similarly, if four different experimental groups receive four different levels of training but the control group does not, the other four groups have gained expertise that the control group has not had a chance of receiving. But should this become an ethical dilemma **preventing** experimental designs with control groups in organizational research? Perhaps not, for at least three reasons. One is that several others in the system who did not participate in the experiment also did not benefit. Second, even in the experimental groups, some would have benefited more than the others (depending on the extent to which the causal factor is manipulated). Finally, if a cause → effect relationship is found, in all probability the system will implement the new-found knowledge sooner or later and everyone will ultimately gain. The assumption that the control group did not gain anything even after participating in the experiment may not be sufficient reason not to use lab or field experiments.

Many universities have a "human subjects committee" to protect the rights of human subjects involved in any type of research activity involving people. The basic function of these committees is to discharge the moral and ethical responsibility of the university system by studying the procedures outlined in the research proposals and giving their stamp of approval to the studies. The human subjects committee might require the investigators to modify their procedures or inform the subjects more fully.

GENERALIZABILITY OF LAB EXPERIMENTS

To what extent would the results found in the lab setting be transferable or generalizable to the actual organizational or field settings? In other words, if we do find a cause → effect relationship after conducting a lab experiment, can we then confidently say that the same cause → effect relationship will also hold true in the organizational setting?

Consider the following situation. If in the lab experimental design in Example 5.1, the groups were given the simple production task of screwing nuts and bolts onto a plastic frame, and the results were that the groups who were paid piece rates were more productive than those who were paid hourly rates, to what extent can we say that this would be true in the live organizational setting? The tasks in organizations are far more complex, and there might be several confounding variables that cannot be controlled, as for example, experience. Under such circumstances, we cannot be sure that the cause → effect relationship found in the lab experiment is necessarily likely to hold good in the field setting. To test the causal relationships in the organizational setting, field experiments are done. These will now be briefly discussed.

THE FIELD EXPERIMENT

A field experiment, as the name implies, is an experiment done in the natural environment in which events normally occur, with treatments given to one or more groups. Thus in the field experiment, even though it may not be possible to control all of the nuisance variables because members cannot be either randomly assigned to groups or matched, treatments can still be manipulated. Control groups could also be set up in field experiments. The experimental and control groups in the field experiment could be made up of the people working at several plants within a certain radius, or from the different shifts in the same plant, or in some other way. If there are three different shifts in a production plant, for instance, and the effects of the piece-rate system are to be studied, similar to Example 5.1, one of the shifts can be used as the control group, and the two other shifts could be given two different treatments or the same treatment—that is, different piece rates or the same piece rate. Any cause → effect relationship found under these conditions would have wider generalizability to other similar production settings, even though we may not be sure to what extent the piece rates alone were the cause of the increase in productivity because some of the other confounding variables could not be controlled.

EXTERNAL VALIDITY

What we just discussed can be referred to as an issue of external validity versus internal validity. External validity refers to the extent of generalizability of the results of a causal study to other people, events, or settings, and internal validity refers to the extent of our confidence in the causal effects—that variable X causes variable Y. Field experiments have more external validity (i.e., the results may be more generalizable to other similar organizational settings); but they have lesser internal validity (i.e., we cannot be certain of the extent to which variable X alone caused variable Y). Note that in the lab experiment, the reverse is true. The internal validity is high but the external validity is rather low. In other words, in lab experiments we can be sure that variable X causes variable Y because we have been able to keep the other confounding exogenous variables under control, but we have so tightly controlled several variables to establish the cause → effect relationship that we do not know to what extent the results of our study could be generalized, if at all, to field settings. In other words, since the lab setting does not reflect the "real world" setting, we do not know to what extent the lab findings validly represent the reality in the outside world.

TRADE-OFF BETWEEN INTERNAL AND EXTERNAL VALIDITY

There is thus a trade-off between internal and external validity. If we want high internal validity, we should be willing to settle for lower external validity and vice versa. To ensure both types of validity, researchers usually try first to test the causal relationships in a tightly controlled artificial or lab setting, and once the relationship has been established, they try to test the causal relationship in a field experiment. Lab experimental designs in the management area have thus far been used to sort out, among other things, gender differences in leadership styles, managerial aptitudes, and so on. However, gender differences and other factors found in the lab settings are frequently not found in field studies (Osborn & Vicars, 1976). These problems of external validity usually limit the use of lab experiments in the management area, even though they are frequently used as a first step to establish cause → effect relationships before extending causal theories to field settings. Because field experiments often have unintended consequences—such as personnel becoming suspicious, rivalries and jealousies being created among departments—researchers conduct field experiments only infrequently.

FACTORS AFFECTING INTERNAL VALIDITY

Even the best designed lab studies could be influenced by factors that might affect the internal validity of the lab experiment. That is, some confounding factors might still be present that could offer rival explanations as to what is causing the dependent variable. These possible confounding factors pose a *threat to internal validity*. The seven major threats to internal validity are the effects of history, maturation, testing, instrumentation, selection, statistical regression, and mortality and are explained below with examples.

History Effects

Certain events (or factors) that would have an impact on the independent variable–dependent variable relationship might unexpectedly occur while the experiment is in progress, and this history of events would confound the cause → effect rela-

Figure 5.3

Illustration of history effects in experimental designs.

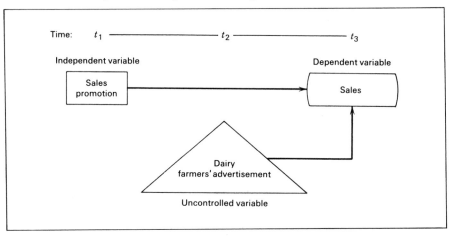

tionship between the two variables, thus affecting the internal validity. For example, let us say that the manager of a Dairy Products Division wants to test the effects of the "Buy one, get one free" sales promotion for a week, on the sales of the company-owned brand of packaged cheese. She carefully records the sales of the packaged cheese during the last two weeks to assess the effect of the promotion. However, on the very day that her sales promotion goes into effect, the Dairy Farmers' Association unexpectedly launches a multimedia advertisement on the virtues of consuming dairy products, especially cheese. The sales of all dairy products, including cheese, go up in all the stores, including the one where the experiment was in progress. Here, because of the unexpected advertisement, one cannot be sure how much of the increase in sales of the packaged cheese in question was due to the sales promotion and how much due to the advertisement of the Dairy Farmers' Association! The effects of *history* have reduced the internal validity or the faith that can be attached to the belief that the sales promotion caused the increase in sales.

The history effects in this case are illustrated in Figure 5.3.

To give another example, let us say a bakery is studying the effects of adding to its bread a new ingredient that is expected to enrich it and offer greater strength and vitality to children under 14 years of age within 30 days, if certain prescribed quantities of the bread are consumed daily. At the start of the experiment the bakery takes a measure of the strength and vitality of thirty children through a special measuring device. Thereafter, the children are given the prescribed quantities of bread daily. Unfortunately, on the twentieth day of the experiment, a flu virus hits the city in epidemic proportions affecting most of the city, including many of the children studied. This unforeseen and uncontrollable specific event, flu, has contaminated the cause → effect relationship study for the bakery.

Figure 5.4
Illustration of maturation effects on cause → effect relationship.

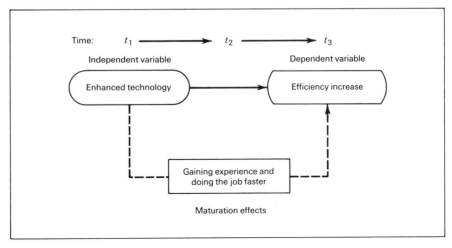

Maturation Effects

Cause → effect inferences can also be contaminated by the effects of the passage of time—another uncontrollable variable. Such contamination is called maturation effects. The maturation effects are a function of the processes—both biological and psychological—operating within the respondents as a result of the passage of time. Examples of maturation processes could include growing older, getting tired, feeling hungry, and getting bored. In other words, there could be a maturation effect on the dependent variable purely because of the passage of time. For instance, let us say that an R & D director contends that increases in the efficiency of workers would result in three months' time by introducing enhanced technology in the worksetting. Supposing, at the end of the three months, increased efficiency is indeed found, it will be difficult to say that the enhanced technology (and it *alone*) increased the efficiency of workers, because with the passage of time employees also gain experience and become faster in how they perform their jobs, which also contributes to their efficiency. Thus, the internal validity also gets reduced owing to the effects of maturation inasmuch as it is difficult to pinpoint how much of the increase is due to the introduction of the enhanced technology alone. Figure 5.4 illustrates the maturation effects in the above example.

Testing Effects

Frequently, to test the effects of a treatment, subjects are given what is called a pretest. That is, first a measure of the dependent variable is taken (the pretest), then the treatment is given, and after the treatment a second test, called the posttest is administered. The difference between the posttest scores and the pretest scores is then attributed to the treatment. However, the very fact that respondents were exposed to the pretest might influence their responses on the posttest, which would adversely impact on internal validity.

For example, if a challenging job is expected to cause increases in job satisfaction, and a pretest on job satisfaction is administered asking for employees' level of satisfaction with the nature of their current jobs, this might sensitize people to the issue of job satisfaction. When a challenging job is introduced and a further job satisfaction questionnaire is administered subsequently, the respondents might now respond to the posttest with a different frame of reference than if they had not originally been sensitized to the issue of job satisfaction through the pretest.

This kind of sensitization through previous testing is called the testing effect, which also affects the internal validity of experimental designs. In the above case, though increases in job satisfaction can legitimately be measured through pre- and posttests, the pretest could confound the cause → effect relationship by sensitizing the respondents to the posttest. Thus, testing effects are another threat to internal validity.

Instrumentation Effects

Instrumentation effects are another source of threat to internal validity. These effects might arise because of a change in the measuring instrument between pretest and posttest, and not because of the treatment's differential impact at the end (Cook & Campbell, 1979). For instance, an observer who is involved in observing a particular pattern of behaviors in respondents before a treatment might start concentrating on a different set of behaviors as time passes by. The frame of measurement of behaviors (in a sense, the measuring instrument) has now changed and will not reflect the change in behaviors that can be attributed to the treatment. This is also true in the case of physical measuring instruments like the spring balance or other finely calibrated instruments that might lose their accuracy due to loss of tension with excessive use, resulting in erroneous final measurement.

In organizations, instrumentation effects in experimental designs are possible when the pretest is done by the experimenter, treatments are given to the experimental groups, and the posttest on measures such as performance are done by different managers. One manager might measure performance by the final units of output, a second manager might assess performance taking into account the number of rejects as well, and a third manager might also take into consideration the amount of resources expended in doing the job! Here, there are at least three different measuring instruments, if we treat each manager as a performance measuring instrument.

Thus, instrumentation effects also pose a threat to internal validity in experimental designs.

Selection Bias Effects

The threat to internal validity could also come from improper or unmatched selection of subjects for the experimental and control groups. For example, if a lab experiment is set up to assess the impact of working environment on employees' attitudes toward work, and if one of the experimental conditions is to have a group of subjects work in a room with some stench, for about two hours, an ethical researcher might disclose this condition to prospective subjects, who may decline participation in the study. However, some volunteers might be lured through incentives (say a payment of $35 for the two hours of participation in the study). The volunteers so selected may be quite different from the others (inasmuch as they may come from deprived backgrounds, etc.) and their responses to the treatment might be quite different. Such bias in the selection of the subjects might contaminate the cause → effect relationships and pose a threat to internal validity as well. Hence, newcomers, volunteers, and others who cannot be matched with the control groups would pose a threat to internal validity in certain types of experiments.

Statistical Regression

The effects of statistical regression occur when the members chosen for the experimental group have extreme scores on the dependent variable to begin with. For instance, if a manager wants to test if he can increase the "salesmanship" repertoire of the sales personnel through Dale Carnegie–type programs, he should avoid choosing those with extremely low abilities or extremely high abilities for the experiment. This is because we know from the laws of probability that those with very low scores on a variable (in this case, current sales abilities) have a greater probability of showing improvement and scoring closer to the mean on the posttest after being exposed to the treatment. This phenomenon of low scorers tending to score closer to the mean is known as "regressing toward the mean" (statistical regression). Likewise, those with very high abilities would also have a greater tendency to regress toward the mean—they will score lower on the posttest than on the pretest. Thus, those who are at either end of the continuum with respect to a variable would not "truly" reflect the cause → effect relationship. The phenomenon of statistical regression is thus yet another threat to internal validity.

Mortality

Another confounding effect on the cause → effect relationship comes from the mortality or attrition of the members in the experimental or control group or both, as the experiment progresses. When the group composition changes over time across the groups, comparison between the groups becomes difficult, because those who dropped out of the experiment may confound the results. Again, we would not be able to say how much of the effect observed arises from the treatment, and how much is attributable to the nature of the members who dropped out; those who stayed with the experiment could be quite different from those who dropped out. Let us see an example.

A sales manager had heard glowing reports about three different training programs that train sales personnel in effective sales strategies. They were all of six weeks' duration. The manager was curious to know which one would offer the best results for his company. The first program took the trainees daily on field trips and demonstrated effective and noneffective sales strategies through practical experience. The second program trained groups indoors in a classroom type of setting, lecturing, role playing, and answering questions from the members. The third program used mathematical models and simulations to increase sales effectiveness.

The manager chose eight trainees each for the three different programs and sent them on training. By the end of the fourth week, three trainees from the first group, one from the second group, and two from the third group had dropped out of the training programs due to a variety of reasons including ill health, family exigencies, transportation problems, and a car accident. This attrition from the various groups has now made it impossible to compare the effectiveness of the various programs.

Thus, mortality can also lower the internal validity of an experiment.

Identifying Threats to Internal Validity

Let us examine each of the possible seven threats to internal validity in the following scenario.

An organizational consultant wanted to demonstrate to the president of a company, through an experimental design, that the democratic style of leadership is the best, if the morale of the employees is to be increased. She set up three experimental groups and one control group for the purpose and assigned members to each of the groups randomly. The three experimental groups were headed by an autocratic leader, a democratic leader, and a laissez-faire leader, respectively.

The members in the three experimental groups were administered a pretest. Since the control group was not exposed to any treatment, they were not given a pretest. As the experiment progressed, two members in the "democratic" treatment group got very excited and started moving around to the other members saying that the participative atmosphere was "great" and "performance was bound to be high in this group." Two members from each of the "autocratic" and "laissez-faire" groups left after the first hour saying they had to go and could no longer participate in the experiment. After two hours of activities, a posttest was administered to all the participants, including the control group members, on the same lines as the pretest.

History Effects: The two members in the "participative" group unexpectedly moving around in an excited manner and remarking that participative leadership is "great" and the "performance is bound to be high in this group" might have boosted the morale of all the members in the group. It would be difficult to separate out how much of the increase in morale was due to the "participative" condition alone and how much to the enthusiasm displayed by the two members.

Maturation: It is doubtful that maturation will have any effects on morale in this situation, since the passage of time, in itself, may not have anything much to do with increase or decrease in morale.

Testing: The pretests are likely to have sensitized the respondents to the post-test. Thus, testing effects would exist. However, if *all* the groups had been given both the pre- and the posttests, the testing effects across all groups would have been taken care of (i.e., nullified) and the posttests of each of the experimental groups could have been compared with that of the control group to detect the effects of the treatment. Unfortunately, the control group was not given the pretest, and thus, this group's posttest scores were not biased by the pretest. Hence, the experimental groups' scores cannot even be really compared with the control group's.

Instrumentation: Since the same questionnaire has measured morale both before and after the treatment for all members, we do not expect instrumentation bias.

Selection Bias: Since members have been randomly assigned to all groups, we do not expect selection bias to exist.

Statistical Regression: Though not specifically stated, we can presume that all the members participating in the experiment were selected randomly from a normally distributed population, in which case, the question of statistical regression does not arise.

Mortality: Since members dropped out of two experimental groups, the effects of mortality could affect internal validity.

In effect, three of the seven threats to internal validity do exist in this case. The history, testing, and mortality effects are of concern and hence the internal validity will be very low.

INTERNAL VALIDITY IN CASE STUDIES

If there are several threats to internal validity even in a tightly controlled lab experiment, it should become quite clear why we cannot draw conclusions about causal relationships from **case studies** that describe the events that occurred during a particular time. Unless a well-designed experimental study, randomly assigning members to experimental and control groups, and successfully manipulating the treatment indicates possible causal relationships, it would be impossible to say which factor causes another. For instance, there are several causes attributed to Slice, the soft drink introduced by Pepsico Inc., for not taking off after its initial success (see *New York Times,* July 15, 1988, D1, D3). Among the reasons given are (1) a cutback in advertisement for Slice, (2) operating on the mistaken premise that the juice content in Slice would appeal to health conscious buyers, (3) Pepsico's attempts to milk the brand too quickly, (4) several strategic errors made by Pepsico, (5) underestimating the time taken to build a brand, and the like. While all the above could provide the basis for developing a theoretical framework for explaining the variance in the sales of a product such as Slice, conclusions about cause → effect relationships cannot be determined from anecdotal events.

FACTORS AFFECTING EXTERNAL VALIDITY

Whereas internal validity raises questions about whether it is the treatment alone or some extraneous factor that causes the effects, external validity raises issues about the generalizability of the findings to other settings. For instance, the extent to which the experimental situation differs from the setting to which the findings are expected to be generalized is directly related to the degree of threat it poses to external validity. To illustrate, subjects in a lab experiment might be given a pretest and a posttest. Those findings, however, cannot be generalized to the organizational world, where a pretest is rarely administered to employees to be followed up by a posttest. Thus the effects of the treatment will not be the same in the field, which reduces the generalizability. Another threat is the selection of the subjects. In a lab setting, the types of subjects selected for the experiment could be very different from the types of employees recruited by the organizations. For example, students in a university might be given an artificial job and a treatment to study the effects on their performance. The findings from this experiment cannot be generalized to the real world of work, however, where the employees and the nature of the jobs would both be quite different. Thus subject selection and its interaction with the treatment would also pose a threat to external validity. These are just some of the factors that restrict generalizability. Maximum external validity can be obtained by ensuring that the experimental conditions are as close and compatible as possible to the real-world situation. It is in this sense that field experiments have greater external validity than lab experiments. That is, the effects of the treatment can be generalized to other settings similar to the one where the field experiment was conducted.

Review of Factors Affecting Internal and External Validity

In summary, at least seven contaminating factors exist that might affect the internal validity of experimental designs. These are the effects of history, maturation, testing, instrumentation, selection, statistical regression, and mortality. However, it is possible to reduce the biases by increasing the sophistication of the experimental design. Whereas some of the more sophisticated designs, discussed below, would help increase the internal validity of the experimental results, they could also become expensive and time consuming.

Threats to external validity can be combated by creating experimental conditions that are as close as possible to the situations to which the results of the experiment are to be generalized. For more extensive discussions on validity, see Cook and Campbell (1979).

WHEN ARE EXPERIMENTAL DESIGNS NECESSARY?

Before embarking on research studies using experimental designs, it is essential to consider whether experimental designs are necessary at all, since they involve special efforts and varying degrees of interference with the natural flow of events. Some questions that need to be addressed are the following:

1. Are causal relationships necessary to be identified, or would tracing the corre-lates that account for the variance in the dependent variable be enough? If the latter would do, experimental designs are not really needed.

2. If causal relationships are important to be identified, is there a greater need for internal validity or external validity or both? If internal validity alone is impor-tant, a carefully designed lab experiment would be the answer; if gener-alizability is the more important criterion, then a field experiment would be called for; if both are equally important, then a lab study should be first under-taken, followed by a field experiment.

3. Is cost an important factor in the study? If cost is a primary consideration, would a less sophisticated rather than a more sophisticated experimental design do?

These decision points can be depicted as per the chart in Figure 5.5.

The various types of experimental designs and the extent of internal validity in each are discussed next.

Figure 5.5
Decision points for embarking on an experimental design.

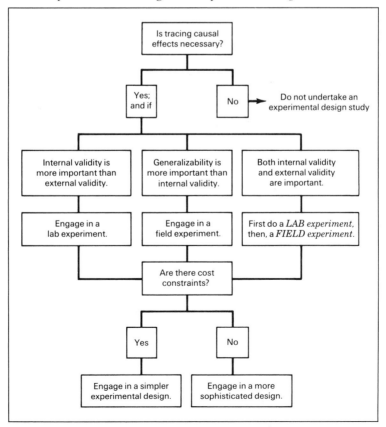

TYPES OF EXPERIMENTAL DESIGNS
AND INTERNAL VALIDITY

Let us consider some of the commonly used experimental designs and determine the extent to which they guard against the seven factors that could contaminate the internal validity of experimental results. It goes without saying that the shorter the time span of the experiments, the less the chances of encountering history, maturation, and mortality effects. Experiments lasting for an hour or two do not usually face many of these problems. It is when experiments take place over an extended period, say several months, that the possibility of encountering more of the confounding factors increases.

Some studies expose an experimental group to a treatment and measure the effects of the treatment. Such an experimental design is the weakest of all designs, and it does not measure any true cause → effect relationship because there is no comparison, nor any recording of the status of the dependent variable as it was prior to the experimental treatment and how it changed after the treatment. In the absence of such control, the study is of no scientific value in determining cause → effect relationships. Hence, such a design is not discussed as an experimental design here.

Pretest and Posttest Experimental Group Design

An experimental group (without a control group) may be given a pretest, exposed to a treatment, and then given a posttest to measure the effects of the treatment. This can be diagrammed as in Figure 5.6, where O refers to some process of observation or measurement, X represents the exposure of a group to an experimental treatment, and the X and Os in the row are applied to the same specific persons. Here, the effects of the treatment can be obtained by measuring the difference between the posttest and the pretest. Note, however, that **testing** and **instrumentation effects** might contaminate the internal validity. If the experiment is extended over a period of time, history effects and maturation effects may also confound the results.

Figure 5.6
Pretest and posttest experimental group design.

Group	Pretest Score	Treatment	Posttest Score
Experimental group	O_1	X	O_2

Treatment effect = $(O_2 - O_1)$

Figure 5.7
Posttest only with experimental and control groups.

Group	Treatment	Outcome
Experimental group	X	O_1
Control group		O_2

$$\text{Treatment effect} = (O_1 - O_2)$$

Posttests Only with Experimental and Control Groups

Some experimental designs are set up with an experimental and a control group, the former being exposed to a treatment and the latter not being exposed to it. The effects of the treatment are studied by assessing the difference in the outcomes—that is, the posttest scores of the experimental and control groups. This is illustrated in Figure 5.7. Here is a case where the testing effects have been avoided because there is no pretest, only a posttest. Care has to be taken, however, to make sure that the two groups are matched for all the possible contaminating "nuisance" variables. Otherwise, the true effects of the treatment cannot be determined by merely looking at the difference in the posttest scores of the two groups. Randomization would take care of this problem.

There are at least two possible threats to validity in this design. If the two groups are not matched or randomly assigned, **selection biases** could contaminate the results. That is, the differential recruitment of the persons making up the two groups would confound the cause → effect relationship. **Mortality** (the dropout of individuals from groups) can also confound the results, and thus pose a threat to internal validity.

Pretest and Posttest Experimental and Control Group Designs

This design can be visually depicted as in Figure 5.8. Two groups—one experimental and the other control—are both exposed to the pretest and the posttest. The only difference between the two groups is that the former is exposed to a treatment whereas the latter is not. Measuring the difference between the differences in the post- and pretests of the two groups would give the net effects of the treatment. Both groups have been exposed to both the pre- and posttests, and both groups have been randomized; thus we could expect that the history, maturation, testing, and instrumentation effects have been controlled. This is true because whatever happened with the experimental group (e.g., maturation, history, testing, and instrumentation) also happened with the control group, and in measuring the net

Figure 5.8
Pretest and posttest experimental and control groups.

Group	Pretest	Treatment	Posttest
Experimental group	O_1	X	O_2
Control group	O_3		O_4

$$\text{Treatment effect} = [(O_2 - O_1) - (O_4 - O_3)]$$

effects (the difference in the differences between the pre- and posttest scores) we have controlled these contaminating factors. Through the process of randomization, we have also controlled the effects of selection biases and statistical regression. **Mortality** could, however, pose a problem in this design. In experiments that take several weeks, as in the case of assessing the impact of training on skill development or technology enhancement on effectiveness, some of the subjects in the experimental group may drop out before the end of the experiment. It is possible that those who drop out are in some way different from those who stay till the end and take the posttest. If so, mortality could offer a plausible rival explanation for the difference between O_2 and O_1.

Solomon Four-Group Design

To gain more confidence in internal validity in experimental designs, it is advisable to set up two experimental groups and two control groups for the experiment. One experimental group and one control group can be given both the pretest and the posttest, as shown in Figure 5.9. The other two groups will be given only the posttest. Here the effects of the treatment can be calculated in several different ways, as indicated in the figure. To the extent that we come up with almost the same results in each of the different calculations, we can attribute the effects to the treatment. This increases the internal validity of the experimental design and its results. This design, known as the Solomon four-group design, is probably the most comprehensive and the one with the least problems with internal validity.

Solomon Four-Group Design and Threats to Internal Validity

Let us examine how the threats to internal validity are taken care of by the Solomon four-group Design. It is important to note that subjects have been randomly selected and randomly assigned to groups. This removes the **statistical regression and selection biases.** Group 2, the control group that was exposed to both the pre- and posttest, helps us to see whether or not history, maturation, testing, instrumentation, regression, or mortality threats to validity exist. If scores O_3 and O_4 (pre- and posttest scores of Group 2) remain the same, then it goes without

Figure 5.9
Solomon four-group design.

Group	Pretest	Treatment	Posttest
1. Experimental	O_1	X	O_2
2. Control	O_3		O_4
3. Experimental		X	O_5
4. Control			O_6

Treatment effect (E) could be judged by:

$$E = (O_2 - O_1)$$
$$E = (O_2 - O_4)$$
$$E = (O_5 - O_6)$$
$$E = (O_5 - O_3)$$
$$E = [(O_2 - O_1) - (O_4 - O_3)]$$

If all Es are similar, the cause $\rightarrow$ effect relationship is highly valid.

saying that neither history, nor maturation, nor testing, nor instrumentation, nor statistical regression, nor mortality has had an impact.

Group 3, the experimental group that was not given a pretest, helps to establish whether or not testing effects have affected internal validity in a given experiment. If O_2 (the posttest score of Group 1, which was exposed to a treatment and also took a pretest) is greater than O_5 (the posttest score of Group 3, which was exposed to a treatment but did not take the pretest), then this can be attributed to the testing effects. If, however, O_2 and O_5 are equal, then the internal validity has not been thwarted by testing effects. Thus, Group 3 (the one exposed to the treatment without the pretest) helps us to establish that there was no interaction between the pretest and the treatment. If this is so, then the external validity of the experiment also increases inasmuch as we can generalize the cause $\rightarrow$ effect relationships to other subjects as well.

Group 4 (which has only the posttest score, without pretest and without having been exposed to any treatment) helps us to see whether or not changes in the posttest scores for our experiment group are a function of the combined effects of history and maturation by comparing O_6 (the posttest score of the control group without the pretest) with O_1 (the pretest score of the experimental group that was exposed to a pretest) and O_3 (the pretest score of the control group that was exposed to a pretest as well). If all three scores are similar, maturation and history effects have not been a problem.

Thus, the Solomon four-group experimental design assures the maximum internal validity, ruling out many other rival hypotheses. Where establishing cause $\rightarrow$

Table 5.2
Major Threats to Internal Validity in Different Experimental
Designs When Members Are Randomly Selected
and Assigned

Types of Experimental Designs	Major Threats to Internal Validity
1. Pretest & posttest with one experimental group only	Testing, history, maturation
2. Posttests only with one experimental and one control group	Maturation
3. Pretest & posttest with one experimental and one control group	Mortality
4. Solomon four-group design	Mortality

effect relationships is critical for the survival of businesses, as for example pharmaceutical companies, which often face lawsuits for questionable products, the Solomon four-group design is extremely useful. However, because of the number of subjects that need to be recruited, the care with which the study has to be designed, the time that needs to be devoted to the experiment, and such, the costs of conducting such an experiment are high. The experimental setup shown in Figure 5.7 with one experimental and one control group, both being exposed to the posttest only, is a viable alternative since it has many of the advantages of the Solomon four-group design and only half the number of subjects required for the experiment.

Referring now to the last two boxes in Figure 5.5, if cost considerations are important, then the simpler "one experimental and one control group posttest only" design is a good choice. If cost is not a consideration, the more sophisticated Solomon four-group design would be the choice.

Table 5.2 summarizes the threats to internal validity covered by the different experimental designs. If the subjects have all been randomly assigned to the groups, then selection biases and statistical regression will be avoided in all cases.

More advanced experimental designs such as the completely randomized design, randomized block design, Latin square design, and the factorial design are noted in the appendix to this chapter for the interested student.

SIMULATION

An alternative to lab and field experimentation currently being used in business research is simulation. Simulation uses a model-building technique to determine the effects of changes, and computer-based simulations are becoming popular in business research. A simulation can be thought of as an experiment conducted in a specially created setting that very closely resembles the natural environment in which events usually occur. In that sense, the simulation lies somewhere in between a lab and a field experiment—insofar as the environment is artificially created but not far different from "reality." Participants are exposed to real-world experiences over a period of time, lasting anywhere from several hours to several weeks, and they can be randomly assigned to different treatment groups. If managerial behavior as a function of a specific treatment is to be studied, subjects will be asked to operate in an environment very much like an office, with desks, chairs, cabinets, telephones, and the like. Members will be randomly assigned to the roles of managers, directors, clerks, and so on, and specific stimuli will be presented to them. Thus, the researcher would retain control over the assignment and manipulation, but the subjects will be free to operate as they would in a real office. In essence, there will be some factors that will be built into or incorporated in the simulated system and others that are free to vary (participants' behaviors, within the rules of the game). Data on the dependent variable can be obtained through observation, videotaping, audio recording, interviews, or questionnaires.

Causal relationships can be tested since both manipulation and control are possible in simulations. Two types of simulations can be done: one in which the nature and timing of simulated events are totally determined by the researcher (called experimental simulation), and the other (called free simulation) where the flow of events is at least partly governed by the reaction of the participants to the various stimuli as they interact among themselves. **Looking Glass,** the free simulation developed by Lombardo, McCall, and DeVries (1983) to study leadership styles has been quite popular in the management area.

Cause → effect relationships are better established in experimental simulations where the researcher has greater control. In simulations involving several weeks, however, there could be a high rate of attrition of members. Experimental and free simulations are both expensive since creating real-world conditions in an artificial setting and collecting data over extended periods of time involve many types of resources. Simulations can be done in specially created settings using subjects, with computers, and with mathematical models. Steufert, Pogash, and Piasecki (1988), who assessed managerial competence through a six-hour computer-assisted simulation, feel that simulation technology may be the only viable method to simultaneously study several types of executive styles. Computer-based simulations are frequently used in the accounting and finance areas. For example, the effectiveness of various analytic review procedures in detecting errors in account balances has been tested through simulations (Knechel, 1986). In the finance area, risk management has been studied through simulations. Simulations have also been used to understand the complex relationships in the financing of pension plans and for making important investment decisions (Perrier & Kalwarski, 1989). It is possible to vary several variables (workforce demographics, inflation rates, etc.) singly or simultaneously in such models.

Simulation has also been used by many companies to test the robustness and efficacy of various products. We are familiar with flight simulators, driving simulators, and even nuclear reactor simulators. Here, the visual patterns presented keep changing in response to the reactions of the individual (the pilot, the driver, or the emergency handler) to the previous stimulus presented, and not in any predetermined order. We can expect simulation as an important decision-making tool in the future with advances in computer technology and the advancement of mathematical models. The day may not be far off when management decisions involving motivation, leadership, and other behavioral and administrative areas will be scientifically simulated as a matter of course using programmed, computer-based simulation models.

SUMMARY

This chapter covered experimental designs, with particular reference to the lab and field experiments. Issues of internal and external validity and the seven factors that could affect internal validity were discussed. Also, some types of experimental designs that can be used to test cause → effect relationships and the usefulness of these in the context of validity versus practicality were examined.

The next chapter discusses how the variables—whether in a field survey or in an experimental design—can be measured.

DISCUSSION QUESTIONS AND POINTS TO PONDER

1. What are the differences between causal and correlational studies?

2. In what ways do lab experiments differ from field experiments?

3. Define the terms *control* and *manipulation*. Describe a possible lab experiment where you would need to control for a variable. Further, include a possible variable over which you would have no control but which could affect your experiment.

4. Explain the possible ways in which you can control "nuisance" variables.

5. What is internal validity and what are the threats to internal validity?

6. Explain the concept of "trade-off between internal and external validity."

7. *Explain fully* how you would demonstrate to machine operators and convince them that thorough knowledge of the operating policies and procedures (by reading the manual) will virtually eliminate all on-the-job accidents.

8. If a control group is a part of an experimental design, one need not worry about controlling for other exogenous variables." Discuss this statement.

9. A researcher wants to set up a lab experiment to test the effects of different kinds of leadership styles on followers' attitudes. The three particular kinds of leadership styles she is interested in testing are autocratic, democratic, and participative. You are asked to enlist some students to play the part of followers. What cover story would you give the participants?

10. "Because the external validity of lab experiments is not usually high, they are useless for investigating cause → effect relationships in organizations." Comment on this statement.

11. "Covariance—that is, two variables varying together either positively or negatively—and control are integral aspects of experimental designs." Discuss.

12. "The Solomon four-group design is the answer to all our research questions pertaining to cause → effect relations because it guards against all the threats to internal validity." Comment on this statement.

APPENDIX TO CHAPTER 5

FURTHER EXPERIMENTAL DESIGNS

In this chapter we discussed experimental designs where groups were subjected to one or more treatments and the effects of the manipulation were measured through various types of experimental designs. However, the simultaneous effects of two or more variables on a dependent variable may sometimes be desired to be assessed, which would call for more complex designs. Among the many advanced experimental designs that are available, we will examine here the completely randomized design, the randomized block design, Latin square design, and the factorial design.

It would be useful to understand some terms before describing the various designs. The term **factor** is used to denote an independent variable—for example, price. The term **level** is used to denote various categories of the factor—for example, high price, medium price, low price—with a clear definition of what these categories mean (e.g., high price is anything over $2 per piece; medium is $1–$2 per piece; low price is anything less than $1 per piece). **Treatment** refers to the various levels of the factors. A **blocking factor** is a preexisting variable in a given situation that might have an effect on the dependent variable in addition to the treatment, the impact of which would be important to assess. In effect, a blocking factor is an independent variable that has an effect on the dependent variable but that is preexisting in a given situation, as for example the number of women and men in an organization; or teenagers, middle-aged men, and senior citizens as customers of a store, and so on.

THE COMPLETELY RANDOMIZED DESIGN

Let us say that a bus transportation company manager wants to know the effects of fare reduction by 5 cents, 7 cents, and 10 cents, on the average daily increase in the number of passengers using the bus as a means of transportation. He may take 27 routes that the buses usually ply, and randomly assign nine routes for each of the treatments (i.e. reduction of fares by 5, 7, and 10 cents) for a two-week period. His experimental design would look as shown in Figure 5.10, where the Os on the left indicate the number of passengers that used the bus for the two weeks preceding the treatment; X_1, X_2, and X_3 indicate the three different treatments (fare reductions of 5c, 7c, and 10c per mile), and the Os on the right indicate the number of passengers that used the bus as the transportation mode during the two weeks when the fares were reduced. The manager will be able to assess the impact of the three treatments by deducting each of the three Os on the left from its corresponding O to the right. The results of this study would provide the answer to the bus company manager's question.

Figure 5.10
Illustration of a completely randomized design.

Routes	# of Passengers BEFORE	Treatment	# of Passengers AFTER
Group 1 of nine routes	O_1	X_1	O_2
Group 2 of nine routes	O_3	X_2	O_4
Group 3 of nine routes	O_5	X_3	O_6

RANDOMIZED BLOCK DESIGN

In the foregoing case, the bus company manager was simply interested in the effects of different levels of price reduction on the increase in the number of passengers, in general. However, he may be more interested in targeting the price reduction on the right routes or sectors. For example, it is possible that the reduction in fares will be more valuable to senior citizens and to the individuals living in crowded urban areas where driving is stressful than to car owners living in the suburbs, who may not be as sensitive to price reduction. Thus, reduction in fares would attract more passengers if targeted to the right groups (i.e., the right blocking factor—the residential areas). In this case, the bus company manager would first segregate the routes according to the three blocks—whether they are in suburbs, crowded urban areas, or retirement areas. Thus, the 27 routes would be assigned to one of three blocks and then randomly assigned, within blocks, to the three treatments. The experimental design would now look as in Figure 5.11.

Through the above randomized block design, not only can the direct effect of each treatment (i.e., the main effect of the level, which is the effect of each type of

Figure 5.11
Illustration of a randomized block design.

Fare Reduction	Blocking Factor: Residential Areas		
	Suburbs	Crowded Urban Areas	Retirement Areas
5c	X_1	X_1	X_1
7c	X_2	X_2	X_2
10c	X_3	X_3	X_3

Note that the Xs above only indicate various levels of the blocking factor and the Os (the number of passengers before and after each treatment at each level) are not shown, though these measures will be taken.

fare reduction), be assessed, but the joint effects of price and the residential area route (the interaction effect) can also be assessed. For example, the general effect of a 5-cent reduction for all routes will be gathered by the increase in passengers across all three residential areas, and the general effect of a 5-cent reduction on those in the suburbs alone will also be known by seeing the effects in the first cell. If the highest average daily number of increased passengers is 75 for a 7-cent decrease for the crowded urban area route, followed by an increase of 30 for the retirement areas for the 10-cent decrease, and an increase of 5 passengers for a 5-cent reduction for the suburbs, the bus company manager can work out a cost–benefit analysis and decide on the course of action to be taken. Thus, the randomized block design is a more powerful technique, offering more information to make a decision. However, the costs of this experimental design will be higher.

LATIN SQUARE DESIGN

Whereas the randomized block design helps the experimenter to minimize the effects of one nuisance variable (variation among the rows) in evaluating the treatment effects, the Latin square design is very useful when two nuisance blocking factors (i.e., variations across both the rows and the columns) are to be controlled. Each treatment appears an equal number of times in any one ordinal position in each row. For instance, in studying the effects of bus fare reduction on passengers, two nuisance factors could be: (1) the day of the week—(a) midweek (Tuesday through Thursday), (b) weekend, (c) Monday and Friday—and (2) the (three) residential locality of the passengers. A three by three Latin square design can be created in this case, to which will be randomly assigned the three treatments (5c, 7c, and 10c fare reduction), such that each treatment occurs only once in each row and column intersection. The Latin square design would look as in Figure 5.12.

After the experiment is carried out and the net increase in passengers under each treatment is calculated, the average treatment effects can be guaged. The price reduction that offers the best advantage can also be assessed.

A problem with the Latin square design is that it presupposes that there is no interaction between the treatments and blocking factors, which may not always be the case. We also need as many cells as there are treatments. Furthermore, it is an uneconomical design compared to some others.

Figure 5.12
Illustration of the Latin square design.

Residential Area	Day of the Week		
	Midweek	Weekend	Monday/Friday
Suburbs	X_1	X_2	X_3
Urban	X_2	X_3	X_1
Retirement	X_3	X_1	X_2

FACTORIAL DESIGN

Thus far we have discussed experimental designs in the context of examining a cause → effect relationship between *one* independent variable and the dependent variable. The *factorial* design enables us to test the effects of *two or more manipulations* on the dependent variable at the same time. In other words, two treatments can be simultaneously manipulated and their single and joint (known as main and interaction) effects assessed.

For example, the manager of the bus company might be interested in knowing passenger increases if he used three different types of buses (Luxury Express, Standard Express, Regular) and manipulated both the fare reduction and the type of vehicle used, simultaneously. Figure 5.13 illustrates the 3 × 3 factorial design that will be used for the purpose.

Here, two factors are used with three levels of each. The above is completely randomized since the fares are randomly assigned to one of nine treatment combinations. A wealth of information can be obtained from this design. For example, the bus company manager would know the increase in passengers for each fare reduction, for each type of vehicle, and for the two in combination. Thus, the main effects of the two independent variables as well as the interactions among them can be assessed. For this reason, the factorial design is more efficient than several single-factor randomized designs.

It is also statistically possible to control one or more variables through **covariance analysis.** For example, it may be suspected that even after randomly assigning members to treatments, there is a further "nuisance" factor. It is possible to statistically block such factors while analyzing the data.

Several other complex experimental designs are also available and can be seen in books devoted to experimental designs.

Figure 5.13
Illustration of a 3 × 3 Factorial Design

Type of Bus	Bus Fare Reduction Rates		
	5c	7c	10c
Luxury Express	X_1Y_1	X_2Y_1	X_3Y_1
Standard Xpress	X_2Y_2	X_1Y_2	X_3Y_2
Regular	X_3Y_3	X_2Y_3	X_1Y_3

CHAPTER 6

MEASUREMENT OF VARIABLES

TOPICS DISCUSSED

CHAPTER OBJECTIVES

After completing Chapter 6 you should be able to:

1. Operationally define (or operationalize) concepts.
2. Distinguish among the characteristics of the four different scales.
3. Know how to use the graphic rating, itemized rating, Likert, and the semantic differential scales.
4. Be conversant with the various forms of validity.
5. Explain what stability and consistency mean and how to establish them.
6. Discuss what "goodness" of measures means and why it is important to establish the goodness of measures.

Measurement of the variables in the theoretical framework is an integral part of research and an important aspect of research design (see shaded portion in figure below). Unless the variables are measured in some way, we will not be able to test our hypotheses and find answers to complex research issues. In this chapter, we will discuss the different ways in which variables lend themselves to measurement.

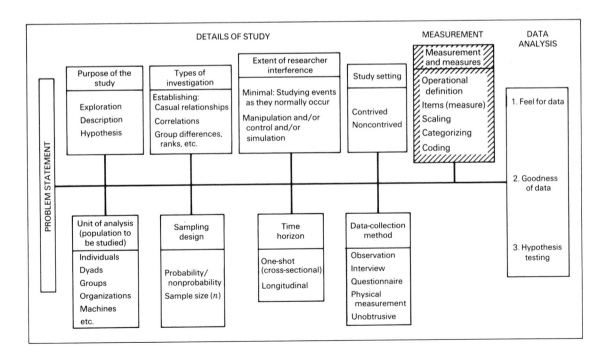

HOW VARIABLES ARE MEASURED

Objects that can be physically measured by some calibrated instruments pose no measurement problems. For example, the length and breadth of an office table can be easily measured with a measuring tape or a ruler. The same is true for measuring the office floor area. Data representing several demographic characteristics of the office personnel are also easily obtained by asking employees simple, straightforward questions, for example:

How long have you been working in this organization?

How long have you been working on this particular assignment?

What is your job title?

What is your marital status?

One can also check the company records to obtain or verify certain types of information. Even certain physiological phenomena pertaining to humans such as blood pressure, heart rates, and body temperature, as well as certain physical attributes such as height and weight, lend themselves to measurement through the use of appropriate measuring instruments. When we get into the realm of people's subjective feelings, attitudes, and perceptions, however, the measurement of these factors or variables becomes difficult. This is one of the aspects of organizational behavior and management research that adds to the complexity of research studies.

There are at least two types of variables: one lends itself to some objective and precise measurement; the other is more nebulous and does not lend itself to precise measurement because of its subjective nature. However, despite the lack of objective physical measuring devices to measure the latter type, there are ways of tapping the subjective feelings and perceptions of individuals. One technique is to reduce the abstract notions, or concepts such as motivation, involvement, or satisfaction, to observable behaviors and characteristics exhibited by those who possess these abstract qualities. In other words, the abstract notions are simplified into observable characteristic behaviors. For instance, the concept of thirst is abstract; we cannot see thirst. However, we would expect a thirsty person to drink a lot of fluids. In other words, the expected behavior of people who are thirsty is to drink fluids. If several people say they are thirsty, then we can measure the thirst levels of each of these individuals by measuring the quantity of fluids that they drink when they say they are thirsty. We would thus be able to measure their levels of thirst, even though the concept of thirst itself is abstract and nebulous. Reducing abstract concepts so that they can be measured is called operationalizing the concepts.

OPERATIONAL DEFINITION

Operationalizing, or operationally defining a concept so that it becomes measurable, is achieved by looking at the behavioral dimensions, facets, or properties denoted by the concept, and categorizing these into observable and measurable elements. This involves a series of steps. An example will help to illustrate how a concept is operationally defined.

Example 6.1   Let us try to operationally define achievement motivation, a concept of interest to educators, managers, and students alike. What behavioral dimensions or facets or characteristics would we expect to find in people high in achievement motivation? Such people would probably have the following five typical broad characteristics, which we might call *dimensions.*

1. They would be driven by work; that is, they would be constantly working in order to derive the feeling of having "achieved and accomplished."
2. Many of them would generally find it hard to relax and think of things other than their work.
3. Because they always want to be achieving and accomplishing, they would prefer to work on their own rather than with others.
4. In order to derive the sense of accomplishment and achievement, they would rather engage in challenging jobs than easy, routine ones. However, they would not want to take on excessively challenging jobs because the probability of accomplishment and achievement in such jobs would not be very high.
5. They would like to know how they are doing in their jobs as they go along. That is, they would like to seek frequent feedback in direct and subtle ways from their superiors, colleagues, and sometimes even their subordinates, to know how they are performing on their jobs.

Thus we would expect those high in achievement motivation to be driven by work, unable to relax, preferring to work alone, engaging in challenging—but not too challenging—jobs, and seeking feedback. Although breaking the concept into these five dimensions has somewhat reduced its level of abstraction, we still have not operationalized the concept into measurable elements of behavior. This could be done by examining each of the five dimensions and breaking it further into its elements, thus delineating the actual behaviors that would be exhibited. These behaviors should somehow be quantitatively measurable so that we can distinguish those who have high motivation from those who have low motivation. Let us see how this can be done.

Elements of Dimension 1

We can describe the behaviors of a person who is driven by work. Such a person will (1) be constantly working, (2) be reluctant to take time off from work, and (3) persevere even if there are some setbacks. All three behaviors would lend themselves to measurement.

For instance, we can count the number of hours employees engage themselves in work-related activities during work hours, beyond working hours at the workplace, and at home where they are likely to carry their unfinished assignments.

Thus, merely observing and keeping track of the number of hours that they work would provide an indication of the extent to which work "drives" them.

Next, keeping track of how frequently people continue to persevere on their job despite failures would give a good idea of how persevering people are in achieving their goals. A student who drops out of school because he could not pass the first exam does not represent a highly persevering, achievement-oriented individual. However, a student who, despite getting D grades on three quizzes, works night after night in order to understand and master a course he considers difficult, would exhibit persevering and achievement-oriented behaviors. Achievement-motivated individuals would not usually want to give up on their tasks when faced by some failures. They would have the drive to persevere. Hence, the extent of perseverance could be measured by counting the number of setbacks people experience on the task, yet continue to work. For example, an accountant might find that she is unable to balance the books. After trying to detect the error for an hour or so, if she has still not detected it, she might give up and leave the workplace. Another employee in the same position might not want to leave until the mistake has been detected and the books are balanced, even if it takes the whole evening to accomplish the task. In this case we would get an idea of who is the more persevering by merely observing the two individuals.

Finally, in order to measure the reluctance to take time off, we need only know how frequently people take time off, and for what reasons. If an employee was found to have taken seven days off during the last six months to watch football games, attend an out-of-town circus, and visit friends, we would have no trouble in concluding that the individual would probably not be reluctant to take time off the job at all. However, if an individual has never missed work even a single day during the past fifteen months, and he is at work even when he is not feeling very well, it is evident that he is perhaps not one who would be willing to take time off from the job.

Thus, if we can measure how many hours per week individuals spend on work-related activities, how persistent they are in completing their daily tasks, and how frequently and for what reasons they take time off from their jobs, we would have a measure of the extent to which employees are driven by work. This variable, when thus measured, would place individuals on a continuum ranging from those who are driven very little by work to those who are driven all the time by work. This, then, would give a partial indication of the extent of their achievement motivation.

Figure 6.1 schematically diagrams the dimensions (the several facets or main characteristics) and the elements (representative behaviors) for the concept of achievement motivation. Frequent reference to this figure will help you follow the ensuing discussions.

Elements of Dimension 2

The extent of inability to relax can be measured by asking persons such questions as (1) how often they think of work while they are at home, (2) whether they have any hobbies, and (3) how they spend their time off the job. Those who are able to relax would indicate that they spend time on hobbies and leisure-time activities,

Figure 6.1
Dimensions (D) and elements (E) of the concept (C) achievement motivation.

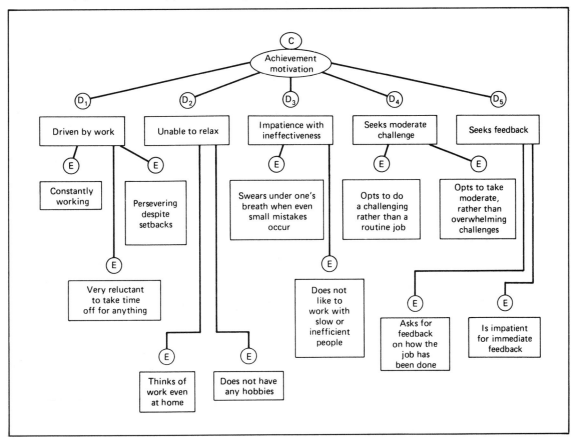

and would say that they do not generally think about work or the workplace while at home. Such people are probably engaged in family or other social or cultural activities while away from work.

Thus we can here place employees on a continuum ranging from those who relax a lot to those who relax very little. This dimension also then becomes measurable.

Elements of Dimension 3

Individuals wanting to achieve on their own can be measured by their reluctance to work with others. Whereas some achievement-motivated persons in the organization may be very high on these behavioral predispositions, there may be others who are not highly achievement motivated. These latter people may not be upset with ineffectiveness in either themselves or others, and may be quite willing to work with almost anybody. Thus impatience with ineffectiveness can also be measured by observing behaviors.

Elements of Dimension 4

The extent to which people seek challenging jobs can be measured by asking employees what kinds of jobs they would prefer. A number of different job descriptions can be presented, with some jobs being described to reflect routineness and others to indicate differing degrees of challenges built into them. Employee preferences for different types of jobs could then be placed on a continuum ranging from those who prefer fairly routine jobs to those who prefer highly challenging jobs. Those opting for medium degrees of challenge are likely to be more achievement motivated than those who opt for lower or higher degrees of challenge. They would represent a set of individuals who are realistic and would choose jobs that are reasonably challenging and yet possible to accomplish. The reckless and overconfident persons would perhaps choose the highly challenging jobs where the probability of success is rather low, oblivious to whether the end results will be achieved or not. Those low in achievement motivation would perhaps choose the more routine jobs. Thus, those who seek moderate challenge can also be identified.

Elements of Dimension 5

Those who want feedback would be seeking it from their superiors, co-workers, and sometimes even from their subordinates. They would want to know others' opinions on how well they are performing. Feedback, both positive and negative, would indicate to them how much they are achieving and accomplishing. If they receive messages indicating a need for improvement, they will act on them. Hence, they would be constantly seeking feedback from several sources. By keeping track of the number of times individuals seek feedback from others during a certain period of time—say, over several months—employees can again be placed on a continuum ranging from those who seek extensive feedback from all sources to those who never seek any feedback from anyone at any time.

Having thus operationalized the concept of achievement motivation by reducing its level of abstraction to observable behaviors, it is possible to develop a measure to tap the concept of achievement motivation. The usefulness of developing a good measure is that others could use the same measure, and replicability is achieved thereby. It should, however, be recognized, that any operational definition is likely to (1) exclude some of the important dimensions and elements, because we may not recognize or be able to conceptualize them, and (2) include certain irrelevant features, which we mistakenly think are relevant. You would recall that we had earlier pointed out that management research cannot be 100 percent scientific because we do not have the "perfect" measuring instruments.

Operationally defining the concept, nevertheless, is the best way to measure it. However, actually observing and counting the number of times individuals behave in particular ways, even if practical, would be too laborious and time consuming. So, instead of actually observing the behaviors of individuals, we could ask them to report their own behavior patterns by asking them appropriate questions, which they can respond to on some scale that we provide. We will discuss the various types of scales to be used, later. In Example 6.2, which follows, we will look at the type of questions that may tap achievement motivation.

Example 6.2   Answers to the following questions from respondents would be one way of tapping the level of achievement motivation.

1. To what extent would you say you push yourself to get the job done on time?
2. How difficult is it for you to keep on continuing to do your work in the face of initial failures or discouraging results?
3. How frequently do you think of your work when you are at home?
4. How disappointed would you feel if you did not reach the goals you had planned for?
5. How much do you concentrate on achieving your goals?
6. How annoyed do you get when you make mistakes?
7. To what extent would you prefer to work with a friendly but incompetent colleague rather than a difficult but competent one?
8. To what extent would you prefer to work by yourself rather than with others?
9. To what extent would you prefer a job that is difficult but challenging to one that is easy and routine?
10. To what extent would you prefer to undertake extremely difficult assignments rather than moderately challenging assignments?
11. During the past three months, how often have you sought feedback from your superiors on how well you are performing your job?
12. How often have you tried to obtain feedback on your performance from your co-workers during the past three months?
13. How often during the past three months have you checked with your subordinates that what you are doing is not getting in their way of efficient performance?
14. To what extent would it frustrate you if people did not give you feedback on how you are progressing?

The foregoing list illustrates a possible way to measure variables relating to the subjective domain of people's attitudes, feelings, and perceptions by first operationally defining the concept. Operational definition implies our reducing the concept from its level of abstraction by breaking it into its dimensions and elements as discussed. Thus, by tapping the behaviors associated with a concept, we can measure the variable. Of course, the questions will ask for responses on some scale attached to them (such as, very little to very much), which we will discuss later in this chapter.

What an Operational Definition Is Not

Just as important as it is to understand what an operational definition *is,* equally important is it to remember what it is *not.* An operational definition does *not* describe the correlates of the concept. For example, performance or success cannot be a dimension of achievement motivation, even though a motivated person is likely to be highly successful in performing the job. Thus, achievement motivation and performance and/or success may be highly correlated, but we cannot measure an individual's level of motivation through success and performance. Performance and success could have occurred as a consequence of achievement motivation, but in and of themselves, the two are not measures of achievement motivation. To elaborate, a person may be high in achievement motivation, but for some reason, perhaps beyond her control, might have failed to perform the job successfully. Thus, if we judge the achievement motivation of this person by looking at performance, we would have measured the wrong concept. Instead of measuring achievement motivation—our variable of interest—we would have measured performance, another variable that we did not intend to measure and in which we were not interested.

Thus, it is clear that operationally defining a concept does *not* consist of delineating the reasons, antecedents, consequences, or correlates of the concept. Rather, it describes the observable characteristics of the concept in order to be able to measure it. This is important to remember because if we either operationalize the concepts incorrectly or confuse them with other concepts, then we will not have valid measures. This means that we will not have "good" data, and our research will not be scientific.

Having seen what an operational definition is and what it is not, let us now operationally define another concept that is relevant to the classroom: the concept of "learning."

Example 6.3   Learning is an important concept in the educational setting. Teachers tend to measure student learning by giving exams. Students quite often feel that exams really do not measure their learning—at least not the multiple-choice questions that are given in exams. The students are probably right.

How then might we measure the abstract concept called learning? As before, we need to define the concept operationally and break it down to observable and measurable behaviors. In other words, we should delineate the dimensions and elements of the concept of learning. The dimensions of learning may well be as follows:

1. Understanding   2. Retention   3. Application.

In other words, we can be reasonably sure that a student in the class is "learning" when the individual is (1) understanding what is going on in the classroom, (2) can remember what is understood, and (3) can apply whatever has been understood and remembered.

Figure 6.2
Dimensions (D) and elements (E) of the concept (C) learning (L).

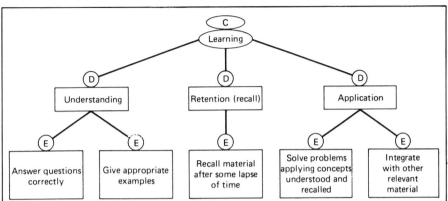

Terms such as understanding, remembering, and applying are still abstract even though they have helped us to get a better grasp of what learning is all about. It is necessary to break these three dimensions into elements so that we can measure the dimensions, and thus the concept of learning. A schematic diagram of the operational definition of the concept of learning is shown in Figure 6.2. The diagram will facilitate our understanding of the discussion that follows.

A teacher can assess whether students have understood by asking them to explain a concept that was just taught and to answer questions. If they answer correctly, the teacher can presume that the students have understood. By giving a test a week or month later, the teacher can measure the extent to which they have remembered what was explained. By asking them to apply the concepts learned in a new problem situation, the teacher can also measure how much they can apply what is understood. If they solve the problem successfully using the material taught to them in class, the teacher will be reasonably assured that learning has taken place. To the extent that they do not successfully apply the concepts taught, learning might not have occurred to the degree expected. Note that in this case, **application** of the relevant concepts subsumes both **understanding** and **retention.** That is, one cannot apply the concepts unless one has understood them *and* retained them. In most multiple-choice questions, understanding and retention are likely to be tested; the application aspects are often not. Exams, when properly designed, could be a good instrument for assessing the learning that takes place during the semester. In other words, exams could reliably measure learning when the questions therein are well constructed to tap the understanding, retention, and ability to apply.

Again, it is very important to remember that learning is not the same as the amount of effort the teacher expends in explaining, or the amount of effort put in by the student to understand, though both of these will tend to enhance understanding. Although both may be correlated to learning, they do not measure actual learning.

A Measure of Student Learning

An exam that partially measures learning would include the following questions (the particular dimensions tapped are shown in parentheses):

1. Define the concept of motivation (*recall*).
2. State the various theories of motivation and explain them, giving examples (*understanding* and *recall*).
3. (a) In the beginning of the semester, the class was split into two debate teams: one was to argue for the manager's role as a motivator, and the other that it is not a manager's job to motivate the employees. State three important arguments put forth by each group (*understanding* and *recall*).
   (b) What is *your* viewpoint regarding the manager's role as motivator (*understanding* and *analysis*).

An exam that measures learning according to our operational definition would include the following questions:

1. Describe three different situations in which a manager in a work organization would use equity theory, the expectancy theory, and job design to motivate employees.
2. In the Concord Camp case, how would Bob have been motivated to take an interest in the camp's activities? Adequately defend your answer, citing the appropriate theories and why they are superior to some of the other possible solutions.
3. How does motivation relate to leadership? How are both of these concepts related to a manager's job?

Review of Operational Definition

We have thus far examined how to operationally define concepts and to ask questions that are likely to measure the concept. Operational definitions are important for abstract concepts, which usually fall into the subjective areas of feelings and attitudes. More objective variables such as age or educational level are easily measured through simple straightforward questions and do not have to be operationally defined. Fortunately, measures for many organization-relevant concepts have already been developed by researchers. While you review the literature in a given area, you might want to note particularly the reference that discusses the instrument to tap the concept.

Now do Exercises 6.1 and 6.2.

SCALES AND MEASUREMENT

Learning how to define concepts operationally has helped us to see what questions might be asked to tap concepts. However, we still need to know how we can measure them. In other words, how would we know the extent to which these subjective feelings, attitudes, or perceptions might exist in different individuals? Is it possible to devise an instrument that would measure these variables?

Certain scales have been devised that will allow us to measure our variables of interest. First we must become familiar with the scales themselves, and then we can examine how they can be used to measure the concepts.

Scales

A scale is a tool or mechanism by which individuals are distinguished on the variables of interest to our study, in some form or the other. The scale or tool could be a gross one in the sense that it would only broadly categorize individuals on certain variables; or it could be a fine-tuned tool that would differentiate individuals on the variables with varying degrees of sophistication.

There are four basic types of scales: nominal, ordinal, interval, and ratio. The degree of sophistication to which the scales are fine-tuned increases as we move from the nominal to the ratio scale. As the calibration or fine tuning of the scale increases in sophistication, the power of the scale increases; that is, more detailed information can be obtained on our variables. With more powerful scales, increasingly sophisticated data analyses can be performed, which means, in turn, that we can find more meaningful answers to our research questions. However, certain variables lend themselves more readily to more powerful scaling than others.

Let us now examine each of these four scales.

Nominal Scale

A nominal scale is one that allows the researcher to assign subjects to certain categories or groups. For example, with respect to the variable of gender, respondents can be grouped in two categories: males and females. These two groups can be assigned code numbers 1 and 2. These numbers serve as simple and convenient category labels with no intrinsic value. What we have done is to simply assign respondents to one of two nonoverlapping or *mutually exclusive* categories. Note that the categories are also *collectively exhaustive*. In other words, there is no third category into which respondents would normally fall. Thus, nominal scales categorize individuals or objects into mutually exclusive and collectively exhaustive groups. The information that can be generated from nominal scaling is to calculate the percentage (or frequency) of males and females in our sample of respondents. For example, if we had interviewed 200 people, and assigned a code number 1 to all male respondents and number 2 to all female respondents, then computer analysis of the data at the end of the survey might reveal that 98 of the respondents were men and 102 were women. This frequency distribution tells us that 49 percent of the survey's respondents are men and 51 percent women. Other than this marginal information, such scaling tells us nothing. Thus the nominal scale gives some basic, categorical, gross information.

Example 6.4   Let us take a look at another variable that could have a nominal scale: the nationality of the individuals. We could nominally scale this variable in the following mutually exclusive and collectively exhaustive categories.

American	Italian
Australian	Polish
German	Swiss
Indian	Zambian
	Other

Note that every respondent has to fit into one of the nine categories and that the scale will allow computation of the percentage of respondents who fit into each of these nine categories.

> **Now answer Exercise 6.3.**

Ordinal Scale

An ordinal scale not only categorizes the variables in such a way as to denote qualitative differences among the various categories, it also rank-orders the categories in some meaningful way. With any variable for which the categories are to be ordered according to some preference, the ordinal scale would be used. The preferences would be ranked (e.g., from best to worst; first to last) and numbered 1, 2, and so on. For example, respondents might be asked to indicate their preferences by ranking the importance they attach to five distinct characteristics in a job that the researcher might be interested in studying. Such a question might take the following form.

Example 6.5

> Rank the following five characteristics in a job in terms of how important they are for you. You should rank the most important item as 1, the second most important as 2, and so on, until you have given each of the five items a rank of 1, 2, 3, 4, or 5.

Job Characteristic	**Ranking of Importance**

The opportunity provided by the job to:

1. Interact with others.   ——
2. Use a number of different skills.   ——
3. Complete a whole task from
   beginning to end.   ——
4. Serve others.   ——
5. Work independently.   ——

The ordinal scale will help the researcher to determine the percentage of respondents who consider interaction with others as most important, those who consider using a number of different skills as most important, and so on. Such knowledge might help in designing jobs that would be seen as most enriched by the majority of the employees.

We can now see that the ordinal scale provides more information than the nominal scale. The ordinal scale not only taps the differences in the categories, but also gives some information as to how respondents distinguish among these items by rank-ordering them. Note, however, that the ordinal scale does not give any indication of the magnitude of the differences among the ranks. For instance, in the job characteristics example, the first-ranked job characteristic might be only marginally preferred over the second-ranked characteristic, whereas the characteristic that is ranked third might be preferred considerably more than the one ranked fourth. Thus, in ordinal scaling, even though we would know there are differences in the ranking of objects, persons, or events investigated, we would not know the magnitude of these differences. This deficiency is overcome by interval scaling, which is discussed next.

Now respond to Exercise 6.4.

Interval Scale

An interval scale allows us to perform certain arithmetical operations on the data collected from the respondents. Whereas the nominal scale only allows us to qualitatively distinguish groups by categorizing them into mutually exclusive and collectively exhaustive sets, the ordinal scale allows us to rank-order the preferences, and the interval scale allows us to compute the means and the standard deviations of the responses on the variables. In other words, the interval scale not only groups individuals according to certain categories and taps the order of these groups; it also measures the magnitude of the differences in the preferences among the individuals. If, for instance, employees think that (1) it is more important for them to have a variety of skills in their jobs compared to doing a task from beginning to end, and (2) it is more important for them to be serving people than to be working independently on the job, then the interval scale would indicate whether the first preference is to the same extent, to a lesser extent, or to a greater extent than the second. This can be done by now changing the scale from the ranking type in Example 6.5 to make it appear as if there were several points on a scale that would signify the extent or magnitude of the importance of each of the five job characteristics. Such a scale could be indicated as follows for the job design example.

Example 6.6

Indicate the extent to which you agree with the following statements as they relate to your job, by *circling* the appropriate number against each, using the scale below.

	Strongly Disagree	Disagree	Neither Disagree Nor Agree	Agree	Strongly Agree
	1	2	3	4	5
The following opportunities offered by the job are very important to me:					
a. Interacting with others	1	2	3	4	5
b. Using a number of different skills	1	2	3	4	5
c. Completing a task from beginning to end	1	2	3	4	5
d. Serving others	1	2	3	4	5
e. Working independently	1	2	3	4	5

Let us illustrate how the interval scale establishes the equality of the magnitude of differences in the scale points. Let us suppose that employees circle the numbers 3, 1, 2, 4, and 5 for the five items in Example 6.6. We can say that the employees are trying to indicate to us that the extent of their preference for skill utilization by the job over doing the task from beginning to end is the same as the extent of their preference for serving customers over their preference for working independently. That is, the magnitude of difference represented by the space between points 1 and 2 on the scale is the same as the magnitude of difference represented by the space between points 4 and 5. Any number can be added to or subtracted from the numbers on the scale, still retaining the magnitude of the difference. For instance, if we add 6 to all five points on the scale, the interval scale will have the numbers 7 to 11 (instead of 1 to 5). The magnitude of the difference between 7 and 8 is still the same as the magnitude of the difference between 9 and 10. Thus, the origin, or the starting point, could be any arbitrary number. The clinical thermometer is a good example of an interval-scaled instrument; it has an arbitrary origin and the magnitude of the difference between 98.6 degrees (supposed to be the normal body temperature) and 99.6 degrees is the same as the magnitude of the difference between 104 and 105 degrees. Note, however, that one may not be terribly upset if the temperature rises from 98.6 to 99.6, but is likely to be very concerned when the temperature increases from 104 to 105!

Thus the interval scale taps the differences, the order, and the equality of the magnitude of the differences in the variable. As such, it is a more powerful scale than the nominal and ordinal scales, and has for its measure of central tendency the arithmetic mean. Its measures of dispersion are the range, the standard deviation, and the variance.

Now respond to Exercises 6.5 and 6.6.

Ratio Scale

The ratio scale overcomes the deficiency of the arbitrary origin point given to the interval scale, in that it has an absolute (in contrast to an arbitrary) zero point which is a meaningful measurement point. Thus the ratio scale not only measures the magnitude of the differences between points on the scale but also taps the proportions in the differences. It is the most powerful of the four scales because it has a unique zero origin (not an arbitrary origin) and subsumes all the properties of the other three scales. The weighing balance is a good example of a ratio scale. It has an absolute (and not arbitrary) zero origin calibrated on it, which allows us to calculate the ratio of differences between the weights of two individuals. For instance, a person weighing 250 pounds is *twice* as heavy as one who weighs 125 pounds. Note that multiplying or dividing both of these numbers (250 and 125) by any given number will preserve the ratio of 2:1. The measure of central tendency of the ratio scale could be either the arithmetic or the geometric mean and the measure of dispersion could be either the standard deviation, or variance, or the coefficient of variation. Some examples of ratio scales are the actual age, income, and the number of organizations an individual has worked for.

The properties of the increased fine tuning of the scales are summarized in Figure 6.3. We can also see from the figure how the power of the statistic increases as we move away from the nominal scale (where we group subjects under some categories), to ranking the categories (ordinal scale), to tapping the magnitude of the differences (interval scale), to measuring the proportion of the differences (ratio scale).

Now respond to Exercise 6.7.

Now that we have looked at the four types of scales, let us see, through various examples, when and how they would be used.

Figure 6.3
Properties of the four scales.

Scale	Highlights			Unique Origin	Measures of Central Tendency	Measures of Dispersion	Some Tests of Significance
	Difference	Order	Distance				
Nominal	Yes	No	No	No	Mode	—	χ^2
Ordinal	Yes	Yes	No	No	Median	Semi-interquartile range	Rank-order correlations
Interval	Yes	Yes	Yes	No	Arithmetic mean	Standard deviation, variance, coefficient of variation	*t, F*
Ratio	Yes	Yes	Yes	Yes	Arithmetic or geometric mean	Standard deviation or variance or coefficient of variation	*t, F*

Note: The interval scale has 1 as an arbitrary starting point.
The ratio scale has the natural origin 0, which is meaningful.

Example 6.7   **Nominal scale** is usually used for obtaining personal data such as gender, department in which one is working, and so on, where grouping of individuals or objects is useful, as in the cases below.

1. Your gender

___ Male
___ Female

2. Your department

___ Production
___ Sales
___ Accounting
___ Finance
___ Personnel
___ R & D
___ Other

Ordinal scale is usually used to rate the preferences or usage of various brands of a product by individuals and to rank order individuals, objects, or events, as per the examples below.

1. Rank the following personal computers with respect to their usage in your office, assigning the number 1 to the most used system, 2 to the next most used, and so on. If a particular system is not used at all in your office, put a 0 against it.

___ IBM PS2/30   ___ Compaq
___ IBM/AT   ___ AT & T
___ IBM/XT   ___ Tandy 2000
___ Apple II   ___ Leading Edge
___ MacIntosh   ___ Next
___ Zenith   ___ Other (Specify)

2. Rank the cities listed below in the order that you consider to be suitable for opening a new plant. The city considered the most suitable will be ranked 1, the next 2, and so on.

___ Cincinnati   ___ Milwaukee
___ Detroit   ___ Pittsburgh
___ Des Moines   ___ St. Louis
___ Houston

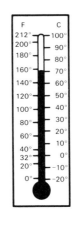

Interval scale is used when responses to various items that measure a variable can be tapped on a five-point (or seven-point or any other number of points) scale, which can thereafter be summated across the items. See example of a Likert scale below.

> Using the scale below, please indicate your response to each of the items that follow by *circling* the number that best describes your feeling.

	Strongly Disagree	Disagree	Neutral	Agree	Strongly Agree
	1	2	3	4	5
1. My job offers me a chance to test myself and my abilities.	1	2	3	4	5
2. Mastering this job meant a lot to me.	1	2	3	4	5
3. Doing this job well is a reward in itself.	1	2	3	4	5
4. Considering the time spent on the job, I feel thoroughly familiar with my tasks and responsibilities.	1	2	3	4	5

Ratio scales usually get used in organizational research when exact figures on objective (as opposed to subjective) factors are called for, as in the following questions:

1. How many other organizations did you work for before joining this system? ____

2. Please indicate the number of children you have in each of the following categories:
   ____ below 3 years of age
   ____ between 3 and 6
   ____ over 6 years but under 12
   ____ 12 years and over

3. How many retail outlets do you operate? ____

The responses could range from 0 to any figure.

Measurement

Whereas the nominal and ordinal scales help us to group and to qualitatively identify the differences between the groups, the interval and the ratio scales help us to get some idea of the quantitative differences in the variables of interest.

Certain variables simply do not lend themselves to quantification, except in a very basic manner. For instance, when we split a sample of blue-collar workers into those having a college degree and those without a college degree, we will, at best, know only the numbers and the percentages of blue-collar workers in each of the two groups. If we ask the supervisors in the system to rank their preferences for workers with a college degree and those without, we would, at best, be able to know which of the two groups is preferred more. However, if we ask the supervisors the extent to which they like working with those who have a college degree and with those without a college degree, say on a scale of 1 to 5, we will not only know which group is preferred but also the magnitude of the difference in the preference. We thus have more and better information through the interval scale.

Because the interval scale gives more information than the nominal and the ordinal scales, we should try, whenever possible, to measure variables on an interval scale. For instance, instead of asking respondents whether they are motivated or not ("yes or no" answer, nominal scale), we can ask them the extent to which they are motivated (on a 5-point or a 7-point interval scale, with 1 denoting very little motivation and 5 or 7 denoting very high motivation).

It would be nice if we could measure all our variables on a ratio scale because we know it is even more powerful than the interval scale. Recall that the ratio scale can identify not only the magnitude but also the proportion of the differences. Unfortunately, however, attitudinal and perceptual variables do not have an absolute zero point. We could say that a person has very little motivation, or even negative motivation (i.e., turned off), but we would be unable to justify that someone can or will have an exact zero motivation, though we may loosely use the term in our conversations. Thus subjective feelings, attitudes, and perceptions do not easily lend themselves for measurement on a ratio scale.

Review of Scales and Measurement

There are four scales that can be applied to the measurement of variables: the nominal, ordinal, interval, and ratio scales. The nominal scale highlights the differences by classifying objects or persons into groups, and of the four scales, provides the least amount of information on the variable. The ordinal scale provides some additional information by rank-ordering the categories provided by the nominal scale. The interval scale, in addition to the ranking, provides us with information on the magnitude of the differences in the variable. The ratio scale indicates not only the magnitude of the differences but also the proportion of the differences. Multiplications or divisions would preserve these ratios. As we move from the nominal to the ratio scale, we obtain more precision in quantifying the data, and greater flexibility in using more powerful statistical tests. Hence, whenever possible, and appropriate, a more powerful rather than a less powerful scale should be used to measure the variables of interest.

DEVELOPING SCALES

From the discussions so far in this chapter, it is clear that measuring variables involves first operationally defining them and then applying the appropriate scales. When we decide to use an interval scale that would indicate the magnitude of the differences, we have to decide how many points in the scale we should use (5, 7, 9, or what?), and what kinds of anchors we would provide for the respondents to relate to, when we use the numbers, say 1, 2, 3, 4, and 5 on the scale (e.g., Very Unimportant to Very Important; Strongly Disagree to Strongly Agree, etc.).

Research indicates that a 5-point scale is just as good as any and that an increase from 5 to 7 or 9 points on a rating scale does not improve the reliability of the ratings (Elmore & Beggs, 1975). We will now examine a few scales used in business research.

Rating Scales and Attitude Scales Commonly Used in Business Research

Scales that are commonly used in business research can be generally classified as **rating** scales and **attitude** scales. The graphic rating scale and the itemized rating scale are the most frequently used rating scales, and the Likert scale and semantic differential scales are among the more commonly used attitudinal scales. The graphic rating scale, the itemized rating scale, and the semantic differential scale offer considerable flexibility in anchoring the scales to suit our specific purposes while tapping a concept. This is helpful for drawing useful interpretive conclusions from the data. Brief descriptions and examples of some of these scales are offered below.

Graphic Rating Scale

Here a graphical representation helps the respondent to indicate the response to a particular question by placing a mark at the appropriate point on the line, as in the following example:

On a scale of 0 to 10, how would you rate your supervisor?

This scale is easy to respond to. The brief descriptions on the scale points are meant to serve as a guide in locating the rating rather than to serve as discrete categories.

Itemized Rating Scale

Here a category of responses is offered (could be any number), out of which the respondent picks the one that is most relevant for answering the question under consideration. This scale is popular in business research because of its adaptability to many situations where variables are to be measured. The following examples illustrate the use of this scale.

Example 6.8 (i)

	Not at all Interested	Somewhat Interested	Moderately Interested	Very Much Interested
How would you rate your interest in changing organizational policies?	1	2	3	4

Example 6.8 (ii)

	Extremely Poorly	Rather Poorly	Quite Well	Very Well	Excellently
How well is the new distribution channel working?	1	2	3	4	5

Likert Scale

This scale, as shown in Example 6.6, specifically utilizes the anchor of **Strongly Disagree, Disagree, Neither Disagree nor Agree, Agree,** and **Strongly Agree.** The respondents indicate the extent to which they agree or disagree to a variety of statements (as shown in the example under Interval Scale), which are then summated.

Semantic Differential

Here a number of bipolar attributes are indicated at the extremes of, usually, a seven-point scale, and respondents indicate their attitudes toward a particular individual, object, or event on these attributes. The bipolar adjectives could represent such words as: Good—Bad; Strong—Weak; Hot—Cold. These can be used to assess respondents' attitudes toward a particular brand, advertisement, object, individual, or the like, on various dimensions. Examples of the semantic differential scale used in the management and marketing areas can be found in the appendix to this chapter.

Though we have discussed operational definition, scales, and scale construction, developing measures (or *instruments* or *scales* as they are also called) is not an easy task. Earlier, we mentioned that in operationally defining perceptual and attitudinal variables, we might overlook some important dimensions and elements

Figure 6.4

Testing goodness of measures—reliability and validity.

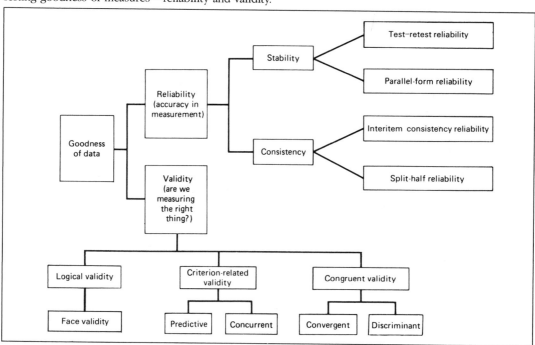

and include some irrelevant ones. Thus, the scales developed are imperfect and there are always errors in measurement. However, the use of better instruments will ensure more accurate results, which in turn, will enhance the scientific quality of the research. Hence, we need to assess the goodness of measures in some way. That is, we need to be reasonably sure that the instruments we use in our research do indeed measure the variables they are supposed to measure (though they may not capture the concept completely) and that they measure them as well as possible.

Let us now examine how we can ensure that the measures developed are reasonably good. The two main criteria for testing the goodness of measures are **validity** and **reliability.** Validity tests how well an instrument that is developed measures *the particular concept* it is supposed to measure. Reliability tests *how consistently* a measuring instrument measures whatever concept it is measuring. In other words, validity is concerned with whether we are measuring the right concept, and reliability is concerned with stability and consistency in measurement. Validity and reliability attest to the scientific rigor applied to the research study. These two criteria will now be discussed. The various forms of reliability and validity are depicted in Figure 6.4.

VALIDITY

Earlier, in Chapter 5, we examined the terms *internal validity* and *external validity* in the context of experimental design. That is, we were concerned about the issue of the authenticity of the cause → effect relationships and their generalizability to the external environment. Now we are going to examine the validity of the measuring instrument itself. That is, when we ask a set of questions (i.e., develop a measuring instrument) in hopes that we are tapping the concept, how can we be reasonably sure that we are measuring the concept we set out to measure and not something else? This can be determined by applying certain validity tests.

Several types of validity tests are used to test the goodness of measures. Writers use different terms to denote these validity tests. For the sake of clarity, we can group validity tests under three broad headings: **content validity, criterion-related validity,** and **construct validity.**

Content Validity

Content validity ensures that the measure includes an adequate and representative set of items that would tap the concept. The more the scale items represent the domain or universe of the concept being measured, the greater the content validity. To put it differently, content validity is a function of how well the dimensions and elements of a concept have been delineated. *Face validity* is a basic, and a very minimum, index of content validity. Face validity indicates that the items that are supposed to measure a concept, do on the face of it, look like they *are* measuring the concepts. Kidder and Judd (1986) cite the example where a test designed to measure degrees of speech impairment can be considered as having validity if it is indeed evaluated by a group of expert judges—in this case, professional speech therapists—as testing speech impairment.

Criterion-Related Validity

Criterion-related validity is established when the measure differentiates individuals on a criterion it is expected to predict. This can be done by establishing concurrent validity or predictive validity, as explained below.

Concurrent validity is established when the scale discriminates individuals who are known to be different; that is, they should score differently on the test. For example, if a measure of work ethic is developed and administered to a group of welfare recipients, the scale should differentiate those who are enthusiastic about accepting a job and being off of welfare from those who do not want to work even when offered a job Obviously, those with high work ethic values would not want to be on welfare and would be enthusiastic about accepting a job. Those who are low on work ethic values, on the other hand, might appreciate the opportunity to survive on welfare without having to work. If both types of individuals score the same on the work ethic scale, then the test would not be a measure of work ethic, but of something else.

Table 6.1
Types of Validity

Validity	Description
Content validity	Does the measure adequately measure the concept?
Face validity	Do "experts" validate that the instrument measures what its name suggests it measures?
Criterion-related validity	Does the measure differentiate in a manner that helps to predict a criterion variable?
Concurrent validity	Does the measure differentiate in a manner that helps to predict a criterion variable currently?
Predictive validity	Does the measure differentiate individuals in a manner as to help predict a future criterion?
Construct validity	Does the instrument tap the concept as theorized?
Convergent validity	Do two instruments measuring the concept correlate highly?
Discriminant validity	Does the measure have a low correlation with a variable that is supposed to be unrelated to this variable?

Predictive validity is the ability of the test or measure to differentiate among individuals as to a future criterion. For example, if an aptitude or ability test, administered to employees at the time of recruitment, is expected to differentiate individuals on their expected future performance, then those who score low on the test should be poor performers and those who score high should be good performers. Tests may have high, moderate, or low predictive validity.

Construct Validity

Construct validity testifies to how well the results obtained from the use of the measure fits the theories around which the test is designed. This is assessed through **convergent** and **discriminant** validity, which are explained below.

Convergent validity is established when the scores obtained by two different instruments measuring the same concept are highly correlated.

Discriminant validity is established when, based on theory, two variables are predicted to be uncorrelated, and the scores obtained by measuring them are indeed empirically found to be so.

Validity can thus be established in different ways. Published measures for various concepts usually report the kinds of validity that have been established for the instrument so that the user or reader can judge the "goodness" of the measure.

Table 6.1 summarizes the kinds of validity discussed here.

RELIABILITY

The reliability of a measure indicates the stability and consistency with which the instrument is measuring the concept and helps to assess the "goodness" of a measure.

Stability of Measures

The ability of a measure to maintain stability over time, despite uncontrollable testing conditions and the state of the respondents themselves, is indicative of its stability and low vulnerability to changes in the situation. This attests to the goodness of the measure, inasmuch as it stably measures the concepts no matter when they are measured. Two tests of stability are test–retest reliability and parallel-form reliability.

Test–Retest Reliability

The reliability coefficient obtained with repetition of an identical measure on a second occasion is called test–retest reliability. That is, when a questionnaire containing some items that are supposed to measure a concept is administered to a set of respondents now, and again to the same respondents, say several weeks to six months later, then the correlation between the scores obtained at the two different times from the same set of respondents is called the test–retest coefficient. The higher it is, the better the test–retest reliability, and hence the stability of the measure across time.

Parallel-Form Reliability

When responses on two comparable sets of measures tapping the same construct are highly correlated, we have parallel-form reliability. Both forms have similar items and the same response format with only the wordings and the ordering of questions changed. What we try to establish here is the error variability resulting from wording and ordering of the questions. If two such comparable forms are highly correlated (say .8 and above), we can be fairly certain that the measures are reasonably reliable, with minimal error variance caused by wording, ordering, or other factors.

Internal Consistency of Measures

The internal consistency of measures is indicative of the homogeneity of the items in the measure that tap the construct. In other words, the items should "hang together as a set" and be capable of independently measuring the same concept such that the respondents attach the same overall meaning to each of the items. Consistency could be tested through split-half reliability and interitem consistency reliability.

Interitem Consistency Reliability

This is a test of the consistency of respondents' responses to all the items in a measure. To the degree that items are independent measures of the same concept, they will be correlated with one another. The most popular test of interitem consistency reliability is the Cronbach's coefficient alpha (Cronbach's alpha; Cronbach, 1946), which is used for multipoint-scaled items, and the Kuder–Richardson formulas (Kuder & Richardson, 1937), used for dichotomous items.

Split-Half Reliability

Split-half reliability reflects the correlations between two halves of an instrument. Split-half reliability estimates would vary depending on how the items in the measure are split into two halves. Split-half reliabilities could be higher than Cronbach's alpha only in the circumstance when there are more than one underlying response dimensions tapped by the measure *and* certain other conditions are met as well (for complete details, refer to Campbell, 1976). Hence, in almost all cases, Cronbach's alpha can be considered a perfectly adequate index of the interitem consistency reliability.

Interrater Reliability

The consistency of the judgment of several raters on how they see a phenomenon or interpret some responses is also a measure of reliability. This interrater reliability is especially relevant when the data are obtained through observations, projective tests, or unstructured interviews, all of which are liable to be subjectively interpreted. More confidence in the measure is obtained when there is a high interrater reliability.

Goodness of Measures

In sum, the goodness of measures is established through different kinds of validity and reliability tests depicted in Figure 6.4. The results of any research can only be as good as the measures that tap the concepts in the theoretical framework. In order for research to be scientific, we need to use well-validated and reliable measures. Fortunately, measures have been developed for many important concepts in organizational research, and the psychometric properties of these measures (i.e., the reliability and validity) have been established by the developers of these instruments in most cases. Thus researchers can use the instruments that have already been reputed to be "good," rather than develop their own measures. When using these measures, however, researchers should cite the source (i.e., the author and reference) so that the reader can seek more information if necessary.

It is not unusual for two or more equally good measures to have been developed for the same concept. For example, there are several different instruments for measuring the concept of job satisfaction. One of the most frequently used scales to measure job satisfaction, however, is the Job Descriptive Index (JDI) developed by Smith, Kendall, and Hulin (1969), which can be found in the appendix to this chapter. When more than one scale exists for any variable, it is better to use the measure that has better reliability and validity and is also more frequently used.

At times, we may also have to adapt an established measure to suit the setting, For example, a scale used to measure job performance, job characteristics, or job satisfaction in the manufacturing industry may have to be modified slightly to suit a utility company or a health care organization. The work environment in each case is different and the wordings in the instrument may have to be adapted. However, in doing this, we are tampering with an established scale, and it would be advisable to test for the adequacy of the validity and reliability once again.

In the appendix to this chapter, a sample of five measures used to tap some frequently researched concepts in each of the management and marketing areas is shown.

SUMMARY

In this chapter, we saw how concepts are operationally defined and what kinds of scales can be used in developing instruments. We also discussed how the goodness of measures can be established in terms of validity and reliability.

In the next chapter, we will see the different methods by which data can be collected.

DISCUSSION QUESTIONS AND POINTS TO PONDER

1. What is meant by operational definition and why is it necessary?
2. Operationally define the following:
   a. Sexual harassment
   b. Diversity-positive environment
   c. Career success
3. Describe the four major scales.
4. Construct a semantic differential scale to assess the properties of a particular brand of cigarette.
5. You have developed a new scale to measure sex-role stereotypes. Explain in some detail how you would go about establishing the "goodness" of the measure that you have developed.
6. Why are reliability and validity important concepts in measurement? Explain the different forms of reliability and validity. How do you think these concepts are related to the concepts of precision and confidence that we had discussed throughout the book?
7. "Whenever available, it is advisable to use instruments that have already been developed and repeatedly used in published studies rather than develop our own instruments for our studies." Do you agree? Discuss the reasons for your answer.
8. "A valid instrument is always reliable, but a reliable instrument may not always be valid." Comment on this statement.

EXERCISES

Exercise 6.1   Schematically depict the operational definition of the concept of **stress** and develop ten questions that would measure stress.

Exercise 6.2   Schematically depict the operational definition of the concept of **enriched job** and develop twelve items to measure the concept.

Exercise 6.3   Think of two variables that would be natural candidates for nominal scales, and set up mutually exclusive and collectively exhaustive categories for each.

Exercise 6.4   Develop an ordinal scale for consumer preferences for different brands of beer.

Exercise 6.5   Measure three variables on an interval scale.

Exercise 6.6   Example 6.2 lists fourteen items directed toward tapping achievement motivation. Take items 6 to 9 and item 14, and use an interval scale to measure them. Reword the questions if you wish, without changing their meaning.

Exercise 6.7   Mention one variable for each of the four scales in the context of a market survey, and explain how or why they would fit into the scale.

APPENDIX TO CHAPTER 6

EXAMPLES OF SOME MEASURES

Some of the measures used in behavioral research can be had from the *Handbook of Organizational Measurement* by Price (1972), and from the *Michigan Organizational Assessment Package* published by the Institute of Survey Research in Ann Arbor, Michigan. Several measures can also be seen in *Psychological Measurement Yearbooks* and in other published books. A sample of measures from the management and marketing areas is provided in this appendix.

MEASURES FROM MANAGEMENT RESEARCH

Below are a sample of five scales used to measure five variables related to management research.

I. **Job Satisfaction** measured by the Job Descriptive Index (JDI) developed by Smith, Kendall, and Hulin (1969).

The following items refer to various aspects of your job.

For each item, for each scale (work, pay, etc.) put in the spaces below:
"Y" if the item applies
"N" if the item does not apply
"?" if you cannot decide

A. My work

____ Fascinating
____ Routine
____ Satisfying
____ Boring
____ Good
____ Creative
____ Respected
____ Hot
____ Pleasant
____ Useful
____ Tiresome
____ Healthful
____ Challenging
____ On your feet
____ Frustrating
____ Simple
____ Endless
Gives sense of
____ accomplishment

B. My supervisor

____ Asks my advice
____ Hard to please
____ Impolite
____ Praises good work
____ Tactful
____ Influential
____ Up-to-date
Doesn't supervise
____ enough
____ Quick-tempered
Tells me where I
____ stand
____ Annoying
____ Stubborn
____ Knows job well
____ Bad
____ Intelligent
____ Leaves me on my own
____ Around when needed
____ Lazy

C. My co-workers in
my work unit (if
you are a manager
this means other
managers)

____ Stimulating
____ Boring
____ Slow
____ Ambitious
____ Stupid
____ Responsible
____ Fast
____ Intelligent
Easy to make
____ enemies
____ Talk too much
____ Smart
____ Lazy
____ Unpleasant
____ No privacy
____ Active
____ Narrow interests
____ Loyal
____ Hard to meet

D. My pay

Income adequate for
____ normal expenses
____ Satisfactory profit sharing
____ Barely live on income
____ Bad
____ Income provides luxuries
____ Insecure
____ Less than I desire
____ Highly paid
____ Underpaid

E. My promotions

____ Good opportunity for advancement
____ Opportunity somewhat limited
____ Promotion on ability
____ Dead-end job
____ Good chance for promotion
____ Unfair promotion policy
____ Infrequent promotions
____ Regular promotions
____ Fairly good chance for promotion

PLEASE MAKE SURE ALL ITEMS ABOVE HAVE EITHER A "Y", "N", OR "?".

Smith, P.C., Kendall, L., and Hulin, C. (1969). *The measure of satisfaction in work and retirement.* Chicago: Rand McNally, 79–84.

II. **Participation in Decision-Making** developed by White and Ruh (1973).

Scale

	Very Little	A Little	To An Average Extent	Much	Very Much
	1	2	3	4	5
1. In general, how much say or influence do you have on how you perform your job?	1	2	3	4	5
2. To what extent are you able to decide how to do your job?	1	2	3	4	5
3. In general, how much say or influence do you have on what goes on in your group?	1	2	3	4	5
4. In general, how much say or influence do you have on decisions that affect your job?	1	2	3	4	5
5. To what extent are your superiors receptive and listen to your ideas and suggestions?	1	2	3	4	5

White, J. K., & Ruh, R. A. (1973). Effects of personal values on the relationship between participation and job attitudes. *Administrative Science Quarterly, 18*(4), 506–514.

III. **Role Conflict** developed by Rizzo, House, and Lirtzman (1970).

Scale: Likert

I have to do things that should be done differently.	1	2	3	4	5
I work under incompatible policies and guidelines.	1	2	3	4	5
I receive an assignment without the manpower to complete it.	1	2	3	4	5
I have to buck a rule or policy in order to carry out an assignment.	1	2	3	4	5
I receive incompatible requests from two or more people.	1	2	3	4	5
I receive an assignment without adequate resources and materials to execute it.	1	2	3	4	5
I work on unnecessary things.	1	2	3	4	5
I have to work under vague directives or orders.	1	2	3	4	5

Rizzo, J. R., House, R. J., and Lirtzman, S. I. (1970). Role conflict and role ambiguity in complex organizations. *Administrative Science Quarterly, 15,* 150–163.

IV. **Communication** from Price (1972).

Scale

	None at All 1	A Little 2	A Moderate Amount 3	Quite a Bit 4	Very Much 5
How much are you informed about:					
1. What is done in your job	1	2	3	4	5
2. Policies and procedures	1	2	3	4	5
3. Priority of the work to be done	1	2	3	4	5
4. How well you do your job	1	2	3	4	5
5. Expectations about your job performance	1	2	3	4	5

Price, J. L. (1972). *Handbook of organizational measurement.* Lexington, Mass.: D.C. Heath.

V. **Least Preferred Co-worker (LPC) Scale.**

QUESTIONNAIRE: Fiedler's Least Preferred Co-worker Scale (LPC)

Think of a person *with whom you have had difficulty working*. It does not have to be a person you really dislike, just someone you *must* work with and with whom working is difficult. Describe the person on each of the scales below by checking the number between each pair of adjectives that best describes that person. Then transfer the numbers to the spaces at the right and total them

Pleasant	:__:__:__:__:__:__:__:__:	Unpleasant	_____
	8 7 6 5 4 3 2 1		
Friendly	:__:__:__:__:__:__:__:__:	Unfriendly	_____
	8 7 6 5 4 3 2 1		
Rejecting	:__:__:__:__:__:__:__:__:	Accepting	_____
	8 7 6 5 4 3 2 1		
Tense	:__:__:__:__:__:__:__:__:	Relaxed	_____
	8 7 6 5 4 3 2 1		
Distant	:__:__:__:__:__:__:__:__:	Close	_____
	8 7 6 5 4 3 2 1		
Cold	:__:__:__:__:__:__:__:__:	Warm	_____
	8 7 6 5 4 3 2 1		
Supportive	:__:__:__:__:__:__:__:__:	Hostile	_____
	8 7 6 5 4 3 2 1		
Boring	:__:__:__:__:__:__:__:__:	Interesting	_____
	8 7 6 5 4 3 2 1		
Quarrelsome	:__:__:__:__:__:__:__:__:	Harmonious	_____
	8 7 6 5 4 3 2 1		

Gloomy	:__:__:__:__:__:__:__:	Cheerful	_____
	8 7 6 5 4 3 2 1		
Open	:__:__:__:__:__:__:__:	Guarded	_____
	8 7 6 5 4 3 2 1		
Backbiting	:__:__:__:__:__:__:__:	Loyal	_____
	8 7 6 5 4 3 2 1		
Untrustworthy	:__:__:__:__:__:__:__:	Trustworthy	_____
	8 7 6 5 4 3 2 1		
Considerate	:__:__:__:__:__:__:__:	Inconsiderate	_____
	8 7 6 5 4 3 2 1		
Nasty	:__:__:__:__:__:__:__:	Nice	_____
	8 7 6 5 4 3 2 1		
Agreeable	:__:__:__:__:__:__:__:	Disagreeable	_____
	8 7 6 5 4 3 2 1		
Insincere	:__:__:__:__:__:__:__:	Sincere	_____
	8 7 6 5 4 3 2 1		
Kind	:__:__:__:__:__:__:__:	Unkind	_____
	8 7 6 5 4 3 2 1		
		Total	========

There are two different leadership styles which are measured by the Least Preferred Co-worker scale.

1. *Relationship-motivated* (High LPC—score of 64 and above). These leaders seem to be most concerned with maintaining good interpersonal relations and accomplishing the task through these personal relationships. Sometimes the high LPC leader becomes so concerned with relating to group members that it interferes with completion of the assignment or mission. In relaxed and well-controlled situations, this type of leader tends to impress the boss.

2. *Task-motivated* (Low LPC—score of 57 or below). These leaders place primary emphasis on task performance. Low LPC leaders work best from guidelines and specific directions and if these are lacking, the low LPC will make the organization and creation of these guidelines the first priority. However, under relaxed and well-controlled situations when the organization is running smoothly, the task-motivated leader takes time to attend to the morale of group members.

Source: Fiedler, *A Theory of Leadership Effectiveness* (New York: McGraw-Hill, 1967).

MEASURES FROM MARKETING RESEARCH

Below is a sample of five scales used to measure five commonly researched concepts in marketing. Bruner and Hensel are currently compiling, and will soon be publishing, the scales available in marketing (**multi-item scales for marketing research**), which will be very useful to marketing researchers.

Attitude toward Advertising in General

Scale 1

	Agree Strongly	Agree Somewhat	Neither Agree nor Disagree	Disagree Somewhat	Disagree Strongly
Most advertising provides consumers with essential information.	1	2	3	4	5
Most adverstising is very annoying.	1	2	3	4	5
Most advertising makes false claims.	1	2	3	4	5
If most advertising were eliminated, consumers would be better off.	1	2	3	4	5
I enjoy most ads.	1	2	3	4	5
Advertising should be more closely regulated.	1	2	3	4	5
Most advertising is intended to deceive rather than to inform consumers.	1	2	3	4	5

Gaski, J. F., and Etzel, M. J. (1986), The index of consumer sentiment toward marketing. *Journal of Marketing, 50* (July), 71–81.

Scale 2

Good _____ | | | | | | _____ Bad

Positive _____ | | | | | | _____ Negative

Favorable _____ | | | | | | _____ Unfavorable

Muehling, D. D. (1987), An investigation of factors underlying attitude-toward-advertising-in-general. *Journal of Advertising, 16* (1) , 32–40.

Satisfaction Scale

> Please indicate how *satisfied* you were with your * by checking the space that best gives your answer.

* Extremely pleased me	—	—	—	—	—	—	—	* Extremely displeased me
Am contented with *	—	—	—	—	—	—	—	Am disgusted with *
I am very satisfied with *	—	—	—	—	—	—	—	I am very dissatisfied with *
* did a good job for me	—	—	—	—	—	—	—	* did a poor job for me
Buying * was a good choice	—	—	—	—	—	—	—	Buying * was a poor choice
Am happy with *	—	—	—	—	—	—	—	Am unhappy with *

Note: * represents the object toward which satisfaction is measured.

Attitude toward Product/Brand Scale

1. Good	—	—	—	—	—	—	—	Bad
2. Dislike	—	—	—	—	—	—	—	Like very much
3. Pleasant	—	—	—	—	—	—	—	Unpleasant
4. Poor Quality	—	—	—	—	—	—	—	High Quality
5. Disagreeable	—	—	—	—	—	—	—	Agreeable
6. Unsatisfactory	—	—	—	—	—	—	—	Satisfactory

7. Foolish	—	—	—	—	—	—	—	Wise
8. Harmful	—	—	—	—	—	—	—	Beneficial
9. Favorable	—	—	—	—	—	—	—	Unfavorable
10. Very distinc- tive	—	—	—	—	—	—	—	Not very dis- tinctive
11. Positive	—	—	—	—	—	—	—	Negative
12. Positive opin- ion	—	—	—	—	—	—	—	Negative opin- ion
13. Seek more information	—	—	—	—	—	—	—	Not seek more information
14. Negative	—	—	—	—	—	—	—	Positive

Note: Score on items 1, 3, 9, 10, 11, 12, is to be reversed.

Credit Usage Scale

	Strongly Disagree 1	Disagree 2	Neutral 3	Agree 4	Strongly Agree 5
1. I buy many things with a credit card or a charge card.	1	2	3	4	5
2. I like to pay cash for everything I buy.	1	2	3	4	5
3. It is good to have charge accounts.	1	2	3	4	5
4. To buy anything, other than a house or a car, on credit is unwise.	1	2	3	4	5

Note: Item 2 is to be reversed.

Opinion Leadership Scale

1. In general, do you talk to your friends and neighbors about XXX.

    Very
    Often   Never
    5 ———— 4 ———— 3 ———— 2 ———— 1

2. When you talk to your friends and neighbors about XXX do you:

    Give a great deal of   Give very little
       information   information
       5 ———— 4 ———— 3 ———— 2 ———— 1

3. During the past six months, how many people have you told about XXX?

    Told a number
       of people   Told no one
       5 ———— 4 ———— 3 ———— 2 ———— 1

4. Compared with your circle of friends, how likely are you to be asked about XXX?

       Very likely   Not at all likely
       to be asked   to be asked
       5 ———— 4 ———— 3 ———— 2 ———— 1

5. In discussions of XXX, which of the following happens most often?

       You tell your   Your friends tell
    friends about XXX   you about XXX
       5 ———— 4 ———— 3 ———— 2 ———— 1

6. Overall in all of your discussions with friends and neighbors are you?

    Often used as a   Not used as a source
    source of advice   of advice
       5 ———— 4 ———— 3 ———— 2 ———— 1

Note: XXX refers to the topic.

CHAPTER 7

DATA-COLLECTION METHODS

TOPICS DISCUSSED

DIFFERENT DATA COLLECTION METHODS
- Interviewing
  - *Unstructured and Structured Interviews*
  - *Tips for Interviewing*
  - *Face-to-Face and Telephone Interviews*
  - *Computer-Assisted Interviewing*
- Questionnaires and Questionnaire Design
  - *Personally Administered Questionnaires and Mail Questionnaires*
  - *Principles of Wording*
  - *Principles of Measurement*
  - *General Appearance of the Questionnaire*
  - *Electronic Questionnaire Design and Surveys*
- Observational Studies
  - *Participant and Nonparticipant Observation*
  - *Structured and Unstructured Observation*
- Projective Tests

SOURCES OF DATA
- Focus Groups
- Panels
- Unobtrusive Sources

MULTIMETHODS AND MULTISOURCES OF DATA COLLECTION

CHAPTER OBJECTIVES

After completing Chapter 7 you should:

1. Be conversant with the various data-collection methods.

2. Know the advantages and disadvantages of each method.

3. Make the logical decisions as to the appropriate data-collection method(s) for specific studies.

4. Demonstrate your skills using interviewing as a data-collection technique.

5. Design questionnaires to tap different variables.

6. Evaluate questionnaires, distinguishing between "good" and "bad" questions therein.

7. Identify and minimize the biases in various data-collection methods.

8. Discuss the advantages of multisources and multimethods of data collection.

9. Apply what you have learned to class assignments and projects.

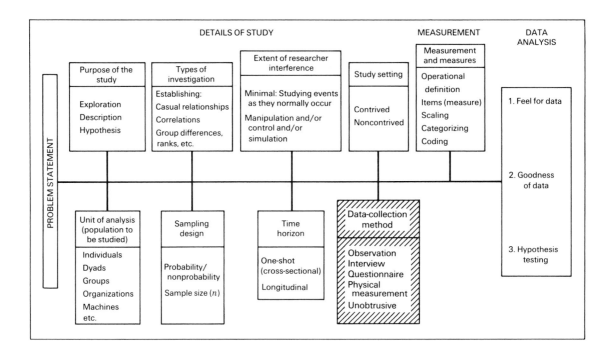

Having examined how variables are measured, we will now discuss how data can be gathered for the purpose of analysis, testing of hypotheses, and answering the research questions. The manner in which data are collected could make a big difference to the rigor of the research project.

Data collection methods are an integral part of research design as shown in the shaded portion in the figure above. There are several data collection methods, each with its own advantages and disadvantages, which will be discussed in this chapter.

DATA-COLLECTION METHODS, SETTINGS, AND SOURCES OF DATA

Data can be collected in a variety of ways, in different settings, and from different sources. **Data collection** methods include face-to-face interviews, telephone interviews, computer-assisted interviews; questionnaires that are either personally administered, sent through the mail, or electronically administered; observation of individuals and events with or without videotaping or audio recording; and a variety of other motivational techniques such as projective tests.

As for the **setting,** data can be collected in any one of the aforementioned ways in the natural environment in which phenomena occur. Data may also be collected in lab experimental settings where variables are controlled and manipulated, or gathered in the homes of the respondents, on the street, in malls, or in a setting where a LAN (Local Area Network) system is available.

Data **sources** can be primary and/or secondary. Individuals, focus groups, and a panel of respondents specifically set up by the researcher whose opinions may be sought on specific issues from time to time are examples of primary data sources. Data can also be obtained from secondary sources, as for example, company records or archives, government publications, industry analysis offered by the media, and so on. In some cases, the environment or particular settings and events may themselves be sources of data, as for example, studying the layout of a plant.

Interviewing, administering questionnaires, and observing people and phenomena are the three main data-collection methods in survey research. Projective tests and other motivational techniques are also sometimes used to tap variables. In such tests, respondents are usually asked to write a story, complete a sentence, or give their reactions to ambiguous cues such as inkblots or unlabeled pictures. It is assumed that the respondents project into the responses their own thoughts, feelings, attitudes, and expectations, all of which can be interpreted.

Although interviewing has the advantage of flexibility in terms of adapting, adopting, and changing the questions as the researcher proceeds with the interviews, questionnaires have the advantage of obtaining data more efficiently in terms of researcher time, energy, and costs. Unobtrusive methods of data collection such as extracting data from company records have the advantage of ensuring the accuracy of the information obtained. For instance, gathering information on the absenteeism of employees from company records will probably give more precise and reliable information than asking the respondents how many days they have been absent during the past year. Projective tests are usually administered by those researchers who have had training in administering them and interpreting the results. Though some management research has been done using projective techniques, they are more frequently used in marketing research, as we shall see later.

Modern technology is playing a key role in shaping data-collection methods for the future. Technological advances are currently facilitating computer surveys, in terms of interviewing (computer-assisted interviewing—CAI), as well as preparing and administering questionnaires (for example, the CAPPA system). These are described later.

The choice of data-collection methods depends on the facilities available from the organization, the extent of accuracy required, the expertise of the researcher, the time span of the study, and other costs and resources associated with and available for data gathering.

We will now examine the various data-collection methods.

INTERVIEWING

One method of collecting data is to interview respondents to obtain information on the issues of interest to the researcher. Interviews can be unstructured or structured, and could be conducted either face to face or by telephone. The unstructured and structured interviews will be discussed first. Next, some important factors to be borne in mind while interviewing will be detailed, the advantages and disadvantages of face-to-face interviewing and telephone interviews will then be enumerated, and finally, computer-assisted interviews will be touched upon.

Unstructured and Structured Interviews

Unstructured Interviews

Unstructured interviews are so labeled because the interviewer does not enter the interview setting with a planned sequence of questions that he will be asking the respondent. The objective of the unstructured interview is to surface some preliminary issues so that the researcher can formulate a good idea of what variables need further in-depth investigation. In Chapter 2 in the discussion of the "Broad Problem Area," we saw several situations where the manager might have a vague idea of certain changes taking place in the situation without knowing what exactly is happening. Such situations call for unstructured interviews with the people concerned. In order to understand the total situation, the researcher will interview employees at several levels. At the initial stages of such conversations, only broad, open-ended questions would be asked, and the replies to these questions would give the researcher an indication of the perceptions of the individuals. The type and nature of the questions asked of the individuals might vary according to the job level and type of work done by respondents. For instance, managers at top and middle levels might be asked more direct questions about their perceptions of the problem and the situation. Employees at lower levels may have to be approached differently.

Clerical and other employees at lower hierarchical levels may be asked broad, open-ended questions about their jobs and the work environment during the unstructured interviews. Supervisors may be asked broad questions relating to their department, their employees and the organization. The following question, for instance, may be put to them during the unstructured interview stage:

"Tell me something about your unit and department, and perhaps even the organization as a whole, in terms of work, employees, and whatever else you think is important."

Such a question might elicit a voluminous response from some people, whereas others may briefly reply that everything is fine. Following the leads from the more vocal persons is comparatively easy, especially when the interviewer listens carefully for the important messages that might be transmitted in a very casual manner while responding to a general, global question. As managers and researchers, we should train ourselves to develop these listening skills and identify the critical topics that are being touched on. However, when some respondents give one-word, crisp, short replies that do not give out much information, the interviewer will have to ask questions that can definitely not be answered in one or two words. Such questions might be phrased as the one below:

> *"I would like to know something about your job. Please describe to me in detail the things you do on your job on a typical day, from eight in the morning to four o'clock in the afternoon."*

Several questions might then be asked as a follow-up to the answer. Some examples of such follow-up questions include:

> *"Compared to other units in this organization, what are the strengths and weaknesses of your unit?"*

> *"If you would like to have one problem solved in your unit, or eliminate one bottleneck, or attend to something that blocks your effectiveness, what would that be?"*

If the respondent answers that everything is fine and she has no problems, the interviewer could say: "That is great! Tell me what contributes to this effectiveness of your unit, because most other organizations usually experience several difficulties." Such a questioning technique usually brings the respondent's defenses down and the respondent then usually shows a greater willingness to share information. Typical of the revised responses to the original question is something like, "Well, it is not that we never have a problem, sometimes, we are late in getting the jobs done, crash jobs have some defective items, . . .". Encouraging the respondent to talk about both the good things and the not-so-good things in the unit can elicit a lot of information. Whereas some respondents do not need much encouragement to speak, others do; and they have to be questioned broadly. Some respondents may be reluctant to be interviewed, and may subtly or overtly refuse to cooperate. The wishes of such people must be respected and the interviewer should pleasantly terminate such interviews.

Employees at the shop-floor level, and other nonmanagerial and nonsupervisory employees, might be asked very broad questions relating to their jobs, work environment, satisfactions and dissatisfactions at the workplace, and the like—for example:

What do you like about working here?

If you were to tell me what aspects of your job you like and which aspects of it you do not like, what would they be?

Tell me something about the reward systems in this place.

If you were offered a similar job elsewhere, how willing would you be to take it?

If I were to seek employment here and request you to describe your unit to me as a newcomer, what would you say?

After a sufficient number of such unstructured interviews have been conducted with employees at several levels, the researcher would have a good idea of the variables that need more focus and where more in-depth information has to be obtained. At this stage, the researcher is ready to conduct structured interviews.

Structured Interviews

Structured interviews are those conducted by the interviewer when he or she knows exactly what information is needed and has a predetermined list of questions that will be posed to the respondents. The interviewer will have written out these questions and/or topics and will refer to this list while conducting the interviews. The questions are likely to focus on factors that were surfaced during the unstructured interviews and considered relevant to the problem. As the respondents express their views, the researcher would note the responses on the schedule. The same questions will be asked of everybody in the same manner. Sometimes, however, based on the exigencies of the situation, the researcher might follow a prospective lead from a respondent's answer by asking other relevant questions not on the schedule. Through this process new factors might be identified and a deeper understanding might result. However, to know when a meaningful response has been obtained, the interviewer must comprehend the purpose and goal of each question. This is particularly important when a team of trained interviewers conducts the survey.

Visual aids such as pictures, line drawings, cards, and other materials are also used sometimes in conducting interviews. The appropriate visuals are shown to the interviewees, who then indicate their responses to the questions posed. Marketing research, for example, benefits from such techniques in order to capture the likes and dislikes of customers to different types of packaging, forms of advertising, and so on. Visual aids, including painting and drawing, are particularly useful when children are the focus of marketing research. Visual aids also come in handy when eliciting certain thoughts and ideas that are difficult to express or are awkward to articulate.

When a sufficient number of interviews has been conducted and the researcher feels he has sufficient information to understand and describe the important factors operating in the situation, the researcher would stop the interviews. The information collected from the various interviews would then be analyzed by tabulating the data. This would help the researcher to describe the phenomena, or quantify them, or identify the specific problem and evolve a theory of the factors that influence the problem or find answers to the research question.

Training Interviewers

When several long interviews are to be conducted, it is often not feasible for one individual to conduct all the interviews. A team of trained interviewers then becomes necessary. Interviewers have to be thoroughly briefed about the research and trained in how to start an interview, how to proceed with the questions, how to motivate respondents to answer, what to look for in the answers, and how to close an interview. They also need to be instructed in taking notes and coding the interview responses. The tips for interviewing, discussed later, should become a part of their repertoire for interviewing.

Good planning, proper training offering clear guidelines to interviewers, and monitoring their work all help in profitably utilizing the interviewing technique as a viable data-collection mechanism. Personal interviews offer rich data that are spontaneously given by the respondents, in the sense that their answers do not typically fall within a constricted range of responses as required in a questionnaire. However, personal interviews are also expensive in terms of time, training costs, and resource consumption.

Review of Unstructured and Structured Interviews

The main purpose of the unstructured interview is to explore the several factors in the situation that might be central to the broad problem area. During this process it might become evident that the problem as identified by the client is only the symptom of a more serious and deep-rooted problem. Conducting unstructured interviews with many people in the organization could result in the identification of several critical factors in the situation. These factors would then be pursued further during the structured interviews for eliciting more in-depth information on the selected factors. This will help in the identification of the critical problem as well as in solving problems. In applied research, a tentative theory of the factors influencing the problem is often conceptualized on the basis of the information obtained from the unstructured and structured interviews. Thereafter, further interviews may even be conducted to find solutions.

Some Tips to Follow While Interviewing

The information obtained during the interviews should be as free as possible of bias. Bias refers to errors or inaccuracies in the data collected. Biases could be introduced by the interviewer, the interviewee, or the situation. The **interviewer** could bias the data if proper trust and rapport are not established with the interviewee or when the responses are either misinterpreted or distorted, or when the interviewer unintentionally encourages or discourages certain types of responses through gestures, facial expressions, and the like. **Interviewees** can bias the data when they do not give their true opinions but provide information that they think is what the interviewer is expecting or wants to hear or would like. Also, if the respondents do not understand questions, they may feel hesitant to ask for clarification. They may then answer questions without knowing what exactly the questions mean, and thus introduce biases. Biases could be **situational** as well, in terms of (1) nonparticipants, (2) trust levels and rapport established, and (3) the physical setting of the interview. **Nonparticipation** can bias data inasmuch as the responses of the participants may be different from those who did not participate (which implies that a biased, rather than a representative, set of responses is being gathered). Bias also occurs when different interviewers establish **different levels of trust and rapport** with their interviewees, thus eliciting answers of varying degrees of openness. The actual **setting** itself in which the interview is conducted might sometimes introduce biases. Some individuals may feel uncomfortable when interviewed at the workplace and not respond frankly and honestly.

Bias can be minimized in several ways. The following strategies will be useful for the purpose.

Establishing Credibility and Rapport, and Motivating Individuals to Respond

Projecting professionalism, enthusiasm, and confidence is important for the researcher. A manager hiring outside researchers would be interested in assessing their abilities and personality predispositions. Researchers must establish rapport with and gain the confidence and approval of the hiring client before they can even start their work in the organization. Knowledge, skills, ability, confidence, articulateness, and enthusiasm are therefore qualities a researcher must demonstrate in order to establish credibility with the hiring organization and its members.

To obtain honest information from the respondents, the researcher-interviewer should be able to establish rapport and trust with the interviewees. In other words, the researcher should be able to make the respondent comfortable enough to give informative and truthful answers without fear of adverse consequences. To this end, the researcher should state the purpose of the interview and assure complete confidentiality about the source of the responses. Establishing rapport with the respondents may not be easy, especially when interviewing employees at lower levels. The employees are likely to be suspicious of the intentions of the researchers; they may believe that the researchers are on the management's "side," and hence are likely to advocate reduction of the labor force, increase in the workload, and so on. Thus it is important to ensure that everyone concerned is aware of the researchers' purpose as simply to understand what is happening in the organization. The respondents must be assured that the researchers are not on any particular side; they are not there to harm the staff, and they will provide the results of research to the organization only in aggregates, without disclosing the identity of the individuals.

The researcher can establish rapport by being pleasant, sincere, sensitive, and nonevaluative. Evincing a genuine interest in the responses and allaying any anxieties, fears, suspicions, and tensions sensed in the situation will help respondents to feel more comfortable with the researchers. If the respondent is told about the purpose of the study and how she was chosen to be one of those interviewed, there will be better communication flow between the parties. Researchers can motivate respondents to give honest and truthful answers by explaining to them that their contribution will help, and that they themselves may stand to gain from such a survey; for example, the quality of life at work for most employees might improve.

The Questioning Technique

Funneling.   In the beginning of an unstructured interview, it is advisable to ask open-ended questions to get a broad impression, for example: "What are some of your feelings about working for this organization?" From the responses to this broad question, further questions that are progressively more focused may be asked as the researcher processes the interviewees' responses and determines some possible key issues relevant to the situation. This transition from broad to narrow themes is called the funneling technique.

Unbiased Questions.   It is important to ask questions in a way that would ensure the least bias in the response. For example, "Tell me how you experience your job" is a better question than saying," Boy, the work you do must be really boring; let me hear how you experience it." The latter question is "loaded" in terms of the interviewer's own perceptions of the job. A loaded question might influence the types of answers the respondent gives. Bias could be also introduced by emphasizing certain words, by tone and voice inflections, and through inappropriate suggestions.

Clarifying Issues.   To make sure that the researcher understands issues as the respondent means to represent them, it is advisable for the researcher to restate or rephrase important information given by the respondent. For instance, if the interviewee says, "There is an unfair promotion policy in this organization; seniority is not counted at all. It is the juniors who always get promoted," the researcher might interject, "So you are saying that juniors always get promoted over the heads of even capable seniors." Rephrasing in this way clarifies the issue of whether or not the respondent considers ability important. If certain things that are being said are not clear, the researcher should seek clarification. For example, if the respondent happened to say, "The facilities here are really poor; we often have to continue working even when we are dying of thirst," the researcher might ask if there is no water fountain or drinking water available in the building. The respondent's reply to this might well indicate that there is a water fountain across the hall, but the respondent would have liked one on his side of the work area.

Helping the Respondent to Think Through Issues.   If the respondent is not able to verbalize her perceptions, or replies, "I don't know," the researcher should ask the question in a simpler way or rephrase it. For instance, if a respondent is unable to specify what aspects of the job he dislikes, the researcher might ask the question in a simpler way. For example, the respondent might be asked which task he would prefer to do: serve a customer or do some filing work. If the answer is "serve the customer," the researcher might use another aspect of the respondent's job and ask the paired-choice question again. In this way, the respondent can sort out which aspects of the job he likes better than others.

Taking Notes.   When conducting interviews, it is important that the researcher makes written notes as the interviews are taking place, or as soon as the interview is terminated. The interviewer should not rely on memory, because information recalled from memory is imprecise and often likely to be incorrect. Furthermore, if more than one interview is scheduled for the day, the amount of information received increases, as do possible sources of error in recalling from memory. In addition, information based solely on recall introduces bias into the research.

It is possible to record the interviews on tape if the respondent has no objection. However, taped interviews might sometimes bias the respondents' answers because they may be uncomfortable knowing that their voices are being recorded, thus making the interview not completely anonymous. Hence, even if the respondents do not object, there could be some bias in their responses. Before taping or videotaping interviews, one should be reasonably certain that such a method of obtaining data is not likely to bias the information received. Any taping or videotaping should always be done only after obtaining the respondent's permission.

Review of Tips to Follow in Interviewing

Establishing credibility as able researchers with the client system and the organizational members is important for the success of the research project. Researchers need to establish rapport with the respondents and motivate them to give responses relatively free from bias by allaying whatever suspicions, fears, anxieties, and concerns they may have about the research and its consequences. This can be done by being sincere, pleasant, and nonevaluative. While interviewing, the researcher has to ask broad questions initially and then narrow the questions to specific areas, ask questions in an unbiased way, and clarify and help respondents to think through difficult issues. The responses have to be transcribed immediately and the information should not be trusted to memory and later recall.

Having looked at unstructured and structured interviews and learned something about how to conduct the interviews, we can now look at the face-to-face and telephone interviews.

Face-to-Face and Telephone Interviews

Interviews can be conducted either face to face or over the telephone. In either case, they could also be computer-assisted, as detailed later. Although most unstructured interviews in organizational research are conducted face to face, structured interviews could be either face to face or through the medium of the telephone depending on the level of complexity of the issues involved, the time that the interview would take, the convenience of both parties, and the geographical area covered by the survey. Telephone interviews are best suited when many respondents are to be reached over a wide geographic area and the time that each interview takes is short—say, less than ten minutes. Many market surveys, for instance, are conducted through structured telephone interviews.

Face-to-face interviews and telephone interviews have their other advantages and disadvantages. These will now be briefly discussed.

Face-to-Face Interviews

Advantages. The main advantage of face-to-face or direct interviews is that the researcher can adapt the questions as necessary, clarify doubts, and ensure that the responses are properly understood by repeating or rephrasing the questions. The researcher can also pick up nonverbal cues from the respondent. Any discomfort, stress, or problems that the respondent experiences can be detected through frowns, nervous tapping, and other body language unconsciously exhibited by the respondent. This would obviously be impossible to detect in a telephone interview.

Disadvantages. The main disadvantages of face-to-face interviews are the geographical limitations they may impose on the surveys and the vast resources needed if such surveys need to be done nationally or internationally. The costs of training interviewers to minimize interviewer biases (e.g., differences in questioning methods, interpretation of responses) are also high. Another drawback is that respondents might feel uneasy about the anonymity of their responses when they are interacting face to face with the interviewer.

Telephone Interviews

Advantages. The main advantage of telephone interviewing, from the researcher's point of view, is that a number of different people can be reached—if need be, across the country or even internationally—in a relatively short period of time. From the respondent's standpoint it would eliminate any discomfort that some respondents might feel in facing the interviewer. It is also possible that most respondents would feel less uncomfortable disclosing personal information over the phone than face to face.

Disadvantages. A main disadvantage of telephone interviewing is that the respondent could unilaterally terminate the interview without warning or explanation by hanging up the phone. To minimize this problem it would be advisable to call the interviewee ahead of time to request participation in the survey, giving an approximate idea of how long the interview would last, and setting up a mutually convenient time. Interviewees tend usually to appreciate this courtesy and are more likely to cooperate. It is a good policy not to prolong the interview beyond the time originally agreed on. As mentioned earlier, another disadvantage of the telephone interview is that the researcher will not be able to see the respondent to read the nonverbal communication.

Interviewing is a useful data-collection method, especially during the exploratory stages of research. Where a large number of interviews is conducted with a number of different interviewers, it is important to train the interviewers with care in order to minimize interviewer biases manifested in such ways as voice inflections, accentuations of particular words, and differences in interpretation. Good training increases interrater reliability.

Additional Sources of Bias in Interview Data

We have already discussed several sources of bias in data collection. Biased data will be obtained when respondents are interviewed while they are extremely busy or are in a bad mood. Responses to issues such as strikes, layoffs, or the like could also be biased. The personality of the interviewer, the introductory sentence, inflection of the voice, and such other aspects could introduce additional biases. Being sensitive to the many sources of bias will enable interviewers to obtain relatively valid information.

Computer-Assisted Interviewing

With computer-assisted interviewing (CAI), thanks to modern technology, questions are flashed onto the computer screen and interviewers can enter the answers of the respondents directly into the computer. The accuracy of data collection is considerably enhanced since the software can be programmed to flag the "off-base" or "out-of-range" responses. CAI software also prevents interviewers from asking the wrong questions or in the wrong sequence since the questions are automatically flashed to the respondent in an ordered sequence. This would, to some extent, eliminate interviewer-induced biases.

CATI and CAPI

There are two types of computer-assisted interview programs: CATI (computer assisted telephone interviewing) and CAPI (computer assisted personal interviewing). Very few use CAPI, owing to the big investments needed for hardware and software. CAPI has an advantage in that it can be self-administered; that is, respondents can use their own computers to run the program by themselves once they receive the software and enter their responses. However, not everyone is comfortable using a personal computer.

The **voice recording system** assists CATI programs inasmuch as the interviewees' responses are recorded. Courtesy, ethics, as well as legal requirements would require that the respondent's permission to record be obtained before the **voice capture system** (VCS) is activated. The VCS allows the computer to capture the respondents' answers, which are recorded in a digital mode and stored in a data file. They can be played back later to listen to customers by region, industry, or any combination of different sets of factors (*Marketing News,* May 9, 1988, p. 3), as desired.

Ci2 is a computer-assisted interviewing package for the IBM/PC. It is very useful for telephone interviews and has the capability to operate by itself. It can be used to conduct interviews in shopping malls with low costs (*American Demographics,* July 1987, p. 52). Ci2 has five basic programs. An introduction to the survey and questions can be typed in by using a Frames program. The Logic program specifies the screen color for each frame and the logic of responses to each question. The Questionnaire program runs the actual interviews (hence it can run by itself and record the responses that are keyed in). The responses can be printed with the Print program and the Data program will tabulate the data and summarize the results.

Hewlett-Packard has a data acquisition software (DACQ/300) that performs tasks such as data collection, storage, analysis, presentation, transmission, and data-base management, mostly used in R & D projects. DACQ/300 is designed to work with a Basic program running on an HP-9000 series.

In sum, the advantages of computer-assisted interviews can be stated simply as quick and more accurate gathering of information, plus faster and easier analysis of data. The field costs are low and automatic tabulation of results is possible. It is more efficient in terms of costs and time, once the initial heavy investment in equipment and software is made. However, to be really cost-effective, the surveys should be large and done frequently enough to warrant the heavy front-end investment and programming costs.

Computer-Aided Survey Services

Since many companies cannot currently afford to make the huge initial investments in the hardware and software for conducting CATI or CAPI, several other sources offer their services to these firms. We will discuss a few of these services.

The National Computer Network provides computer survey services to smaller companies to conduct marketing studies. Some of the many advantages of using the services are that (1) the researcher can start analyzing the data even as the field survey is progressing, since results can be transmitted to clients through modem in raw or tabulated form; (2) data can be automatically "cleaned up" and errors fixed even as they are being collected; (3) biases due to ordering questions in a particular way (known as the ordering effects) can be eliminated since meaningful random start patterns can be incorporated into the questioning process (discussed later in the chapter); (4) skip patterns (e.g., If the answer to this question is NO, skip to question #19) can be programmed into the process; and (5) questions can be customized to incorporate the respondent's terminologies of concepts into subsequent questions (*Marketing News,* May 9, 1988).

Computer surveys can be conducted either by mailing the disks to respondents or through on-line surveys with the respondents' personal computers being hooked up to computer networks. Survey System provided by Creative Research Systems and Interview System provided by Compaq Co. are two of the several computer survey systems available in the market.

Other Advantages of Computer Packages

Field notes taken by interviewers as they collect data have generally to be transcribed, hand coded, hand tabulated, and so on—all of which are tedious and time consuming. However, computers can vastly facilitate the interviewers' job as they relate to these activities. Automatic indexing of the data can be done with special programs, such as the ZuIndex. The two modes in operation are (1) **indexing** such that specific responses are coded in a particular way; and (2) **retrieval** of data with a fast search speed—going through 10,000 pages in less than five seconds. Text-oriented database management retrieval program allows the user to go through the text, inserting marks that link related units of text. The associative links formed are analytical categories specified by the researcher. Once the links are created, the program allows the user to activate them by opening multiple windows on the screen.

We thus see that computers have made their debut and will have a big impact on data collection in the future. With greater technological advancement and a lowering of hardware and software costs in the future, computer-assisted interviewing will catch up and become a very popular data-collection mechanism.

Review of Interviewing

Interviews are one method of obtaining data; they can be either unstructured or structured and can be conducted face-to-face or over the telephone. Unstructured interviews are usually conducted to obtain more definite ideas about what is and is not important and relevant to particular problem situations. Structured interviews give more in-depth information about specific variables of interest. To minimize bias in responses, the interviewer must establish rapport with the respondents and ask unbiased questions. The face-to-face interview and the interview conducted over the telephone each has its advantages and disadvantages; both are useful under different circumstances. Computer-assisted interviewing, which entails a heavy initial investment, is having an impact on interviewing and in the analyses of qualitative, spontaneous responses. We can expect CAI to become more frequently used in the future. We will now see how data can be gathered through questionnaires.

QUESTIONNAIRES

A questionnaire is a preformulated written set of questions to which respondents record their answers, usually within rather closely defined alternatives.

A questionnaire is an efficient data-collection mechanism when the researcher knows exactly what is required and how to measure the variables of interest. Questionnaires can be administered personally or mailed to the respondents. Information can also be obtained by electronically administering the questionnaire.

Personally Administered Questionnaires

When the survey is confined to a local area, and the organization is willing and able to assemble groups of employees to respond to the questionnaires at the workplace, personally administering the questionnaires is the best way to collect data. The main advantage to this is that the researcher or a member of the research team can collect all the completed responses within a short period of time. Any doubts that the respondents might have regarding any question could be clarified on the spot. The researcher also has the opportunity to introduce the research topic and motivate the respondents to give their honest answers. Administering questionnaires to large numbers of individuals simultaneously is less expensive and less time consuming than interviewing; it also requires fewer skills to administer the questionnaire than to conduct interviews. Wherever possible, it is advantageous to administer questionnaires personally to groups of people because of these advantages. However, organizations often are not able or willing to allow company time for data collection, and other ways of getting the questionnaires completed and returned may have to be found. In such cases, employees may be given blank questionnaires that will be collected from them later personally, or they can be provided with self-addressed, stamped envelopes and asked to have them completed and mailed to the researcher by a certain date. Scanner sheets (the answer sheets that are usually provided for answering multiple-choice questions in exams) are usually sent with the questionnaire so that respondents can circle their answers to each question on the sheet in pencil, which can then be directly entered into the computer as data without someone having to code and then manually enter the data in the computer. Disks containing the questions can also be sent to such respondents who have and can use personal computers.

Mail Questionnaires

The main advantage of a mail questionnaire is that a wide geographical area can be covered in the survey. The questionnaires are mailed to the respondents, who can complete them at their own convenience, in their homes, and at their own pace. However, the return rates of mail questionnaires are typically not as high as might be desired; sometimes they are very low. Another disadvantage to the mail questionnaire is that any doubts the respondents might have cannot be clarified. Also, with very low return rates it is difficult to establish the representativeness of the sample, because those who responded to the survey may be totally different from the population they were intended to represent. However, some effective techniques exist for improving the rates of response to mail questionnaires. Sending follow-up letters, enclosing some small monetary incentives with the questionnaire, providing the respondent with self-addressed, stamped return envelopes, and keeping the questionnaire as short as possible will all help to increase return rates of mail questionnaires (Kanuk & Berenson, 1975).

The choice of using the questionnaire as a data-gathering method might be restricted if the researcher has to reach subjects with very little education. Adding pictures to the questionnaires, if feasible, might help in such cases. For most organizational research, however, after the variables for the research have been identified and the measures for them have been found or developed, the questionnaire is a convenient data-collection mechanism. Field studies, comparative surveys, and experimental designs often use questionnaires to measure the variables of interest. Because questionnaires are commonly used in surveys, it is necessary to know how to design an effective questionnaire. A set of guidelines for questionnaire construction follows.

Figure 7.1
Principles of questionnaire design.

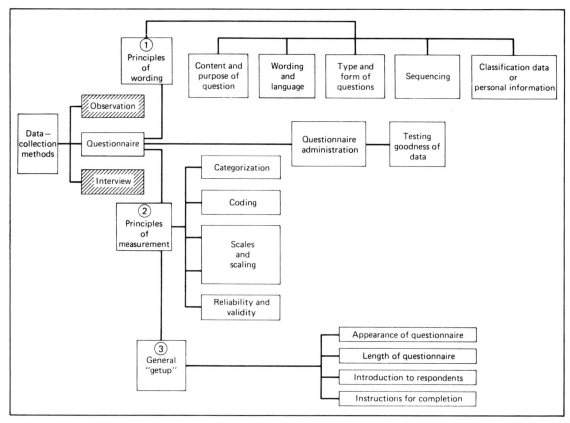

GUIDELINES FOR QUESTIONNAIRE DESIGN

Good questionnaire design principles should focus on three areas. The first relates to the wording of the questions. The second refers to issues of how the variables will be categorized, scaled, and coded after the questionnaire responses are received. The third pertains to the general appearance of the questionnaire. All three are important issues in questionnaire design because they can minimize biases in research. These issues are discussed below. The important aspects are schematically depicted in Figure 7.1.

Principles of Wording

The principles of wording refer to such factors as (1) the appropriateness of the content of the questions (2) how questions are worded and the level of sophistication of the language used, (3) the type and form of questions asked, (4) the sequencing of the questions in the questionnaire, and (5) the personal data sought from the respondents. Each of these is explained below.

Content and Purpose of the Question

The nature of the variable tapped—subjective feelings or objective facts—will determine what kinds of questions will be asked. If the variables tapped are of a subjective nature (e.g., satisfaction, involvement), where respondents' beliefs, perceptions, and attitudes are being measured, the questions asked should tap the dimensions and elements of the concept (Lazarsfeld, 1935; Payne, 1951). Where objective variables such as age and educational levels of respondents are tapped, a single direct question—preferably a question that has an ordinally scaled set of categories—would be appropriate. Thus the purpose of each question should be carefully considered so that the variables are adequately measured and yet no unnecessary questions are asked.

The Language and Wording of the Questionnaire

The language in the questionnaire should approximate the level of understanding of the respondents. The choice of words would depend on the educational level of the respondents sampled, the usage of terms and idioms in the culture, and the frames of reference of the respondents. For instance, even when English is the spoken or is the official language in two cultures, certain words may be alien to one culture. Terms such as "working here is a *drag*," and "she is a *compulsive* worker," may not be interpreted the same way in different cultures. Some blue-collar workers may not understand terminologies such as "organizational structure." Thus it is essential to word the questions in such a way that they are understood by the respondent. If some questions either are not understood or are interpreted differently by the respondent, the researcher will be getting the wrong answers to the questions, and responses will thus be biased. Hence, the questions asked, the language used, and the wording should be appropriate to tap respondents' attitudes, perceptions, and feelings.

Type and Form of Questions

Type of question refers to whether the question will be open-ended or closed. Form of the question refers to positively and negatively worded questions.

Open-Ended versus Closed Questions.

Open-ended questions allow respondents to answer them in any way they choose. An example of an open-ended question is asking the respondent to state five things that are interesting and challenging in the job. Another example is asking what the respondents like about their supervisors or their work environment. A third example is to ask them the investment portfolio of the firm.

A *closed* question, in contrast, would ask the respondents to make choices among a set of alternatives given by the researcher. For instance, instead of asking the respondent to state any five aspects of the job that are interesting and challenging, the researcher might list ten or fifteen characteristics that might seem interesting or challenging in jobs and ask the respondent to rank the first five among these. All items in a questionnaire using a nominal, ordinal, or Likert or ratio scale are considered closed.

Closed questions help the respondent to make quick decisions by making a choice among the several alternatives that are provided. They also help the researcher to code the information easily for subsequent analysis. Of course, care has to be taken to ensure that the alternatives are mutually exclusive and collectively exhaustive. If there are overlapping categories, or if all possible alternatives are not given (i.e., the categories are not exhaustive), the respondents might get confused and the advantage of their being able to make a quick decision may thus be lost.

Some respondents may find even well-delineated categories in a closed question rather confining and might like the opportunity to make additional comments. This is the reason that many questionnaires end with open-ended questions that invite respondents to comment on topics that may not have been covered or might have been inadequately covered in the questionnaire. The responses to such open-ended questions have to be edited and categorized for subsequent data analysis.

Positively and Negatively Worded Questions.   Instead of phrasing all questions positively, it is advisable to include some negatively worded questions as well, so that it minimizes the tendency in respondents to mechanically circle the points toward one end of the scale. For example, let us say that a set of six questions are used to tap the variable "perceived success" on a five-point scale, with 1 being "very low" and 5 being "very high" on the scale. A respondent who is not particularly interested in completing the questionnaire is more likely to stay involved and remain alert while answering the questions when positively and negatively worded questions are interspersed in the questionnaire. For instance, if the respondent had circled 5 for a positively worded question such as, "I feel I have been able to accomplish a number of different things in my job," he cannot circle number 5 again to the negatively worded question, "I do not feel I am very effective in my job." The respondent is now shaken out of any tendency that he might have had to mechanically respond to one end of the scale. In case this does still happen, the researcher has an opportunity to detect such biases. A good questionnaire should therefore include both positively and negatively worded questions. The use of double negatives and excessive use of the words *not* and *only* should be avoided in the negatively worded questions because they tend to confuse respondents. For instance, it is better to say "Coming to work is no great fun" than to say "Not coming to work is greater fun than coming to work." Likewise, it is better to say "The strong people need no tonics" than to say "Only the strong should be given no tonics."

Double-Barreled Questions.   A question that lends itself to different possible answers to its subparts is called a double-barreled question. Such questions should be avoided and two or more separate questions should be asked instead. For example, the question "Do you think there is a good market for the product and that it will sell well?" could bring a "yes" response to the first part (i.e., there is a good market for the product) and a "no" response to the latter part (i.e., it will not sell well—for various other reasons). In this case, it would be better to ask two questions: (1) "Do you think there is a good market for the product?" and (2) "Do you think the product will sell well?" The answers might be "yes" to both, "no" to both, "yes" to the first and "no" to the second, or "yes" to the second and "no" to the first. If we combined the two questions and asked a double-barreled question, we would confuse the respondents and obtain ambiguous responses. Hence, double-barreled questions should be avoided.

Ambiguous Questions. Even questions that are not double-barreled might be ambiguously worded and the respondent may not be sure exactly what they mean. An example of such a question is "To what extent would you say you are happy?" Respondents might not be sure whether the question refers to their state of feelings at the workplace, or at home, or in general. Because it is an organizational survey, she might presume that the question relates to the workplace. Yet the researcher might have intended to inquire about the general, overall degree of satisfaction that the individual experiences in everyday life—a very global feeling not specific to the workplace alone. Thus, responses to ambiguous questions have built-in bias inasmuch as different respondents might interpret such items in the questionnaire differently. The result would be a mixed bag of ambiguous responses that do not accurately reflect the correct answer to the question.

Recall-Dependent Questions. Some questions might require respondents to recall experiences from the past that are hazy in their memory. Answers to such questions might have bias. For instance, if an employee who has had thirty years' service in the organization is asked to state when he first started working in a particular department and for how long, he may not be able to give the correct answers and may be way off in his responses. A better source for obtaining that information would be the personnel records.

Leading Questions. Questions should not be phrased in such a way that they lead the respondent to give the responses that the researcher would like to, or may come across as wanting to, elicit. An example of such a question is: "Don't you think that in these days of escalating costs of living, employees should be given 'good' pay raises?" By asking such a question as this, we are signaling and pressuring respondents to say "yes." Tagging the question to rising living costs makes it difficult for most respondents (unless they are the top bosses in charge of budget and finances) to say, "No; not unless their productivity increases too!" Another way of asking the question about pay raises to elicit less biased responses would be: "To what extent do you agree that employees should be given higher pay raises?" If respondents think that the employees do not deserve a higher pay raise at all, their response would be "Strongly Disagree"; if they think that respondents should be definitely given a high pay raise, they would respond to the "Strongly Agree" end of the scale, and the in-between points would be chosen depending on the strength of their agreement or disagreement. In this case, the question is not framed in a suggestive manner as in the previous instance.

Loaded Questions. Another type of bias in questions occurs when they are phrased in an emotionally charged manner. An example of such a loaded question is asking employees: "To what extent do you think management is likely to be vindictive if the Union decides to go on strike?" The words "strike" and "vindictive" are emotionally charged terms polarizing management and unions. Hence, asking a question such as the above would elicit strongly emotional and highly biased responses. If the purpose of the question is twofold—that is, to find (1) the extent to which employees are in favor of a strike and (2) the extent to which they fear adverse reactions if they did go on strike—then these are the two specific questions that need to be asked. It may turn out that the employees are not strongly in favor of a strike and they also do not believe that management would retaliate if they did go on strike!

Social Desirability.   Questions should not be worded so that they elicit socially desirable responses. For instance, a question such as "Do you think that older people should be laid off?" would elicit a response of "no," mainly because society would frown on a person who would say that the elderly people should be fired even if they are capable. Hence, irrespective of the true feelings of the respondent, a socially desirable answer would be provided. If the purpose of the question is to gauge the extent to which organizations are seen as obligated to retain those above sixty-five years of age, a differently worded question with less pressure toward social desirability would be: "There are advantages and disadvantages to retaining senior citizens in the workforce. To what extent do you think companies should continue to keep the elderly on their payroll?"

Sometimes certain items that tap social desirability are deliberately introduced at various points in the questionnaire and an index of each individual's social desirability tendency is calculated therefrom. This index is then applied to all other responses given by the individual in order to adjust for his social desirability biases (Crowne & Marlowe, 1980; Edwards, 1957).

Length of Questions.   Finally, simple, short questions are preferable to long ones. As a rule of thumb, a question or a statement in the questionnaire should not exceed twenty words, or exceed one full line in print (Horst, 1968; Oppenheim, 1986).

In sum, the language and wording of the questionnaire focus on such issues as the type and form of questions (i.e., open-ended and closed questions, and positively and negatively worded questions), as well as avoiding double-barreled questions, ambiguous questions, leading questions, loaded questions, questions prone to tapping socially desirable answers, and those soliciting distant recall. Questions should also not be unduly long.

Sequencing of Questions

The sequence of questions in the questionnaire should be such that the respondent is led from questions of a general nature to those that are more specific; and from questions that are relatively easy to answer to those that are progressively more difficult. This funnel approach, as it is called (Festinger & Katz, 1966), facilitates the easy and smooth progress of the respondent through the items in the questionnaire. The progression from general to specific questions might mean that the respondent is first asked questions of a global nature that pertain to the organization, and then is asked more incisive questions regarding the specific job, department, and the like. Easy questions might relate to issues that do not involve a lot of thinking; the more difficult ones might call for more thought, judgment, and decision making.

In determining the sequence of questions, it is advisable not to place consecutively a positively worded and a negatively worded question tapping the same element or dimension of a concept. For instance, placing two questions such as the following, one right after the other, is not only awkward but might also seem insulting to the respondent.

1. I have an opportunity to interact with my colleagues during work hours.

2. I have few opportunities to interact with my colleagues during work hours.

First, there is no need to ask exactly the same question in a positive and a negative way. Second, if for some reason this is deemed necessary (e.g., to check the consistency of the responses), the two questions should be placed in different parts of the questionnaire, as far apart as possible.

The way questions are sequenced could also introduce certain biases, frequently referred to as the ordering effects. Though randomly placing the questions in the questionnaire would reduce any systematic biases in the response, it is very rarely done, because of subsequent confusion while categorizing, coding, and analyzing the responses.

Classification Data or Personal Information

Classification data, also known as personal information or demographic questions, consist of such information as age, educational level, martial status, and income. Unless absolutely necessary, it is best not to ask for the name of the respondent. If, however, the questionnaire has to be identified with the respondents for any reason, then the questionnaire could be numbered and connected by the researcher to the respondent's name, in a separately maintained, private document. This procedure should be clearly explained to the respondent, however. The reason for using the numerical system in questionnaires is to ensure the anonymity of the respondent even if the questionnaires should fall into someone else's hands.

Whether questions seeking personal information should appear in the beginning or at the end of the questionnaire is a matter of choice for the researcher. Some people advocate asking for personal data at the end rather than at the beginning of the questionnaire (Oppenheim, 1986). Their reasoning may be that by the time the respondent reaches the end of the questionnaire she would have been convinced of the genuineness of the inquiry made by the researcher. Other researchers may prefer to elicit most of the personal information at the very beginning, on the grounds that respondents might have psychologically identified with the questionnaire and feel committed to responding, once they have said something about themselves at the very beginning. Thus whether one asks this information in the beginning or at the end of the questionnaire is a matter of individual choice. However, questions regarding details of income, or other highly sensitive information, if such information is absolutely necessary, are best placed at the very end of the questionnaire.

It is also a wise policy to ask for information regarding age, income, and other sensitive personal questions by providing a range of response options. For example, the variables can be tapped as shown below:

Example 7.1

Age (years)	Annual Income
☐ Under 20	☐ Less than $10,000
☐ 20–30	☐ $10,000–20,000
☐ 31–40	☐ $20,001–30,000
☐ 41–50	☐ $30,001–40,000
☐ 51–60	☐ $40,001–60,000
☐ Over 60	☐ $60,001–80,000
	☐ Over $80,0000

In organizational surveys, it is advisable to obtain certain demographic data such as age, sex, educational level, job level, department, and number of years in the organization, even if the theoretical framework does not include these variables. Such data will help to describe the sample characteristics while one is writing the report. However, when there are only one or two respondents in a department, then asking information that might reveal their identity might be threatening to employees. For instance, if there is only one female in a department, then she might not respond to the question on gender, because it might reveal the source of the data and this is understandable.

Review of Principles of Wording for Questionnaires

Certain principles of wording need to be followed while designing a questionnaire. The questions asked must be appropriate for tapping the variable. The language and wording of the questionnaire should be at a level that is meaningful to the employees. The form and type of questions should be geared to minimizing respondent biases. The sequencing of the questions should facilitate the smooth progression of the respondent through the questionnaire. The personal data should be gathered with sensitivity to the respondents' feelings, and with respect for privacy.

Principles of Measurement

Just as there are rules or guidelines that have to be followed to ensure that the wording of the questionnaire is appropriate to minimize bias, so also are there some principles of measurement that are to be followed to ensure that the data collected are appropriate to test our hypotheses. These principles of measurement encompass the scales and scaling techniques used in measuring concepts, as well as the assessment of reliability and validity of the measures used, which were all discussed in Chapter 6. As we have seen, appropriate scales have to be used depending on the type of data that needs to be obtained. The different scaling mechanisms help us to anchor our scales appropriately. Once data are obtained, the "goodness of data" is assessed through tests of validity and reliability. Validity establishes how well a technique, instrument, or process measures a particular concept, and reliability indicates how stably and consistently the instrument taps the variable. The data have to be obtained in a manner that lends itself to easy categorization and coding, both of which are discussed later.

General Appearance or "Getup" of the Questionnaire

Not only is it important to address issues of wording and measurement in questionnaire design; it is also necessary to pay attention to how the questionnaire looks. An attractive and neat questionnaire with appropriate introduction, instructions, and a well-arrayed set of questions and response alternatives will make it easier for the respondents to answer the items in the questionnaire. A good introduction, well-organized instructions, and neat alignment of the questions are all important. These elements are briefly discussed with examples.

A Good Introduction

A proper introduction that clearly discloses the identity of the researcher and the purpose of the survey is absolutely necessary. It is also essential to establish some rapport with the respondents and motivate them to respond to the questions in the questionnaire willingly and enthusiastically. Assuring confidentiality of the information provided by respondents will ensure less biased answers. The introduction section should end with a courteous note thanking the respondent for taking the time to respond to the survey. The following is an example of an appropriate introduction.

Example 7.2

Southern Illinois University at Carbondale
Carbondale, Illinois 62901
Department of Management

Dear Participant

This questionnaire is designed to study aspects of life at work. The information you provide will help us better understand the quality of our work life. Because *you* are the one who can give us a correct picture of how you experience your work life, I request you to respond to the questions frankly and honestly.

Your response will be kept *strictly confidential.* Only members of the research team will have access to the information you give. In order to ensure the utmost privacy, we have provided an identification number for each participant. This number will be used by us only for follow-up procedures. The numbers, names, and questionnaires will not be made available to anyone other than the research team.

A summary of the results will be mailed to you after the data are analyzed.

Thank you very much for your time and cooperation. I greatly appreciate your organization's and your help in furthering this research endeavor.

Cordially,

(Sd)

Uma Sekaran, Ph.D.
Professor

Organizing Questions, Giving Instructions and Guidance, and Good Alignment

Organizing the questions logically and neatly in appropriate sections and providing instructions on how to complete the items in each section will help the respondents to answer the questions without difficulty. Questions should also be neatly and conveniently organized in such a way that the respondent can read and answer the questionnaire without eyestrain, and with a minimum amount of time and effort.

A specimen of a portion of a questionnaire incorporating the above points follows.

Example 7.3 SECTION TWO: ABOUT WORK LIFE

> The questions below provide descriptions about how you experience your work life. Think in terms of your everyday experience and accomplishments on the job and *circle* the most appropriate response for you.

	Strongly Agree 1	Agree 2	Slightly Agree 3	Neutral 4	Slightly Disagree 5	Disagree 6	Strongly Disagree 7
1. I do my best work when my job assignments are fairly difficult.	1	2	3	4	5	6	7
2. When I have a choice, I try to work in a group instead of by myself.	1	2	3	4	5	6	7
3. In my work assignments, I try to be my own boss.	1	2	3	4	5	6	7
4. I seek an active role in the leadership of a group.	1	2	3	4	5	6	7
5. I try very hard to improve on my past performance at work.	1	2	3	4	5	6	7
6. I pay a good deal of attention to the feelings of others at work.	1	2	3	4	5	6	7
7. I go on my own way at work, regardless of the opinion of others.	1	2	3	4	5	6	7
8. I avoid trying to influence those around me to see things my way.	1	2	3	4	5	6	7
9. I take moderate risks sticking my neck out to get ahead at work.	1	2	3	4	5	6	7
10. I prefer to do my own work letting others do theirs.	1	2	3	4	5	6	7
11. I disregard rules and regulations that hamper my personal freedom.	1	2	3	4	5	6	7

Personal Data. Demographic or personal data could be organized as in the specimen that follows. Note the scaling of the age variable.

Example 7.4   SECTION ONE: ABOUT YOURSELF

Please *circle* the numbers representing appropriate responses for the following items.

---

1. Your Age (years)

1 Under 20
2 20–35
3 36–50
4 51–65
5 Over 65

2. Your Highest Completed Level of Education

1 Elementary school
2 High school
3 College degree
4 Graduate degree
5 Other (specify)

3. Your Sex

1 Female
2 Male

4. Marital Status

1 Married
2 Single
3 Widowed
4 Divorced or separated
5 Other (specify)

5. Number of Preschool Children (under 5 Years of Age)

1 None
2 One
3 Two or more

6. Age of the Eldest Child in Your Care (years)

1 Under 5
2 5–12
3 13–19
4 Over 19
5 Not applicable

7. Number of Years Worked in the Organization

1 Less than 1
2 1–2
3 3–5
4 6–10
5 Over 10

8. Number of Other Organizations Worked for before Joining this Organization

1 None
2 One
3 Two
4 Three
5 Four or more

9. Present Work Shift

1 First
2 Second
3 Third

10. Job Status

1 Top management
2 Middle management
3 First-level supervisor
4 Nonmanagerial

Information on Income and Other Personal Data

Though demographic information can be asked either at the beginning or at the end of the questionnaire, information of a very private and personal nature such as income, if considered absolutely necessary for the survey, should be asked at the end of the questionnaire rather than at the beginning. Also, such questions should be justified by explaining why this information might contribute to knowledge and problem solving, so that respondents do not perceive the questions to be of a prying nature. Shifting such questions to the end would help reduce respondent bias in case the respondent gets irritated by the personal nature of the question. See the example below.

Example 7.5

> Because many people believe that income is a significant factor in explaining employment decisions, the following two questions are very important. Like all other items in this questionnaire, the responses to these two questions will be kept confidential. Please check the most appropriate box that describes your position.

Roughly, my *total yearly* income before taxes and other deductions is

☐ Less than $36,000
☐ $36,001–50,000
☐ $50,001–70,000
☐ $70,001–90,000
☐ Over $90,000

Roughly, the *total yearly income* before taxes and other deductions *of my immediate family*—including my own income, income from other sources, and the income of my spouse—is

☐ Less than $36,000
☐ $36,001–50,000
☐ $50,001–70,000
☐ $70,001–90,000
☐ $90,001–120,000
☐ $120,001–150,000
☐ Over $150,000

Open-Ended Question at the End

The end of the questionnaire could include an open-ended question allowing respondents to comment on any aspect they choose. The questionnaire would end with sincere thanks to respondents. The last part of the questionnaire could look like the following.

Example 7.6   The questions in the survey may not have allowed you to report some things you may want to say about your job, organization, or yourself. Please make additional comments in the space provided.

How did you feel about completing this questionnaire? Check the face in the following diagram that truly reflects your feelings.

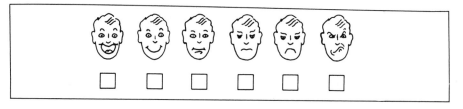

I sincerely appreciate your time and cooperation. Please check to make sure that you have not skipped any questions, and then return the questionnaire.

Review of Questionnaire Design

We have devoted a lot of attention to questionnaire design because questionnaires are one of the most common methods of collecting data. Managers who administer questionnaires or comment on questionnaires to be administered by consultants to members of the organization, as well as those who might be asked to participate in several organizational surveys by other researchers, will find that it is important to know the difference between good and bad questionnaires. The principles of questionnaire design relate to how the questions are worded and measured, and how the entire questionnaire is organized. To minimize respondent biases and measurement errors, all the principles have to be followed carefully.

Questionnaires are most useful as a data-collection method, especially when large numbers of people are to be reached in different geographical regions. Questionnaires are a popular method of collecting data because researchers can obtain data fairly easily, and the questionnaire responses are easily coded. When well-validated instruments are used, the findings of the study benefit the scientific community through replicated results and additions to the theory base.

Do Exercise 7.1.

ELECTRONIC QUESTIONNAIRE DESIGN AND SURVEYS

On-line questionnaire surveys for respondents are possible when microcomputers are hooked up to computer networks. Data disks can also be mailed to respondents, who can use their own personal computers for responding to the questions. These can, of course, be used only when the respondents know how to use the computer and feel comfortable responding in this manner.

Green, Kedia, and Nikhil (1985) have a computer package, CAPPA, which facilitates the preparation and administration of questionnaires, particularly useful for marketing research. The CAPPA system includes ten programs enabling the user to design a sophisticated computerized questionnaire, computerize the data-collection process, and analyze the data collected. It can be run with an IBM/PC, color monitor, and mouse. Better data are expected to result because the respondent can go back and forth and easily change a response, and various on- and off-screen stimuli are provided to sustain respondents' interest.

A program is designed into the CAPPA system that checks for syntactical or logical errors in the coding. Even as the survey is in progress, descriptive summaries of the cumulative data can be obtained either on the screen or in printed form. After data collection is complete, a data-editing program identifies missing or out-of-range data (e.g., a 6 responded to a question on a five-point scale). The researcher can set the parameters for either deleting the missing responses where there are too many, or computing the mean on other responses and substituting this figure for the missing response. CAPPA also includes data analytic programs such as cross-tabs, ANOVA, multiple regression, and others (discussed later in the book). Randomization of questions and the weighting of respondents to assure more representative results (in cases where the sample either overrepresents or underrepresents certain population groups—these are discussed later, in the chapter on Sampling) are stated to be some of the attractive features of CAPPA.

No doubt, in the years to come, several programs will be developed to administer questionnaires electronically. With inexpensive disks, mailing them across the country will not be a problem. Computer literacy would have also advanced significantly by then and nonresponse rates may not be any lower than in mail questionnaires. We can anticipate electronic questionnaire administration to increase in the next decade.

OTHER METHODS OF DATA COLLECTION

Observational Surveys

Whereas interviews and questionnaires elicit responses from the subjects, it is possible to gather data without asking questions of the respondents by observing people in their natural work environment or in the lab setting and recording their behaviors. The researcher can play one of two roles while gathering field observational data: nonparticipant-observer or participant-observer.

Nonparticipant-Observer

The researcher can collect the data in the role of a pure researcher without trying to become an integral part of the organizational system. For example, a researcher might sit in the corner of an office and see and record how the manager spends her time. These activities, carried out over a period of time and including observation of several managers, can allow the researcher to make some generalizations on how managers typically spend their time. By merely observing the activities and recording them on paper, the researcher comes up with some findings. Observers must naturally be physically present at the workplace for extended periods of time; thus observational studies are time consuming.

Participant-Observer

The researcher can also play the role of the participant-observer. Here, the researcher enters the organization or the research setting actually becoming a part of the work team. For instance, if a researcher wants to study group dynamics in work organizations, then she may enter the organization in the role of an employee and observe the dynamics in groups while being a part of the work organization and work groups. Much anthropological research is conducted in this manner, where the researcher becomes a part of the alien culture about which he is interested in knowing more.

Structured versus Unstructured Observational Studies

Thus, observational studies could be of either the nonparticipant-observer or the participant-observer type. Both of these, again, could be either structured or unstructured. Where the observer has a predetermined set of categories of activities or phenomena that she plans to study, it is a structured observational study. Forms for recording the observations can be specifically designed for the purpose. If, however, the observer has no definite ideas of the particular aspects that she wants to focus on in the observation, but records practically everything that is observed, is an unstructured observational study.

Biases in Observational Studies

Data observed from the researcher's point of view are likely to be prone to observer biases. Moreover, where several observers are involved, interobserver reliability has to be established before the data can be accepted. Observer fatigue could also be a source of bias. Observing the happenings day in and day out over extended periods of time could fatigue or bore the observers and introduce biases in the recording of the observations. To minimize observer bias, observers are usually given training on how to observe and what to record. Good observational studies would also establish interobserver reliability.

Respondent bias could also be a threat to the validity of the results of observational studies, because those who are observed may behave differently during the period the study is conducted, especially if the observations are done for a short period of time. However, in studies of longer duration, as the study progresses, the employees become more relaxed and tend to behave more normally. For these reasons, researchers doing observational studies discount the data recorded in the initial few days, if they seem to be quite different from what is observed later.

Projective Methods

Certain ideas and thoughts that cannot be easily verbalized or that remain on unconscious levels in the respondents' minds can usually be brought to the surface through motivational research. This is typically done by trained professionals who apply different probing techniques in order to surface deep-rooted ideas and thoughts in the respondents. Familiar techniques for gathering such data are word associations, sentence completion, thematic apperception tests (TAT), inkblot tests, and the like.

Word-association techniques, such as asking the respondent to quickly associate a word—say, *work*—with the first thing that comes to mind, are often used. The reply is an indication of what work means to the individual. Similarly, sentence completion would have the respondent quickly complete a sentence, such as "Work is _____." One respondent might say, "Work is a lot of fun," whereas another might say "Work is a drudgery." These responses may provide some insights into individuals' feelings and attitudes toward work.

Thematic apperception tests ask the respondent to develop a story around a picture that is shown. Several need patterns and personality characteristics in employees could be traced through these tests. Inkblot tests, another form of motivational research, use colored inkblots that are interpreted by the respondents, who explain what they see in the various patterns and colors.

Although these types of projective tests are useful for tapping attitudes and feelings that are difficult to obtain otherwise, they cannot be engaged in by researchers who are not trained to do such research.

Consumer preferences, buying attitudes and behaviors, product development, and other marketing research strategies make substantial use of in-depth probing. TAT and inkblot tests are on their way out in marketing research since advertisers and others are now utilizing the sentence completion tests and word association tests more frequently. Sketch drawings, collages from magazine pictures, filling in the balloon captions of cartoon characters, and other strategies are now being followed to see how individuals associate different products, brands, advertisements, and so on. Agencies frequently ask subjects to sketch "typical" users of various brands and narrate stories about them. The messages conveyed through the unsophisticated drawings are said to be very powerful, helping different marketing strategies to be developed (see *New York,* May 8, 1989, pp. 33–40).

The idea behind motivational research is that "emotionality" ("I identify with it" feeling) rather than "rationality" ("it is good for me" thought)—which is what keeps a product or practice alive—is captured. Emotional bonds are difficult to overcome and are powerful motivators of action. Capturing them is hence useful. The failed attempts to trade in the New Coke for Coke Classic is as an oft-cited example of the failure to capture the emotionality aspect. Emotionality is clearly at the nonrational, subconscious level, lending itself to be captured by projective techniques alone.

SOME SPECIAL DATA SOURCES

Focus Groups

Focus groups are relatively inexpensive and can provide fairly dependable data within a short time frame. Focus groups typically consist of eight to twelve members randomly chosen, with a moderator leading discussions regarding a particular topic, item, or product. Focus groups have been credited with illuminating why certain products are not doing well, why certain advertising strategies are effective, why specific management techniques do not work, and so on.

Static and Dynamic Panels

Where the effects of certain interventions or changes are to be studied over a period of time, panel studies are very useful. Several individuals are chosen to serve as panel members for a research study. For instance, if the effects of a proposed advertisement for a certain brand of coffee are to be assessed quickly, the panel members can be exposed to the advertisement and their intentions of purchasing the brand can be assessed. This can be taken as the response that could be expected of consumers if, in fact, they were exposed to the advertisement. Six months later, the product manager might think of changing the flavor of the same product and might explore the effects of it on this panel. Thus, a continuing set of "experts" will provide the sample base or serve as the sounding board for assessing the effects of change—that is, the introduction of a new variable. Such members are called a panel, and research that uses this panel is called a panel study.

The Nielsen Television Index is based on the television viewing patterns of a panel. The index is designed to provide estimates of the size and nature of the audience for individual television programs. The data are gathered through Audimeter instruments attached to the television sets in approximately 1200 cooperating households. The Audimeters are connected to a central computer, which records when the set is on and to what channel it is tuned. From these data, Nielson develops estimates of the number and percentage of all TV households viewing a given TV show (Churchill, 1987). Other panels used in marketing research include the National Purchase Diary Panel, the National Family Opinion Panel, and the Consumer Mail Panel.

Panels can be either static (i.e., the same members serve on the panel over extended periods of time) or dynamic (i.e., the members are changed from time to time in order to test the effects of different changes). The main advantages of the static panel is that it offers a good and sensitive measurement of the changes that take place between two points in time—a much better measure than using two different groups at two different times. The disadvantage, however, lies in the fact that the panel members could become so sensitive to the changes as a result of being continuously interviewed that their opinions might no longer be representative of what the others in the population might think. Members could also drop out of the panel from time to time for various reasons. The advantages and disadvantages of the dynamic panel are the reverse of the ones discussed for the static panel.

Unobtrusive Measures

Another important source of data consists of sources that are not people. For instance, the wear and tear on journals in a university library could be a good indication of their popularity, their usage, or both. The number of different brands of soft drink cans found in trashbags could be a measure of the consumption levels of different brands of soft drinks. Signatures on checks exposed to ultraviolet rays could be indicative of the extent of forgery and frauds; actuarial records are good sources for determining the births, marriages, and deaths in a community; company records disclose a lot of personal information about employees, the extent of company efficiency, and other data as well. Thus these unobtrusive sources of data and their use are also important in research.

MULTIMETHODS OF DATA COLLECTION

Because almost all data-collection methods have some biases associated with them, collecting data through multimethods and from multisources lends rigor to research. For instance, if the responses collected through interviews, questionnaires, and observation are strongly correlated with each other, then we will have more confidence about the goodness of the data that are being collected. If there are discrepancies in how the respondent answers the same question when interviewed, as opposed to how she answers the question in a questionnaire, then we would be inclined to discard the data as being biased.

Likewise, if data obtained from several sources are highly similar, we would have more faith in the goodness of the data. For example, if an employee rates his performance as four on a 5-point scale, and his supervisor rates him the same way, we may be inclined to think that he is perhaps a better than average worker. In contrast, if he gives himself a five on the 5-point scale and his supervisor gives him a rating of two, then we will not know to what extent there is a bias and from which source. Therefore, high correlations among data obtained regarding the same variable from different sources lend more credibility to the research instruments and to the data obtained through these instruments (refer to the discussions in the previous chapter). Good researchers try to obtain data from multiple sources and through multiple data-collection methods. Such research, though, would be more costly and time consuming.

REVIEW OF THE ADVANTAGES AND DISADVANTAGES OF VARIOUS DATA—COLLECTION METHODS AND WHEN TO USE EACH

Having discussed the various data-collection methods, we will now briefly recount the advantages and disadvantages of the three most commonly used data-collection methods—interviews, questionnaires, and observation—and see when each method can be most profitably used.

Face-to-face interviews provide rich data, offer the opportunity to establish rapport with the interviewees, and help to explore and understand complex issues. Many ideas that are ordinarily difficult to articulate can also be surfaced and discussed during such interviews. On the negative side, face-to-face interviews have the potential for introducing interviewer bias and can be expensive if a big sample of subjects is to be personally interviewed. Where several interviewers are involved, adequate training becomes a necessary first step.

Face-to-face interviews are best suited at the exploratory stages of research when the researcher is trying to get a handle on concepts or the situational factors.

Telephone interviews help to contact subjects dispersed over various geographic regions and obtain responses from them immediately on contact. This is an efficient way of collecting data when one has specific questions to ask, needs the responses quickly, and has the sample spread over a wide geographic area. On the negative side, the interviewer cannot observe the nonverbal responses of the respondents, and the interviewee can block a call.

Telephone interviews are best suited for asking structured questions where responses need to be obtained quickly from a sample that is geographically spread.

Personally administering questionnaires to groups of individuals helps to establish rapport with the respondents while introducing the survey, provide clarifications sought by the respondents on the spot, and collect the questionnaires immediately after they are completed. In that sense, there is a 100 percent response rate. On the negative side, administering questionnaires personally is expensive, especially if the sample is geographically dispersed.

Personally administered questionnaires are best suited when data are collected from organizations that are located in close proximity to each other and groups of respondents can be conveniently assembled in the company's conference (or other) rooms.

Mailed questionnaires are advantageous when responses to many questions have to be obtained from a sample that is geographically dispersed and when conducting telephone interviews to obtain the same data is difficult, more expensive, or not feasible. On the negative side, mailed questionnaires usually have a low response rate and one cannot be sure if the data obtained are biased because the nonrespondents may be different from the those who did respond.

The mailed questionnaire survey is best suited (and perhaps the only alternative open to the researcher) when a substantial amount of information is to be obtained through structured questions, at minimal costs, from a sample that is widely dispersed geographically.

Observational studies help to comprehend complex issues through direct observation (either as a participant- or a nonparticipant-observer) and then, if possible, asking questions to seek clarifications on certain issues. The data obtained are rich and uncontaminated by self-report biases. On the negative side, they are expensive since long periods of observation (usually encompassing several months) are required, and observer bias may well be present in the data.

Because of the costs involved, very few observational studies are done in business. Henry Mintzberg's study of managerial work is one of the best known published works that used an observational data-collection method. Observational studies are best suited for research requiring non-self-report descriptive data. That is, when behaviors are to be understood without asking the respondents themselves for the information. Observational studies can also capture "in-the-stores buying behaviors."

SUMMARY

In this chapter we examined various data-collection methods and different primary sources of data. We discussed the advantages and disadvantages as well as the biases embedded in each data-collection method. We also traced the current level of impact of personal computers in data collection. Because of the inherent biases in each of the data-collection methods, obtaining data from multiple sources and through multiple methods was recommended. The choices, of course, will be governed by cost considerations and the extent of rigor desired for a given research goal.

In the next chapter we will discuss sampling designs and how data can be collected from samples to make the results generalizable to the population.

DISCUSSION QUESTIONS AND POINTS TO PONDER

1. As a manager who has invited a research team to come in, study, and offer some suggestions on how to improve the performance of your staff, what steps would you take to allay the apprehensions of your employees even before the research team sets foot in your department?
2. What is bias, and how can it be reduced while interviewing?
3. Explain the principles of wording, stating how these are important in questionnaire design, citing examples not in the book.
4. What are projective techniques and how can they be profitably used?
5. Describe the different data sources, explaining their usefulness and disadvantages.
6. How are multiple methods of data collection and from multiple sources related to the reliability and validity of the measures?

7. "Every data-collection method has its own built-in biases. Therefore, resorting to multimethods of data collection is only going to compound the biases." How would you critique this statement?

8. "One way to deal with discrepancies found in the data obtained from multiple sources is to average the figures and take the mean as the value on the variable." What is your reaction to this?

9. The fewer the biases in measurement and in the data-collection procedures, the more scientific the research. Why?

EXERCISES

Exercise 7.1   The president of Serakan Co. suspects that most of the 500 male and female employees in her organization are somewhat alienated from work. She also suspects that those who are more involved (less alienated) are also the ones who are more satisfied with their work lives.

Design a questionnaire the president could use to test her hypotheses.

Exercise 7.2   The president of Anisha, Inc. suspects that most of the 150 male and female managerial employees in her company are concerned that promotion would mean relocation sooner or later, and hence are not accepting promotions. This also apparently has an effect on their satisfaction with working for the organization.

Design a questionnaire for the president that would shed some light on what exactly is happening.

Exercise 7.3   A production manager wants to assess the reactions of the blue-collar workers in his department (including foremen) to the introduction of computer-integrated manufacturing (CIM) systems. He would particularly like to know how they would perceive the effects of (CIM) on:

a. their future jobs
b. additional training that they will have to receive
c. future job advancement.

Design a questionnaire for the production manager.

CHAPTER 8

SAMPLING

TOPICS DISCUSSED

POPULATION, ELEMENT, POPULATION FRAME, SAMPLE, SUBJECT

SAMPLING

REASONS FOR SAMPLING

REPRESENTATIVENESS OF THE SAMPLE

PROBABILITY SAMPLING
- Simple Random Sampling
- Systematic Sampling
- Stratified Random Sampling: Proportionate and Disproportionate
- Cluster Sampling: Single-stage and Multistage Clusters
- Area Sampling
- Double Sampling

NONPROBABILITY SAMPLING
- Convenience Sampling
- Judgment Sampling
- Quota Sampling

ISSUES OF PRECISION AND CONFIDENCE IN DETERMINING SAMPLE SIZE

PRECISION AND CONFIDENCE—TRADE-OFFS

SAMPLE DATA AND HYPOTHESIS TESTING

SAMPLE SIZE

EFFICIENCY IN SAMPLING

CHAPTER OBJECTIVES

After completing this chapter you should be able to:

1. Define sampling, sample, population, element, subject, and population frame.
2. Describe and discuss the different sampling designs.
3. Identify the use of appropriate sampling designs for different research purposes.
4. Explain how to use sample data to test hypotheses.
5. Discuss precision and confidence.

6. Estimate sample size.

7. Discuss the factors to be taken into consideration for determining sample size.

8. Discuss efficiency in sampling.

9. Discuss generalizability in the context of sampling designs.

10. Apply the material learned in this unit to class assignments and projects.

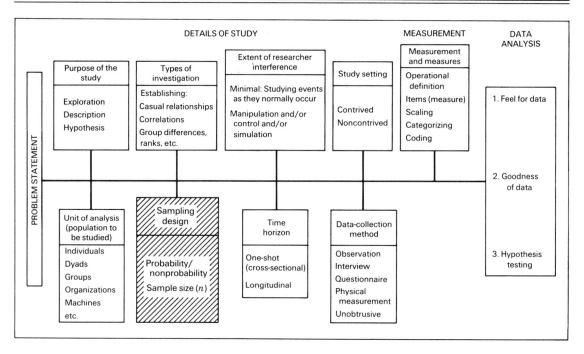

Consider the following two items from the *Wall Street Journal* and *Inc.*

1. Surveys, "properly prepared and correctly targeted, can provide invaluable information on product and market trends and customer attitudes. It can position a company as a concerned and well-informed expert with potential customers and purchasing executives," wrote Senior Vice President of Minolta Corp.'s Business Equipment Division, Mr. Al Kusada, in *Wall Street Journal* (February 1, 1988, p. 26).

2. "Using customers to help develop new products, experts warn, is a dangerous proposition. Often their advice will take you nowhere. Sometimes it can lead you catastrophically astray". *But Technosonic Industries don't buy this. They bet their business on the focus group* (*Inc*, September 1989, p. 91).

The above two messages, individually and jointly, drive home a very important point for researchers. Surveys are useful and powerful, but they can do more harm than good if not *correctly targeted*. In a sense, this *correct targeting* is what a sampling design is all about. We had earlier noted in Chapter 4 that sampling is one of the critical research design decisions (see shaded portion in figure prepage). We will discuss sampling, which includes both the methods used to select the sample from the population and the sample size necessary to generalize the findings from the sample data to the total population, in some depth in this chapter. But first, we need to understand some terms that will be frequently used in the discussions that follow.

POPULATION, ELEMENT, POPULATION FRAME, SAMPLE, AND SUBJECT

Population

Population refers to the entire group of people, events, or things of interest that the researcher wishes to investigate. If the researcher is interested in investigating the savings habits of blue-collar workers in the plastics industry in the United States, then all blue-collar workers in the plastics industry throughout the country will form the population. If an organizational consultant is interested in studying the effects of a four-day workweek on the white-collar workers in a telephone company in Southern Illinois, then all white-collar workers in the telephone company in Southern Illinois will form the population. If regulators want to know how patients in nursing homes run by Beverly Enterprises are cared for, then all the patients in all the nursing homes run by Beverly Enterprises will form the population. If, however, the regulators are interested in only a particular nursing home in Michigan run by Beverly Enterprises (see *Business Week,* November 7, 1988, p. 124), then only the patients in that specific nursing home will form the population.

Element

An element is a single member of the population. If 1000 blue-collar workers in a particular organization happen to be the population of interest to a researcher, each single blue-collar worker in this population is an element. If 500 pieces of machinery are to be approved after inspecting a few, there would be 500 elements in this population.

Population Frame

The population frame is a listing of all the elements in the population from which the sample is to be drawn. The payroll of an organization could be the population frame, if members of the organization are to be studied. Likewise, the university registry containing a listing of all students, faculty, administrators, and support staff in the university during a particular academic year or semester could serve as the population frame for a study of the university population. Likewise, a roster of class students could be the population frame for the study of students in a class. The telephone directory is also frequently used as a population frame for some types of studies, even though it has an inherent bias inasmuch as some numbers are unlisted.

Although the population frame is useful in providing a listing of each element in the population, it may not always be a current, updated document. For instance, members who have just left the organization or dropped out of the university, as well as members who have just joined the organization or the university may not appear in the organization's payroll or the university registers on a given day. Telephones newly installed during the last few days or disconnected during that time, likewise will not be represented in the current telephone directory. Hence, though the population frame may be available in many cases, it may not always be current. The researcher might recognize this problem and may not be too concerned about it, because a few additions and deletions may not make much difference to the study. Even if the researcher is concerned about it, and spends time and effort trying to obtain an updated population frame, there is no guarantee that the new population frame will give an accurate listing of all the elements, for the reasons already discussed.

Sample

A sample is a subset of the population. It comprises some members selected from the population. In other words, some, but not all, elements of the population would form the sample. If 200 members are drawn from a population of 1000 blue-collar workers, these 200 members form the sample for the study. That is, by studying these 200 members, the researcher would draw conclusions about the entire population of the 1000 blue-collar workers considered in the study.

A sample is thus a subgroup or subset of the population. By studying the sample, the researcher would be able to draw conclusions that would be generalizable to the population of interest.

Subject

A subject is a single member of the sample, just as an element is a single member of the population. In the above example, 200 members from the total population of 1000 blue-collar workers formed the sample for the study; each blue-collar worker in the sample is a subject. If a sample of 50 machines from a total of 500 machines is to be inspected, then every one of the 50 machines is a subject, just as every single machine in the total population of 500 machines is an element.

SAMPLING

Sampling is the process of selecting a sufficient number of elements from the population so that by studying the sample, and understanding the properties or the characteristics of the sample subjects, we will be able to generalize the properties

Figure 8.1

The relationship between sample and population

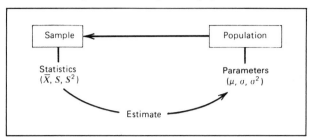

or characteristics to the population elements. The characteristics of the population such as μ (the population mean), σ (the population standard deviation), and σ^2 (the population variance) are referred to as the *parameters* of the population. The central tendencies, the dispersions, and other statistics in the sample of interest to the research are treated as approximations of the central tendencies, dispersions, and other parameters of the population. As such, all conclusions drawn about the sample being studied are generalized to the population. In other words, the sample statistics are used as estimates of the population parameters. Figure 8.1 shows the relationship between the sample and the population.

Reasons for Sampling

The reasons for using a sample rather than collecting data from the entire population are fairly obvious. In research investigations involving several hundreds and even thousands of elements, it would be practically impossible to collect data from, or to test, or to examine every element. Even if it were possible, it would be prohibitive in terms of time, costs, and other human resources. Studying a sample rather than the entire population is also sometimes likely to lead to more reliable results, mostly because there will be less fatigue, and hence fewer errors in collecting data, especially when the elements involved are many in number. In a few cases, it would also be impossible to use the entire population to know or test something. Consider, for instance, the case of electric bulbs. In testing the life of a batch of bulbs, if we were to burn every bulb produced, there would be none to sell!

Representativeness of Samples

The opening statements in the chapter quoting the *Wall Street Journal* and *Inc.* underscore the need for choosing the right sample for any study. Rarely will a sample be the exact replica of the population from which it is drawn. For instance, very few sample means ($\bar{X}$) are likely to be exactly equal to the population means (μ). Nor is the standard deviation of the sample (S) going to be the same as the standard deviation of the population (σ). However, if we choose the sample in a scientific way, we can be reasonably sure that the sample statistic (e.g., $\bar{X}$, S, S^2) will be as close to the population parameters as possible (i.e., μ, σ, σ^2). To put it differently, we should be able to choose the sample in such a way that it is representative of the population it is expected to characterize.

NORMALITY OF DISTRIBUTIONS

Many attributes or characteristics in the population are generally normally distributed. That is, attributes such as height and weight are such that most people will be clustered around the mean and there will be a few people at the extremes who are either very tall or very short, very heavy or very light, and so on, as indicated in Figure 8.2. If we are to estimate the population characteristics reasonably precisely from the characteristics represented in a sample, the sample has to be chosen such that the distribution of the characteristics of interest follows the same type of normal distribution in the sample as it does in the population. From the central limit theorem, we know that the sampling distribution of the sample mean is normally distributed. Irrespective of whether or not the attributes in the population are normally distributed, if we take *large enough* samples and *choose* the sample carefully, we will have a sampling distribution of the mean that has normality. This is the reason that the two important issues in sampling are the sample size (n) and the sampling design. When the properties of the population are not overrepresented or underrepresented in the sample, we will have a representative sample. When a sample consists of elements in the population that have extremely high values on the variable we are studying, the sample mean $\bar{X}$, will be far higher than the population mean μ. If, in contrast, the sample subjects consist of elements in the population with extremely low values on the variable of interest, the sample mean $\bar{X}$ will be much lower than the true population mean μ. If our sampling design and sample size are right, however, the sample mean $\bar{X}$ will be within close range of the true population mean μ. Thus through appropriate sampling designs, we can ensure that the sample subjects are not chosen from the extremes, but are representative of the true properties of the population. The more representative the

Figure 8.2
Normal distribution in a population.

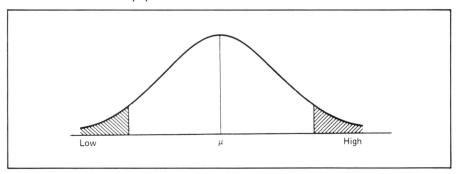

sample is of the population, the more generalizable are the findings of the research. Recall that generalizability is one of the hallmarks of scientific research, as we saw in Chapter 1.

Though we may be concerned about generalizability, and hence be particular about choosing representative samples for most research, at some stages of research we may not be very concerned about generalizability. For instance, at the exploratory stages of fact finding, the researcher may be interested only in "getting a handle" on what is going on in the situation, for which purpose the most conveniently available people may be interviewed. The same is true when time is of the essence in getting some information rather than getting the most accurate information. For instance, a film agency might want to find out quickly the impact on the viewers of a newly released film exhibited the previous evening. The interviewer might ask questions of the first twenty people she can find. On the basis of their replies, the interviewer may form an opinion as to the possible success of the film. In such cases, having some quick information may be more important than having the most representative facts. It should, however, be noted that the results obtained from such convenience samples are not reliable and can never be generalized to the population. We will discuss the different types of sampling designs now.

PROBABILITY AND NONPROBABILITY SAMPLING

There are two major types of sampling designs: probability and nonprobability sampling. In probability sampling, the elements in the population have some known chance or probability of being selected as sample subjects. In nonprobability sampling, the elements do not have a known or predetermined chance of being selected as subjects. Probability sampling designs are used when the representativeness of the sample is of importance for purposes of wider generalizability. When time or other factors rather than generalizability become critical, nonprobability sampling is generally used.

Each of these two major designs has different sampling strategies. Depending on the extent of generalizability desired, the availability of time and other resources, and the purpose for which the study is done, different types of probability and nonprobability sampling designs will be chosen. The various types available are discussed next.

Probability Sampling

Probability sampling can be either unrestricted (or simple random sampling) or restricted (or complex probability sampling) in nature.

Unrestricted or Simple Random Sampling

In the unrestricted probability sampling design, more commonly known as simple random sampling, every element in the population has a *known* and *equal* chance of being selected as a subject. For instance, let us say there are 1000 elements in the population, and we need a sample of 100. Suppose we were to drop chits in a hat, each bearing the name of one of the elements, and we were to draw 100 of those names from the hat with our eyes closed. We know that each one of those elements has a 100/1000 chance of being drawn. In other words we know that the probability of any one of them being chosen as a subject is .1, and we also know that each single element in the hat has the same or equal probability of being chosen. When we thus draw the elements from the population, it is most likely that the distribution patterns of the characteristics we are interested in investigating in the population are also likewise distributed in the subjects we draw for our sample. This sampling design, known as simple random sampling, has the least bias and offers the most generalizability. However, this sampling process could become cumbersome and expensive, in addition to the fact that an entirely updated listing of the population may not always be available, as discussed earlier. For these and other reasons, other probability sampling designs are often chosen instead.

Restricted or Complex Probability Sampling

As an alternative to the simple random (unrestricted) sampling design, several complex probability sampling (restricted probability) designs can be used. These probability sampling procedures offer a viable, and sometimes more efficient alternative to the cumbersome unrestricted design we just discussed. Efficiency is gained in that more information can be obtained for a given sample size using some of the complex probability sampling procedures than using the simple random sampling design. The five most common complex probability sampling designs—systematic sampling, stratified random sampling, cluster sampling, area sampling, and double sampling—will now be discussed.

Systematic Sampling. The systematic sampling design involves drawing every nth element in the population starting with a randomly chosen element between 1 and n. The procedure follows the example cited below.

If we want a sample of 35 households from a total population of 260 houses in a particular locality, then we could sample every seventh house starting from a random number from 1 to 7. Let us say that the random number is 7, then houses numbered 7, 14, 21, 28, and so on, would be sampled until the 35 houses are obtained for the sample.

The one problem that the researcher has to be aware of in the systematic sampling design is the probability of a systematic bias creeping into the sample. In the above example, for instance, let us say that every seventh house happens to be a corner house. If the focus of research in the study conducted by the construction industry is to control "noise pollution" experienced by residents using appropriate filtering materials, then the residents of corner houses may not be exposed to as much noise from the neighboring houses as the houses that are in between. Hence, when information on noise levels is gathered from corner house dwellers, the researcher might be collecting biased data. The likelihood of drawing incorrect conclusions from such data is very high. Thus the scope for systematic bias is present in systematic sampling, and the researcher must consider his plans carefully and make sure that the systematic sampling plan is appropriate for the study before making the decision to use it. For market surveys, consumer attitude surveys, and the like, the telephone directory—which, as stated before, has its inherent biases—frequently serves as the population frame for systematic sampling plans.

Stratified Random Sampling. While sampling helps to estimate population parameters, there may be identifiable subgroups of elements within the population that may be expected to have different parameters on a variable of interest to the researcher. For example, the entire organization will form the population for study for the Human Resources Management Director interested in assessing the extent of felt training needs of employees in the system. But the extent, quality, and intensity of training desired by middle-level managers, lower-level managers, first-line supervisors, computer analysts, clerical workers, and so on, will be different for each group. Knowing the kinds of differences that exist will help in the development of useful and meaningful training programs in the organization. For this purpose, data will have to be collected in a manner that would help the assessment of needs at each subgroup level in the population. The unit of analysis then, would be at each group level—middle-level managers, lower-level managers, and so on. The stratified random sampling process will allow data to be collected and meaningfully analyzed in this manner.

Stratified random sampling, as its name implies, involves a process of stratification or segregation, followed by random selection of subjects from each stratum. In stratified random sampling the population is first divided into mutually exclusive groups that are relevant, appropriate, and meaningful in the context of the study. For instance, if the President of a company is concerned about low motivational levels or high absenteeism rates among the employees, it makes sense to stratify the population of organizational members according to their job levels. When the data are collected and the analysis done, it may so happen that contrary to expectation, it is the middle-level managers that are found to be not motivated. This information will help the President to focus on taking action at the right level and think of better ways to motivate middle-level managers. Tracing the differences in the parameters of the subgroups within a population would not have been possible without the stratified random sampling procedure. If either the simple random sampling or the systematic sampling procedure was used in a case such as this, then the high motivation at some job levels and the low motivation at other levels would have canceled each other out, thus masking the real problems that exist at a particular level or levels.

Stratification also helps when research questions such as the following are to be answered:

1. Are the machinists more accident prone than clerical workers?
2. Are Hispanics more loyal to the organization than American Indians?

Stratifying customers on the basis of life stages, income levels, and the like to study buying patterns, and stratifying companies according to size, industry, profits, and so forth to study stock market reactions, are all common examples of the use of stratification as a sampling design technique.

Stratification is an efficient research sampling design; that is, it provides more information with a given sample size. Stratification should follow the lines that are appropriate to the research question. If we are studying consumer preferences for a product, stratification of the population could be by geographical areas, market segments, consumer age, consumer gender, or various combinations of these. If an organization is contemplating budget cuts, the effects of these cuts on employee attitudes can be studied with stratification by department, function, or region. Stratification ensures homogeneity within each stratum (i.e., very few differences or dispersions on the variable of interest within each stratum), but heterogeneity between strata. In other words, there will be more between-group differences than within-group differences.

Proportionate and Disproportionate Stratified Random Sampling.   Once the population has been stratified in some meaningful way, a sample of members from each stratum can be drawn using either a simple random sampling or a systematic sampling procedure. The subjects drawn from each stratum can be either proportionate or disproportionate to the number of elements in the stratum. For instance, if an organization consists of 10 top managers, 30 middle managers, 50 lower-level managers, 100 supervisors, 500 clerks, and 20 secretaries, and a stratified sample of about 140 people is needed for a survey, the researcher might decide that 20 percent of members from each stratum will be included in the sample. That is, members represented in the sample from each stratum will be proportionate to the total number of elements in the respective strata. This would mean that 2 from the top, 6 from the middle, and 10 from the lower levels of management will be included in the sample. In addition, 20 supervisors, 100 clerks, and 4 secretaries will be represented in the sample, as shown in the third column of Table 8.1. This type of sampling is called a proportionate stratified random sampling design.

In situations like the one above, researchers might sometimes be concerned that obtaining information from just 2 members at the top and 6 from the middle levels would not be representative of how members at those levels would respond. Therefore, a researcher might decide to use a disproportionate stratified random

Table 8.1
Proportionate and Disproportionate Stratified Random Sampling

Job Level	Number of Elements	Number of Subjects in the Sample	
		Proportionate Sampling (20% of the elements)	Disproportionate Sampling
Top management	10	2	7
Middle-level management	30	6	15
Lower-level management	50	10	20
Supervisors	100	20	30
Clerks	500	100	60
Secretaries	20	4	10
Total	710	142	142

sampling procedure instead. Keeping the sample size the same, the number of subjects from each stratum will now be altered. Such a sampling design is illustrated in the far right-hand column in Table 8.1. The idea here is that the 60 clerks might be considered adequate to represent the population of 500 clerks; 7 out of 10 managers at the top level would also be considered an adequate representation of the top managers, and likewise 15 out of the 30 managers at the middle level. This redistribution of the numbers in the strata would be considered more appropriate and representative for the study than the previous sampling design.

Disproportionate sampling decisions are made either when some stratum or strata are too small or too large, or when there is more variability suspected within a particular stratum—for example, the educational levels among supervisors may range from elementary school to master's degrees, and educational level might be expected to influence perceptions—in which case more people will be sampled at this level. Disproportionate sampling is sometimes done when it is easier, simpler, and less expensive to collect data from one or more strata than from others.

In summary, stratified random sampling involves stratifying the elements along meaningful lines and taking proportionate or disproportionate samples from the strata. This sampling design is more efficient than the simple random sampling design because, for the same sample size, we get more representativeness from each important segment of the population and obtain more valuable and differentiated information with respect to each group.

Cluster Sampling. Groups or chunks of elements that, ideally, would have heterogeneity among the members within each group are chosen for study in cluster sampling. This is in contrast to choosing some elements from the population as in simple random sampling, or stratifying and then choosing members from the strata as in stratified random sampling, or choosing every nth element in the population as in systematic sampling. When several groups with intragroup heterogeneity and intergroup homogeneity are found, then a random sampling of the clusters or groups can ideally be done with information gathered from each of the members in the randomly chosen clusters. Ad hoc organizational committees drawn from various departments to offer inputs to the Company President, to enable him to make decisions on product development, budget allocations, marketing strategies, and the like, are a good example of different clusters. Each of these clusters or groups contains a heterogeneous collection of members with different interests, orientations, values, philosophy, and vested interests, drawn from different departments to offer a variety of perspectives. Drawing on their individual and combined insights, the president is able to make final decisions on strategic moves for the company. Cluster samples offer more heterogeneity within groups and more homogeneity among groups—the reverse of what we find in stratified random sampling, where there is homogeneity within each group and heterogeneity across groups.

Cluster sampling technique is not very common in organizational research since, as in the case of the committee example cited above, duplication of members in several clusters is possible. Moreover, naturally occurring clusters, such as clusters of residents, buyers, students, or shops, do not have much heterogeneity among the elements. In fact, there is more intracluster homogeneity than heterogeneity in such clusters. Hence, cluster sampling, though less costly, does not offer much efficiency in terms of precision or confidence in the results. In many cases, though, cluster sampling offers convenience. For example it is easier to inspect an assortment of units packed inside, say, four boxes (i.e., all the elements in four clusters) than to open thirty boxes in a shipment in order to inspect a few units at random.

Single-stage and Multistage Cluster Sampling.   We have thus far been discussing single-stage cluster sampling, which involves the division of the population into convenient clusters, randomly choosing the required number of clusters as sample subjects, and investigating all the elements in each of the randomly chosen clusters. Cluster sampling can also be done in several stages, and is then called multistage cluster sampling. If we were to do a national survey of the average monthly bank deposits, for instance, cluster sampling would first be used to select the urban, semiurban, and rural geographical locations for study. At the next stage, particular areas in each of these locations would be chosen. At the third stage, banks within each area would be chosen. In other words, multistage cluster sampling involves a probability sampling of the primary sampling units; from each of these primary units, a probability sample of the secondary sampling units is then drawn; in turn, a third level of probability sampling is done from each of these secondary units, and so on, until we have reached the final stage of breakdown for the sample units, when we will sample every member in those units.

Area Sampling.   When the research pertains to populations within identifiable geographical areas such as counties, city blocks, or particular boundaries within a locality, area sampling can be done. Area sampling is a form of cluster sampling within an area. Sampling the needs of consumers before opening a 24-hour convenience store in a particular part of the town would involve area sampling. Area sampling is less expensive than most other probability sampling designs, and it is not dependent on a population frame. A city map showing the blocks of the city would be adequate information to allow a researcher to take a sample of the blocks and obtain data from the residents therein.

Double Sampling.   When a sample is used in a study to collect some preliminary information of interest, and later a subsample of this primary sample is used to examine the matter in more detail, such a sampling design is called double sampling. For example, a structured interview might indicate that a subgroup of the respondents has more insight into the problems of the organization. These respondents might be interviewed again with additional questions. This research would have adopted a double sampling procedure.

Review of Probability Sampling Designs

There are two basic probability sampling plans: the unrestricted or simple random sampling, and the restricted or complex probability sampling plans. In the simple random sampling design, every element in the population has a known and equal chance of being selected as a subject. The complex probability plan consists of five different sampling designs. Of these five, the cluster sampling design is probably the least expensive as well as the least dependable. The stratified random sampling design is probably the most efficient in the sense that for the same number of sample subjects it offers more precise and detailed information. The systematic sampling design has the built-in hazard of possible systematic bias. Area sampling is a form of cluster sampling, and double sampling takes place when a subgroup of a sample is used a second time to obtain more information.

Nonprobability Sampling

In nonprobability sampling designs, the elements in the population do not have any probabilities attached to their being chosen as sample subjects. This means that the findings from the study of the sample cannot be confidently generalized to the population. As stated earlier, however, researchers may at times be less concerned about generalizability than they are about obtaining some preliminary information in a quick and inexpensive way. They would then resort to nonprobability sampling. Some of the nonprobability sampling plans are more dependable than others and could offer some important leads to potentially useful information with regard to the population. The nonprobability sampling designs, which fit into the broad categories of convenience and purposive sampling, will be discussed next.

Convenience Sampling

As its name implies, convenience sampling involves collecting information from members of the population who are conveniently available to provide this information. One would expect that the "Pepsi Challenge" contest was administered on a convenience sampling basis. Such a contest, with the purpose of determining whether people prefer one product over another, might be set up at a shopping mall visited by many shoppers. Those who would be inclined to take the test might form the sample for the study of how many people prefer Pepsi over Coke or product X over product Y. Such a sample is a convenience sample.

Consider another example. A convenience sample of five officers who attended the competitor's showcase demonstration at the County Fair the previous evening offered the Vice President of the company a good idea of the "new" products of the competitor and their pricing strategies.

Purposive Sampling

Instead of obtaining information from those who are most conveniently available, it might sometimes become necessary to obtain information from specific targets—that is, specific types of people who will be able to provide the desired information, either because they are the only ones who can give the needed information, or because they conform to some criteria set by the researcher. Such types of sampling designs are called purposive sampling, and the two major types—judgment sampling and quota sampling—will now be explained.

Judgment Sampling. Judgment sampling involves the choice of subjects who are in the best position to provide the information required. For instance, if a researcher wants to find out what it takes for women managers to make it to the top, the only people who can give firsthand information are the women managers who are the presidents, vice-presidents, and important top-level executives in work organizations. Having themselves gone through the experiences and processes, they might be expected to have expert knowledge, and perhaps be able to provide good data or information to the researcher. Thus, the judgment sampling design is used when a limited category of people have the information that is sought. In such cases, any type of probability sampling across a cross section of people is purposeless and not useful. Although judgment sampling may curtail the generalizability of the findings due to the fact that we are using a sample of experts who are conveniently available to us, it is the only viable sampling method for obtaining the type of information that is required from very specific pockets of people who possess the knowledge and can give the information sought.

Quota Sampling.   Quota sampling is a form of proportionate stratified sampling, in which a predetermined proportion of people are sampled from different groups, but on a convenience basis. For instance, it may be surmised that the work attitudes of blue-collar workers in an organization are quite different from those of white-collar workers. If there are 60 percent blue-collar workers and 40 percent white-collar workers in this organization, and if a total of 30 people are to be interviewed to find the answer to the research question, then a quota of 18 blue-collar workers and 12 white-collar workers will form the sample, because these numbers represent 60 and 40 percent of the sample size. The first 18 conveniently available blue-collar workers and 12 white-collar workers will be sampled according to this quota. Needless to say, the sample may not be totally representative of the population; hence the generalizability of the findings will be restricted. However, the convenience it offers in terms of effort, costs, and time makes quota sampling attractive for some research efforts. Quota sampling also becomes a necessity when a subset of the population is underrepresented in the organization—for example, minority groups, foremen, and so on.

Review of Nonprobability Sampling Designs

There are two main types of nonprobability sampling designs: convenience sampling and purposive sampling. Convenience sampling is the least reliable of all sampling designs in terms of generalizability, but sometimes it may be the only viable alternative when quick and timely information is needed. Purposive sampling plans fall into two categories: judgment and quota sampling designs. Judgment sampling, though restricted in generalizability, may sometimes be the best sampling design choice, especially when there is a limited population that can supply the information needed. Quota sampling, though not very reliable for generalization, is often used for cost and time considerations. The generalizability of all nonprobability sampling designs is very restricted, but they have other advantages and are sometimes the only viable alternative for the researcher.

Table 8.2 summarizes the probability and nonprobability sampling designs discussed thus far, and Figure 8.3 offers some decision choice points as to which design might be usable for specific goals.

Table 8.2
Probability and Nonprobability Sampling Designs

Sampling Design	Description	Advantage/Disadvantage
Probability Sampling		
1. Simple random sampling	All elements in the population are considered and each element has an equal chance of being chosen as the subject.	High generalizability of findings. Not as efficient as stratified sampling.
2. Systematic sampling	Every nth element in the population is chosen starting from a random point in the population frame.	Easy to use if population frame is available. Systematic biases are possible.
3. Stratified random sampling (Str.R.S.) Proportionate Str.R.S. Disproportionate Str.R.S.	Population is first divided into meaningful segments; thereafter subjects are drawn: in proportion to their original numbers in the population. based on criteria other than their original population numbers.	Most efficient among the probability designs. Population frame for *each* stratum is essential. Would adequately represent strata with low numbers.
4. Cluster sampling	Groups that have heterogeneous members are first identified; then some are chosen at random; all the members in each of the randomly chosen groups are studied.	In geographical clusters, costs of data collection are low. The least reliable among all the probability sampling designs.
5. Area sampling	Cluster sampling within a particular area or locality.	Cost-effective. Useful for decisions regarding location.
6. Double sampling	The same sample or a subset of the sample is studied twice.	Offers more detailed information on the topic of study. Original biases, if any, will be carried over.
Nonprobability Sampling		
7. Convenience sampling	The most easily accessible members are chosen as subjects.	Quick, convenient, less expensive. Not generalizable at all.
8. Judgment sampling	Subjects selected on the basis of their expertise in the subject investigated.	Sometimes, the only meaningful way to investigate.

(*continued*)

Table 8.2 (*Continued*)

Sampling Design	Description	Advantage/Disadvantage
		Generalizability is questionable.
9. Quota sampling	Subjects are conveniently chosen from targeted groups according to some predetermined number or quota.	Very useful where minority groups' participation in a study is critical.
		Not easily generalizable.

Examples of When Certain Sampling Designs are Appropriate

1. Simple Random Sampling. This sampling design is best fitted when generalizability of the findings to the whole population is the objective of the study. Consider the following two examples.

Example 8.1 The Vice President of a company employing eighty-two people has been asked to consider formulating an implementable drug testing policy. The V.P. feels that such a policy is not necessary for the company since there have been no drug-related issues encountered, and formulating such a policy will only create problems with the personnel. To convince the president that there is no need for such a move, she wants to resort to a simple random sampling procedure to do an initial test. She feels that the results will convince the president to drop the matter.

New paragraph: Since simple random sampling offers the greatest generalizability of the results to the entire population, and the president needs to be convinced, it is important to resort to this sampling design.

Example 8.2 The V.P. in charge of sales in a medium-sized company having twenty retail stores in each of the four geographical regions in which the company is operating wants to know what types of sales gimmicks worked best for the company overall during the past year. The purpose of this information is to formulate some general policies for the company as a whole and prioritize sales promotion strategies for the coming year.

Instead of studying each of the eighty stores, some *dependable* (i.e., *representative* or *generalizable*) information can be had based on the study of a few stores drawn through a simple random sampling procedure. That is, every one of the eighty stores would have an equal chance of being chosen as a sample and the results of the study will be the most generalizable.

Figure 8.3
Choice points in sampling designs.

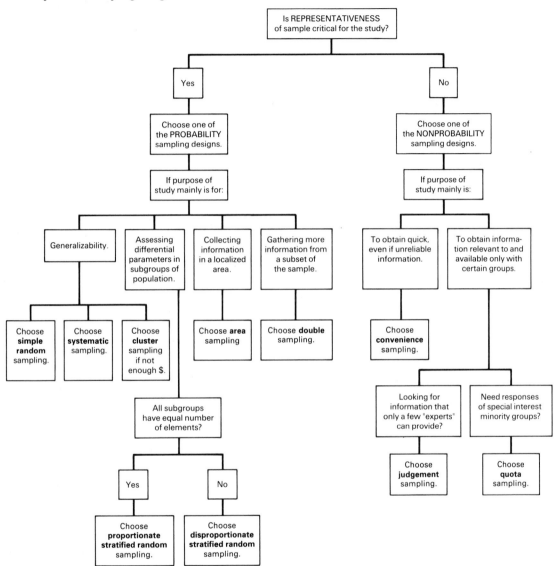

A simple random sampling procedure is recommended in this case since the policy is to be formulated for the company as a whole. This implies that the most representative information has to be obtained that can be generalized to the entire company. This is best accomplished through this design.

Note: In some cases, where *cost* is a primary consideration (i.e., resources are limited) and the number of elements in the population is very large and/or geographically dispersed, the simple random sampling design may not be the most desirable, because it is so cumbersome.

Thus, both the criticality of generalizability and cost considerations come into play in the choice of this sampling design.

2. Stratified Random Sampling.   This sampling design, which is the most efficient, is a good choice when differentiated information is needed regarding various strata within the population known to differ in their parameters. See Examples 8.3 and 8.4 below.

Example 8.3   The HRM Director of a manufacturing firm wants to offer stress-management seminars to the personnel who experience high levels of stress. He conjectures that three groups are most prone to stress: the workmen who constantly handle dangerous chemicals, the foremen who are held responsible for production quotas, and the counselors who, day in and day out, listen to the problems of the employees, internalize them, and offer them counsel, not knowing to what extent they have really helped the clients.

To get a feel for the experienced level of stress within each of the three groups and the rest of the firm, the director would stratify the sample into four distinct categories: (1) the workmen handling the dangerous chemicals, (2) the foremen, (3) the counselors, and (4) all the rest. He would then choose a **disproportionate random sampling** procedure [since group (3) can be expected to be very small, and groups (2) and (1) are much smaller compared to group (4)].

This is the only sampling design that would enable the offering of stress management seminars, targeted at the right groups to be designed in a meaningful way.

Example 8.4   If in Example 8.2 the V.P. had wanted to know which sales promotion gimmick offered the best results for *each* of the geographical areas, so that different sales promotion strategies (according to regional preferences) can be developed, then first the eighty stores would be stratified on the basis of the geographical region, and then a representative sample of stores would be drawn from each of the geographical regions (strata) through a simple random-sampling procedure. In this case, since each of the regions has twenty stores, a *proportionate stratified random sampling* process (say, five stores from each region) would be appropriate. If, however, the northern region had only three stores, the southern had fifteen, and the eastern and western regions had twenty-four and thirty-eight stores, respectively, then a *disproportionate stratified random sampling* procedure would be more appropriate.

If the sample size is retained at twenty, then the four regions will probably have samples of three (all in the northern region because of the small number of elements in the population), four (south), five (eastern), and eight (western).

Note: Sometimes, when stratified random sampling might seem logical, it may not really be necessary. For example, when test-marketing shows that Cubans, Puerto Ricans, and Mexicans perceive and consume a particular product the same way, there is no need to segment the market and study each of the three groups using a stratified sampling procedure (see, for instance, the article entitled, "If you want a big new market" in *Fortune,* November 21, 1988, pp. 181–188).

3. Systematic Sampling. If the population frame is large, and a listing of the elements is conveniently available in one place (as in the telephone directory, company payroll, chamber of commerce listings, etc.), then a systematic sampling procedure will offer the advantages of ease and quickness in developing the sample, as illustrated in the following two examples.

Example 8.5 An administrator wants to assess the reactions of employees to a new and improved health benefits scheme that requires a modest increase in the premiums to be paid by the employees for their families. The administrator can assess the enthusiasm for the new scheme by using a systematic sampling design. The company's records will provide the population frame, and every nth employee can be sampled. A stratified plan is not called for here since the policy is for the entire company.

Example 8.6 If customers' interest in a highly sophisticated telephone answering machine is to be gauged by an entrepreneur, a systematic sampling procedure with the telephone directory as the population frame will be the easiest and quickest way to obtain the information, while still ensuring representativeness of the population studied.

Note: Systematic sampling will be inadvisable where systematic biases can be expected to be present if data were collected on this basis. For example, systematic sampling from the personnel directory of a company (especially when it has an equal number of employees in each department), which lists the names of the individuals department-wise, with the head of the department listed first, and the secretary listed next, has inherent biases. The possibility of systematic biases creeping into the data cannot be ruled out since the selection process may end up in picking each of the heads of the department or the departmental secretaries as the sample subjects. The results from such a sample will clearly be biased and not generalizable at all, despite the fact that a probability sampling procedure has been used. Systematic sampling will have to be scrupulously avoided in such cases.

4. Cluster Sampling. This sampling design would be most useful when a heterogeneous group is to be studied at one time. The unit costs of such a study are much lower compared to the other probability sampling designs of simple or stratified random sampling or systematic sampling. Two examples of cluster sampling are offered below.

Example 8.7   Cluster sampling can be used for conducting exit interviews on specific days of all members completing their final papers in the Personnel Department before resigning. The interviews would help to understand the reasons for turnover of a heterogeneous group of individuals (i.e., from various departments), and the study could be conducted at a low cost. Clusters on different days can be studied at random.

Example 8.8   A financial analyst desires to study the lending practices of pawnbrokers in Contra Costa County, California. All the pawnbrokers in each city would form a cluster. By randomly sampling the clusters, the analyst would be able to draw conclusions regarding the lending practices.

Note: Cluster sampling lends itself to greater biases and is the least generalizable of all the probability sampling designs because most naturally occurring clusters in the organizational context do not contain heterogeneous elements. In other words, the conditions of intracluster heterogeneity and intercluster homogeneity are often not met.

5. Area Sampling.   Geographical clusters are what constitute the area sampling design. Retail stores location plans, advertising focused specifically on local populations, TV and radio programs beamed at specific areas could all use an area sampling design to gather information on the interests, attitudes, predispositions, and behaviors of the local area people. Area sampling is thus best suited when the goal of the research is confined to a particular locality or area as per the example below.

Example 8.9   A telephone company wants to install a public telephone outlet in a locality where crime is most rampant so that victims can have access to a telephone. Studying the crime statistics and interviewing the residents in a particular area will help to install the phone in the right location.

6. Double Sampling.   This plan is resorted to when more complete or comprehensive information needs to be obtained from a group from which some information has already been collected. A subset of the original sample is used for the purpose. This results in minimal additional expenditure for further data gathering. See example below.

Example 8.10   In Example 8.7 (exit interview example), some individuals (i.e., a subset of the original cluster sample) might have indicated that they were resigning because of philosophical differences with the company's policies. The researcher might want to do an in-depth interview with these individuals, to obtain more information regarding the nature of the policies disliked, what exactly were the philosophic differences, and why these particular issues were central to the individuals' value systems. Such additional detailed information from the target group through the double sampling design will help the company to search for ways in which it might retain more people in the future.

7. *Convenience Sampling.* This nonprobability design is not generalizable at all and is not appropriate for "scientific" research. It may, however, be used at times to get some "quick" information, knowing the risks involved in using the results of such a study. At best, data obtained through convenience sampling might offer a "feel" on some variable or variables of interest, as per the example below.

Example 8.11   The Accounts Executive has established a new bookkeeping and accounting system to make the utmost use of the computer facilities available in the company. Before making further changes, he would like to get a feel for how the accounting clerks are reacting to the new system without making it seem that he has doubts about the acceptability of the changes. He may then "casually" talk to the first three accounting personnel that walk into his office, trying to gauge their reactions.

Convenience sampling should be resorted to in the interests of expediency, with the full knowledge that the results are not generalizable at all.

Purposive Sampling

8. *Judgment Sample.* This nonprobability sampling design is used where gathering "specialized informed inputs" on the topic area researched is vital and using any of the probability sampling design would not offer opportunities to gain the specialized information. Though not a probability design, purposive sampling still calls for special efforts to locate and gain access to the individuals who do have the requisite information, as can be seen from the example below.

Example 8.12   A pharmaceutical company wants to trace the effects of a new drug on patients with specific health problems (muscular dystrophy, sickle cell anemia, rheumetoid arthritis, etc.). It then contacts such individuals and, with the voluntary group of consenting patients, tests the drug. This is a judgment sample because data are collected from a special group.

9. *Quota Sample.* This sampling design ensures that certain groups are adequately represented in the study through the assignment of a quota. Generally, the quota fixed for each subgroup is based on the total numbers of each group in the population. However, since this is a nonprobability sampling plan, the results are not generalizable to the population.

In a workplace and society that will be increasingly heterogeneous because of the changing demographics, quota sampling can be expected to be used more frequently in the future. For example, quota sampling can be used to have some idea of the buying predispositions of various ethnic groups, for getting a feel for how employees from different nationalities perceive the organizational culture, and so on. Below is an example of quota sampling.

Example 8.13   A company is seriously thinking of operating an on-site day-care facility. But before making a decision, it wants to get the reactions of four groups to the idea: (1) employees who are parents and where both spouses are working outside of home, (2) employees who are parents where the other spouse is not working outside of home, (3) single parents, and (4) those without children. If the four groups represent 60, 7, 23, and 10 percent, respectively, in the population of 420 employees in the company, then a quota sampling will be appropriate to represent the four groups. The last group is also included in the sample since there is a possibility that they may perceive this as a facility that favors the parents only and may resent the idea.

Note: (1) Quota sampling is not generalizable like stratified random sampling, but does offer some basis for further investigation. (2) Sometimes, it is possible that the first stage of research will use a nonprobability design, and when more information is obtained, a probability design will be resorted to. The converse is also possible. A probability sampling design might indicate new areas for research, to explore the feasibility of which nonprobability sampling designs might be used.

As can be seen from the discussions on sampling designs thus far, decisions on which design to use is dependent on many factors, including the following:

1. Extent of prior knowledge in the area of research undertaken.
2. The main objective of the study—generalizability, efficiency, knowing more about subgroups within a population, obtaining some quick (even if unreliable) information, etc.
3. Cost considerations—is exactitude and/generalizability worth the extra investment of time, cost, and other resources? Even if it is, is suboptimization because of cost or time constraints necessary? (See also Figure 8.3.)

ISSUES OF PRECISION AND CONFIDENCE IN DETERMINING SAMPLE SIZE

Having discussed the various probability and nonprobability sampling designs, we now need to focus attention on the second aspect of the sampling design issue—sample size. Suppose we select thirty people from a population of 3000 through a simple random sampling procedure. Will we be able to generalize our findings to the population with confidence, having chosen a probability design that has the most generalizability? What is the sample size that would be required to make reasonably precise generalizations with confidence? What do precision and confidence mean? These issues will be considered now.

A reliable and valid sample should enable us to generalize the findings from the sample to the population we are investigating. In other words, the sample statistics should be good estimates and reflect the population parameters as closely as possible within a narrow margin of error. No sample statistic ($\bar{X}$, for instance) is going to be exactly the same as the population parameter (μ, for instance), no matter how sophisticated the probability sampling design. Remember that the very reason for a probability design is to increase the probability that the sample statistics will be as close as possible to the population parameters! Though the point estimate $\bar{X}$ may not accurately reflect the population mean μ, an interval estimate can be made within which μ will lie, and this estimate can be made with probabilities attached—that is, at particular confidence levels. The issues of confidence interval and confidence level are addressed in our discussions of precision and confidence.

Precision

Precision refers to how close our estimate is to the true population characteristic. Usually, we would estimate the population parameter to fall within a range, based on the sample estimate. For example, let us say that from a study of a simple random sample of 50 of the total 300 employees in a workshop, we find that the average daily production rate per person is 50 pieces of a particular product ($\bar{X} = 50$). We might then (by doing certain calculations, as we shall see later) be able to say that the true average daily production of the product would be anywhere between 40 and 60 for the population of employees in the workshop. In saying this, we are offering an interval estimate, within which we expect the true population mean production to be ($\mu = 50 \pm 10$). The narrower this interval, the greater the precision. For instance, if we are able to estimate that the population mean would fall anywhere between 45 and 55 pieces of production ($\mu = 50 \pm 5$) rather than 40 and 60 ($\mu = 50 \pm 10$), then we would have more precision. That is, we would now be estimating the mean to fall within a narrower range; in other words, we are estimating with greater exactitude or precision.

Precision is a function of the extent of variability in the sampling distribution of the sample mean. That is, if we take a number of different samples from a population, and take the mean of each of these, we will usually find that they are all different, are normally distributed, and have a dispersion associated with them. The smaller this dispersion or variability, the greater the probability that the sample mean will be closer to the population mean. We need not necessarily take several different samples to estimate this variability. For instance, even if we take only one sample of thirty subjects from the population, we will still be able to estimate the variability of the sampling distribution of the sample mean. This variability is called the standard error, denoted by $S_{\bar{X}}$. The standard error is calculated by the following formula:

$$S_{\bar{X}} = \frac{S}{\sqrt{n-1}}$$

where S is the standard deviation of the sample, n is the sample size, and $S_{\bar{X}}$ indicates the standard error or the extent of precision offered by the sample.

Note that the standard error varies inversely with the square root of the sample size. Hence, if we want to reduce the standard error given a particular standard deviation in the sample, we need to increase the sample size. Another noteworthy point is that the smaller the variation in the population, the smaller the standard error, which in turn implies that the sample size need not necessarily be large when there is very low variability in the population.

Thus, the closer we want our sample results to reflect the population characteristics, the greater will be the precision we would be aiming for. The greater the precision required, the larger will be the sample size needed, especially when the variability in the population itself is large.

Confidence

Whereas precision denotes how close we are in estimating the population parameter based on the sample statistic, confidence denotes how *certain* we are that our estimates will really hold true for the population. In the previous example of production rate, we know we are more precise when we estimate the true mean (μ) production to fall somewhere between 45 and 55 pieces than when we say it will be somewhere between 40 and 60. However, we may have more confidence in the latter estimation than in the former. After all, anyone can say with 100 percent certainty or confidence that the mean production (μ) will fall anywhere between zero and infinity! The narrower the range, other things being equal, the lower the confidence. In other words, there is a trade-off between precision and confidence for any given sample size, as we shall see later in this chapter.

In essence, confidence reflects the level of certainty with which we can state that our estimates of the population parameters, based on our sample statistics, will hold true. The level of confidence can range from 0 to 100 percent. A 95 percent confidence is the accepted level for most business research, most commonly expressed by the significance level $p \leq .05$. In other words, we say that 95 times out of 100, our estimate will reflect the true population characteristic.

SAMPLE DATA, PRECISION AND CONFIDENCE IN ESTIMATION

Precision and confidence are important issues in sampling because when we use sample data to draw inferences about the population, we hope to be fairly "on target," and have some idea of the amount of possible error. Because a point estimate provides no measure of possible error, we do an interval estimation to ensure a *relatively accurate* estimation of the population parameter. Statistics that have the same distribution as the sampling distribution of the mean are used in this procedure, usually a z or a t statistic.

For example, we may want to estimate the mean dollar value of purchases made by customers when they shop at department stores. From a sample of fifty customers sampled through a systematic sampling design procedure, we may find that the sample mean $\bar{X} = 105$, and the sample standard deviation $S = 10$. $\bar{X}$, the sample mean, is a point estimate of μ, the population mean. We could construct a confidence interval around $\bar{X}$ to estimate the range within which μ would fall. The standard error $S_{\bar{X}}$ and the percentage or level of confidence we require will determine the width of the interval, which can be represented by the following formula, where K is the t statistic for the level of confidence desired.

$$\mu = \bar{X} \pm K S_{\bar{X}}$$

we already know that:

$$S_{\bar{X}} = \frac{S}{\sqrt{n-1}}$$

Here,

$$S_{\bar{X}} = \frac{10}{\sqrt{49}} = 1.43$$

From the table of critical values for t in any statistics book (see Table II, page 410, last line in columns 5, 6, and 9, of this book), we know that:

For 90 percent confidence level, the K value is 1.645.

For 95 percent confidence level, the K value is 1.96.

For 99 percent confidence level, the K value is 2.576.

If we desire a 90 percent confidence level in the above case, $\mu = 105 \pm 1.645(1.43)$ (i.e., $\mu = 105 \pm 2.352$), and μ would thus fall between 102.648 and 107.352. These results indicate that using a sample size of 50, we could state with 90 percent confidence that the true population mean $\$$ value for purchases for all customers would fall anywhere between 102.65 and 107.35. If we now want to be 99 percent confident of our results without increasing the sample size, we would necessarily have to sacrifice our precision, as can be seen from the following calculation: $\mu = 105 \pm 2.576(1.43)$. The value for μ now falls between 101.317 and 108.683. In other words, the width of the interval has increased and we are now less precise in estimating the population mean, though we are a lot more confident about our estimation. It is not difficult to see that if we want to maintain our original precision while increasing the confidence, or we want to increase the confidence while maintaining the same precision, or we want to increase both the confidence and the precision, we need a larger sample size.

Figure 8.4

Illustration of the trade-off between precision and confidence. (*a*) More precision but less confidence. (*b*) More confidence but less precision.

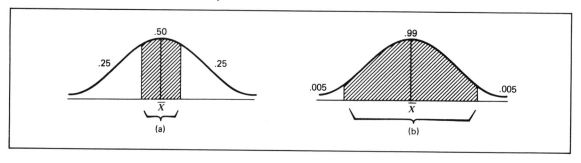

THE TRADE-OFF BETWEEN CONFIDENCE AND PRECISION

From the foregoing it is clear that if we want more precision, or more confidence, or both, the sample size needs to be increased—unless, of course, there is very little variability in the population itself. However, if the sample size (*n*) cannot be increased, for whatever reason—say, we cannot afford the costs of increased sampling—then, with the same *n,* the only way to maintain the same level of precision would be by forsaking the confidence with which we can predict that our estimates will be precise (i.e., be close to the target μ). That is, we are reducing the confidence level or the certainty of our estimate. This trade-off between precision and confidence is illustrated in Figures 8.4*a* and *b*. Figure 8.4*a* indicates that 50 percent of the time the true mean μ will fall within the narrow range indicated in the figure, the .25 in each tail representing the 25 percent nonconfidence or the probability of making errors in our estimation on either side. Figure 8.4*b* indicates that 99 percent of the time we would expect the true mean μ to fall within the much wider range indicated in the figure and there is only a .005 percent chance that we would be making an error in this estimation. That is, in Figure 8.4*a*, we have more precision but less confidence (our confidence level is only 50 percent). In Figure 8.4*b*, we have high confidence (99 percent), but then we are far from being precise—that is, our estimate falls within a broad interval range.

It thus becomes necessary for researchers to consider at least four aspects while making decisions on the sample size needed to do the research: (1) How much precision is really needed in estimating the population characteristics of interest— that is, what is the *margin* of error we can make? (2) How much confidence is really needed—that is, how much *chance* can we take of making errors in estimating the population parameters? (3) To what extent is there a *variability* in the population on the characteristics investigated? (4) What is the *cost–benefit* analysis of increasing the sample size?

SAMPLE DATA AND HYPOTHESIS TESTING

So far we have discussed sample data as a means of estimating the population parameters, but sample data can also be used to test hypotheses about population values rather than simply to estimate population values. The procedure for this testing incorporates the same information as in interval estimation, but the goals behind the two methods are somewhat different.

Referring to the earlier example of the average dollar value purchases of customers in a department store, instead of trying to estimate the average purchase value of the store's customers with a certain degree of accuracy, let us say that we now wish to determine whether or not customers expend the same average amount in purchases at Department Store A as compared to Department Store B. From Chapter 3, we know that we would first set the null hypothesis, which would state that there would be no difference in the dollar values expended by customers shopping at the two different stores. This would be expressed as:

$$H_0 : \mu_A - \mu_B = 0$$

The alternate hypothesis of differences would be stated nondirectionally (since we have no idea about any differences that might exist) as:

$$H_A : \mu_A - \mu_B \neq 0$$

If we take a sample of twenty customers from each of the two stores and find that the mean dollar value purchases of customers in Store A is 105 with a standard deviation of 10 and the mean and standard deviation for Store B is 100 and 15, respectively, we see that:

$$\bar{X}_A - \bar{X}_B = 105 - 100 = 5$$

whereas our null hypothesis had postulated no difference (difference = 0). Should we then conclude that our alternate hypothesis is to be accepted? We cannot say! To determine this we must first find the probability or likelihood of the two group means having a difference of 5 in the context of the null hypothesis of a difference of 0. This can be done by converting the difference in the sample means to a *t* statistic and seeing what the probability is of finding a *t* of that value. The *t* distribution has known probabilities attached to it (see *t*- table in the appendix at the end of the book). Looking at the *t* distribution table, we find that with a sample size of 20, for the *t* value to be significant at the .05 level (with 2 tails since we do not know whether the difference between Store A and Store B will be positive or negative), it should be at least 2.086 (see *t* table column 6 against v 20). For even a 90 percent probability, it should be at least 1.725 (see the figure to the left of 2.086). The t statistic can be calculated for testing our hypothesis as follows:

$$t = \frac{(\bar{X}_1 - \bar{X}_2) - (\mu_1 - \mu_2)}{S_{\bar{X}1} - S_{\bar{X}2}}$$

$$S_{\bar{X}1} - S_{\bar{X}2} = \sqrt{\frac{n_1 s_1^2 + n_2 s_2^2}{(n_1 + n_2 - 2)} \left(\frac{1}{n_1} + \frac{1}{n_2}\right)}$$

$$= \sqrt{\frac{(20 \times 10^2) + (20 \times 15^2)}{(20 + 20 - 2)} \left(\frac{1}{20} + \frac{1}{20}\right)}$$

$$t = \frac{(\bar{X}_A - \bar{X}_B) - (\mu_A - \mu_B)}{4.136}$$

We already know that

$$\bar{X}_A - \bar{X}_B = 5 \quad \text{(the difference in the means of the two stores)}$$

and

$$\mu_A - \mu_B = 0 \quad \text{(from our null hypothesis).}$$

Then

$$t = \frac{5 - 0}{4.136} = 1.209$$

This t value of 1.209 is much below the value of 2.086 required for the conventional 95 percent probability, and even for the 90 percent probability, which requires a value of 1.725. We can thus say that the difference of \$5 that we found between the two stores is not significantly different from 0. The conclusion, then, is that there is no significant difference between how much customers buy (dollars expended) at Department Store A and Department Store B.

Thus the sample data can be used not only for estimating the population parameters, but also for testing hypotheses about population values, population correlations, and so forth, as we will see more fully later in Chapter 10.

DETERMINING THE SAMPLE SIZE

Now that we are aware of the fact that the sample size is governed by the extent of precision and confidence desired, how do we determine the sample size required for our research? The procedure can be illustrated through an example.

Suppose a manager wants to be 95 percent confident that the expected monthly withdrawals in a bank will be within an interval of ±\$500. Let us say that a study of a sample of clients indicates that the average withdrawals made by them has a standard deviation of $3500. What would be the sample size needed in this case?

We noted earlier that the population mean can be estimated by using the formula:

$$\mu = \bar{X} \pm k\, S_{\bar{X}}$$

Since the confidence level needed here is 95 percent, the applicable K value is 1.96 (t table). The interval estimate of $\pm \$500$ will have to encompass a dispersion of $\pm(1.96 \times \text{standard error})$. That is,

$$500 = 1.96 \times S_{\bar{X}}$$

$$S_{\bar{X}} = 500/1.96 = 255.10$$

We already know that

$$S_{\bar{X}} = \frac{S}{\sqrt{n-1}}$$

$$255.10 = \frac{3500}{\sqrt{n-1}}$$

$$n = 187$$

Another way of stating the formula for determining the sample size is as follows:

$$n = \left(\frac{S^2}{S_{\bar{X}}^2} \right) + 1$$

The sample size needed in the above was 187. Let us say that this bank has a total clientele of only 185. This means we cannot sample 187 clients. We can in this case apply the correction formula and see what sample size would be needed to have the same level of precision and confidence given the fact that we have a total of only 185 clients. The correction formula is as follows:

$$S_{\bar{X}} = \frac{S}{\sqrt{n-1}} \times \sqrt{\frac{N-n}{N-1}}$$

where N is the total number of elements in the population, n is the sample size to be estimated, $S_{\bar{X}}$ is the standard error of estimate of the mean, and S is the standard deviation of the sample mean.

Applying the correlation formula, we find that

$$255.10 = \frac{3500}{\sqrt{n-1}} \times \sqrt{\frac{185-n}{184}}$$

$$n = 94$$

We would now sample 94 of the total 185 clients.

To understand the impact of precision and/or confidence on the sample size, let us try changing the confidence required in the bank withdrawal exercise, which needed a sample size of 187 for a confidence level of 95 percent. Let us say that the bank manager now wants to be 99 percent sure that the expected monthly withdrawals will be within the interval of ±$500. What will be the sample size now needed?

$$S_{\bar{X}} \quad \text{will now be} \quad \frac{500}{2.576} = 194.099$$

$$194.099 = \frac{3500}{\sqrt{n-1}}$$

$$n = 324$$

The sample has now to be increased 1.73 times (from 187 to 324) to increase the confidence level from 95 to 99 percent!

Try calculating the sample size if the precision has to be increased from $500 to $300 for a 95 and a 99 percent confidence level! Your answers should show the sample sizes needed as 522 and 902, respectively. These results dramatically highlight the costs of increased precision, confidence, or both. It is hence a good idea to think through how much precision and confidence one really needs before embarking on a research project.

So far we have discussed sample size in the context of precision and confidence with respect to one variable only. However, in research, the theoretical framework has several variables of interest, and the question arises how one should come up with a sample size when all the factors are taken into account. Krejcie and Morgan (1970) greatly simplified the sample size decision by providing a table that ensures a good decision model. Table 8.3 provides that generalized scientific guideline for sample size decisions. The interested student is recommended to read Krejcie and Morgan (1970) as well as Cohen (1969) for decisions on sample size.

IMPORTANCE OF SAMPLING DESIGN AND SAMPLE SIZE

It is now possible to see how both sampling design and sample size are important to establish the representativeness of the sample for generalizability. If the appropriate sampling design is not used, a large sample size will not, in itself, allow the findings to be generalized to the population. Likewise, unless the sample size is adequate for the desired level of precision and confidence, no sampling design, however sophisticated, can be useful to the researcher in meeting the objectives of the study. Hence, sampling decisions should consider both the sampling design and the sample size. Too large a sample size, however (say, over 500) could also become a problem inasmuch as we would be prone to committing Type II errors. That is, we would be accepting the findings of our research, when in fact we should be rejecting them. In other words, with too large a sample size, even weak rela-

Table 8.3
Table for Determining Sample Size from a Given Population

N	S	N	S	N	S
10	10	220	140	1200	291
15	14	230	144	1300	297
20	19	240	148	1400	302
25	24	250	152	1500	306
30	28	260	155	1600	310
35	32	270	159	1700	313
40	36	280	162	1800	317
45	40	290	165	1900	320
50	44	300	169	2000	322
55	48	320	175	2200	327
60	52	340	181	2400	331
65	56	360	186	2600	335
70	59	380	191	2800	338
75	63	400	196	3000	341
80	66	420	201	3500	346
85	70	440	205	4000	351
90	73	460	210	4500	354
95	76	480	214	5000	357
100	80	500	217	6000	361
110	86	550	226	7000	364
120	92	600	234	8000	367
130	97	650	242	9000	368
140	103	700	248	10000	370
150	108	750	254	15000	375
160	113	800	260	20000	377
170	118	850	265	30000	379
180	123	900	269	40000	380
190	127	950	274	50000	381
200	132	1000	278	75000	382
210	136	1100	285	1000000	384

N is population size.
S is sample size.

tionships (say a correlation of .10 between two variables) reach significance levels, and we would be inclined to believe that these significant relationships found in the sample are indeed true of the population, when in fact they may not be. Thus, neither too large nor too small sample sizes help research projects.

Roscoe (1975) proposes the following rules of thumb for determining sample size:

1. Sample sizes larger than 30 and less than 500 are appropriate for most research.
2. Where samples are to be broken into subsamples (males/females, juniors/ seniors, etc.), a minimum sample size of 30 for each category is necessary.

3. In multivariate research (including multiple regression analyses), the sample size should be several times (preferably 10 times or more) as large as the number of variables in the study.

4. For simple experimental research with tight experimental controls (matched pairs, etc.), successful research is possible with samples as small as 10 to 20 in size.

EFFICIENCY IN SAMPLING

Efficiency in sampling is attained when for a given level of precision (standard error), the sample size could be reduced, or for a given sample size (n), the level of precision could be increased. Some probability sampling designs are more efficient than others. The simple random sampling procedure is not always the most efficient plan to adopt; some other probability designs are often more efficient. A stratified random sampling plan is often the most efficient, and a disproportionate stratified random sampling design has been shown to be more efficient than a proportionate sampling design in many cases. Cluster sampling is less efficient than simple random sampling because there is generally more homogeneity among the elements in the clusters than is found in the population. Multistage cluster sampling is more efficient than single-stage cluster sampling when there is more heterogeneity found in the earlier stages. There is often a trade-off between time and cost efficiencies (as achieved in nonprobability sampling designs) and precision efficiencies (as achieved in many probability sampling plans). The choice of a sampling plan thus depends on the objectives of the research, as well as on the extent and nature of efficiency desired.

Review of Sample Size Decisions

We can summarize the factors affecting decisions on sample size as (1) the extent of precision desired (the confidence interval); (2) the amount of risk allowable in predicting that level of precision (confidence level); (3) the amount of variability in the population itself; (4) the cost and time constraints; and, in some cases, (5) the size of the population itself. As a rule of thumb, sample sizes between 30 and 500 could be effective depending on the type of research questions investigated.

SUMMARY

Decisions regarding sampling are important aspects of research design. Sampling design decisions include both the sampling plan to be used and the sample size that will be needed. Probability sampling plans lend themselves to generalizability and nonprobability sampling designs do not. Some probability plans are more efficient than others. Though nonprobability sampling designs are not readily generalizable, they are often useful for obtaining certain types of information quickly and relatively inexpensively. The sample size is determined by the level of precision and accuracy desired in estimating the population parameters, as well as the variability in the population itself. The generalizability of the findings from a study of the sample to the population is dependent on the sophistication of the sampling designs used, which includes the sample size used in the study. In all research, care should also be taken not to overgeneralize the results of the study to populations that are not represented by the sample. This is a common problem in many research studies. Sample data are used for both estimating population parameters and hypothesis testing.

In the next two chapters, we will see how the data that are gathered from a sample of respondents in the population will be analyzed to test the hypotheses generated and answer the research questions.

DISCUSSION QUESTIONS AND POINTS TO PONDER

1. Identify the relevant population for the following research foci, and suggest the appropriate sampling design to investigate the issues, explaining *why* they are appropriate. Wherever necessary, identify the population frame as well.
   a. A gun manufacturing firm would like to know the types of guns possessed by various age groups in Washington, D.C.
   b. A hospital administrator wants to find out if the single parents working in the hospital have a higher rate of absenteeism than parents who are not single.
   c. A researcher would like to assess the extent of pilferage in the materials storage warehouses of manufacturing firms in the East Coast.
   d. An HRM Director wants to investigate the relationship between drug abuse and dysfunctional behaviors of blue-collar workers in a particular plant.

2. a. Why is cluster sampling a probability sampling design?
   b. What are the advantages and disadvantages of cluster sampling?
   c. Describe a situation where you would consider using cluster sampling.

3. a. Explain what precision and accuracy are and how they influence sample size.
   b. Discuss what we mean when we say that there is a trade-off between precision and confidence under certain conditions.

4. A convenience sample used in organizational research is all right because all members share the same organizational stimuli and go through almost the same kinds of experiences in their organizational lives. Comment.

5. Having a sample of 5000 is not necessarily better than having a sample of 500. How would you react to this statement?

6. Nonprobability sampling designs ought to be preferred to probability sampling designs in some cases. Explain with example.

7. Because there seems to be a trade-off between accuracy and precision for any given sample size, accuracy should be always considered more important than precision. Explain with reasons why you would or would not agree.

8. Overgeneralizations give rise to a lot of confusion and other problems for researchers who try to replicate the findings. Explain what is meant by this.

9. Double sampling is probably the least used of all sampling designs in organizational research. Do you agree? Provide reasons for your answer.

EXERCISES

> For the situations presented in Exercises 8.1 to 8.6 below, indicate what would be the relevant population and the most appropriate sampling design. Make sure you discuss the reasons for your answers.

Exercise 8.1   A medical inspector desires to estimate the overall average monthly occupancy rates of the cancer wards in eighty different hospitals that are evenly located in the northwestern, southeastern, central, and southern suburbs of New York City.

Exercise 8.2   The Director of University Women's Professional Advancement (UWPA), appointed by the President of SIUC to enhance the status of women on campus some two years ago, was listening to a speech made by the President of the Women's Caucus. It suddenly occurred to the Director that it would be a great idea to get the opinion of members of this vocal group on how effective they perceived UWPA to be in enhancing the status of women on campus. She thought she could ask a few quick questions as the audience left the meeting room. What should be her sampling design and how should she proceed?

Exercise 8.3   The *Fortune* magazine (February 1, 1988) suggests "Consumers 35 to 44 will soon be the nation's biggest spenders, so advertisers must learn how to appeal to this over-the-thrill crowd." If this suggestion appeals to an apparel manufacturer, what should be the sampling design to assess the tastes of this group?

Exercise 8.4   Carbondale is a university town with about 24,000 students—a number of whom come from various parts of the world. For instance, there are about 200 Indian and 600 Malaysian students—about half of each category being women—and a further 1000 students attend Southern Illinois University at Carbondale coming from over 55 other countries.

　　Martha Ellenden, a talented and adventurous seamstress, desires to open a tailoring shop (so rare these days!) in Carbondale, close to the University Mall, where she lives. She has a good sewing machine and would start her business immediately if she knew there was a demand for her services. To assess the market potential, Martha would like to talk to a few women to estimate how many clients she might attract. While the American women buy ready-made clothes from the University Mall, she knows that the international women, particularly the Indians and the Malays, buy plain material from the Mall and either stitch their own blouses or send them to their native homes to have them stitched. Martha would like to talk to forty-five or so individuals to estimate what demand might exist. How would Martha go about selecting the forty-five individuals?

Exercise 8.5   The McArthur Co. produces special vacuum cleaners that can be conveniently used to clean the inside of cars. About a thousand of these are produced every month with serial numbers attached to them and stored serially in a stock room. Once a month an inspector comes and does a quality control check on fifty of the units. When he certifies them to be of acceptable quality, the units are released from the stock room for sale. The production and sales managers, however, are not satisfied with the quality control check since, quite often, many of the units sold are returned by customers for various types of defects. What would be the most useful sampling plan to test the fifty units?

Exercise 8.6   A consultant had administered a questionnaire to some 285 employees using a simple random sampling procedure. As he looked at the responses, he felt that two of the items in the questionnaire might not have been clear to the respondents. He would like to know if this is true.

CHAPTER 9

A REFRESHER ON SOME STATISTICAL TERMS AND TESTS

TOPICS DISCUSSED

DESCRIPTIVE STATISTICS
- Frequencies
- Measures of Central Tendency and Dispersion
- *Mean, Median, Mode*
- *Range, Variance, Standard Deviation, Interquartile Range*

INFERENTIAL STATISTICS
- Pearson Correlation
- Relationship Between Two Nominal Variables: χ^2 test
- Significant Mean Differences Between Two Groups: *t*-Test
- Significant Mean Differences Among More Than Two Groups: ANOVA
- Multiple Regression Analysis

OTHER TESTS AND ANALYSES

CHAPTER OBJECTIVES

The purpose of this chapter is to merely refresh your memory about the various terms and statistical tests that you might have studied earlier. After reading this chapter, you should be able to explain what types of analyses are appropriate, under what conditions, and for what purposes. Knowing this will help you to follow the data analyses discussed in the next chapter in a relatively easy manner.

In research, we seek scientific facts and answers to the research questions we have, by analyzing the data we obtain. *Data* refers to the available raw information gathered, say, through interviews, questionnaires, or observations, or to secondary data bases. By organizing the data in some fashion, analyzing them, and making sense of the results, we find the answers we seek.

In most organizational research, at the very minimum, we would be interested in knowing how frequently certain phenomena occur (frequencies), and what is the average score when a set of figures are involved, as well as the extent of variability in the set (i.e., the central tendencies and dispersions of the dependent and independent variables). These are known as **descriptive statistics** (statistics that describe the phenomena of interest). Beyond this, we might want to know how variables relate to each other, whether there are any differences between two or more groups, and the like. These are called **inferential statistics** (i.e., statistical results that let us draw inferences from a sample to the population, as we discussed in Chapter 8). Inferential statistics can be categorized as **parametric** or **nonparametric.** The use of parametric statistics is based on the assumption that the population from which the sample is drawn is normally distributed. Parametric statistics can be used only when data are collected on an interval or ratio scale. Nonparametric statistics, on the other hand, makes no explicit assumption regarding the normality of distribution in the population and is used when the data are collected on a nominal or ordinal scale.

Both descriptive and inferential statistics can be obtained through computer programs that are already designed to produce results for various types of data. These canned computer programs are extensively used in social science research. Before discussing data analysis, it would be useful to quickly refresh your memory regarding some of the statistical concepts and their uses.

Here, we will very briefly explain some of the terms and tests used in the next chapter on data analysis such as **frequencies, measures of central tendencies and dispersions, correlation, regression,** and the like. The idea is to give an overview of these and their relevance, rather than to offer a tutorial in statistical formulas and interpretations, which you might have studied earlier in a course in statistics.

DESCRIPTIVE STATISTICS

Frequencies

Frequencies simply refer to the number of times various subcategories of a certain phenomenon occur, from which the percentage and the cumulative percentage of the occurrence of the subcategories can be easily calculated. An example will make this clear. Let us say the President of a company wants to know how many blacks, Hispanics, Asians, whites, and "others" (subcategories of the phenomenon "employees") are on the payroll of the company. A frequency count of these distinct subcategories of employees would provide the answer and might look something like the figures in Table 9.1.

The President now knows that there are 8 blacks, 2 Hispanics, 6 Asians, 182 whites, and 2 American Indians (others) in the company. He also has the percentages and cumulative percentages for each category. This information can also be presented in the form of a **histogram** or a **bar chart.** If the President desires to have at least 10 percent blacks without increasing the total number of employees, then at a minimum, 12 more blacks have to be recruited, and a decision made as to which of the other 12 employees will be dispensed with.

Examples of other instances where frequency distributions would be useful are

Table 9.1
Frequency Distribution of Types of Employees

Category	Frequency	Percent	Cumulative Percent
Blacks	8	4.0	4.0
Hispanics	2	1.0	5.0
Asians	6	3.0	8.0
Whites	182	91.0	99.0
Others (American Indians, etc.)	2	1.0	100.0
Total	200	100.0	100.0

when (1) a marketing manager wants to know how many units (and what proportions or percentages) of each brand of coffee sells in a particular region during a given period, (2) a tax consultant desires to keep count of the number of times different sizes of firms (small, medium, large) are audited by the IRS, and (3) the financial analyst wants to keep track of the number of times the shares of manufacturing, industrial, and utility companies lose or gain more than ten points on the New York Stock Exchange over a six-month period.

In all the foregoing cases, it may be noted that we desired to obtain the frequencies on a **nominally scaled** variable. That is, these variables have been grouped into various nonoverlapping subcategories, such as the different brands of coffee, sizes of firms, and nature of companies, and the number of occurrences under each category has been determined (see Chapter 6 for **nominal** scale). Frequencies are generally obtained for nominal variables such as gender, the departmental unit in which one works, type of organization, and the like.

Measures of Central Tendencies and Dispersion

It is often useful to characterize a series of observations parsimoniously in a meaningful way. That is, one or two statistics could serve as a shorthand description of the entire data set, which would enable individuals to get an idea of the basic characteristics, or "a feel" for the data. Measures of central tendencies and measures of dispersions enable us to achieve this goal. There are three measures of central tendencies: the **mean,** the **median,** and the **mode.** Measures of dispersion include the **range,** the **standard deviation,** and the **variance** (where the measure of central tendency is the mean), and the **interquartile range** (where the measure of central tendency is the median).

Mean

The mean or the average is a measure of central tendency that offers a general picture of the data without unnecessarily inundating one with each of the observations in a dataset. For example, the Production Department might keep detailed records on how many units of a product are being produced each day. However, to estimate the raw materials inventory, all that the manager might want to know is how many units per month, *on an average,* the department has been producing over the last six months. This measure of central tendency, that is, the *mean*, might offer the manager a good idea of the quantity of materials that need to be stocked.

Likewise, a marketing manager might want to know how many cans of soup are being sold, *on an average,* each week, or a banker might be interested in the number of new accounts that are opened each month, *on an average.* The mean or average of a set of say, ten observations, is the sum of the ten individual observations divided by ten (the number of observations).

Apart from knowing the mean or the average, one would also like to know the variability that exists in the set of observations. For example, if Company A sold 30, 40, and 50 units of a product during the months of April, May, and June, respectively, and Company B sold 10, 40, and 70 units, during the same period, the average units sold per month by both companies is the same—that is, 40 units—but the variability or the **dispersion** in the latter company is larger. The three measurements of dispersion connected with the mean are the range, the variance, and the standard deviation. The range refers to the extreme values in a set of observations. The range is between 30 and 50 for Company A (a dispersion of 20 units), while the range is between 10 and 70 units (a dispersion of 60 units) for Company B. A more useful measure of dispersion is the variance. The variance is calculated by subtracting each of the observations in the data set from the mean, taking the square of this difference, and dividing the total of these by the number of observations. In the above example, the variance for each of the two companies is:

$$\text{Variance for Company A} = \frac{(30 - 40)^2 + (40 - 40)^2 + (50 - 40)^2}{3} = 66\tfrac{2}{3}.$$

$$\text{Variance for Company B} = \frac{(10 - 40)^2 + (40 - 40)^2 + (70 - 40)^2}{3} = 600$$

Standard deviation is another measure of dispersion, which is most commonly used and which is calculated simply as the square root of the variance. In the above case, the standard deviation for the two companies A and B would be $\sqrt{66\tfrac{2}{3}}$ and $\sqrt{600}$ or approximately 8.165 and 24.49, respectively.

The mean and standard deviation are the most common descriptive statistics. The standard deviation, in conjunction with the mean, is a very useful tool because of the following statistical rules, in a normal distribution:

1. Practically all observations fall within three standard deviations of the average or the mean.

2. More than 90 percent of the observations are within two standard deviations of the mean.

3. More than half of the observations are within one standard deviation of the mean.

What this indicates to the manager then, is that when the average is 40 units, and the standard deviation for Company A is 8.16, he would need anywhere between 15 and 65 units for the next month [$40 \pm (3 \times 8.165)$]. In other words, in all probability, he would need no more than 65 units. For Company B, on the other hand, the demand could be as high as 114 units. The demand could vary anywhere between 0 and 114 [$40 \pm (3 \times 24.495)$]—a much wider spread.

As can be readily seen, if the manager wants to estimate the optimum number of units to be manufactured for the next month, based on the three months' sales data, he will be more in a predicament if he is the manager in Company B than in Company A, even though both companies sold 40 units on an average. Rather than try to estimate how many units should be produced based on the past three months' average, the manager in Company B might opt to trace the trends during the same months in the previous year and make his estimation based on this, since there is so much variability in the sales!

In the foregoing example, the calculation of the **mean** (or the **average**) and the **standard deviation** were possible since the observations pertained to values measured on a ratio scale—that is, they were not nominal or ordinal in nature. Whenever observations are measured either on an interval or a ratio scale, it is possible to calculate the mean. It would be useful to refer to discussions on scales and to Figure 6.3 in Chapter 6, where the mean is shown to be appropriate as a measure of central tendency and the variance and standard deviation are indicated as appropriate indicators of the dispersion when either the interval or ratio scale is used as the basis of measurement.

Median

Sometimes we may be interested in knowing where we stand in comparison to others—are we in the middle, in the upper 10 or 25 percent, or in lower 20 or 25 percent, or what. For instance, if in a company-administered test, Mr. Chou scores 78 out of a possible total of 100 points, he would be unhappy if he is in the bottom 10 percent among his colleagues (the test-takers), but will be reasonably pleased if he is in the top 10 percent, despite the fact that his score remains the same. His position in relation to the others can be determined by the central tendency **median** and the dispersion.

The median is the central item in a group of observations when they are arrayed in either ascending or descending order. Let us take an example to examine how the median is determined as a measure of central tendency. Let us say the salaries of nine employees in a department are $65,000, $30,000, $25,000, $64,000, $35,000, $63,000, $32,000, $60,000, and $61,000. The mean salary here works out to be about $46,300, but the median is $60,000. That is, when arrayed in the ascending order, the figures will be as follows: $25,000, $30,000, $32,000, $35,000, $60,000, $61,000, $63,000, $64,000, $65,000, and the figure in the middle is $60,000.

With the median as the measure of central tendency, percentiles, deciles, and quartiles become meaningful. Just as the median divides the total area of observations into two equal halves, the quartile divides it into 4 equal parts, the decile into 10, and the percentile to 100 equal parts. The percentile is useful when huge masses of data, such as the GRE or GMAT scores, are handled. When the area of observations is divided into 100 equal parts, there are 99 percentile points, each with a probability of .01 that any given score will fall in any one of those points. If John's score is in the sixteenth percentile, it indicates that 84 percent of those who took the exam scored better than he did, while 15 percent did worse.

The measure of dispersion for the median is the **interquartile range,** which is calculated by taking the ratio of (1) the difference between the first and third quartiles and (2) their sum. In the above example of the salary of the nine individuals in the department, the individual who earns $32,000 is in the first quartile,

Figure 9.1a
Box and whisker plot

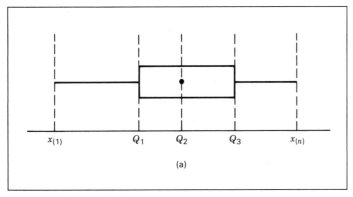

(a)

Figure 9.1b
Comparison of telephone bills in three cities. (*Source:* Salvia, A. A. (1990). *Introduction to Statistics.* Philadelphia: Saunders.)

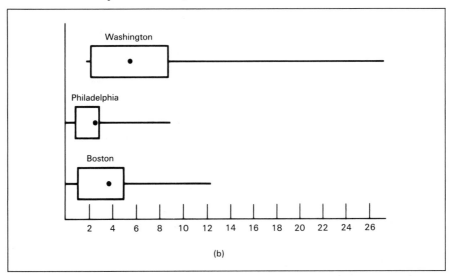

(b)

and the one who earns $63,000 is in the third quartile, since the median obviously falls in the second quartile.

When comparisons are to be made among several groups, the interquartile range could be very useful. For instance, telephone companies can compare long-distance charges of customers in several areas by taking samples of customer bills from each of the cities to be compared. By plotting the first and third quartile and comparing the median and the spread, they can get a good idea of where billings tend to be highest, to what extent customers vary in how much use they make of long-distance calls, and so on. This is done by the box-and-whisker plot for each area, where a box is drawn extending from the first to the third quartile and lines are drawn from either side of the box to the extreme scores, as shown in Figure 9.1. The median is represented by a dot within each box. Side-by-side comparisons of the various plots clearly indicate the highest value, the range, and the spread for each area or city. For a fuller discussion on this, refer to Salvia (1990).

Mode

In some cases, a set of observations would not lend itself to be meaningfully represented through either the mean or the median, but can be described by the most frequently occurring phenomenon within the set of observations. For instance, in a department where there are 10 white women, 24 white men, 3 black women, and 2 Asian women, the most frequently occurring number—the **mode**—is the white men. Neither a mean nor a median is calculable in this case. There is also no way of indicating any measure of dispersion. As is evident from the above, nominal data lend themselves only to be described by the mode as a measure of central tendency (see discussions in Chapter 6 and Figure 6.3). It is possible that a data set could contain bimodal observations. For example, using the foregoing scenario, there could also be 24 Asian men who are specially recruited for a project. Then we have two modes, the white men and the Asian men.

We have illustrated how the mean, median, and the mode can be useful measures of central tendencies, based on the type of data we have. Likewise, we have shown how the standard deviation (and variance, which is the square of standard deviation), and the interquartile range are useful measures of dispersion.

INFERENTIAL STATISTICS

Thus far, we have discussed descriptive statistics. Many times, however, we will be interested in inferential statistics. We might be interested in knowing the relationship between two variables, differences in a variable among different subgroups, how several independent variables might explain the dependent variable, and so on. We will discuss some of these types of analyses now.

Correlations

In a research project that includes several variables, beyond knowing the means and standard deviations of the dependent and independent variables, we would often like to know how one variable is related to another. That is, we would like to

Figure 9.2a
Scatter diagram with no discernible pattern.

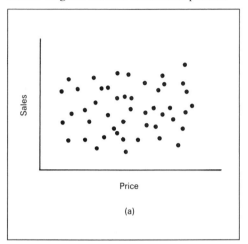

(a)

Figure 9.2b
Scatter diagram indicating a downward or negative slope.

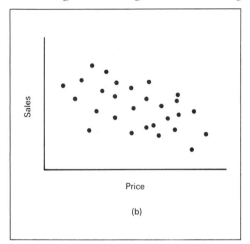

(b)

see the nature, direction, and significance of the bivariate relationships (i.e., relationship between two variables). A Pearson correlation matrix will provide this information—that is, will indicate the direction, strength, and significance of the bivariate relationships among the variables in the study.

The correlation is derived by assessing the variations in one variable as another variable also varies. For the sake of simplicity, let us say we have collected data on two variables: price and sales. The volume of sales at every price level can be plotted as shown in the scatter diagrams in Figure 9.2*a* and 9.2*b*. Figure 9.2*b* indicates a discernible pattern in how the two factors vary simultaneously (the trend of the scatter is that of a downward straight line), whereas Figure 9.2*a* does not indicate any pattern. Looking at the scatter diagram in Figure 9.2*b*, it would seem there is a direct negative correlation between price and sales. That is, as price increases, the sales of the product drop consistently. Figure 9.2*a* suggests no interpretable pattern. A correlation coefficient that indicates the strength and direction of the relationship can be computed by applying a formula that takes into consideration the two sets of figures—different sales volume at different prices.

Theoretically, there could be a perfect positive correlation between two variables, which is represented by 1.0, or there could be a perfect negative correlation which would be −1.0. However, neither of these will be found in reality when assessing the correlations between two variables that are expected to be different from each other. While the correlation could range between −1.0 and +1.0, we need to know if a correlation between two variables is significant or not (i.e., if it has occurred by chance alone or if there is a high probability of its true existence). As we know, a significance of $p \leq .05$ is the generally accepted conventional level in social science research. This indicates that 95 times out of 100, we can be sure that there is a true or significant correlation between the two variables, and there is only a 5 percent chance that the relationship does not exist. If there is a correlation of .56 (denoted as $r = .56$) between two variables A and B, with $p < .01$, then we know that there is a positive relationship between the two variables and the probability of this not being true is 1 percent or less. That is, over 99 percent of the time we would expect this correlation to exist. The correlation of .56 also indicates that the variables would explain the variance in one another to the extent of 31.4 percent $(.56^2)$.*

We would not know which variable *causes* which, but we would know that the two variables are associated with each other. Thus, a hypothesis that postulates a significant positive (or negative) relationship between two variables can be tested by examining the correlation between the two. The Pearson Correlation, which indicates the strength of relationship (r) between two variables, can be mean-ingfully generated for variables measured on an interval or ratio scale. Other nonparametric tests are available to assess the relationship between variables not measured on an interval or ratio scale. See Table 9.4 for some of these.

Relationship Among Nominal Variables: χ^2 Test

We might sometimes want to know if there is a relationship between two nominal variables or whether they are independent of each other. As examples: (1) Is viewing television advertisement of a product (yes/no) related to the buying of that product by individuals (buy/don't buy)? (2) Is the type of jobs done by individuals (high level white-collar jobs vs. low level blue-collar jobs) a function of the color of the employee's skin (white vs. nonwhite)? We might collect data from a sample of 55 individuals whose color of skin and nature of jobs, culled from a frequency count, might be illustrated as in Table 9.2 in a two-by-two contingency table.

Just by looking at Table 9.2 a clear pattern seems to emerge that those who are white hold white-collar jobs. Very few of those who are nonwhite hold white-collar jobs. Thus, there does seem to be a relationship between the color of the skin and the type of job handled; the two do not seem to be independent. This can be statistically confirmed by the chi-square (χ^2) test—a nonparametric test—which would indicate whether the observed pattern is due to chance or not. The χ^2 test operates on the principle of expected (based on probability) and actual frequencies and the χ^2 statistic is obtained by the formula:

$$\chi^2 = \sum \frac{(O_i - E)^2}{E_i}$$

where χ^2 is the chi-square statistic; O_i is the observed frequency in the ith cell; and E_i is the expected frequency of the ith cell. Computers can be programmed to give the χ^2 statistic for any given set of data, with the level of significance of the χ^2 statistic indicated on the output.

χ^2 statistic can also be used for multiple levels of both the variables. For instance, one might be interested in knowing if four groups of employees—production,

---

*For a detailed discussion of the inferences drawn and some problems associated with it, the advanced student is referred to Jacob Cohen's (1990, December) article titled, "Things I Have Learned (So Far)" in the *American Psychologist*, pp. 1304–1312.

Table 9.2
Contingency Table of Skin Color and Job Type

		Job Type		
		White Collar	Blue Collar	Total
SKIN C O L O R	White	30	5	35
	Nonwhite	2	18	20
	Total	32	23	55

sales, marketing, and R & D personnel—react to a policy in four different ways, with no interest at all, with mild interest, moderate interest, and intense interest. Here the χ^2 value for the test of independence will be generated by cross-tabulating the data in 16 cells—that is, classifying the data in terms of the four subgroups of humans and the four categories of interest.

The χ^2 test of significance thus helps us to see whether or not two nominal variables are related. There are other alternatives to the χ^2 test such as the **Fisher exact probability test,** which is used when the expected frequencies are small.

Significant Mean Differences Between Two Groups: The t-Test

There are many instances when we would be interested in knowing whether two groups are different from each other on a particular variable of interest. For example, would men and women indicate their preference for the introduction of flexitime at the workplace to the same extent or would they differ in their need for it? Do MBAs perform better in organizational settings than business students who have only a bachelor's degree? Do individuals in the urban area have a different investment pattern of their savings than those in semi-urban areas? To find answers to such questions, a t-Test is used to see if there are any significant differences in the means for two groups in the variable of interest. That is, a **nominal** variable that is split into *two* subgroups (as for example, smokers and nonsmokers; employees in the marketing department and employees in the accounting department; younger and older employees) is tested to see if there is a significant mean difference between them on a dependent variable, which is measured on an **interval** or **ratio** scale (as for instance, extent of well-being; pay; comprehension level).

The t-Test takes into consideration the means and standard deviations of the two groups on the variable and examines if the numerical difference in the means is significantly different from 0 (zero) as postulated in our null hypothesis. We examined this under **sample data and hypothesis testing** in the last chapter.

When we compare the mean differences between two different groups on a variable, we have a t-Test done on two independent samples. The t-Test can also be used to examine the differences in the same group before and after a treatment. For example, would a group of employees who have undergone training perform better *after* receiving the training than they did *before?* In this case, the formula for the *t*-Test is adjusted to take into account correlation between the two scores, if any. In other words, the adjusted *t*-Test for the matched sample or other type of dependent samples reflects the true mean differences.

Significant Mean Differences Among Multiple Groups: ANOVA

Whereas the *t*-Test would indicate whether or not there is a significant mean difference in a dependent variable between two groups, an **Analysis of Variance** (ANOVA) will help to examine if there are significant mean differences among more than two groups. For example, would there be a significant difference in the sales made by the following four groups of salespersons: those who are sent to training schools; those who are given on-the-job training during field trips; those who have been tutored by the sales manager; and those who have had none of these three. Another example would be to see if the rate of promotion is significantly different for those who have assigned mentors, for those who choose their own mentors, and for those who have no mentors in the organizational system.

The results of ANOVA will indicate whether or not the means of the various groups are significantly different *from one another* or not. If there are significant mean differences among the groups as indicated by the significance level of the F statistic, there is no way of knowing from the ANOVA results alone where the differences lie. That is, whether the significant difference is between groups A and B, or between B and C, or A and C, and so on. Here it would be unwise to use multiple *t*-Tests, taking two groups at a time, because the greater the number of *t*-Tests done, the lower is the confidence we can place on our results. For example, doing three *t*-Tests simultaneously decreases the confidence from 95 percent to 86 percent $(.95)^3$. However, several tests such as Scheffe's test, Duncan Multiple Range test, Tukey's test, and Student-Newman-Keul's test are available and can be used, as appropriate, to detect where exactly the mean differences lie.

Multiple Regression

Whereas the correlation coefficient *r* indicates the strength of relationship between two variables, it gives us no idea of how much of the variance in the dependent variable will be explained when several independent variables are theorized to *simultaneously* influence it. For example, when the variance in a dependent variable *X* (say performance) is expected to be explained by four independent variables, *A, B, C,* and *D* (say, pay, task difficulty, supervisory support, and organizational culture), it should be noted that not only are the four independent variables correlated to the dependent variable in varying degrees, but they might also be intercorrelated (i.e., among themselves). For example, task difficulty is likely to be related to supervisory support, pay might be correlated to task difficulty, and all three might influence the organizational culture. When these variables are jointly regressed against the dependent variable in an effort to explain the variance in *A,* the individual correlations get collapsed into what is called a **multiple *r*** or multi-

Table 9.3
Statistical Techniques and Tests Classified According to Type, Number, and Measurement Scale of Variables[a]

		Criterion Variables					
		One			Two or More		
		Nominal	Ordinal	Interval	Nominal	Ordinal	Interval
Variates — One	Nominal	Chi-square test for independence Contingency coefficient Cochran Q test Fisher exact probability Test for 2 × 2 tables	Sign test Median test Mann–Whitney U test Kruskal-Wallis one-way analysis of variance	Analysis of variance			Multiple discriminant analysis
	Ordinal		Spearman's rank correlation Kendall's rank correlation	Analysis of variance with trend analysis			
Variates — Two or More	Interval	Analysis of variance		Regression analysis (multiple correlation coefficient)	Analysis of variance		Multiple regression analysis
	Nominal		Friedman two-way analysis of variance	Analysis of variance (factorial design)			Analysis of variance
	Ordinal						
	Interval	Multiple discriminant analysis		Multiple regression analysis	Multiple discriminant analysis		Canonical correlation

[a]Taken from R. L. Baker & R. E. Schultz (Eds.). *Instructional product research.* New York: Van Nostrand Co., 1972, p. 110.

ple correlation. The square of multiple r, R-square or R^2 as it is commonly known, is the amount of variance explained in the dependent variable by the predictors. Such analysis, where more than one predictor are jointly regressed against the criterion variable, is known as **multiple regression** analysis. When the R-square value, the F statistic, and its significance level are known, we can interpret the results. For example, if the R^2 is .63 with an F value of say, 25.56, and a significance level of $p <$ .005, then we can say that 63 percent of the variance has been significantly ex-

Table 9.4

Information on Some Nonparametric Tests

Test	When Used	Function
Chi-Square	With **nominal** data for one sample or two or more independent samples.	Tests for independence of variables.
Cochran Q	With more than two related samples measured on **nominal** scale.	Helps when data fall into two natural categories.
Fisher Exact Probability	With two independent samples measured on **nominal** scale.	More useful than χ^2 when expected frequencies are small.
Sign test	With two related samples measured on **ordinal** scale.	A good test for ranked data.
Median test	With one sample, to see if randomly drawn measurements are from a population with a specified median.	In a symmetric distribution, the mean and median will be the same.
Mann-Whitney U test	With two independent samples on **ordinal** data.	Analogue of the two independent sample *t*-Test.
Kruskal-Wallis one-way ANOVA	With more than two independent samples on an **ordinal** scale.	An alternative to one-way ANOVA where normality of distributions cannot be assumed.
Friedman two-way ANOVA	With more than two related samples on **ordinal** data.	A good alternative to two-way ANOVA where normality cannot be assumed.
Kolmogorov-Smirnov	With one sample or two independent samples measured on an **ordinal** scale.	Is a more powerful test than χ^2 or Mann-Whitney U.

plained by the set of predictors. The chance of this not being true is only .005 percent!

In sum, multiple regression analysis helps us to understand how much of the variance in the dependent variable is explained by a set of predictors. If we want to know which, among the set of predictors, is the most important in explaining the variance, which is the next most important, and so on, a stepwise multiple regression analysis can be done. If we want to know whether a set of job-related variables (e.g., job challenge, job variety, and job stress) would significantly add to the variance explained in the dependent variable (say, job satisfaction) by a set of organizational factors (e.g., participation in decision making, communication, supervisory relationship), a hierarchical regression analysis can be done. A discussion of these is beyond the scope of this book.

Other Tests and Analyses

Several other tests and statistical techniques, not discussed here, are shown in Table 9.3. These include nonparametric tests such as the Sign test and the Mann–Whitney U test and also other multivariate analytic techniques such as discriminant analysis, and canonical correlations. The table is helpful since it shows the statistical techniques and tests that are appropriate for data that are measured on different scales for the dependent and independent variables. Table 9.4 also provides some additional information on some of the other nonparametric tests—when they can be used and how they are useful.

ANALYSIS OF QUALITATIVE DATA

When responses to open-ended questions are obtained through interviews, or data are collected through observations or through open-ended questions in a questionnaire, they can be categorized and coded according to some meaningful classification scheme. Thereafter, frequency counts can be taken, and χ^2 or other appropriate nonparametric tests can be done. In Chapter 7, we saw how personal computers can be programmed to record and analyze such data.

As an example, a manager might be concerned about the productivity at the workplace, especially since a diverse group of individuals work together. The researcher who assists the manager might want to know how people of different ethnic origins might perceive their white bosses. Would these individuals feel they are respected and treated well at the workplace, that they are not being stereotyped in different ways, and that their being different is valued rather than devalued? In addition, the researcher might want to know if there are any special needs expressed by individuals based on their parenting status. For instance, women with infants and small children might like flexi-time or flexi-place or part-time jobs, which might improve their productivity.

The researcher might talk to several employees about these issues, make a note of the ethnic origin, parenthood status, and responses to a number of open-ended questions. These may be later tabulated and coded. The data can then be entered in the computer. For example, if a Hispanic woman feels that communicating with the boss is a problem for her, this could be coded as a communication concern. If a black man indicates that he is being discriminated against in the nature of the tasks assigned to him, then it could be coded under "discrimination:task," and so on. All the items coded, including the ethnic origin, parenthood status, and so on, can then be submitted for cross tabulation and a χ^2 test.

Table 9.5 illustrates a tabulation of the responses obtained from 25 employees to

Table 9.5

Tabulation of Responses Obtained from 25 Interviewees

Nature of Responses	Physical	Psychological	Substantive
FAVORABLE	# Relieves physical exhaustion. ## Will reduce muscular pains. ### Can sleep better at night.	@ Don't have to worry about personal responsibility for meeting targets. @@ Mind is free to think about other things as well.	* Production will increase. ** Just-in-time systems can be easily incorporated. + Less supervision needed.
UNFAVORABLE	$ Sedantary life not good for physical fitness. = Muscles will get flabby.	x Sooner or later there will be layoffs. xx I am not sure what I am now! xxx Do I have to learn new things now? At my age will I be able to?	& Will the heavy investment really pay off in the long run? ^ Maintenance costs can be very high. % Too much time will be spent on training—meantime, production will suffer.
Respondents	Respondents	Respondents	
# 6, 8, 15, 22 ## 8, 15, 19 ### 6, 8, 15, 19	@ 1, 11, 16, 17 @@ 3, 8, 9, 13, 16 $ 2, 20, 24 = 9	* 4, 7, 10 ** 7, 12, 18 + 10, 12, 14	
x 1, 9, 21 xx 2, 3, 22, 24 xxx 9, 23	& 10, 18, 25 ^ 4, 12, 18 % 7, 12, 14	Top Managers: 4, 7, 10 Middle Managers: 12, 14, 18, 25 Blue Collar: All the rest	

the open-ended, unstructured interview asking the question: "What is your reaction to the computerized production system recently introduced?" Frequency counts can then be obtained based on these tabulations and the applicable nonparametric tests used to interpret data.

SUMMARY

In this chapter, we briefly revisited some statistical terms and tests. Now that we have refreshed our memory with the necessary background materials, in the next chapter, we will discuss how the data are actually analyzed. The Supplementary Readings List offered for this chapter at the end of the book will be useful if more in-depth understanding of the various statistical tests is needed.

DISCUSSION QUESTIONS

1. Which measures of central tendency and dispersion are appropriate in the following cases, and why?
   a. The ages of individuals who are grouped as follows:

Under 25	3
25–35	120
36–55	80
Over 55	22

   b. The performance ratings (on a 100-point scale) given by the head of the department to the top six performers:

Top scorer	87 percent
Second in rank	82 percent
Third	81 percent
Fourth	76 percent
Fifth	74 percent
Sixth	68 percent

   c. The weights of eight boxes of raw materials purchased: 275, 263, 298, 197, 275, 287, 263, and 243 pounds.

2. What is the chi-square test? Give the example of a research hypothesis (not in the examples given in the book) that would call for a χ^2 test.

3. If you want to know whether three groups of employees—those who have been with the organization between four and six years, between seven and nine years, and between ten and twelve years—are different in the number of trips they have taken outside of the city on business work, what statistical test would you use and why?

4. Explain in your own words what a multiple regression analysis is. Give an organizational situation that would call for the use of multiple regression analysis.

CHAPTER 10

DATA ANALYSIS AND INTERPRETATION

TOPICS DISCUSSED

GETTING DATA READY FOR ANALYSIS
- Editing Data
- Handling Blank Responses
- Coding
- Categorizing

THE SPSSX PROGRAM

BASIC OBJECTIVES IN DATA ANALYSIS
- Feel for the Data
- Testing Goodness of Data
- Hypothesis Testing
- Use of Several Data-Analytic Techniques
- Descriptive Statistics
- Inferential Statistics

INTERPRETATION OF RESULTS

CHAPTER OBJECTIVES

After completing Chapter 10 you should be able to:

1. Edit questionnaire and interview responses.
2. Be able to handle blank responses.
3. Set up the coding key for the data set and code the data.
4. Categorize data.
5. Create a data file.
6. Do SPSSX or SAS or other programming.
7. Get a feel for the data.
8. Test the goodness of data.
9. Interpret the computer results.

10. Deal with any data set given to you or collected by you.

11. Have an idea of how to use the SPSS/PC$^+$ software package.

After data have been collected from a representative sample of the population, the next step is to analyze the data so that the research hypotheses can be tested. Before we can do this, however, some preliminary steps need to be completed. These steps help to prepare the data for analysis, ensure that the data obtained are reasonably good, and allow the results to be meaningfully interpreted. Figure 10.1 shows these steps and identifies the four steps in data analysis as (1) getting data ready for analysis, (2) getting a feel for the data, (3) testing the goodness of data, and (4) testing the hypotheses. We will now examine each of these steps.

Figure 10.1
Flow diagram of data analysis process.

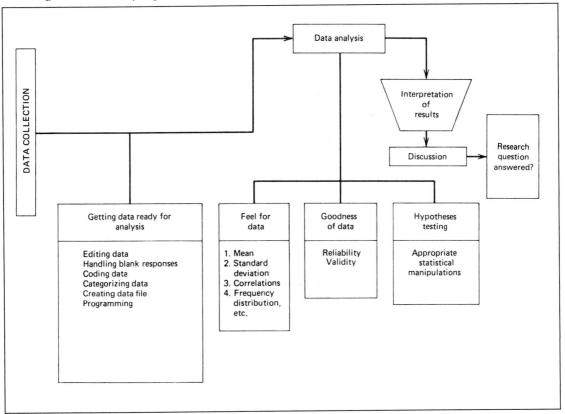

GETTING DATA READY FOR ANALYSIS

After the questionnaire or interview responses or the observational data have been obtained, the data need to be edited. The blank responses, if any, have to be handled in some way; the data then have to be coded, categorized, and keyed in; and decisions need to be made as to how they will be computer analyzed. Each of these stages of data preparation will be briefly discussed.

Editing Data

Especially when the data come from interviews, observations, and questionnaires containing open-ended questions, the data have often to be edited. In other words, information that may have been written by the interviewer, observer, or respondent in a hurry must now be clearly deciphered so that all of it can be coded systematically. Lack of such clarification at this stage will result in confusion when the coding starts and the data have to be categorized under broad heads, and errors in categorization may result from misinterpretation. Also, if there are some inconsistencies in the responses that can be logically corrected, they should be rectified and edited at this stage. For instance, on a questionnaire, the respondent might have inadvertently not answered the question whether or not she is married. In the column asking for the number of years married, she might have responded 12 years; in the number of children column, she might have marked 2, and for ages of children, she might have answered 8 and 4. The latter three responses would indicate that the respondent is married. The first response could then be edited by the researcher to read "yes." However, it is possible that the respondent deliberately omitted responding to the item because she is either a widow or has just been separated or widowed. If such is the case, we would be introducing a bias in the data by editing the data to read "yes." Hence, whenever possible, it would be better to follow up with the respondent and get the correct data while editing. The example we saw is a clear case for editing, but some others may not be so simple, and omissions could be left unnoticed and not rectified. Thus some respondent biases could affect the goodness of the data, and the researcher may have no control over them. The validity and the replicability of the study could thus be impaired. Currently, technology is available where corrections in responses can be automatically taken care of by the computer as discussed in Chapter 7 under Data Collection Methods. However, until such time as the collection of data through computers and automatic editing of data become more feasible, the data collected will have to be carefully edited manually.

Handling Blank Responses

Not all respondents answer every item in the questionnaire. Questions may have been left blank because the respondent did not understand the question, was not willing to answer, or was simply indifferent to responding to the entire questionnaire. If the latter is the case, the respondent may have left many of the items blank.

If more than, say, 25 percent of the questionnaire has been left blank, it may be a good idea to throw out the questionnaire and not include it in the data set for analysis. If, however, only two or three items are left blank in a questionnaire with, say, 30 or more items, we need to decide how these blank responses should be handled.

One way to handle a blank response to an interval-scaled item with a midpoint would be to assign the midpoint in the scale for that particular item. Another way of handling it is to allow the computer to ignore the blank responses when the analyses are done. This, of course, will reduce the sample size for analyses using that variable. A third way is to assign the item the mean value of the responses of all those who have responded to that particular item. A fourth way is to give the item the mean of the responses of this particular respondent to all other questions. A fifth way of dealing with it is to give the missing response a random number within the range of numbers that could occur. As can be seen, there are several ways of handling blank responses; a common way of dealing with this problem, however, is either to give the midpoint in the scale as the value or to ignore the particular item during the analysis. The computer can be programmed to do this. The latter is probably the best way to handle missing data to enhance the validity of the study, especially if the sample size is big.

Where items have a "do not know" response, they can be treated as a missing value and ignored in the analysis. If many of the respondents have answered "do not know" to a particular item or items, however, it might be worth further investigation to find out whether the question was not clear or something else is happening in the organization that might need further probing.

Coding

The next step is to code the responses. In Chapter 7, we discussed the convenience of using scanner sheets for collecting questionnaire data; such sheets will facilitate the entry of the responses directly into the computer without manual keying in of the data. However, if for whatever reason this cannot be done, then it is perhaps better to use a coding sheet first to enter the data from the questionnaire and then key in the data, to avoid confusion, especially when there are many questions in the questionnaire. The easiest way to illustrate a coding scheme is through an example. Let us take the correct answer provided for Exercise 7.1, the questionnaire design exercise to test the job involvement–job satisfaction hypothesis in the Serakan Co. case and set up a coding key (coding system) for it.

Coding Key for the Serakan Co. Data

In the Serakan Co. questionnaire, we have five demographic variables and sixteen items measuring involvement and satisfaction. To follow the points being made here, refer frequently to the code key in Table 10.1. The responses for the demographic variables can be coded from 1 to 5 for the variables age, education, and number of years in the organization, depending on which box in the columns was checked by the respondent. Sex can be coded as 1 or 2 depending on whether the

Table 10.1
Setup of Coding Key for the Serakan Co. Questionnaire

Age (years)	Education	Job level	Sex
① Under 25	① High school	① Manager	① M
② 25–35	② Some college	② Supervisor	② F
③ 36–45	③ Bachelor's degree	③ Clerk	
④ 46–55	④ Master's degree	④ Secretary	
⑤ Over 55	⑤ Doctoral degree	⑤ Technician	
		⑥ Other (specify)	

Number of Years in this Organization
① Less than 1
② 1–3
③ 4–8
④ 9–15
⑤ More than 15

Coding Demographic Variables		
Variable	Column No.	Variable No. (V)
1. Age	7	1
2. Education	8	2
3. Job level	9	3
4. Sex	10	4
5. No. of years in organization	11	5

Here are some questions that ask you to tell us how you experience your worklife in general. Please <u>circle</u> the appropriate number on the scales below.

To what extent would you agree with the following statements, on a scale of 1 to 7, 1 denoting very low agreement, and 7 denoting very high agreement?

		Column No.	Variable No. (V)
1. The major happiness of my life comes from my job.	1 2 3 4 5 6 7	12	6
2. Time at work flies by quickly.	1 2 3 4 5 6 7	13	7
3. I live, eat, and breathe my job.	1 2 3 4 5 6 7	14	8
4. My work is fascinating.	1 2 3 4 5 6 7	15	9
5. My work gives me a sense of accomplishment.	1 2 3 4 5 6 7	16	10
6. My supervisor praises good work.	1 2 3 4 5 6 7	17	11
7. The opportunities for advancement are very good here.	1 2 3 4 5 6 7	18	12

Table 10.1 continued

8. My co-workers are very stimulating.	1 2 3 4 5 6 7	19	13
9. People can live comfortably with their pay in this organization.	1 2 3 4 5 6 7	20	14
10. I get a lot of cooperation at the workplace.	1 2 3 4 5 6 7	21	15
11. My supervisor is not very capable.	1 2 3 4 5 6 7	22	16
12. Most things in life are more important than work.	1 2 3 4 5 6 7	23	17
13. Working here is a drag.	1 2 3 4 5 6 7	24	18
14. The promotion policies here are very unfair.	1 2 3 4 5 6 7	25	19
15. My pay is barely adequate to take care of my expenses.	1 2 3 4 5 6 7	26	20
16. My work is not the most important part of my life.	1 2 3 4 5 6 7	27	21
Respondent no. (questionnaire no.)		76–80	

response was from a male or a female. The job levels can be coded from 1 to 6 depending on the actual job level of the respondent as in the numbers given in the boxes in the table. Item numbers 1 to 16 on the questionnaire can be coded by using the actual number circled by the respondents. If, for instance, 3 has been circled for the first question, then the response will be coded as 3; if it was circled 4, we would code it as 4, and so on, for each of the next 15 items. Note that in this questionnaire, every item can have only a single-digit response. Contrast this with asking the *actual* age without giving a range. In this case, one would expect to find double-digit number responses from organizational members (age is 35, 46, etc.). If only a one-digit number is to be coded, it is enough to provide one column for the variable; if, however, some variables are likely to have either single- or double-digit numbers (e.g., age 9 or 90), then we need to allocate two columns for entering such variables. The 9 will be in the second column, and the 90 in columns 1 and 2 as 9 and 0. Age 9 can also be coded as 09 in columns 1 and 2.

Every record (or line of data entered) usually has 80 columns. Coding and entering data could start from any column. You could start coding from column 1, or you could leave, say, the first six columns blank and start coding from column 7 as shown in Table 10.2. The last four of the 80 columns can be kept for coding the number of the questionnaire. This may prove useful later to identify errors in coding and rectifying them. As the questionnaires are received, they could be sequentially numbered. We do not normally expect to administer more than 9999 questionnaires, so the last four of the 80 columns are considered more than adequate to record the questionnaire number.

Table 10.2

Code Setup for the Serakan Co. Responses

Taking the Serakan Co. questionnaire, we could start coding from column 7 and end the coding of the five demographic variables and the other 16 items in column 27. See the column number specified to the immediate right of the items in Table 10.1. This questionnaire is fairly short and hence a simple one to code. What if one had a questionnaire with 120 items in it for coding? In this case, instead of only one record (i.e., one line of 80 columns), two or more records will be required for coding each respondent's answers.

Note that coding could start from column 1 of each record. Each subject could also be given an identification number, in addition to every record being given a running serial number.

Because coding can become monotonous if the number of questionnaires to be coded is large and the number of questions in the questionnaire are also many, human errors can occur while coding. Therefore, at least 10 percent of the coded questionnaires should be checked for coding accuracy. Questionnaires may be selected using a systematic sampling procedure for this purpose. That is, every *n*th form coded will be verified for accuracy. If many errors are found in the sample, *all* items may have to be checked.

Variables Listing

Now that the variables have been coded, they need to be given sequential variable numbers starting with V1 (for variable 1, which is the age variable). Because we have a total of twenty-one variables (five demographic plus sixteen to measure involvement and satisfaction), we will number them as V1 to V21. See the variable numbers so identified to the extreme right of the items in Table 10.1. Instead of giving each variable a number such as V1, V2, and V3, and so on, the variables can be identified as **age, educn, job,** and so on (no more than eight letters to represent a variable); or they can be identified as VAR001, VAR002, VAR003, and so on. Identifying the variables thus will help in setting up the computer program to analyze the data.

Categorization

At this point it is useful to categorize the variables such that the several items measuring the concept are all grouped together for feeding into the computer later. Responses to some of the negatively worded questions have to be reversed so that all answers are in the same direction. Note that with respect to negatively worded questions, a response of 7 on a seven-point scale, with 7 denoting "strongly agree," really means "strongly disagree," which actually is a 1 on the seven-point scale. Thus the item has to be reversed so as to be in the same direction as the positively worded questions. This can be done on the computer through a RECODE statement as described later. In the Serakan Co. data, variables V16 to V21, will have to be recoded such that scores of 7 are read as 1; 6 as 2; 5 as 3; 3 as 5; 2 as 6; and 1 as 7.

If the questions measuring a concept are not contiguous but are scattered over various parts of the questionnaire, care has to be taken to include all the items without any omissions or wrong inclusions. The reversal of the appropriate items is also important. This categorization will be used when the computer programs are to be run.

Keying Data

If questionnaire data are not collected on scanner answer sheets, which can be directly entered into the computer as a data file, the raw data will have to be manually keyed into the computer. Mistakes can occur at this stage as well. To ensure that the correct figures are entered into the right columns, initially every tenth record or so can be spot-checked for accuracy. If mistakes are detected, it would then become necessary for one person to read each of the figures on the code sheet as another checks for the accuracy of the keyed-in data (from a printout of the raw data entered into the computer). Because the results obtained from data analyses can only be as good as the raw data entered, care should be taken to minimize errors at this stage. The coding error problem is avoided when the data are collected through computer surveys as discussed in Chapter 7.

Once the data are checked for accuracy, it would be a good idea to have them transferred on to a magnetic tape and/or to a disk, as a backup. The procedure to do these will be readily available from the computer departments in universities.

When the raw data have been entered into the computer, they are ready for analysis. Several statistical packages are available for data analysis such as the SPSSX, SAS, Stat-Easy, and Minitab. The most commonly used ones in business are the **Statistical Package for the Social Sciences** (SPSSX) and the **Statistical Analysis System** (SAS). Data can be analyzed using the mainframe or the personal computer (PC). Several user-friendly software programs are also available for data analysis on PCs, including SPSSX and SAS programs. These will be briefly discussed, later in this chapter.

DATA ANALYSIS: PROGRAMMING

We will elaborate, in the rest of this chapter, on the various statistical tests and the interpretation of the results of the analyses. Though the results shown in this chapter were generated through the SPSSX program, any other program would also produce similar results, and the data will be interpreted in the same manner. If the mainframe is used, the results can be obtained by submitting batch files or through the interactive system. In the batch system, the job that is submitted gets into a queue with all other jobs and has to wait its turn to be processed based on the time, memory, and so on, that is required to compute the results. In the interactive system, the job gets processed right away without entering the queue and, hence, the turnaround of results is fast.

The programming procedures, integral to the specific computer programs used, should be readily available in your system and should be followed while analyzing data. Different statistical tests call for different procedure statements, and once these are entered, the results are computed.

BASIC OBJECTIVES IN DATA ANALYSIS

In data analysis we have three objectives: getting a feel for the data, testing the goodness of data, and testing the hypotheses developed for the research. The feel for the data will give preliminary ideas of how good the scales are, how well the coding and entering of data have been done, and so on. Suppose an item tapped on a seven-point scale has been improperly coded and/or entered as 8; this will be highlighted by the maximum values on the descriptive statistics and can be corrected. The second objective—testing the goodness of data—can be accomplished by submitting the data for factor analysis, obtaining the Cronbach's alpha or the split-half reliability of the measures, and so on. The third objective—hypotheses testing—is achieved by programming the computer to test each of the hypotheses with the appropriate statistical test, the results of which will determine whether or not the hypotheses are substantiated. We will now discuss data analysis with respect to each of these three objectives in detail.

Feel for the Data

We can acquire a feel for the data by checking the central tendency and the dispersion. The mean, the range, the standard deviation, and the variance in the data will give the researcher a good idea of how the respondents reacted to the items in the questionnaire and how good the items and measures are. If the responses do not have a good spread and show very little variability, then the researcher would suspect that the question was probably not properly worded and respondents did not quite understand what was intended to be asked. Biases, if any, could also be detected if the respondents have tended to respond similarly to all items—that is, stuck to certain points on the scale. The mean, standard deviation, maximum and minimum scores, range, skewness, and so on, can be easily obtained through the CONDESCRIPTIVE command or other appropriate commands if using other programs. It is important to obtain these statistics, which indicate whether the responses range over the scale. Researchers go to great lengths obtaining the central tendency, the range, the dispersion, and other statistics for every single item measuring the dependent and independent variables, especially when the measures are being developed and tested.

It is also important to get a feel for the demographic characteristics of the respondents. A frequency distribution of the nominal variables of interest, together with visual displays of the frequencies through histograms/bar charts can be obtained by appropriately programming the computer. In addition to the frequency distributions and the means and standard deviations, it is good to know how the dependent and independent variables are related to each other. For this purpose, an intercorrelation matrix of these variables should also be obtained. It is always prudent to obtain (1) the frequency distributions for the demographic variables, (2) the mean, standard deviation, range, and variance on the other dependent and independent variables, and (3) an intercorrelation matrix of the variables, irrespective of whether the hypotheses are directly related to these analyses or not. These statistics give a feel for the data. In other words, looking at the results of these analyses, we would know how the respondents perceive the work environment or any other variable that is assessed, by examining the mean, median, or mode, and also see how clustered or dispersed these perceptions happen to be by looking at the dispersions. The correlations would also give an indication of how closely related or unrelated the variables under investigation are. If the correlation between two variables happens to be high—say, over .75—we might start wondering whether there are really two different concepts, or whether they are measuring the same concept. If two variables that are theoretically stated to be related do not seem to be significantly correlated to each other in our sample, we would begin to wonder if we have measured the concepts validly and reliably. Recall our discussions on convergent and discriminant validity in Chapter 7. Such concerns for goodness of our data surface even as we go through the preliminary steps discussed here. Hence, getting a feel for the data becomes the necessary first step in all data analysis. Based on this initial feel, further detailed analyses can be done to test the goodness of the data.

Testing Goodness of Data

The reliability and validity of the measures can now be tested.

VALIDITY

Factorial validity can be established by submitting the data for factor analysis. The results of factor analysis (a multivariate technique) will confirm whether or not the theorized dimensions emerge. Recall from Chapter 3 that measures are developed by first delineating the dimensions, so as to operationalize the concept. Factor analysis would reveal whether the theorized dimensions are indeed tapped by the items in the measure. Criterion-related validity can also be established by testing for the power of the measure to differentiate individuals who are known to be different (refer to discussions regarding concurrent and predictive validity in Chapter 6). Convergent validity can be established when there is a high degree of correlation between two different sources responding to the same measure (e.g., both supervisors and subordinates respond similarly to a **perceived reward system** measure administered to them). Discriminant validity can be established when two distinctly different concepts are not correlated to each other (as for example, courage and honesty; leadership and motivation; attitudes and behavior). Convergent and discriminant validity can be established through the multitrait–multimethod matrix, a full discussion of which is beyond the scope of this book. The student interested in knowing more about factor analysis and the multitrait–multimethod matrix is referred particularly to Gorsuch (1974) and Campbell and Fiske (1959), respectively.

RELIABILITY

As discussed in Chapter 6, the reliability of a measure is established by testing for both consistency and stability. Consistency indicates how the items measuring a concept hang well together as a set. **Cronbach's alpha** is a reliability coefficient that reflects how well the items in a set are positively correlated to one another. Cronbach's alpha is computed in terms of the average intercorrelations among the items measuring the concept. The closer Cronbach's alpha is to 1, the higher the internal consistency reliability.

Another measure of consistency reliability used in specific situations is the **split-half** reliability coefficient. Since this reflects the correlations between two halves of a set of items, the coefficients obtained will *vary* depending on how the scale is split. Sometimes split-half reliability is obtained to test for consistency when more than one scale, dimension, or factor, is assessed, and the items across each of the dimensions or factors are split based on some predetermined logic (Campbell, 1976). In almost every case, Cronbach's alpha is an adequate test of internal consistency reliability.

As discussed in Chapter 6, the stability of a measure can be assessed through **parallel form** reliability and **test–retest** reliability. When a high correlation between two similar forms of a measure (see Chapter 6) is obtained, parallel form reliability is established. Test–retest reliability can be established by computing the correlation between the same test administered at two different time periods.

HYPOTHESIS TESTING

Once the data are cleaned up (i.e., out-of-range/missing responses, etc., are taken care of) and the goodness of the measures is established, the researcher is ready to test the hypotheses developed for the study. In the previous chapter, we discussed the statistical tests that would be appropriate for different hypotheses and for data obtained on different scales. We will now examine the results obtained from data analyses and how they are interpreted.

DATA ANALYSIS AND INTERPRETATION

Data analysis and interpretation of results can be most meaningfully explained by referring to a business research project. After a very brief description of the background of the company in which the research was carried out and the sample, we will discuss the data analysis done for testing each hypothesis and how the results were interpreted.

RESEARCH DONE IN KRIYA ENTERPRISES

Kriya Enterprises is a medium-sized company, manufacturing and selling instruments and supplies needed by the health care industry, including blood pressure instruments, surgical instruments, dental accessories, and so on. The company, with a total of 320 employees working three shifts, is doing reasonably well but could do far better if it did not experience employee turnover at almost all levels and in all the departments. The President of the Company called in a research team to study the situation and to make recommendations regarding the turnover problem.

Since tracing those who left the company and getting access to them was difficult, the research team suggested to the President that they talk to the current employees, and based on their inputs and a literature survey, try to understand the factors associated with employees' **intentions to stay with, or leave,** the company. Since intention to leave has been shown to be an excellent predictor of actual turnover, the President thought this was a good idea and agreed.

The team first conducted an unstructured interview of about fifty employees at various levels and from different departments. Their broad statement was: "We are here to find out how you experience your worklife. Tell us whatever you consider is important for you in your job, as issues relate to your work, the environment, the organization, supervision, and whatever else you think is relevant. If we get a good handle on the issues involved, we may be able to make appropriate recommendations to management after talking to you and administering a questionnaire survey thereafter."

Each interview typically lasted about forty-five minutes, and the responses were written down verbatim by the team. When the responses were tabulated, it became clear that the issues most frequently brought up by the respondents in one form or another, related to three main areas: the **job** (employees said the jobs were dull or too complex; not enough freedom to do the job as one wanted to, etc.), **perceived inequities** (remarks such as: "other companies pay more for the kind of jobs we do"; "compared to the work we do, we do not get paid enough"; etc); and **burnout** (comments such as, "there is so much work to be done that by the end of the day we are physically and emotionally exhausted"; "we frequently feel the need to take time off because of exhaustion"; etc.).

A literature survey confirmed that these were good predictors of intention to leave and subsequent turnover. In addition, **job satisfaction** was also found to be a useful predictor. A theoretical framework was developed based on the interviews and the literature survey, and five hypotheses (stated later) were developed.

Next, a questionnaire was designed incorporating well-validated and reliable measures for the four independent variables of job characteristics, perceived inequity, burnout, and job satisfaction, and the dependent variable of intention to leave. Demographic variables such as age, education, gender, tenure, job title, department, and work shift were also included in the questionnaire.

The questionnaire was administered personally to 174 employees who were chosen on a stratified (on the basis of department and job level) random sampling basis. The responses obtained on scanners were entered directly into the computer. Thereafter, the data were submitted for analysis to test the following hypotheses, which were formulated by the researchers:

1. Men will perceive more inequities than women.
2. The job satisfaction of individuals will vary depending on the shift they work.
3. Employees' intentions to leave will vary according to their job title. In other words, there will be significant differences in the ITL of top managers, middle-level managers, supervisors, and the clerical and blue-collar employees.
4. There will be a relationship between the shifts that people work (day, evening, night shift) and the part-time versus full-time status of employees. In other words, these two factors will not be independent.
5. The four independent variables of job characteristics, distributive justice, burnout, and job satisfaction will significantly explain the variance in intention to leave.

Though not directly related to data analysis, it may be pertinent to point out here that the five hypotheses derived from the theoretical framework are particularly relevant for finding some answers to the turnover issue in direct and indirect ways. For example, if men perceived more inequity (as could be conjectured from the interview data), it would be important to set right their (mis)perceptions so that they are less inclined to leave (if indeed a positive correlation between perceived inequities and ITL is found). If work shift has an influence on job satisfaction (irrespective of its influence on ITL), the matter will have to be further examined since job satisfaction is also an important outcome variable for the organization. If employees at particular levels have greater intentions of leaving, further information can be gathered as to what can be done for these groups. If there is a pattern to the part-time/full-time employees working for particular shifts, this might offer some suggestions for further investigation, such as: "Do part-time employees who are concentrated in the night-shift have some special needs that may not be addressed currently?" The results of testing the last hypothesis, of course, will offer insights into how much of the variance will be explained by the four independent variables, and what corrective action, if any, needs to be taken.

The researcher submitted the data for computer analysis using the SPSSX program. We will now proceed to discuss the results of these analyses and their interpretation. In particular, we will examine the following:

1. The establishment of Cronbach's alpha for the measures.
2. The frequency distribution of the variables.
3. Descriptive statistics such as the mean and standard deviation.
4. The Pearson correlation matrix.
5. The results of hypotheses testing.

Checking the Reliability of Measures: Cronbach's Alpha

Since, even when well-validated measures are used, it is always a good idea to check for the interitem consistency reliability of the independent and dependent variables, the Cronbach's alpha reliability coefficient was obtained for the five variables. Output 10A shows the result of the program submitted to ascertain the reliability for the dependent variable—Intention to Leave—through the SPSSX program.

The result indicates that the Cronbach's alpha for the six-item Intention to Leave measure is .82. Cronbach's alpha for the other four independent variables were found to range from .80 to .85. Reliabilities less than .60 are generally considered to be poor, those in the .7 range, to be acceptable, and those over .8 to be good. The closer the reliability coefficient gets to 1.0, of course, the better. Thus, the internal consistency reliability of the measures used in this study can be considered to be good.

It is important to note that all the negatively worded items in the questionnaire should first be reversed through a RECODE statement before the items are submit-

Output 10A
Cronbach's alpha.

RELIABILITY VARIABLES = V195 TO V200/
  SCALE (V325) = V195 TO V200/

RELIABILITY ANALYSIS—SCALE
(V325)

1. V195
2. V196
3. V197
4. V198
5. V199
6. V200

RELIABILITY COEFFICIENTS
N OF CASES = 174.0   N OF ITEMS = 6
ALPHA = 0.8172

ted for reliability tests. Unless all the items measuring a variable are in the same direction, the reliabilities obtained will be incorrect.

Descriptive Statistics

Frequency Distributions

Frequency distributions were obtained for all the personal data or classification variables through the **Frequencies** command together with the **Histograms/ Barcharts** pictorially illustrating the frequency distributions.

The frequencies for the number of individuals in the various Departments with the histograms and bar charts for this sample are shown in Outputs 10B and 10B(1). The results show that the greatest number of individuals in the sample came from the Production Department (28.2%), followed by the Sales Department (25.3%). Only 3 individuals (1.7%) came from Public Relations, and five individuals came from each of Finance, Maintenance, and Accounting Departments (2.9% from each). The low numbers in some of the departments are a function of the total population (very few members) in those departments.

From the frequencies obtained for the other variables (outputs not shown here) it was found that 86 percent of the respondents were men and 14 percent were women; about 68 percent worked the morning shift, 19 percent the evening shift, and 13 percent the night shift. Sixteen percent of the respondents worked part time, and 84 percent worked full time. About 8 percent had Elementary School

Output 10B
Frequency distribution.

```
FREQUENCIES VARIABLES = V5/
  STATISTICS = ALL/
  HISTOGRAM/
```

V5   DEPARTMENT

Value Label	Value	Frequency	Percent	Valid Percent	Cum Percent
Marketing	1	13	7.5	7.5	7.5
Production	2	49	28.1	28.1	35.6
Sales	3	44	25.3	25.3	60.9
Finance	4	5	2.9	2.9	63.8
Servicing	5	34	19.5	19.5	83.3
Maintenance	6	5	2.9	2.9	86.2
Personnel	7	16	9.2	9.2	95.4
Public Relations	8	3	1.7	1.7	97.1
Accounting	9	5	2.9	2.9	100.0
	Total	174	100.0	100.0	

```
Count   Value   One symbol equals approximately 1.00 occurrence

 13     1.00    *************
 49     2.00    *************************************************
 44     3.00    ********************************************
  5     4.00    *****
 34     5.00    **********************************
  5     6.00    *****
 16     7.00    ****************
  3     8.00    ***
  5     9.00    *****
                I........I........ I........ I........ I........ I
                0       10       20       30       40       50
                          Histogram frequency
```

Mean	3.701	Std err	.154	Median	3.000
Mode	2.000	Std dev	2.029	Variance	4.118
Kurtosis	−.156	S E Kurt	.366	Skewness	.825
S E Skew	.184	Range	8.000	Minimum	1.000
Maximum	9.000	Sum	644.000		

Valid cases	174	Missing cases	0

Output 10B(1)
Horizontal bar chart.

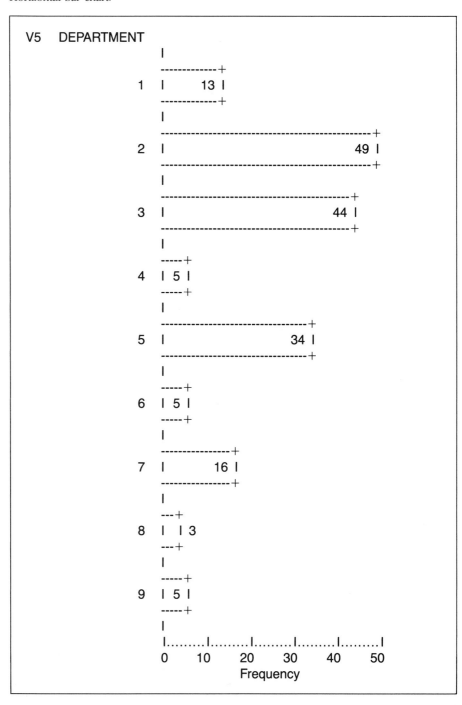

education, 28 percent had a High School diploma, 23 percent had a Bachelor's degree, 30 percent had a Master's degree, and 11 percent had doctoral degrees. About 21 percent of the respondents had worked for the organization for less than a year, 20 percent had worked between one and three years, 20 percent between four and six years, the balance 39 percent had worked for the organization for over six years, including 8 percent who had worked for over twenty years.

Measures of Central Tendencies and Dispersion

By using the CONDESCRIPTIVE statement, statistics such as means, standard deviations, variance, etc., were obtained for the interval-scaled independent and dependent variables. The results of the computer output are shown in Computer Output 10C.

All variables excepting ITL have been tapped on a five-point scale. ITL was tapped on a four-point scale. It can be seen that the **mean** on perceived equity (termed distributive justice) is rather low (less than the average—2.38 on a five-point scale), as also the mean on experienced burnout (2.67). Job satisfaction is about average (3.12 on a five-point scale), and the job is perceived as somewhat enriched (3.47). The mean of 2.12 on a four-point scale for ITL indicates that most of the respondents are not quite bent on leaving (i.e., the intention to leave is not high). The **minimum** of 1 indicates that there are some who do not intend to leave at all, and the maximum of 4 indicates that some are seriously considering leaving. For the major part, however, respondents are firm on neither staying nor on leaving.

The **variance** for burnout, job satisfaction, and the job characteristics is very small. The variance for ITL and perceived equity (distributive justice) is only slightly more, indicating that most respondents are very close to the mean on all the variables.

In sum, the perceived equity is rather low, there is not much burnout experienced, the job is perceived to be fairly enriched, there is average job satisfaction, and there is neither a strong intention to stay with the organization nor a strong intention to leave it.

Inferential Statistics

Pearson Correlation

The Pearson correlation matrix obtained through the **PEARSON CORR** command is shown in Output 10D. From the results, we can see that the upper diagonal of the matrix is a mirror image of the lower diagonal. Intention to leave is, as would be expected, significantly, negatively correlated to perceived equity, job satisfaction, and enriched job. That is, the intention to leave is low if equitable treatment, an enriched job, and job satisfaction are experienced. However, when individuals experience burnout (physical and emotional exhaustion), their intention to leave also increases (positive correlation of .33). Job satisfaction is also positively correlated to perceived equity or justice, and to an enriched job. It is negatively correlated to burnout and ITL. The correlations are all in the expected direction.

Output 10C
Measures of central tendency.

CONDESCRIPTIVE V319,V320,V321,V328,V325/
  STATISTICS = ALL

Variable V319   DIST JUSTICE

Mean	2.379	S.E. Mean	.057	Std. Dev	.755
Variance	.570	Kurtosis	−.246	S.E. Kurt	.367
Skewness	.075	S.E. Skew	.185	Range	4.000
Minimum	1.00	Maximum	5.00	Sum	411.600

Valid observations −   173   Missing observations −   1

Variable V320   BURNOUT

Mean	2.671	S.E. Mean	.040	Std. Dev	.521
Variance	.271	Kurtosis	.580	S.E. Kurt	.367
Skewness	.045	S.E. Skew	.185	Range	3.333
Minimum	1.00	Maximum	4.33	Sum	462.111

Valid observations −   173   Missing observations −   1

Variable V321   JOB STATIS

Mean	3.117	S.E. Mean	.039	Std. Dev	.507
Variance	.257	Kurtosis	.409	S.E. Kurt	.370
Skewness	−.508	S.E. Skew	.186	Range	2.667
Minimum	1.61	Maximum	4.28	Sum	529.833

Valid observations −   170   Missing observations −   4

Variable V328   TOTAL JOB CHAR

Mean	3.474	S.E. Mean	.040	Std. Dev	.518
Variance	.268	Kurtosis	−.512	S.E. Kurt	.374
Skewness	.027	S.E. Skew	.188	Range	2.375
Minimum	2.31	Maximum	4.69	Sum	580.187

Valid observations −   167   Missing observations −   7

Variable V325   ITL

Mean	2.212	S.E. Mean	.051	Std. Dev	.673
Variance	.453	Kurtosis	.191	S.E. Kurt	.366
Skewness	.633	S.E. Skew	.184	Range	3.000
Minimum	1.00	Maximum	4.00	Sum	384.833

Valid observations −   174   Missing observations −   0

Output 10D
Pearson correlation matrix.

PEARSON CORR V319,V320,V321,V328,V325/

PEARSON CORRELATION COEFFICIENTS

	Dis. Jus	Burnout	Job. Sat	Job Char	ITL
Dist. Justice	1.0000 (173) P= .	−.3735 (172) P= .000	.5884 (169) P= .000	.1685 (166) P= .015	−.3574 (173) P= .000
Burnout	−.3735 (172) P= .000	1.0000 (173) P= .	−.4744 (169) P= .000	−.2985 (166) P= .000	.3279 (173) P= .000
Job Satis.	.5884 (169) P= .000	−.4744 (169) P= .000	1.0000 (170) P= .	.3283 (163) P= .000	−.5347 (170) P= .000
Job Charac.	.1685 (166) P= .015	−.2985 (166) P= .000	.3283 (163) P= .000	1.0000 (167) P= .	−.2737 (167) P= .000
ITL	−.3574 (173) P= .000	.3279 (173) P= .000	−.5347 (170) P= .000	−.2737 (167) P= .000	1.0000 (174) P= .

It is important to note that no correlation exceeded .59. If correlations were higher (say, .75 and above), we might have wondered whether or not the correlated variables are two different and distinct variables and would have doubted the validity of the measures.

Hypothesis Testing

Five hypotheses were generated in this research as earlier stated. These call for the use of a *t*-Test (for hypothesis 1), an ANOVA (for hypotheses 2 and 3), a chi-square test (for hypothesis 4), and a multiple regression analysis (for hypothesis 5). The results of these tests and their interpretation are discussed below.

***Hypothesis 1: Use of* t-Test.** Hypothesis 1 can be stated in the null and alternate as follows:

$H1_O$: There will be no difference between men and women in the inequities they perceive.

Statistically expressed: $H1_O$: $u_1 = u_2$

where u_1 = the equity perceived by women and u_2 = the equity perceived by men.

$H1_A$: Men will perceive less equity than women, or women will perceive more equity than men.

Statistically expressed: $H1_A$: $u_1 > u_2$

The results of this *t*-Test are shown in Computer Output 10E. Since the two groups are independent, we will be looking for the significance of the *t* value under the **separate variance estimate** column in the output. If we had had matched groups, or if we did a "before" and "after" test on the same group as in experimental designs, we would be examining the significance of the *t* value under **pooled variance estimate** column. As can be seen, the *t* value of 1.46 is not significant (2 tail probability is .154). The results thus indicate that the difference in the means for the women and men on perceived equity (or distributive justice) of 2.53 and 2.34 (see under the column **MEAN** in Output 10E) with standard deviations of .75 and .76 (see next column) is not significantly different. In effect, there are no significant differences between men and women in how they perceive (in)equities. Thus, **hypothesis 1 is not substantiated.**

Hypothesis 2: Use of ANOVA.   The second hypothesis can be stated in the null and alternate as follows:

$H2_O$: The job satisfaction of individuals will be the same irrespective of which shift they work (whether it is shift 1 or 2 or 3).

Statistically expressed: $H2_O$: $u_1 = u_2 = u_3$

where $u_1, u_2,$ and u_3 signify the means on the job satisfaction of employees working in shifts 1, 2, and 3, respectively.

$H2_A$: The job satisfaction of individuals will vary depending on which shift they work.

Statistically expressed: $H2_A$: $u_1 \neq u_2 \neq u_3$

Since there are more than two groups (three different shifts) and job satisfaction is measured on an interval scale, ANOVA is appropriate to test this hypothesis. The results of ANOVA are shown in Computer Output 10F.

The first column **Source of Variation** has Main Effects, and Explained printed. Both refer to the independent variable, work shift. The term Residual in the same column refers to the effects not explained by the independent variable. The second column, **Sum of Squares,** is a measure of variation. The total variation in the dependent variable, job satisfaction, is 41.304, which is derived from two sources:

1. Between-group variation, or that which is explained by the independent variable, work shift, which is 1.659.

Output 10E
Results of t-test.

T-TEST GROUPS = V3(1,2)/VARIABLES = V325/

--------------------------------- T - T E S T ---------------------------------

GROUP 1 - V3 EQ 1
GROUP 2 - V3 EQ 2

							Pooled Variance Estimate			Separate Variance Estimate		
						*				*			
Variable	Number of Cases	Mean	Standard Deviation	Standard Error	F Value	2-tail Prob.	*	t Value	Degrees of Freedom	2-tail Prob.	*	t Value	Degrees of Freedom	2-tail Prob.
V325 ITL							*				*			
GROUP 1	24	2.1181	.756	.154			*				*			
					1.30	.352	*	-.74	171	.460	*	-.67	28.98	.506
GROUP 2	149	2.2282	.663	.054			*				*			

Output 10F
Results of ANOVA with job satisfaction as D.V.

ANOVA V321 BY V8 (1,3)/

```
***ANALYSIS  OF  VARIANCE***

        V321    JOB SATIS
    by  V8      SHIFT
```

Source of Variation	Sum of Squares	DF	Mean Square	F	Sig of F
Main Effects	1.659	2	.830	3.327	.038
V8	1.659	2	.830	3.327	.038
Explained	1.659	2	.830	3.327	.038
Residual	39.645	159	.249		
Total	41.304	161	.257		

174 cases were processed.
12 cases (6.9 pct) were missing.

2. Within-group variation, or that which cannot be explained, called residual or error sum of squares, which is 39.645.

DF in the third column refers to the degrees of freedom, and each source of variation has associated degrees of freedom. For the Explained Variance, DF = $(K - 1)$, where K is the number of groups or levels. Because there were three shifts, we have $(3 - 1) = 2$ DF. The DF for the residual sum of squares equals $(N - K)$, where N is the total number of respondents and K is the total number of groups. If there were no missing responses on any of the variables, $(N - K)$ should be $(174 - 3) = 171$. However, since there were 12 missing cases, the Residual DF is $(162 - 3) = 159$.

The mean square for each source of variation (column 4 of the results) is derived by dividing the sum of squares by its associated DF. Finally, the F value itself equals the explained mean square divided by the residual mean square.

$$F = \frac{\text{MS explained}}{\text{MS residual}}$$

In this case, F = 3.327. This F value is significant at the .04 level. This implies that **hypothesis 2 is substantiated.** That is, there are significant differences in the mean satisfaction levels of workers in the three shifts, and the null hypothesis can be rejected.

The F test used here is called the overall or omnibus F test. To determine among which groups the true differences lie, other tests need to be done, as discussed in Chapter 9. The **Duncan Multiple Range** test was performed for the purpose, the results of which are shown in Computer Output 10G. We can see that the mean job satisfaction for the three groups working on the three shifts was 2.91 for the second shift, 3.15 for the first shift, and 3.23 for the third shift. Thus, the second shift (the evening shift) is the one that is low on job satisfaction and is significantly different.

Hypothesis 3: Use of ANOVA. Hypothesis 3 can be stated in the null and the alternate as follows:

$H3_O$: There will be no difference in the intention to leave of employees at the five different job levels.

Statistically expressed: $H3_O$: $u_1 = u_2 = u_3 = u_4 = u_5$
where the five us represent the five means on ITL of employees at the five different job levels.

$H3_A$: The ITL of members at the five different job levels will vary significantly.

Statistically expressed: $H3_A$: $u_1 \neq u_2 \neq u_3 \neq u_4 \neq u_5$

The results of ANOVA shown in Computer Output 10H do not indicate any significant differences in the intention to leave among the five groups ($F = 1.37$; $p = .24$). Thus, **hypothesis 3 was not substantiated.**

Hypothesis 4: Use of Chi-Square Test. Hypothesis 4 can be sated in the null and alternate as under:

$H4_O$: Shifts worked and employment status (part-time vs. full-time) will be independent (i.e., will not be related).

$H4_A$: There will be a relationship between the shifts that people work and their part-time vs. full-time status.

Since both variables are nominal, a chi-square (χ^2) test was done, the results of which are shown in Computer Output 10I. The cross-tabulation (see the six cells) indicates that, of the full-time employees, 103 work the first shift, 25 work the second shift, and 18 work the third shift (first column of cells). Of the part-time employees, 16 work the first shift, 8 work the second shift, and 4 work the third shift (second column of cells).

It can be seen that the χ^2 value of 2.31, with two degrees of freedom, is not significant. In other words, the part-time/full-time status and the shifts worked are not related. Hence **hypothesis 4 has not been substantiated.**

Output 10G
Results of Duncan Multiple Range test.

```
ONEWAY V321 BY V8 (1,31)/
   RANGES = DUNCAN/
```

O N E W A Y

Variable   V321   JOB SATIS
By Variable   V8   SHIFT

ANALYSIS OF VARIANCE

SOURCE	D.F.	SUM OF SQUARES	MEAN SQUARES	F RATIO	F PROB.
BETWEEN GROUPS	2	1.6592	.8296	3.3272	.0384
WITHIN GROUPS	159	39.6448	.2493		
TOTAL	161	41.3040			

Variable   V321   JOB SATIS
By Variable   V8   SHIFT

MULTIPLE RANGE TEST

DUNCAN PROCEDURE
RANGES FOR THE 0.050 LEVEL –

    2.80   2.94

THE RANGES ABOVE ARE TABLE RANGES.
THE VALUE ACTUALLY COMPARED WITH MEAN(J)–MEAN(I) IS..
    $0.3531 * RANGE * DSQRT(1/N(I) + 1/N(J))$

(*) DENOTES PAIRS OF GROUPS SIGNIFICANTLY DIFFERENT AT
    THE 0.050 LEVEL

```
                            G  G  G
                            r  r  r
                            p  p  p
      Mean       Group      2  1  3

      2.9149     Grp 2
      3.1539     Grp 1      *
      3.2255     Grp 3
```

Output 10H
Results of ANOVA with ITL as D.V.

ANOVA V325 BY V8 (1,3)/

```
***ANALYSIS OF VARIANCE***

          V325      ITL
      by  V8        SHIFT

                  Sum of              Mean              Sig
Source of Variation  Squares    DF    Square      F     of F

Main Effects        1.156       2     .578       1.254   .288
   V8               1.156       2     .578       1.254   .288
Explained           1.156       2     .578       1.254   .288
Residual           75.106     163     .461
Total              76.262     165     .462

174 cases were processed.
8 cases (4.6 pct) were missing.
```

Hypothesis 5: Use of Multiple Regression Analysis. The last hypothesis can be stated in the null and alternate as under:

H5$_O$: The four independent variables will not significantly explain the variance in intention to leave.

H5$_A$: The four independent variables will significantly explain the variance in ITL.

To test this hypothesis, multiple regression analysis was done. The results of regressing the four independent variables against Intention to Leave can be seen in Computer Output 10J. The four independent variables are listed on the top of the computer output. The **Multiple R** (.548) is the correlation of the four independent variables with the dependent variable after all the intercorrelations among the four independent variables are taken into account. The **R Square** (.30) is actually the square of the multiple $R(.548)^2$. The DF (degree of freedom) in the numerator is the number of independent variables (4), and in the denominator (156) is the total number of complete responses for all the variables in the equation (N), minus the number of independent variables (K) minus 1. ($N - K - 1$) in this case is (161 − 4 − 1) = 156. The F statistic produced (F = 16.71) is significant at the .00001 level.

What this means is that 30 percent of the variance (R-square) in intention to leave has been significantly explained by the four independent variables. Thus, **hypothesis 5 is substantiated.**

Output 10I
Results of chi-square test.

```
CROSSTABS VARIABLES = V600 (1,3) V9 (1,2)/
    TABLES = V600 TO V9/
    STATISTICS CHISQ
```

V600   by   V9   FULL/PART TIME

```
                    V9              Page 1 of 1
           Count  I
                  I
                  I                  Row
                  I    1 I     2 I   Total
           --------+------+------+
               1  I 103 I   16 I     119
     S         I      I      I     68.4
     H         +------+------+
     I       2  I  25 I    8 I      33
     F         I      I      I     19.8
     T         +------+------+
               3  I  18 I    4 I      22
                  I      I      I     12.6
                  +------+------+
         Column    146     28       174
          Total    83.9    16.1     100.0
```

Chi-Square	Value	DF	Significance
Pearson	2.31202	2	.31474
Likelihood Ratio	2.16343	2	.33901
Mantel-Haenszel	1.10347	1	.29351

Minimum Expected Frequency −   3.540
Cells with Expected Frequency < 5 −   1 OF   6 (16.7%)

Number of Missing Observations: 0

If we want to figure out which among the four independent variables is the most important in explaining the variance in ITL, we can look at the column **Beta** under the **Variables in the Equation** line. We see that the highest number in the **BETA** is −.37 which is significant at the .0001 level (see under **Sig T**). It can also be seen that this variable V321 is job satisfaction, which is the only independent variable that is significant. The negative beta weight indicates that if ITL is to be reduced, enhancing the job satisfaction of employees will help.

Output 10J
Results of Multiple Regression Analysis.

```
REGRESSION VARIABLES = V325,V319,V320,V321,V328/
  DEPENDENT = V325/ENTER
```

```
★ ★ ★ M U L T I P L E   R E G R E S S I O N ★ ★ ★


Listwise Deletion of Missing Data
Equation Number 1   Dependent Variable..  V325   ITL
Beginning Block Number  1.  Method:  Enter

Variable(s) Entered on Step Number  1..  V328    TOTAL  JOB  CHAR
                                     2..  V319    DIST JUSTICE
                                     3..  V320    BURNOUT
                                     4..  V321    JOB SATIS
```

		Analysis of Variance			
Multiple R	.54775		DF	Sum of Squares	Mean Square
R Square	.30003				
Adjusted R Square	.28208	Regression	4	22.36577	5.59144
Standard Error	.57835	Residual	156	52.17978	.33449

$$F = 16.71653 \quad \text{Signif } F = .0000$$

---------------------------------- Variables in the Equation ----------------------------------

Variable	B	SE B	Beta	T	Sig T
V328	−.111702	.095258	−.084643	−1.173	.2427
V319	−.115044	.078736	−.121272	−1.461	.1460
V320	.143558	.103029	.108814	1.393	.1655
V321	−.497767	.120777	−.370178	−4.121	.0001
(Constant)	4.048175	.603055		6.713	.0000

End Block Number 1   All requested variables entered.

Overall Interpretation and Recommendations to the President

Of the five hypotheses tested, two were substantiated and three were not. From the results of the multiple regression analysis, it is clear that job satisfaction is a critical factor in explaining employees' intentions to stay with the organization. Hence, whatever is done to increase job satisfaction will help employees to think less about leaving.

It is also clear from the results that ITL does not differ by job level. That is, employees at all levels feel neither too strongly inclined to stay with the organization nor to leave it. Hence, if retaining employees is a top priority for the President, it is important to pay attention to employees at all levels and create policies and practices systemwide that will have an impact on the job satisfaction of all employees organizationwide. Also, since job satisfaction is found to be significantly lower for employees working the evening shifts, further interviews with them might shed some light on what is making them dissatisfied. Corrective action can then be taken.

It is informative to find that the perceived equity, though not significantly different for men and women as originally hypothesized, is nevertheless rather low for all (see Computer Output 10C). The Pearson correlation matrix (Computer Output 10D) indicates that perceived equity (or distributive justice) is positively correlated to job satisfaction and negatively correlated to ITL. Hence, the President will be well advised to rectify inequities if they do really exist, or clear misperceptions of inequities, if such is actually the case.

While increasing job satisfaction will help to reduce people's intentions to quit, the fact that only 30 percent of the variance in intention to leave was significantly explained by the four independent variables considered in this study suggests that 70 percent of the variance in ITL is still not explained. In other words, there are also other variables that are important in explaining ITL that have not been considered in this study. So further research might be necessary to explain more of the variance in ITL, if the President so desires.

Computer Programs

Having interpreted the overall results and made some suggestions for further action, we will now briefly discuss data analysis using microcomputers. The appendix to this chapter gives the programming details for the SPSSX and SAS for those who are interested in using these common computer programs on the mainframe. It should be noted that the format of the first few lines (four or so) may vary across computer systems.

DATA ANALYSIS USING MICROCOMPUTERS

Statistical analyses can now be done on personal computers using SPSS or SAS without accessing the mainframe. The software programs that have been developed for the purpose are mostly adaptations of the packages used for the mainframe. The **SPSS/PC$^+$** is a package that can be used to generate frequencies, descriptive statistics such as the mean and standard deviation, correlations, *t*-test, the ANOVA, multiple regression, and other analyses. It can also produce tables and graphs. An advanced supplementary program is also available for more sophisticated multivariate analyses such as factor analysis, cluster analysis, discriminant analysis, and multivariate analysis of variance. The program consists of nine software disks and requires a hard disk on the PC. Data can be retrieved from tape or from an ASCII file. We will explain the SPSS/PC$^+$ *Studentware* in a little more detail later.

There are other packages available for data analysis as well. For instance, marketing research survey and analysis become easier with the **CAPPA,** which is an IBM/PC package, as mentioned in Chapter 7. Apart from helping in questionnaire surveys, CAPPA computes weights for each respondent's "representativeness" while analyzing the data. Among other things, CAPPA generates measures of central tendency and dispersion, gives cross-tabulations (both weighted and unweighted), performs χ^2 tests, ANOVA, regression analysis, and discriminant analysis.

Hewlett Packard has also designed a software package meant especially for scientists and engineers—the **Data Acquisition Manager (DACQ/300 program).** This program provides subroutine tools to perform tasks such as data collection, storage, analysis, presentation, transmission, and database management (Drenkow, 1987). DACQ also organizes data into archives, books, pages, columns, and rows as we usually tend to prefer. The program also performs statistical analyses and allows research scientists and engineers to tailor the subroutines to match their specific needs, which may vary from project to project.

Software packages are tailored to meet the data analysis requirements of researchers in different fields. For instance, RATS—Regression Analysis of Time Series—is used by econometricians; SYSTAT is a package used in the field of Education; Time Line and Project Management are software packages used for generating PERT and GANTT charts in the Production/Operations Management field; and TSP—Time Series Programming—is used for forecasting. Obviously, the development of software programs for data analysis on the personal computer is gaining increasing attention. In the next few years, we can expect to see more and more sophisticated packages being developed that are tailored and fine-tuned for the specific data-collection and data-analytic needs of researchers in different fields (e.g., business) and subfields (e.g., marketing, accounting).

SPSS/PC⁺ STUDENTWARE

It is useful to briefly explain the **SPSS/PC⁺ Student Software** program since it is being used in classes such as this. The program is menu-driven and easy to use. The program disk comes with data collected from the General Social Survey so that you can practice the various commands and familiarize yourself with data analysis and interpretation. If you want to use your own data collected from a survey, you can key in and store the data on a floppy or hard disk. However, no more than twenty variables can be entered. Details regarding creation of a new data file using the text editor REVIEW, and the various program commands are available from the Manual that comes with the program. As in the SPSS program, DATA LIST (to identify and specify the location of the data on the file), VARIABLE LABELS (giving descriptions of the variables), MISSING VALUES (indicating the codes used for data that are missing), and BEGIN DATA, {DATA CARDS}, and END DATA are necessary. A sample set-up is as below:

DATA LIST / SEX 1 EDUC 2 AGE 3–4 ASSETS 5–8 PROFITS 9–11 SALES
 12–14 IND 15–19 V1 20.

VARIABLE LABELS	SEX "GENDER OF SALES MANAGER"
	EDUC "EDUCATIONAL LEVEL OF SALES
	    MANAGER"
	AGE "AGE OF ORGANIZATION IN YEARS"
	ASSETS "TOTAL ASSETS IN MILLIONS OF
	    DOLLARS"
	PROFITS "AVERAGE PROFITS OVER THE LAST
	    THREE YEARS IN 000's OF $"
	SALES "CURRENT YEAR'S SALES IN 000's OF $"
	IND "INDUSTRY SALES FOR CURRENT YEAR IN
	    MILLIONS OF $"
	V1 "POSITION IN BUSINESS".

VALUE LABELS	SEX 1 'WOMEN' 2 'MEN'/ EDUC 1 'HIGH SCHOOL' 2 'SOME COLLEGE' 3 'BACHELOR'S' 4 'MASTERS' 5 'OTHER'.
MISSING VALUE	SEX, EDUC, AGE, ASSETS, PROFITS, SALES, IND (0).

RECODE   V1   (1=4)   (2=3)   (3=2)   (1=4).

BEGIN DATA.

⟨DATA⟩

END DATA.

The file is now ready to be SAVED under any name you desire, for future use. This is done by the command:

SAVE OUTFILE = 'FILENAME.SYS'.

All other analyses can be done after this at any time by entering:

GET FILE = 'FILENAME.SYS'.

The commands for the various types of analyses discussed earlier are as per the following example:

FREQUENCIES VARIABLES=SEX/ BARCHART.

FREQUENCIES VARIABLES=V1/ HISTOGRAM.

FREQUENCIES VARIABLES=IND/ STATISTICS ALL. [gives mean, median, mode, maximum, minimum, std dev, variance, skewness, kurtosis, etc.]

CORRELATION ASSETS SALES PROFITS.

CROSSTABS TABLES=EDUC BY SEX/ OPTIONS 14 15/ STATISTIC 1.

[Options 14 15 calculate the expected cell frequencies and the residuals, and Statistic 1 generates the χ^2.]

ANOVA   SALES BY EDUCATION(1,4).   [The 1,4 refers to the four levels of education we are interested in.]

REGRESSION VARIABLES=PROFITS SALES ASSETS AGE
    /DEPENDENT=PROFITS
    /METHOD=ENTER
    /METHOD=STEPWISE.

As can be seen, the commands are not far different from the regular SPSSX commands. Note the **.** after the end of each command.

Data analysis on microcomputers is becoming more popular because of its convenience (no mainframe is needed), and we can expect businesses to use this mode more frequently in the future. User-friendly microcomputer data analytic programs will be the wave of the future.

EXPERT SYSTEMS IN DATA ANALYSIS

An Expert System employs unique programming techniques to model the decisions that experts make. A considerable body of knowledge fed into the system and some good software and hardware help the individual using the Expert System to make good decisions about the problem that he or she is concerned about. In sum, an Expert System can be thought of as an "advisor," clarifying or resolving problematic issues that are confusing to the individual.

The use of Expert Systems in data analysis is slowly gaining momentum. For example, choosing the most appropriate statistical procedure to find answers to a research question may be perplexing to a researcher. The *Statistical Navigator* is an Expert System that will recommend one or more statistical procedures after seeking information on the **goals** (i.e., the purpose of the analysis—say, to understand the relationship between two variables), the **data** (i.e., categories, scales), and the **audience** for whom the results are to be disseminated.

Procedures suggested by the *Statistical Navigator* may include the less obvious but more appropriate solutions than what one would have initially thought of (Blank, 1989). It also prints a report explaining the reasoning behind its recommendations in the context of the goals, data, and audience. The *Statistical Navigator* is a useful guide for those who are not well versed in statistics but want to ensure that they are using the appropriate statistical techniques.

Expert Systems will also be useful for making decisions regarding the **nature, time horizon,** and **type of research** study to be conducted (correlational/causal; cross-sectional/longitudinal; exploratory/descriptive/predictive); **study setting** (laboratory/field), **unit of analysis** (individuals/groups/etc.); appropriate **sampling designs, data collection methods,** and the like.

Other applications of Expert Systems for business decisions using available data include *Auditor* for a company's decisions on allowing for bad debts, and *Taxadvisor,* which helps audit firms to advise clients on estate planning. As suggested by Luconi, Malone, and Morton (1986), Expert Systems can be used for making decisions in operational control (accounts receivable, inventory control, cash management, production scheduling), management control (budget analysis, forecasting, variance analysis, budget preparation), and strategic planning (warehouse and factory location, mergers and acquisitions, new product planning). Thus, the scope for developing expert systems to aid managerial problem solving and decision making is infinite.

SUMMARY

In this chapter we covered the procedure for analyzing data after they have been collected. By means of an example, we saw the steps necessary to get the data ready for analysis—editing, coding, and categorizing. Through the example of the research on KRIYA Enterprises, we saw various statistical analyses and tests used to examine the different hypotheses to answer the research question. We also saw how the computer results are interpreted. We also described some microcomputer programs and discussed the *SPSS/PC* $^{+}$ Studentware in some detail. Some expert systems for data analysis and managerial decision making and problem solving were also mentioned.

In the next chapter we will learn how to write a research report after the data have been analyzed and the results are interpreted.

DISCUSSION QUESTIONS AND POINTS TO PONDER

1. What kinds of biases do you think could be minimized or avoided during the data-analysis stage of research?

2. In the case of directional hypotheses (i.e., $\mu_1 > \mu_2$ or $\mu_1 < \mu_2$), how would we know whether the results of the *t*-Test obtained are significant or not?

3. When we collect data on the effects of treatment in experimental designs, which statistical test would be most appropriate to test the treatment effects?

4. A tax consultant is wondering whether he should be more selective about the class of clients he serves so as to maximize his income. He usually deals with four categories of clients: the very rich, rich, upper middle class, and middle class. He has records of each and every client served, the taxes paid by them, and how much he charged them. Since many factors varied for the clients, such as the number of their dependents, business deductibles, and such, irrespective of which category the clients belonged to, he would like to do some kind of analyses to see which among the four categories of clientele he should choose to serve in the future.

What kind of analysis should be done in the above case and why?

5. Below are the results of a computer output tabulated in Tables 10.3 to 10.6. The research was conducted in a sales organization that operates in 50 different areas with a total salesforce of about 500. The number of salesmen sampled for the study was 150.

Table 10.3
Means, Standard Deviations, Minimum, and Maximum

Variable	Mean	Standard Deviation	Minimum	Maximum
Sales (in 1000s of $)	75.1	8.6	45.2	97.3
No. of salesmen	25	6	5	50
Population (in 100s)	5.1	0.8	2.78	7.12
Per capita income (in 1000s)	20.3	20.1	10.1	75.9
Advertisement (in 1000s of $)	10.3	5.2	6.1	15.7

Table 10.4
Correlations Among the Variables

	Sales	Salesmen	Population	Income	Advertisement
Sales	1.0				
No. of salesmen	.76	1.0			
Population	.62	.06	1.0		
Income	.56	.21	.11	1.0	
Advertisement expenditure	.68	.16	.36	.23	1.0

All figures above .15 are significant at $p \leq .05$.
All figures above .35 are significant at $p \leq .001$.

Table 10.5
Results of ANOVA: Sales by Level of Education

Source of Variation	Sum of Squares	DF	Mean Square	F	Significance of F
Main effects	50.7	4	12.7	3.6	.01
Explained	50.7	4	12.7	3.6	.01
Residual	501.8	145	3.5	3.6	.01
Total	552.5	150			

Table 10.6

Results of Regression Analysis

Multiple R	.65924	DF	
R square	.43459	5	F = 5.27799
Adjusted R square	.35225	144	Sig. F = .00001
Standard error	.41173		

Variables in the Equation

Variable	Beta	T	SIG T
Training of salesmen	.28	2.768	.0092
No. of salesmen	.34	3.55	.00001
Population	.09	0.97	.467
Per capita income	.12	1.200	.089
Advertisement	.47	4.54	.00001

You are to:

a. Interpret the information contained in each of the tables, in as much detail as possible.

b. Summarize the results for the CEO of the company.

c. Make recommendations based on your interpretation of the results of the tables.

APPENDIX TO CHAPTER 10

SPSSX AND SAS PROGRAMMING

Since SPSSX and SAS are commonly used mainframe computer programs, the programming for these with respect to the types of analyses discussed by us is provided in Tables 10.7 and 10.8. A short explanation on SPSSX programming follows immediately.

NOTES ON TABLE 10.7: GUIDE TO SPSSX PROGRAMMING

Table 10.7 gives a visual representation of what will be explained here, and the lines in the table are numbered in parentheses at the end of each line merely to facilitate the explanations. It should be noted that the SPSSX is constantly updated and the discussions here pertain to Version 3.1. Updated versions usually call for only minor changes, and you can easily find out what the changes are. If the interactive system is utilized, the first five lines and the very last line shown in Table 10.7 will not be necessary. It should also be noted that the format of the first four lines will *vary* with different systems.

The first five lines on Table 10.7 are the job control cards. These cards are necessary for **batch** jobs. If the interactive system is accessed, these are not necessary. You can then log on to the computer and start with the sixth line directly.

The GA2068 on the *first* line is the computer number assigned to me. Each individual will be assigned a distinct computer number, which is what should be entered. Note that the last two digits (in this case 68) denote the bin number in which the computer output can be found when the program is run and from where it can be picked up. The word SEK can be substituted by your name. The Time (=29) denotes that we expect the job that is submitted for analysis to be completed within 29 seconds. For most jobs, this is ample time. For smaller jobs, 10 seconds might be enough. Generally, the shorter the time specified, the quicker the job is run.

The *second* line directs the computer to show the results of the analysis on the computer terminal itself (line 2) or to route it to the printer (line 2A). Note that these two lines are programmed as per our requirements here at my university. You need to use what is appropriate for your system. *Lines 3 to 5* are SPSSX job controls. The *sixth* line, which is optional, identifies the title of the job—in this case SERAKIN Co. The *seventh* line and the *eighth* line indicate where the variables can be located in the raw data. Line *seven* indicates that the data are in fixed format (i.e., no decimal places) and (in this case) the data are all to be found in a single record (Records=1). If there are two records, then this will be indicated by **Records**=2 The seventh line here indicates that in record 1 (/1) the variables V1 to V21 are to be found in columns 7 to 27. That is, the first six columns are blank and the 21

Table 10.7
Setup for SPSSX Programming

```
Col
1
//GA2068 JOB (1,2068),SEK,TIME(=29),CLASS=A,REGION=4096K          (1)
/*ROUTE PRINT SIUCVMPB.GA2068                                      (2)
            or
/*ROUTE PRINT SIUCHVSA                                             (2A)
// EXEC SPSSX                                                      (3)
//FT06F001 DD SYSOUT=A,OUTLIM=5000                                 (4)
//SYSIN DD *                                                       (5)

TITLE SERAKIN CO DATA                                             (6)
DATA LIST FIXED RECORDS=1                                         (7)
   /1 V1 TO V21 7-27                                              (8)
MISSING VALUES V6 TO V21 (4)                                      (9)
RECODE V8,V9,V11,V15,V18,V21 (7=1) (6=2) (5=3) (3=5)              (10)
   (2=6) (1=7)                                                    (10A)
COMPUTE V100=(V6+V7+V8+V9+V10+V11)/6                              (11)
COMPUTE V101=(V12+V13+V14+V15+V16+V17+V18+V19+V20+V21)/10         (12)
VAR LABELS   V1,AGE/V2,EDUCATION/V3,JOB LEVEL/V4,GENDER/          (13)
             V5,TENURE/V100,INVOLVEMENT/V101,SATISFACTION         (13A)
BEGIN DATA                                                        (14)

⟨DATA⟩                                                           (15)

END DATA                                                         (16)
FREQUENCIES   VARIABLES=V1 TO V5/                                (17)
              HISTOGRAM/                                          (17A)
CONDESCRIPTIVE  V100,V101/                                        (18)
   STATISTICS        ALL                                          (18A)
PEARSON CORR   V100,V101/                                         (19)
Col
1
T-TEST           GROUPS=V4(1,2)/VARIABLES=V100,V101/              (20)
ANOVA            V100 BY V9(1,6)/                                 (21)
CROSSTABS        VARIABLES=V2 (1,5) V9 (1,6)/                     (22)
   TABLES        V2 BY V9/                                        (22A)
   STATISTICS    CHISQ                                            (22B)
REGRESSION       VARIABLES=V100,V101,V1,V5                        (23)
                 DEPENDENT=V100/ENTER                             (23A)
FINISH                                                           (24)
//                                                               (25)
```

variables are entered consecutively from column 7 to 27 (each variable occupying one column). If a variable is coded in two or more columns, this should be so indicated. For example, suppose we have two extra variables V22 and V23, which occupy 2 and 3 columns, respectively, we would program the eighth line as below:

/1 V1 TO V21 7-27, V22 28-29, V23 30-32

If data are continued on a second record, this will be indicated on the next line by:

/2 V---- (ENTER THE APPROPRIATE VARIABLES AND COLUMNS)

If values that were missing were left blank or coded by any other specific number, then this information has to be fed to the computer. This is done by line 9, which reads:

MISSING VALUES V1 to V21 (4)

As we have already seen there are different ways of handling missing values. By default, the computer will *not* include cases that have missing values in the computations.

Line 10 has the RECODE command, which is self-explanatory. All the negatively worded items have been reversed through this statement. *Lines 11 and 12* have the COMPUTE statements. These statements add up the responses to the individual items in a scale and average out the responses for each individual. *Line 13* labels the variables for which numbers have been given so that from the computer printouts we can readily infer the variables by name.

Line 14 indicates that the data set will begin on the next line. After this line, all the data entries will follow. *Line 16* indicates that the last data entry is over with the previous line. *Lines 17 to 23A* are the programs for the various statistical analyses that we have already discussed in this chapter. *Line 24* with the FINISH command indicates that all the programs that are necessary to be processed have been entered. *Line 25* is necessary only when a batch file is submitted and is not required for the interactive mode.

Note:

1. If we did *not* have the RECODE statement (lines 10 and 10A), our Compute Statements for V100 and V101 would have looked like:

   COMPUTE $V100=(V6+V7+(8-V8)+(8-V9)+V10+(8-V11))/6$
   COMPUTE $V101=(V12+V13+V14+(8-V15)+V16+V17$
   $+(8-V18)+V19+V20+(8-V21))/10$

   In the above two Compute Statements, we have reversed the negative items, by adding 1 to the highest point on the scale (i.e., 7 + 1 = 8), and then subtracting the actual response on the negatively worded items.

   Thus, if someone had circled 3 for an item, the actual score would be generated by the computer as (8 − 3 =) 5, which is the same number stipulated in the RECODE statement.

2. Missing values have been assigned the average or the center point on the 7-point scale (=4) for the items comprising the variables of Involvement and Satisfaction, through the Missing Value statement on line 9. Thus, wherever a response is left blank on the items involved, it will be assigned a value of 4 by the computer.

Table 10.8
Setup for SAS Programming

```
Col
1
//(Same first card as for SPSSX)                                    (1)
/*ROUTE PRINT SIUCVMB.GA2068    (whatever is applicable to          (2)
                                your setting)
// EXEC SAS                                                         (3)
//SYSIN DD *                                                        (4)
TITLE SERAKIN CO DATA;                                             (5)
DATA SERAKIN;                                                       (6)
INPUT (V1−V21) (21*1.);                                            (7)
IF V6=.  THEN V6=4;                                               (8)
IF V7=.  THEN V7=4;                                               (9)


IF V20=. THEN V20=4;                                              (22)
IF V21=. THEN V21=4;                                              (23)

V8=8−V8;                                                          (24)
V9=8−V9;                                                          (25)
V11=8−V11;                                                        (26)
V15=8−V15;                                                        (27)
V18=8−V18;                                                        (28)
V21=8−V21;                                                        (29)
V100=(V6+V7+V8+V9+V10+V11)/6;                                     (30)
V101=(V12+V13+V14+V15+V16+V17+V18+V19+V20+V21)/10;                (31)
LABEL   V1=AGE;                                                   (32)
LABEL   V2=EDUCATION;                                             (33)
LABEL   V3=JOB LEVEL;                                             (34)
LABEL   V4=GENDER;                                                (35)
LABEL   V5=TENURE;                                                (36)
LABEL   V100=INVOLVEMENT;                                         (37)
LABEL   V101=SATISFACTION;                                        (38)
CARDS;                                                             (39)
        ⟨DATA SET⟩
PROC FREQ;                                                        (40)
    TABLES  V1*V2   V1*V3   V1*V4   V1*V5                         (41)
            V2*V3   V2*V4   V2*V5   V3*V5                         (42)
            V3*V5   V4*V5;                                        (43)
PROC CHART;                                                       (44)
   VBAR   V1−V5;                                                 (45)
PROC MEANS;                                                       (46)
   VAR   V1−V5;                                                  (47)
PROC CORR;                                                        (48)
   VAR   V100 V101;                                              (49)
PROC TTEST;                                                       (50)
    CLASS V4;                                                    (51)
    TITLE V100 V101;                                             (52)
```

Table 10.8   continued

PROC ANOVA;	(53)
CLASSES V9 (1,6);	(54)
MODEL V100=V9 (1,6);	(55)
PROC FREQ;	(56)
TABLES V2*V9/CHISQ;	(57)
PROC GLM;	(58)
MODEL V100=V101 V1 V5;	(59)

Notes on Table 10.8

Lines 1 to 5 need no explanation. *Line 6* gives the DATA name and *IS* required. *Line 7,* the Input statement, indicates that the variables 1 to 21 are to be read consecutively. *Lines 8 to 23* indicate that the *Missing Values* for the variables V6 to V21 should be treated as 4. *Lines 24 to 29 Recode* the relevant variables. *Lines 30 and 31* serve as the *Compute* statements. *Lines 32 to 38 label* the variables. *Line 39* indicates that the data begin, and the data set comes right after this.

The rest correspond to the programming in the SPSSX.

CHAPTER 11

THE RESEARCH REPORT

TOPICS DISCUSSED

THE WRITTEN REPORT
- Purpose
- Different Types of Reports
- Audience
- Basics
- Details

CONTENTS OF THE RESEARCH REPORT
- Title of the Report
- Table of Contents
- Synopsis
- The Introductory Section
- Method Section
- Results Section
- Discussion Section
- Recommendations and Implementation
- Summary
- Acknowledgments
- References
- Appendix

ORAL PRESENTATION

CHAPTER OBJECTIVES

After completing this chapter you should:

1. Know what the contents of a research report are.

2. Write a good synopsis.

3. Tailor the report format to meet the needs of different audiences.

4. Know the components of a good oral presentation.

5. Write a good introductory section to a written report explaining
   a. The background for the research.
   b. Preliminary data gathering.
   c. Literature review.

   d. Problem statement.
   e. Theoretical framework.
   f. Hypotheses.
   g. Details of research design.
6. Write a method section describing
   a. The population, sample, and sample characteristics.
   b. Variables and measures.
   c. Data-collection methods.
   d. Data-analytic methods to be used.
7. Write the results section, using tables and pictorial representations where appropriate, giving
   a. A feel for the data.
   b. A correlation matrix among the primary variables of interest.
   c. Results of hypothesis testing.
8. Discuss the results, stating the generalizability of your findings and the limitations of your study.
9. Give your recommendations and suggestions for implementation in the case of applied research.
10. Write the summary and acknowledgment.
11. Give the appropriate references.
12. Include appropriate materials in the appendix.
13. Critique research reports and published studies.

Once the data analyses are completed and conclusions drawn from the findings, the investigator is ready to present the results of the research study and make the recommendations. These are usually done in the form of a written report, sometimes followed up by an oral presentation. The contents and organization of both the written report and the oral presentation depend on the purpose for which the research study was done and the target audience for whom they are intended. The relevant details for the written and oral reports are discussed in this chapter.

THE WRITTEN REPORT

The written report enables the decision maker to weigh the facts and arguments presented in the document and implement the final solution(s), with a view to closing the gap between the desired and present state of affairs in any given problem area. To achieve its goal, the written report has to focus on the issues discussed below.

The Written Report and Its Purpose

Writing a research report requires careful thinking and planning. It is necessary to know what the **purpose** of the report is. If the purpose is simply to offer details on some specific factors as requested by a manager, the report can be very narrowly focused and provide the desired information to the manager in a brief format, as discussed in Example 11.1. If, on the other hand, the report is intended to sell an idea to management, then it has to be more detailed and convincing as to why the proposed idea is an improvement and should be adopted. Here the emphasis would be on presenting all the relevant information backed by the necessary data, to influence the reader to "buy into the idea," as indicated in Example 11.2. A third kind of report may be elicited in some cases, where a manager asks for several alternative solutions or recommendations for rectifying a problem in a given situation, so that the manager can make the final decision. In this case, a detailed report surveying past studies, the methodology used for the present study, different perspectives generated from interviews and current data analysis, and alternative solutions based on the results of the study will have to be provided, detailing how each alternative will help to improve the problem situation. The advantages and disadvantages of each of the proposed solutions, together with a cost–benefit analysis in terms of dollars and/or other resources, will also have to be provided since it would be very useful to the manager in making the decision. In other words, a detailed report such as the one warranted in Example 11.3 will have to be provided.

Yet another type of report might require the researcher to identify the problem and provide the final solution as well. That is, the researcher might be called in to study a situation, determine what the problem is, and offer a report of findings and recommendations. Such a report has to be very detailed, as found in Report 3 in the Appendix to this chapter. A fifth kind of research report is the very scholarly publication presenting the findings of a basic study that one usually finds published in academic journals.

Example 11.1   A VERY SIMPLE REPORT

If a study is undertaken to *understand the details* (e.g., characteristics, composition, etc.) of certain variables of interest in a given situation, then a report describing the phenomena of interest in the manner desired is all that is necessary. Let us say that a Personnel Manager wanted to know how many employees were recruited during the past twelve months in the organization, their gender composition, educational level, and the average number of days that these individuals had remained absent during the twelve-month period; a simple report giving the desired information is all that would be necessary.

A statement of the **purpose** of the report will be first given (e.g.: It was desired that details of the number of employees recruited during the past months in the company be provided. This report offers those details). The **methods** or **procedures** adopted to find the data will then be given (e.g., the payroll of the company and the personal files of the employees were examined to collect the data). Finally, a narration of the actual **findings** or **results** reinforced with visual forms of representation of the data [tables of crosstabs and frequency distributions, illustrations of bar charts (for gender), pie charts (to indicate the proportions of individuals at various educational levels)] will be provided. This section will summarize the data by saying that there were *xx* number of total employees recruited during the past twelve months, of which 45 percent were women and 55 percent were men. Of the total employees, 20 percent had a Master's degree, 68 percent had a Bachelor's degree, and 12 percent had a High School diploma. The average number of days that these employees remained absent during the past twelve months was *z*. These details will suffice for the manager to get the information that she requires. It is not unwise to provide a further genderwise breakdown of the educational levels and mean number of days of absence of the employees in an appendix as well, even though this information might not have been specifically requested.

A short simple report of the type discussed above is provided in Report 1 in the appendix to this chapter.

Example 11.2   A REPORT TO "SELL" AN IDEA

The purpose of a report may be to *sell an idea to top management*. For example, the Information Systems Manager might want to convince the top administration executives that an **Executive Information System (EIS)** is necessary for the organization. The manager would like to convince the executives that EIS would improve the benefits of the existing paper reporting system by using electronic information delivery that increases the data's timeliness and usability. When the executives realize that they can perform their information-intensive activities with ease and speed, and that their decision making will become more effective, they will readily buy into the idea. But then the research report for this purpose will have a different thrust and will focus more on the following:

1. Explain in clear and simple terms what an EIS is in terms of its being a powerful executive tool for effective decision making.
2. What it would do (e.g., give immediate access to the specific information the executive needs without having to go through the frustration of shuffling reams of paper materials and not finding what is required).
3. How it would be better than the present system (e.g., it will provide the latest sales, inventory, purchase, and other data necessary for more informed decision making, since all information will be updated on a daily basis).
4. Offer a detailed cost–benefit analysis. That is, compare the costs of (a) training executives to use the system—a two-day seminar and helping them through the initial stages until they become comfortable with using the system, and (b) updating information on a daily basis, *versus* the savings accruing due to timely information—for example, updated information facilitating the establishment of viable "just-in-time" systems, which saves a lot of money, making more *informed*

decisions compared to best hunches, which enhances the probability of effective decision making that offers the best results, and so on.

5. Give examples from past experiences (within the past two months, if possible) of how an EIS system would have facilitated the executives to make decisions easier, and/or how it could have saved the system more money/resources.

6. A final convincing recommendation to adopt EIS as a way of life.

A specimen of the type of report discussed above with respect to recommending sabbaticals for managers is provided in Report 2 in the appendix to this chapter.

Example 11.3   A COMPREHENSIVE REPORT OFFERING ALTERNATIVE SOLUTIONS AFTER STUDYING A SITUATION THOROUGHLY

The President of a tire company wants several recommendations to be made on how the future growth of his company should be planned, taking into consideration the manufacturing, marketing, accounting, and financial strategies that should be followed. In this case only a broad objective is stated: corporate growth. There may currently be several impediments to such growth, or at least some forces restraining growth. One has to carefully examine the situation to determine the obstacles to growth and how these may be overcome through strategic planning from a production, marketing, management, financial, and accounting perspective. Identifying the problems or impediments in the situation would require intensive interviewing, literature review, industry analysis, formulation of a theoretical perspective, generation of several hypotheses to come up with different alternative solutions, data gathering, data analyses, and then exploring alternative ways of attaining corporate growth through different strategies. To enable a good assessment of the alternatives proposed, the pros and cons of implementing the various alternative solutions and a statement of the costs and benefits attached to each would follow.

This report will be more elaborate, detailing each of the steps in the study, emphasizing the data analysis and results, and providing a strong basis for the various recommendations. Such a report is likely to follow the format of Report 3 in the appendix, without the recommendation of the final solution.

Thus, the contents and format of a report will depend on the purpose for which the study is conducted and the needs of the audience.

The Written Report and Its Audience

The organization of a report depends on its intended audience. Its length, focus on details, and illustrations and data displays will also be a function of the audience. Some executives are averse to reading a lot of material and want to know only the critical aspects of the survey and the findings in a brief format. A Synopsis or an Executive Summary that offers just the right amount of detail (say, in less than three pages) will help them to quickly grasp the essentials of the study, and they can turn to the pages in the report that offer more detailed information on aspects that are of greater interest to them, if they so desire.

Some managers are distracted by data presented in the form of tables and feel more comfortable with graphs and charts, while others want to see "facts and figures" (Williams, 1990). Whereas both tables and figures are visual forms of representation and need to be presented in reports, which one is prominently displayed in the report and which is relegated to an appendix is a function of the idiosyncracies of the ultimate consumer of the report. If a report is to be handled by different executives, with different orientations, the report should be packaged such that the individuals know where they can find the information that meets their preferred mode of processing information. For example, after discussing market share illustrated through a pie chart, the raw data can also be presented in a tabular form.

Thus, the length, organization, and presentation modes of the report will, among other things, depend on the target audience. Some businesses might also prescribe their own format for report writing. In all cases, it is good to know who the audience is and what exactly is the purpose of the report. Some reports may have to be long and detailed while others may have to be brief and specific.

The Written Report: Basics

Despite the fact that report writing is a function of purpose and audience and has to be tailored to meet the needs of both, certain basic features are integral to all written reports. Clarity, conciseness, coherence, proper emphasis on important aspects, meaningful organization of paragraphs, appropriate transitions from one topic to another, apt choice of words, and specificity are all important for a good report. Any assumptions made by the researcher should be clearly stated in the report, and facts, rather than opinions, should be provided. The report should be organized in a manner that enhances the smooth flow of materials in a meaningful fashion as the reader goes through it.

Appropriate headings and subheadings help to organize the report in a logical manner and help the reader to follow the transitions that the author makes. A double-spaced, typed report with at least 1.25-inches wide margin on all sides enables the reader to make notes/comments while going through the report.

All reports will have an introductory section detailing the purpose of the study to set the stage for what the reader can expect in the rest of the report. The body of the report will contain details regarding the framework for the study, the research question, hypotheses if any, the methodology pursued in conducting the study, analysis of data and the results obtained, and the conclusions drawn. Where appropriate, recommendations will be made. These details will enable the reader to judge the thoroughness of the study and how much confidence can be placed on the results and on the recommendations made.

Good descriptions and lucid explanations, smooth and easy flow of materials, adherence to recommendations that follow logically from the data analysis, and acknowledgment of any limitations to the study help the report to take on a more scientific character. The Executive Summary (or Synopsis) and the transmittal letter can be written with a personal touch, wherever appropriate, focused toward the relevant audience. In the absence of any specific requirements regarding the format of the report, the model prescribed in the APA *Manual* (1983), which is followed by most scholarly journals, should serve well. Doctoral dissertations usually follow the APA format.

In sum, a well done study that is not presented properly is of very little use. The report should clearly present the problem studied, provide good rationale, present the data fully and adequately, and interpret the data for the reader. The conclusion should indicate how the problem can be resolved. The report can be organized in various parts or chapters and should be tailored to meet the needs of the situation. Good, crisp, and clear writing; figures, charts, and tables that succinctly support or highlight the written message; and attractive packaging are some of the essential characteristics of a good report. The writing style has to be interesting, precise, and comprehensible. Unbiased and objective presentation of the findings pointing out the limitations of the study lends credibility to the research work. The format and style of reporting should be tailored to the audience and meet the purpose for which the study was initiated.

The Written Report: The Details

The research report should bear a title that indicates in a straightforward manner what the study is about. It should have a table of contents, a synopsis, and as indicated earlier, an introductory section, the main body describing the framework for the study, the methodology, the data analysis, results, conclusions, and recommendations. The report will end with a summary and acknowledge the help received from various individuals. A list of references cited in the report will then follow. Any appendix should be attached to the report.

We will now discuss each of the above. A copy of a student's report on a supermarket, written as part of the requirements for a research methods course is provided in the appendix (Report 3) to serve as an illustration of how to document the literature survey and to write the method, the results, and the discussion sections for a comprehensive study undertaken to solve a problem in any business system.

INTEGRAL PARTS OF THE REPORT

The Title of the Research Report

The report title should succinctly describe what the study is all about. Examples of study report titles are as follows:

1. A Study of Customer Satisfaction with the Pizza Hut at Sunshine City, Illinois.
2. Factors Influencing the Burnout of Nurses in Monroe Hospital.
3. Antecedents and Consequences of White-Collar Employees' Resistance to Mechanization in Service Industries.

4. Factors Affecting the Upward Mobility of Women in Accounting Firms.

5. A Study of Portfolio Rebalancing and Risk Management in Investment Companies.

The first two projects will be applied research, whereas the last three will be basic research.

Apart from the title of the project, the title page will also cite the name or names of the researchers, their affiliations, for whom the study was conducted (if appropriate), and the date of the final report.

Table of Contents

The table of contents indicates, with page references, the important headings and subheadings of the report. A separate list of tables and figures, if any, should follow the listing of the written contents of the report.

The Synopsis

The synopsis or Executive Summary is an account of the research study that, although very brief, should give all the important information with respect to the study in order to furnish the reader with a good overview of the problem investigated, the hypotheses tested, the data-collection methods used, the sampling design resorted to, and the findings, recommendations, and suggestions for implementation of the recommendations. The synopsis will usually be one to two pages long.

A Synopsis or the Executive Summary for the study on customer satisfaction with the Pizza Hut in Sunshine City, for instance, might be as follows.

Synopsis

At the request of the Pizza Hut manager in Sunshine City, a survey was conducted to assess customer satisfaction with Pizza Hut. The sample was comprised of 240 customers who were administered a short questionnaire during a period of two months from July 15 to September 14. Each day, one customer who walked into the Pizza Hut at 12:00 noon, 3:00, 6:00, and 9:00 p.m. was requested to respond to a short questionnaire on site, after he or she had eaten the pizza. The questionnaire, which took less than five minutes to complete, asked respondents to indicate on an interval scale the extent of their satisfaction with (1) the flavor and texture of the pizza, (2) its taste and (3) nutritional value, (4) the price they paid for the pizza, (5) the service they received, and (6) the ambiance. Customers were also asked to comment on whatever else they wished to.

Analysis of the data indicated that about 60 percent of the respondents were men and 40 percent were women. Most of them were over 25 years of age. Customers expressed greatest satisfaction with the taste of the pizza (a mean of 4.5 on a 5-point scale), followed by its flavor and texture (mean of 4 on 5-point scale). They were neither pleased nor displeased with the price they paid or the service they received (3 on a 5-point scale). However, they were not particularly satisfied with the ambiance (mean of 2.8) or the nutritional value (mean of 2.5). The written comments of some 25 individuals indicated that they thought that the amount of cheese in the pizza might increase their cholesterol level.

It would seem that customers do like the pizza and have no complaints about the price or the service. Should the manager be concerned about the displeasure of the customers about the ambiance or the nutritional value, these two aspects can be taken care of fairly easily. It is possible to improve the ambiance by having flowers and hanging baskets of plants in the Pizza Hut. Candle lights on the tables in the evenings will also enhance the ambiance. Information can also be disseminated through the menu card and through advertisements that, in the interests of customer health, only low fat cheese is being used in the pizza at this Hut.

The Introductory Section

In the case of applied research, the introductory section starts with an introduction to the problem that is investigated and why it is important, and the background information about the organization studied. Among other things, this background information briefly covers pertinent details about the physical, environmental, financial, business, and human aspects of the organization. Any structural and process details that are relevant to the study will also find a place in this background section. In applied research, the next important information in the introductory section would be the details of the circumstances under which the study was done. For example, it may be indicated that the researchers were called in by top management to study certain aspects of the organization or its work; or the research was undertaken by a team of research students who were allowed entry into the organization in order that both students and the organization might benefit from the study. Next, the gist of the unstructured and structured interviews conducted is presented in a manner that does not disclose the identity of the individuals who were interviewed. Then, using the interviews as a basis, the tentative problem arrived at, with subproblems if any, is stated. This is followed by a literature review, a more refined problem statement, a theoretical framework, and several hypotheses for testing. In sum, the introductory section thus includes the background information of the organization studied, an account of the interviews conducted, the problem statement, the literature review, the theoretical framework, and hypotheses for testing. As noted earlier, in the case of descriptive studies or other applied research studies, where changes are proposed (see Examples 11.1 and 11.2), the format for the report will vary considerably.

In the case of basic research the introductory section would offer an idea of the topic that is researched, and why or how it is important to study it. The arguments would focus on the relevancy, timeliness, and appropriateness of the research in the context of current factors and trends in society and/or organizations. This is followed by a literature review, the problem statement, theoretical framework, and several hypotheses for testing if the study is analytical or predictive in nature. The end of the introductory section in a research report usually indicates the nature and type of study, the time horizon, the field setting, and the unit of analysis.

Points to Be Covered in the Introduction Section are:

1. Enunciating the broad problem or issue that is researched.
2. Providing the background and the rationale for the study.
3. Literature review.
4. Specifying the problem statement and clearly identifying the research questions to be addressed.
5. Developing a theoretical framework and hypotheses in the case of analytical studies.
6. Describing the nature and type of study, the time horizon, the study setting, and the unit of analysis.
7. A good transition to the next chapter or section, which would describe the methodology for the research.

A *very brief sketch* of what an introductory section for the basic research study on the factors affecting the upward mobility of women in public accounting would include is given below.

Factors Affecting the Upward Mobility of Women in Public Accounting

Introduction

A substantial number of women have entered the public accounting profession in the last ten years or so. However, less than 4 percent of the partners in the Big Eight accounting firms are women, indicating a lack of upward mobility for women in the accounting profession. Against the backdrop of the fact that the women students perform significantly better during their academic training than the men students, it is unfortunate that the intellectual power and knowledge of the women remain untapped when they start working. The recent costly litigation and discrimination suits filed, make it imperative for us to study the factors that affect the upward mobility of the women and see how the situation can be rectified.

A Brief Literature Survey

Studies of male and female accounting majors indicate that since 1977, the percentage of women accounting students has increased several fold (Kurian, 1988). Mutchler, Turner, and Williams (1987), found that women students' grades in senior accounting courses were higher than that of the male students' by an average of 5.5 percent, based on the analysis of longitudinal data collected over an 18-year period. This higher level of academic performance has been theorized as due to women having a higher need to achieve in order to overcome stereotypes (Messing, 1985), having higher success and career orientation (Tinsley et al., 1983), or having a higher aptitude for accounting (Deboer, 1984; Pallas & Alexander, 1983). Empirical studies by Fraser, Lytle, and Stolle (1978) and Johnson and Dierks (1982), however, have found no significant differences in personality predispositions or behavioral traits among men and women accounting majors.

A recent survey of women accountants in the Chicago area by Walkup and Fenzau (1980) indicated that the reasons for women not advancing in their profession may be (1) the long hours they have to work (a factor that conflicts with family demands), (2) lack of professional development opportunities (career counseling, more responsible assignments, mentoring), and (3) discrimination.

In sum, the lack of upward mobility seems to be due to factors over which the organization has some control.

Research Question

Do long work hours, lack of developmental opportunities, and discrimination account for the lack of upward mobility of women in public accounting?

Theoretical Framework

The variance in the dependent variable, **upward mobility,** can be explained by the three independent variables: long hours of work, lack of developmental opportunities, and discrimination. Since women are expected to take on, and do indeed take on, responsibility for household work and childrearing, they are not able to work after regular work hours at the workplace. This gives the wrong impression to higher-ups in the organization that women are not committed to their work. Because of this perception, women are not given significant responsibilities. This further hinders their progress since women do not get exposure to the intricacies of accounting practices as much as men. So when the time for promotion comes, women are overlooked. Deliberate discriminatory practices due to sex-role stereotypes, as evidenced in the well-known case of *Hopkins* vs. *Price Waterhouse & Co.,* also arrest women's progress. If women are not rated on their performance and are expected to conform to sex-typed behaviors (which is to play an inconspicuous role), their chances of moving up the career ladder are significantly reduced.

Thus, the three independent variables considered here should significantly explain the variance in the upward mobility of women in public accounting.

Hypotheses

1. If women are not judged by the number of hours they work after regular work hours, they will be given greater responsibilities.
2. If women are given higher responsibilities, and are trained for higher level jobs, chances for their upward mobility will increase.
3. If women are judged purely by their performance and not discriminated against, their chances for upward mobility will increase.

Study Design

This will be a correlational field study where the three independent variables and the dependent variable will be studied in several public accounting organizations.

The unit of analysis will be the individuals who respond to the survey, and the study will be cross sectional.

Method Section

The method section includes all the research design issues, such as the population and sample, variables and the measures used, data-collection methods, and the data-analysis techniques to be used in the study.

Population and Sample

The population and sample for the study are described in sufficient detail to permit the readers to develop a good feel for both, and to come to their own conclusions about the validity of the results and their generalizability. The population considered in the study should be clearly specified; for example, the population studied was blue-collar workers in the steel industry, or the board of directors of the Fortune 500 Companies, or the white-collar workers in the banking industry in Australia, Egypt, India, the United Kingdom, and the United States. The sampling design, the actual sample size used, and the sample characteristics should be fully detailed so that replications of the study are possible. The demographic characteristics of the sample include the age, educational levels, gender composition, tenure, job levels and other relevant information. Histograms of these characteristics from the frequency-distribution analysis could also be presented. For the white-collar employees' resistance to mechanization study, the description of the population and sample might look as described below.

Population and Sample for the Mechanization Study

The population for the study consisted of white-collar workers in three specific service industries in four cities in the United States. The three service industries chosen were hospitals, telephone systems, and banks. The four cities from which data were collected were New York City, Los Angeles, Chicago, and Houston. It was felt that, by studying a sample of white-collar workers in the four metropolitan cities in these three service industries, it may be possible to generalize the findings to the white-collar workers in metropolitan cities in this country since all geographical regions were covered, as were the main service industries.

Three organizations from each of the three industries were chosen for the study in each of the cities. To ensure representation of big, medium-sized, and small organizations, all hospitals, telephone companies, and banks were first categorized as big, medium-sized, or small. Thereafter, one organization from each of these categories was chosen through a simple random sampling procedure. Once permission was obtained from the organizations to administer questionnaires to their employees, a **stratified proportionate random sampling** procedure was adopted to include employees at the managerial and nonmanagerial levels.

About 350 individuals comprised the sample from each of the four cities. Of the total sample of 1400 individuals sampled, about 75 percent were women, and the rest were men. Roughly 15 percent of the respondents were managers; the rest had nonmanagerial positions. About 70 percent were Whites, 10 percent Blacks, and the rest constituted Hispanics, Asians, American Indians, and others. The mean age of the respondents was 34, and the mean number of years of their tenure in the organization was 12 years.

Note that the researcher has described the population, the sampling design and the sample size, and the sample characteristics. By taking care to represent big, medium-sized, and small organizations in each industry, and by sampling both the managerial and nonmanagerial white-collar employees, the researcher has laid the foundation to generalize the findings to at least these three service industries in these four cities.

Variables and Measures Used

Next, the variables and the measures used in the study are detailed. That is, starting with the dependent variable, each variable is briefly defined. If the measure for the variable has been taken from another published source, the reference to the source should be given. A brief description of the validity and reliability of the measure claimed by the developer of the instrument should also be provided. A rigorous research study would also state the reliabilities for the particular sample in the study. If, however, the measures for the variables have been newly developed specifically for the research, then the number of items used, an example item, and the Cronbach's alpha and split-half reliabilities for the measure should be given. The validity of the measures should also be established. For class projects, at least the face validity and the factorial validity should be discussed. The questionnaire should be placed in the appendix with a tabulation of the items in the questionnaire that measures each of the variables in the study.

Let us illustrate how a variable is defined and described in this section.

Enabling.   This dependent variable indicates the extent to which support systems exist for an individual to pursue the career without too much difficulty (Rapoport and Rapoport, 1977). Sekaran (1986) developed seven items to measure this variable, an example item being: *I am actively encouraged to set my goals high.* The measure is reported to have convergent and discriminant validity, and the Cronbach's alpha interitem consistency reliability for the seven items is .86.

Data-Collection Methods

The data-collection methods should be discussed next. Two examples of such a discussion are given here:

A convenience sample of 15 organizational members representing the top, middle, and clerical levels were interviewed to surface the important variables. Next, structured interviews were held with 10 people chosen from among the first-level managers, supervisors, and clerks. This, again, was a convenience sample. After developing the theoretical framework for the study, questionnaires were developed and personally administered to 165 employees using a proportionate random sampling procedure, as explained earlier. Groups of 30 individuals were assembled in the company's conference room, and the researcher personally explained the purpose of the survey, assured anonymity, and administered the questionnaires. Respondents typically took about 15 minutes to answer the questionnaire and hand it back to the researcher.

Another example is as follows:

Questionnaires were mailed to 280 employees in the organization with a cover letter requesting that they return the completed questionnaires within 7 days in the stamped, self-addressed envelope that was enclosed with the questionnaire. Within 15 days, 148 completed questionnaires were received. At the end of the second week a reminder was sent to all of the participants to return the completed questionnaire immediately if they had not already done so. This was followed by another reminder, 10 days later. At the end of the sixth week, a total of 188 questionnaires was received—a return rate of 67 percent. Of these, 185 questionnaires became usable for further analysis. Three had to be discarded because too many questions were left blank.

Data-Analysis Techniques

Next, the data-analytic techniques used in the data analysis are specified. Especially when new or relatively unknown techniques are used, they should be explained in detail so that the reader will be able to follow the subsequent analysis.

For class projects, the types of statistical analyses and tests proposed to be used in the study—for example, frequency distributions; descriptive statistics such as mean and standard deviation through use of the condescriptive command, the Pearson correlation analysis, χ^2 tests, ANOVA procedures, and so on—should be detailed. An example of this section follows:

Frequency distributions will be used to describe the sample. Cronbach's alpha will be established for the dependent and independent variables for this sample. The means and standard deviations for all the independent and dependent variables will be obtained through the SPSSX CONDESCRIPTIVE command. The intercorrelations among the variables will be examined through the PEARSON CORR command.

For the first hypothesis postulating differences in perceived enabling between men and women, a t-Test will be done. To test the last hypothesis, which indicates that all seven independent variables will significantly explain the variance in the dependent variable, a multiple regression analysis will be done. For all the rest of the hypotheses, which postulate bivariate relationships, the Pearson correlation analysis will provide the answer.

Results Section

The results section addresses two main things: the results of the analyses and their interpretation. First, the analyses, giving a feel for the data (such as the mean, standard deviation, etc., and the Pearson correlation matrix) are presented in tabular form and briefly discussed. See Tables 1 and 2 presented later in Report 3. All tables are sequentially numbered and given a heading.

Next, the hypotheses are stated, one at a time, both in the null and in the alternate form. The appropriateness of the test used is explained, and the results of the test are then presented, using tables wherever necessary. See Table 3 in the example study in Report 3 of the appendix. A brief interpretation of the results in the context of the hypothesis or research question then follows as we saw in the Kriya Enterprises example in the previous chapter.

Discussion Section

This section discusses the meaning of the interpretation of the results in the previous section. It details what the substantiation of the hypotheses means in terms of this research and why some of the hypotheses (if any) may not have been supported. The reasons for the nonsubstantiation of the hypotheses might be addressed through intuitive but appropriate and logical speculations about inadequacies in the sampling design, the measures, the data-collection methods, control of critical variables, respondent bias, questionnaire design, and so on. An example of this follows.

Example 11.5 The unanticipated nonsignificant correlation between vacation benefits and employee satisfaction (hypothesis 2 that was not substantiated) is intriguing at first. However, in hindsight, the results should not come as a total surprise. There are at least two factors operating in the situation that would explain the results. One is that, due to paucity of staff, very few employees get to take their vacation days. Talking to some of the employees subsequently also indicated a possible second reason. Many employees seemed to be reluctant to take their vacation for fear of being conveniently laid off during the recession period, with no job to come back to. For all practical purposes, then, though vacation benefits do exist, they are not utilized. The lack of a positive correlation between employee vacation benefits and satisfaction may be attributed to these factors.

The discussion section is the place to discuss the limitations of the study. Even if all or most of the hypotheses are substantiated, the researcher should beware of making tall claims and overgeneralizing the findings of the study. Limitations of the study in terms of any of the methodological or theoretical and conceptual aspects should be stated so that the reader is aware and appreciative of the researcher's concerns for scientific rigor. Some of the methodological deficiencies are likely to pertain to inadequacies in sampling design (using convenience sample, volunteers, etc.), data-collection methods (using same-source, self-report data), measurement problems (failure to establish high reliability and/or validity), respondent and interviewer biases (moods, biases toward topics investigated, etc.), and low response rates.

The discussion section should pull together the interpretations of the results section and give an overall picture of what the results and the interpretation mean to the study. Appropriate conclusions and implications are drawn from the findings and presented to the reader. A sample statement from the discussion section could be as follows:

> *This research is aimed at identifying the critical factors influencing the motivation of employees in this organization. The results of the study indicate that almost 65 percent of the variance in employee motivation is explained by the variables: (1) employee feelings of control over their work, (2) flexibility in scheduling work time, (3) being upbeat about the organization, letting employees set their own goals, (4) building social support among staff members, and (5) providing benchmarks of progress for long-term projects.*
>
> *The results provide various avenues for enhancing employee motivation at very low cost. Employees can be encouraged to plan and organize their work by themselves and set their own goals with minimal imposition from superiors. They can also be provided periodic feedback about their progress. Whether or not flexible time schedules are feasible, "talking up" the organization from time to time should be possible at all levels, from the President of the company to the immediate supervisor. It would thus seem feasible to increase employee motivation by taking action as elaborated in the next section.*
>
> *One limitation of this study should, however, be noted. There was an underrepresentation of the night-shift workers in the sample. However, since only 15 percent of the entire workforce works during the night shift, we need not perhaps be too much concerned about this.*

The discussion section should put forth all the relevant arguments with respect to the findings, and draw conclusions and implications therefrom. If it is basic research, the discussion section will end with implications of the findings and future directions of research in the area. If it is applied research, the discussion section is followed by a recommendations and implementation section as found in the student example in Report 3 in the Appendix.

Recommendations and Implementation

Based on the conclusions drawn in the discussion section, several alternatives for solving the problem, as well as a recommended solution, will find a place in this section. The pros and cons of implementing the recommendation should also be discussed in sufficient detail, with cost and other implications highlighted wherever possible. How these recommendations are to be implemented should also be discussed with the reasons explained in some detail. For example, for the conclusions drawn about enhancing employee motivation in the discussion section example above, the following recommendations could be made.

As discussed above, employee motivation can be increased by paying attention to such factors as goal setting, offering feedback, and the like. It will, however, be necessary to raise the consciousness of managers and supervisors to the benefits of employees managing their own work and setting their own goals. Once managers and supervisors have internalized the value of this, they should be offered training in providing timely, constructive, and realistic feedback to the employees. There are consulting agencies that would provide the training either in the company or outside. The costs of training some 300 managers and supervisors over a 12-month period and offering them assistance during the initial period immediately after training will be around $500,000 (details in worksheet). However, this investment is likely to result in the desired outcome of increased employee motivation, which, in turn, is likely to result in increased productivity of the workers (as evidenced from the article in Wall Street Journal, *October 31, 1990, B1). Even if the productivity increases by 15 percent, the expenses incurred in training the managers will be recovered in less than two years (see worksheet). It should be noted that, for the scheme to be successful, a built-in reward system for the managers who have achieved the goal of increasing the productivity of their employees (through enhanced motivation) would also be necessary.*

SUMMARY SECTION

The summary section highlights the research question and the answers found by doing the study, and also briefly recounts the recommendations and the implementation. It should be less elaborate than the synopsis.

ACKNOWLEDGMENTS

An acknowledgment of the help received from others is made in the acknowledgments section. Usually, the people who allowed the researcher(s) access to the organization are thanked, as well as those who assisted in the study by collecting the questionnaires, acting as liaison persons, helping in data analysis, and so on. Each person is individually acknowledged, with mention being made of the service rendered. Organizational members are thanked in general for responding to the survey.

REFERENCES

Immediately after the acknowledgments, starting on a fresh page, appears a list of the references cited in the literature review and at other places in the report. The format of the references has been discussed and illustrated in Section 3 of the appendix to Chapter 2. Footnotes, if there are any in the text, are referenced either separately at the end of the report, or at the bottom of the page where the footnote occurs.

APPENDIX

The appendix, which comes last, is the appropriate place for the organization chart, for newspaper clippings or other materials that substantiate what is said in the text of the report, for verbatim narration of interviews with organizational members, and for anything else that is considered useful for following the text. The appendix should also contain a copy of the questionnaire administered to the respondents, together with a table showing the location of the items in the questionnaire that tap the variables if they are not labeled in the questionnaire itself in the section heading. This could be tabulated as shown in Table 11.1 and placed before the questionnaire in the appendix. If there are several appendixes, they could be referenced as Appendix A, Appendix B, and so on, and appropriately labeled.

Table 11.1
Items in the Questionnaire Tapping the Variables

| | | Questionnaire Location | |
| | | --- | --- |
Variable	Number of Items	Section No.	Item Nos.
Demographics	6	1	1–6
Involvement	6	2	1–6
Satisfaction	20	2	7–13
		3	1–13
Challenge	8	2	14–18
		3	14–16
Organizational climate	10	4	1–10
Open-ended question regarding job	1	3	17
Open-ended question: General	1	4	11

PICTORIAL REPRESENTATION

It was earlier stated that the frequency distributions and other descriptive data can be depicted pictorially in the form of graphs and pie charts, bar charts, and other types of art. Let us illustrate several of these.

Example of a Vertical Bar Chart Representation of the Number of
Employees in an Entrepreneurial Firm from Its Inception to 1990

Figure 11.1
Vertical bar chart of employees on a yearly basis.

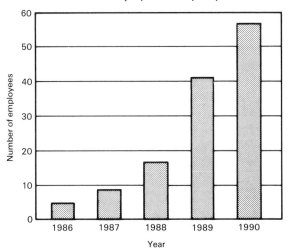

Example of a Horizontal Bar Chart of the Usage Levels
of Four Types of Wordprocessing Programs in an Office

Figure 11.2
Horizontal bar chart of wordprocessing software usage.

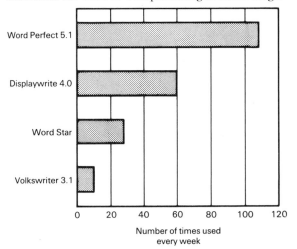

Example of a Vertical Bar Chart Representing Three Different Pain Relievers Used in a Hospital During Four Different Time Periods

Figure 11.3
Vertical bar chart depicting the usage of three different pain relievers during four different time periods.

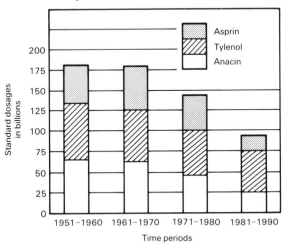

Example of a Pie Chart Depicting the Share of a Company's Profits from Various Product Lines

Figure 11.4
Pie chart showing share of profits from the various product lines of XYZ Company in 1990.

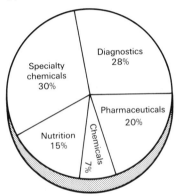

***Example of a Graph Depicting the Actual
and Projected Labor Force from 1975 to 2000***

Figure 11.5
Actual and projected labor force from 1975 to 1990.

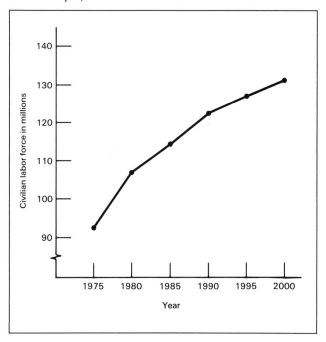

===

ORAL PRESENTATION

Usually organizations (and instructors in classes) require about a twenty- to thirty-minute oral presentation of the research project. This presentation is generally followed by a question and answer session.

The oral presentation requires considerable planning. A study that took several months to conduct has to be presented in twenty minutes to a live audience! The important aspects of the study have to be highlighted in an interesting manner while still emphasizing the statistical and quantitative details. Different stimuli (overheads, slides, charts; pictorial vs. tabular depiction, etc.) have to be creatively provided to the audience so that their interest is consistently sustained throughout the presentation. These are not possible unless time and effort are expended in planning, organizing, and rehearsing the presentation.

Deciding on the Content

Since a lot of material has to be packed in a twenty-minute presentation, it is necessary to decide what points will be focused on, and how much weight will be given to each in terms of time. Obviously, the purpose of the study, the problem investigated, the design of the study, details of the sample, data-collection methods, data analysis, results, the conclusions drawn, the limitations of the study, and the recommendations and how they can be implemented are all important aspects of the presentation. However, depending on the audience, different aspects will get stressed more. For example, if the presentation is made to a group of statisticians in the company or in a research methods class, the data analyses and results will receive more time than if the project is presented to a group of managers who are mainly interested in knowing how the problem can be solved and how the recommendations can be implemented. Thus, the time and attention devoted to the various components of the study will vary, depending on the audience.

Visual Aids

Graphs, charts, and figures help to drive home the points one wishes to make, rather effectively, within a short period of time. Thus, visual aids are vital for presentations. They also provide a different sensory stimulus, thus sustaining the attention of the audience. With modern technology, color graphics can be produced on personal computers and projected onto the screen. Slides, transparencies, flip charts, and handout materials also help the audience to easily follow what the speaker is focusing on. The selection of the visual mode of presentation will depend, among other things, on the size of the room, the availability of a good screen for projection, and the cost constraints of developing sophisticated visuals.

Delivery

An effective presentation is a function of how "unstressed" the presenter is, being able to maintain eye-contact with the audience, speaking audibly and understandably, being sensitive to the nonverbal reactions of the audience, focusing on what the audience is most interested in knowing about, and being able to time the presentation well. Extreme nervousness throughout the presentation, fumbling for words or with the notes or audiovisuals, speaking inaudibly and/or with distracting mannerisms, straying away from the main focus of the study, and exceeding the time limit given for the presentation, all detract from effectiveness. One should also not underestimate the importance of dress, posture, and how one carries oneself on the impression created on the audience. Simple things such as covering the materials on the visuals until the point is discussed and voice modulation make a big difference to the attention span of the audience and their focusing on what is being said.

Handling Questions

Having worked on the research topic for several months, the presenter is the one who knows more about the project than anyone in the audience. Hence, handling the questions from the members should not be difficult, provided one does not get flustered. It is important to feel and come across as relatively relaxed and non-defensive during the question-and-answer session. The audience might sometimes come up with a very good idea or recommendation that the researcher had not thought of. It would be graceful to acknowledge the merit of the proposed idea and say it is definitely worth considering. If a question or a suggestion from a member in the audience happens to be flawed, this can be discussed in a nonjudgmental fashion. Such handling can also be expected to elicit discussions among several members in the audience itself. The presentation can then become an exciting experience.

As can be readily seen, a twenty- to thirty-minute presentation does call for planning, psychological preparedness, and good impression management skills.

SUMMARY

The components of various types of written research reports were discussed in this chapter. It was emphasized that the purpose of the report and the intended audience are critical factors in deciding what aspects of the study will be stressed the most. Tips regarding oral presentation were also offered. Three different styles of report writing, referred to and discussed in the text, are provided in the appendix to this chapter.

DISCUSSION QUESTIONS AND POINTS TO PONDER

1. "A good description of the sample is extremely important in any research study." Discuss this statement.
2. "The limitations of the study need not necessarily be delineated because the reader will see the flaws in the study anyway." Comment.
3. "The literature survey section in the report is really a waste of space." Refute the statement.
4. "A synopsis does not really give the details of the research study that would testify to its scientific quality, so it serves no useful purpose." Critique.
5. "Applied research need not be as rigorous as basic research." Discuss.

EXERCISE

Exercise 11.1   Critique the student Report 3 in the Appendix. Discuss it in terms of good and bad research, suggesting what could have been done to improve the study, what aspects of the study are good, and how scientific the study is.

APPENDIX TO CHAPTER 11

REPORT 1: SAMPLE OF A REPORT INVOLVING A DESCRIPTIVE STUDY

Sekras Company

August 25

TO: The Chairman
Competition Gaining on Sekras Committee

FR: Cathy McWilliams, Manager
Public Relations

RE: The information requested by Mr. Griffin

Attached is the report requested by Mr. Griffin.

If any further information or clarification is needed, please contact me.

REPORT FOR THE "COMPETITION GAINING ON SEKRAS" COMMITTEE

Introduction

Vice President Griffin, Chairman of the "Competition Gaining on Sekras Committee," requested the following:

1. He wanted the revenue figures for the top five retailers in the country in 1971 and in 1988.
2. He also wanted us to conduct a quick survey of our customers to assess what *they thought* should be the improvements that we should be making in our company.

Methods Used for Obtaining the Requisite Information

The revenues of the top five retailers in the country and their revenues in 1971 were obtained from Moody's and from *Business Week*'s estimates.

To assess customers' inputs regarding improvements, a short personalized questionnaire (specimen in Appendix A) was sent through mail to 300 of our customers—100 who most frequently used our charge card in the last 18 months, 100 who most infrequently used it, and 100 medium users. Questionnaires in three different colors were sent to the three groups. As is evident from the questionnaire, the respondents were offered a complimentary pen and pencil set if their responses were received within two weeks; they were also told that if any of their suggestions were implemented, they would be sent a complimentary bread toaster or tree mug set, as per their choice.

The questionnaire asked for responses to three questions:

1. What are some of the things you like best about shopping at Sekras?
2. What are some of the things that you dislike and would like to see improved at Sekras? Please explain in as much detail as possible.
3. What are your specific suggestions for enhancing our service to customers?

Findings

I. Revenues of Top Five Retailers

Information regarding the revenues of the top five retailers in 1988 and in 1971 are offered in Table 1 below. It is evident from this table that the top retailer continues to be Sears, Roebuck & Co, though its share among the top five is eroding (from 44% in 1971 to 29% in 1988). K Mart has been progressing consistently, moving to the top second position in terms of revenues. J.C. Penney has slid from second to fourth position currently, while Wal-Mart, which was not in the top five list in 1971, is now the third.

II. Customer Suggestions for Improvement

Of the 300 surveys sent out, 225 were received, a 75 percent response rate. Of the 100 customers who most frequently used our credit card, 80 responded; among the

Table 1
Revenues of Top Five Retailers

Top Retailers in 1988			Top Retailers in 1971		
Company	Revenues in Billions of $	Share Among Top Five	Company	Revenues in Billions of $	Share Among Top Five
Sears, Roebuck	30.2	29%	Sears, Roebuck	10.1	44%
K Mart	27.3	26%	J.C. Penney	4.8	21%
Wal-Mart	20.6	20%	Kresege (now K Mart)	3.1	13%
J.C. Penney	15.2	14%	Woolworth	2.8	12%
Dayton-Hudson	12.2	11%	Montgomery Ward	2.3	10%

most infrequent users, 60 responded; and among the middle-level users, 85 responded.

The responses to the three open-ended questions were analyzed. The information needed by the Committee on the Suggested Improvements is tabulated below in Table 2. Responses to the other two questions on features liked by the customers, and their specific suggestions for improvement, are provided in Tables 3 and 4 in the Appendix. The following are suggestions received from one or two respondents only:

1. Have more water fountains on each floor.

2. The pushcarts are heavy.

3. Some chairs for resting after long shopping would help.

4. Prices of luxury items are too high.

Table 2
Suggested Areas for Improvement

Features	Frequent Users No.	Medium Users No.	Infrequent Users No.	Total No.	Total %
Small appliances such as mixers, blenders are often not to be found. This is irritating.	30	48	22	100	44%
The cafeteria serves only bland, uninteresting food. How about some spicy international food?	26	14	5	45	20%
Often, we are unable to locate where the items we want are!	3	6	14	23	10%
It would be nice if you could have a childcare service so we can shop without distractions.	28	32	25	85	38%
It is often difficult to locate a store person who can help us with our questions.	29	49	22	100	44%
I wish it were a 24-hour store.	17	13	7	37	16%
Sometimes, there is a mistake in the billing received by us. We have to make some telephone calls before the charges are corrected. This is a waste of our time.	4	12	14	20	16%

5. It would be good to have a company doctor on premises.

6. Have space for children to play videogames.

7. Import more Eastern apparel like the Kimono, Sarees, Sarongs.

8. Regulate the temperature better; sometimes it is too cold or too hot.

A Note of Caution

We are not sure how representative our sample is. We thought that a mix of high, medium, and infrequent users would provide us some useful insights. If a more detailed study using a simple random sampling procedure is considered necessary, we will initiate it quickly. We are also interviewing a few of the customers who shop here. If we find something significant from these interviews, we will surely inform you.

(Sd)
Cathy Williams

REPORT 2: SAMPLE OF A REPORT WHERE THE IDEA HAS TO BE "SOLD"

Mueller Pharmaceuticals

June 15

TO: The Board of Directors
FR: Harry Wood, V.P.
Through: President Michael Osborn
RE: Sabbatical for Managers

Enclosed is a brief report on the need for a sabbatical policy for our managers and R & D personnel, for discussion at our next board meeting. We will also plan on a more detailed presentation at that time.

WHY SABBATICAL FOR MANAGERS IS NECESSARY

Introduction

At the company's board meeting last month, the members were concerned that no new products have been developed during the last four years and that the profits of the company are considerably down. One of the Board members had suggested that a sabbatical given to the managers and key staff of our company might rejuve-nate them, and creativity might flow again. At that time, the matter was treated lightly and not given any further consideration. Feeling the need to consider this option seriously, I have since talked to a few companies who do offer this benefit to their managers. I have further obtained some data from them, which demonstrate the efficacy of sabbaticals.

Based on the available information, there is a strong case for us incorporating the sabbatical policy. Details of my discussions with other companies and their data are presented below.

Telephone Conversations with Vice Presidents and Presidents of Companies

I talked to the presidents, vice presidents, and directors of IBM, Tandem, Apple Computers, Eli Lilly, and Time Warner Inc. All these companies have had sabbatical policies for at least the past seven years. Some presidents to whom I spoke said they initiated the policy because they found that their own productivity went up after they had had some time away from their jobs doing different kinds of things. Some said that they introduced the sabbatical because they felt that their manageri-al staff experienced burnout after long years of nonstop work at a hectic pace and became ineffective.

Without exception, everyone said that it makes good business sense to offer managers a chance to refurbish their lives and recharge their batteries every six years or so, so that they come back to work with renewed vigor. Among the many advantages recounted by those to whom I spoke are:

1. More enthusiasm and zest for work.
2. Better working relationships with staff.
3. A fresh approach to problem solving with less competitiveness among the differ-ent departments.
4. More creative flow of ideas, new marketing strategies, product development ideas.
5. A more dynamic workplace in terms of interpersonal interactions, interdepart-mental colleagiality, and joint problem solving.

Some Hard Data

The Appendix, which contains the information provided by two companies, shows that the number of new products developed quadrupled in one company and increased fivefold in the other during the seven years since the introduction of the sabbatical. As they themselves acknowledge, the increase cannot be attributed to the sabbatical alone, but they have also documented that most of the new products developed were under the leadership of the managers *after* their return from a six-month sabbatical. You will note that the *before-* and *after*-sabbatical new product statistics for these managers are indeed compelling! Reinforcing this is also the decline in the figures after the fourth or fifth year of their return from sabbatical and the pick up again after the next sabbatical. Noteworthy also is that the "pick up" years were no different from the others in terms of technology advancement or other factors that might have a direct impact on innovation!

I also enclose with this report a copy of the article on Executive Life, which appeared in *The New York Times* of June 3, 1990, which you have probably already read. Is it not amusing that many of the executives who try something new ultimately want to get back to their old jobs (like the law firm partner, Axinn, who missed the rigors of his old job and could just not shake off the lawyer in him when he tried to be a rabbi-in-training during his sabbatical)?

Benefits of Sabbatical

The benefits of sabbatical to the managers are obvious; they refresh themselves trying their hands at new things or doing the things they have dreamed of (such as learning to play the flute or paint or write). These activities seem to offer them a new lease on their professional lives. But the benefits to the corporation seem to be even greater, as experienced by the companies that already have this scheme in place. Apple Computer's revenues are stated to have quadrupled under the leadership of Mr. John Sculley, who took nine-week sabbaticals; again no one is attributing cause–effect relationships, but there might be a strong correlation possible there! Mr. Lerman, partner of Wilmer, Cutler & Pickering strongly affirms that when managers come back from sabbatical, they are more effective and invigorated.

Recommendation

Given the qualitative and quantitative evidence generated from a number of organizations that have implemented the sabbatical policy, I strongly recommend that we also establish a policy to offer a paid, three-month sabbatical for all our managerial and executive staff, after every six years of service. The costs of implementing this with respect to our 42 managers and executives are worked out and shown in Exhibit 4 of the Appendix. The likely benefits within 10 years of our initiating such a policy in terms of new product development, increased sales, and joint problem solving endeavors due to higher energy levels of department heads is also shown in the same exhibit.

I will ask the HRM Director to collect information from more companies having sabbatical policies and ask him to make a presentation to the Board at our next meeting. In the meantime, if you need more information or clarification, feel free to give me a call.

Our company is at the crossroads and our managers need to be energized to enhance their performance and productivity. Constant pressure and ceaseless toil are wearing them out. Many are frustrated by the demands imposed by the jobs. "All work and no play" has banished their zest for working and drained their creative ideas. It is high time we inject some vitality into our system through sabbaticals.

REPORT 3: SAMPLE OF A PROBLEM-INVESTIGATION REPORT

NATURAL SUPERMARKET: A STUDY OF THE FACTORS THAT ENHANCE THE ORGANIZATIONAL COMMITMENT OF EMPLOYEES

Mike Conner
Management Major
Southern Illinois University
Carbondale, Illinois

Paper submitted in partial fulfillment
of the requirements for Research Methods Mgmt. 361
December 1991

CONTENTS

Literature Survey

Problem Statement

Theoretical Framework

Hypotheses

The Research Design Details

Method Section

Population and Sample

Data-Collection Methods

Sample Characteristics

Variables and Measures

Data-Analysis Methods

Results

Feel for the Data (Means, Standard Deviation and Variance; Pearson Correlations)

Hypotheses Testing

Discussion, Conclusion, and Recommendations

Possible Courses of Action and Recommendation

Implementation

Costs and Benefits of Implementing the Recommendations

Summary

Acknowledgments

References

Appendix

Table 1: Means, Standard Deviations, and Variances of the Three
Multiple-Item Variables in the Natural Supermarket Sample

Table 2: Pearson Correlation Matrix for the
Natural Supermarket Sample

Table 3: Results of the Multiple Regression Analysis
Regressing the Five Independent Variables
Against Organizational Commitment

Figure 1: Schematic Diagram of the Theoretical Framework

SYNOPSIS

The purpose of this research project was to investigate the organizational commitment of the employees at the Natural Supermarket store located in Rollinghills, Illinois. The dependent variable in this study was organizational commitment, and the independent variables considered were age, gender, opportunity for advancement, number of years served in the organization, and job satisfaction. Our data-collection methods comprised unstructured and structured interviews, and a 29-item questionnaire. A random sample of 40 employees was chosen for this study. The data analysis to test the several hypotheses included the use of Pearson correlations, t-Tests, and multiple regression analysis. The results showed that 40 percent of the variance in organizational commitment was explained by the five independent variables, and that opportunity for advancement was the most significant predictor of commitment. The women employees perceived fewer opportunities for advancement in the organization than the men, though there were no significant differences in the organizational commitment expressed by men and women. Job satisfaction was the second most significant variable predicting organizational commitment. As a matter of fact, organizational commitment, job satisfaction, and opportunities for advancement were significantly intercorrelated.

Several recommendations have been made to enhance the organizational commitment of employees at the Natural Supermarket. Suggestions include (1) holding meetings to clarify and explain the policies regarding promotion, (2) enhancing job satisfaction through job enrichment, and (3) instituting a simple but effective evaluation system. A phased plan for implementation of the various suggestions and a new appraisal form are discussed in detail in the report.

Our research team wishes to thank Dr. Usha Kiren, Mr. Larry Begee, and all the employees at Natural Supermarket who participated in the survey for making this research project possible.

RESEARCH PROPOSAL

Southern Illinois University
Carbondale, Illinois 62901
October 16, 1991

Mr. Larry Begee
Manager, Natural Supermarket
212 West Mauris
Rollinghills, IL 62901

Dear Mr. Begee:

Following our various interviews with you and your employees at Natural Supermarket, our team has decided on two potential areas of study within your organization: job satisfaction and organizational commitment.

The next step in our research will involve administering questionnaires to a sample of forty to fifty employees. A copy of the questionnaire will be made available to you prior to administration. We will distribute the questionnaires to the employees to be completed during the break periods, and we will take them back personally. These questionnaires will require approximately ten minutes for completion. This phase of our study will start on October 20, 1991, and end by October 26, 1991.

As was the case with our employee interviews, we will make sure that the normal flow of work is not obstructed by our presence and data gathering. A summary of our findings will be made available to you by January 20, 1992.

If you have any questions to ask, please contact Mike Conner of our team at 529-4758.

We wish to thank you sincerely for your cooperation and assistance in making this survey possible. We anticipate that our findings will be useful to you.

Yours truly,

(Sd)

Mike Conner
Bruce McClain
S.I.U. Research Project Team

INTRODUCTORY SECTION

Introduction

Organizational commitment has been the focus of many research studies because of its importance to employing organizations. With today's mobile and floating working population, it has become increasingly important for organizations to know how they can retain employees and gain their loyalty. Because organizations continually search for ways to increase employees' commitment to the organization, it was hoped that the study would offer some general insights.

More specifically, this study investigates the correlates of organizational commitment among employees in a supermarket.

Background Information of the Supermarket

Natural Supermarkets are a chain of food stores located throughout the midwestern United States. These stores are wholly owned subsidiaries of the Resson Company. There are presently four divisions located in Milwaukee, Minneapolis, New Orleans, and St. Louis (corporate headquarters).

In 1972, Natural opened a store at 212 W. Mauris in Rollinghills, and it has remained in operation for the past eight years. The store's present manager is Larry Begee, who is currently serving his third year in this position. Mr. Begee's association with Natural began eighteen years ago when he was a stockboy at the store in Belleville, Illinois. Mr. Begee was the successor to two previous managers when he was transferred to his present location from Centralia, Illinois, in 1977. He is an active supporter of the high school job program and knows most of the customers personally.

Mike Garrison is the associate manager and Ken Thompson is the assistant manager; both men are currently being trained to become future store managers.

Natural presently has a workforce of nearly 80, with college and high school students comprising the bulk of the employees. Twenty-five percent of these students hold their jobs even during the summer.

Natural's products are very similar to the lines of other supermarket chain stores. It has a full line of grocery products, a bakery department, a deli department, and a limited line of generic products. The store's income fluctuates between $30,000 and $40,000 per month, with summer being the slowest season of the year. Its organizational structure, according to Mr. Begee, is typical of most other supermarkets.

The Unstructured and Structured Interviews

Our research team interviewed the first set of employees on September 19, 1991. Through a previous meeting with the manager, we arranged to conduct the meetings in the employee's lounge, located in the rear of the store. This particular location was chosen so as not to interfere with the normal daily workflow of employees.

Although we sensed some initial apprehension among the employees in the store, they seemed to overcome it and we were able to communicate with them in a cordial and open manner, explaining to them that this project is a part of our coursework.

During the course of our discussions, our research team attempted to surface the employees' overall impressions of the store, their fellow workers, and their respective managers and supervisors. A brief summary of the results follows, organized under three main headings. The verbatim conversations can be seen in Appendix A.

Employee Responses Regarding Their Jobs and the Store in General

During the course of our interviews, we addressed questions to the employees concerning their present job and the store. Employee reactions and responses were many and diverse.

One group expressed great pleasure over their jobs and with the entire organization. They said that their work was enjoyable and challenging, and that they found a great deal of gratification in working for Natural Supermarket. It is interesting to note that the vast majority of workers expressing these views had been employees of the company for a considerable length of time.

On the other hand, there was a group of employees who expressed very little satisfaction with their jobs or with the organization. This set of workers communicated to us that they were "there for the money, and that's all." When questioned about their attitudes concerning their job, one employee responded that she did not much care for it, whereas another worker stated that she was simply there to do a job "and that's it." These same attitudes were repeated when most other women were questioned about the Natural Supermarket as a place to work. Some of the younger male employees also expressed a similar opinion.

Employees' Impressions About Their Fellow Workers

Nearly all of the employees we talked to expressed positive attitudes toward their fellow workers. One respondent, when asked about the working relationships of the personnel, stated that it was just like a family within a store. Identical remarks were echoed by several others. However, some employees did not express this same attitude toward their fellow workers. There seemed to be an unhealthy competition for promotions and recognition, and concerns were expressed over the tensions, dishonesty, and rivalry among fellow workers. One respondent described the situation using such terms as "backstabbing" and "brownnosing."

Through subsequent structured interviews, it was gathered that the dissatisfactions among the employees revolved around the promotions within the system. Our team felt that the variables of opportunities for advancement and job satisfaction should be considered important for the research.

Employees' Reactions to Management

Opinions were decidedly split among the employees about management in general, and about the supervisors. About half the employees expressed negative attitudes toward their superiors, whereas the other half expressed more positive feelings toward their supervisors and the management of the store in general.

Those workers who communicated negative emotions cited reduction in work hours, management style, and promotional policy as a few of the underlying reasons for their negative attitude. Through more detailed discussions, we found out that women employees appeared to be very concerned that they would not be considered for promotion because of their gender. Some employees expressed dissatisfaction with management in general, citing no particular reasons for their dissatisfaction.

Of those workers who expressed more positive attitudes toward their superiors, feelings of friendship and respect for the individuals were often voiced. Moreover, this group felt that the store was better organized and run more efficiently now than in the past. Both these factors were attributed to Mr. Begee's management.

Upon concluding the interviews with the employees, our group attempted to identify the prospective variables of concern to the study. Four areas appeared to be potential topics for investigation: job satisfaction, organizational loyalty, attitudes toward promotion policies, and employee relations.

Our next phase of research was to interview Mr. Begee, the manager of Natural Supermarket.

Our discussion with Mr. Begee covered many topics and areas of concern in a relatively short period of time. He informed us that when he came to Rollinghills three years ago, the store was in a state of disarray. He worked diligently with the union and attempted to incorporate more efficient and organized methods of operation in the store. He stated that he still works closely with the union and he runs a very efficient operation.

When questioned about his employees, Mr. Begee expressed concern over the lack of integration between departments, and the need for a general feeling of organizational commitment. Although he believed that the employees at higher levels were extremely committed, he expressed his conviction that the part-time workers lacked work commitment and were dedicated to their work and the supermarket only to the extent of retaining their jobs. Mr. Begee suggested that we do our research to see how the organizational commitment of all employees in Natural Supermarket at Rollinghills can be increased.

Upon completion of our interviews with all levels of employees at Natural Supermarket, our team worked to come up with a problem statement and drew up a list of important variables that were surfaced in the interviews. In light of the fact that most employees felt very little satisfaction with their jobs and expressed no loyalty or commitment to the organization, and that Mr. Begee had stated that commitment was an area of his concern, we concluded that the variable to be studied in this research project would be organizational commitment. We also decided to examine the effects of job satisfaction, years of service, age, opportunities for advancement, and gender of the employee on the dependent variable. These five variables appeared to be important in explaining the variance in organizational commitment based on the responses of the employees in the unstructured and structured interviews described earlier.

Literature Review

Porter, Steers, Mowday, and Boulin (1974) defined organizational commitment (OC) as the "relative strength of an individual's identification with, and involvement in a particular organization." Mowday, Steers, and Porter (1979) further clarified the concept by stating that commitment can be said to exist when the individual links his or her identity to the organization, and the goals of the individual and the organization become increasingly integrated and congruent. OC has been found to be a predictor of job search behaviors, absenteeism, intentions to stay or leave, and subsequent turnover (Pierce & Dunham, 1987; Sekaran & Jeanquart, 1991).

OC has been studied in the context of several demographic factors such as age, gender, and tenure (Pierce & Dunham, 1984; Werbel, 1990). Age was found to be positively correlated to the organizational commitment of managers in service industries (Glisson, 1988; Morris, 1990). Strasser (1991) found that employees who had served in the organization for longer periods of time were more committed to the system than those who just joined the organization. Conflicting reports have been found as to the association of gender with OC (see for instance, Chapman, 1987; Derrick, 1989; Vanslow, 1990). However, it has been found in the study by Sekaran (1991) that women who are past 40 are more committed to the organization than men. It would thus seem from the current research that age, tenure, and gender would have an impact on the organizational commitment of members.

Studying a sample of teachers and nurses, Digboy and Pritcher (1987) found that perceived opportunities for advancement prompted employees to remain committed to the organization. This has been further confirmed in the studies done by Sergo (1988) and Peluchette (1990) with industrial workers and hospital staff. Satisfaction with the work, with the work environment, and with pay have also been found to significantly influence OC (Mueller, 1990; Sekaran & Jeanquart, 1991; Mather, 1990). Interestingly enough, the type of industry in which people work does not seem to make any difference in how the demographic and organizational factors, just discussed, seem to influence OC.

To sum up, a review of the literature suggests that organizational commitment can be best examined using age, gender, work experience, opportunities for advancement, and job satisfaction as predictors. The fact that similar variables were surfaced in our unstructured and structured interviews reinforced our original thinking that we could use these five variables in our research to predict organizational commitment.

Problem Statement

To what extent do age, gender, job satisfaction, opportunities for advancement, and number of years served in the organization predict organizational commitment?

Theoretical Framework

The variable of primary interest to this research is the dependent variable of organizational commitment. Five independent variables are used in an attempt to explain the variance in employees' commitment to the organization. These five variables are age, opportunity for advancement, job satisfaction, years in the organization, and sex of the employee.

The greater the chances are for advancement within the organization, the higher is likely to be the level of organizational commitment expressed by the employee. When employees know that they are going to grow and prosper in the current organization, their level of commitment to stay with the organization is expected to be high. If, however, there are no opportunities for advancement perceived in the present organization, employees—especially those who want to climb up the organizational ladder—are likely to search for other jobs offering greater opportunities. Their level of commitment to stay with the present organization and get involved in its goals and activities will be low. Similarly, if employees are highly satisfied with their jobs and derive high levels of job satisfaction, they are more likely to be committed to the organization than if they are not satisfied. One usually feels obligated to be loyal and committed to the source that offers satisfaction and happiness. Also, as the period of time served in the organization increases, the amount of commitment to the organization increases. When people stay long enough with an organization, they tend to form an attachment to the place, the fellow workers, the customers, and so on, and feel reluctant to leave the place and join another institution. Their involvements in and loyalty to the existing organization would usually preclude their wanting to quit. Therefore, organizational commitment will be less among those employees who have served in the organization for the shortest period of time.

Somewhat following the lines of the preceding arguments, age also has an influence on organizational commitment. Older employees, who usually have served the organization longer, are generally more committed to the organization than their younger counterparts. This is not only because seniority carries with it some status and prestige, but also because as one advances in age, there are limited opportunities for finding a better job elsewhere. This induces more commitment and loyalty to the present organization where the employee is working. Hence, age would seem to have a positive correlation with organizational commitment. Contrary to popular opinion, female employees would be more committed to the organization than male employees, as found in Hrebiniak and Alutto's study cited earlier. This stronger commitment could be a result—especially in the case of married women—of their being dual-income family members who would thus not be unduly concerned about making more money, but would rather tend to derive greater satisfaction by doing the best possible job where they are. Thus, they may remain with the same organization for a long time. However, if the need patterns of women are high—a variable not explored in the present study—they may not be as highly committed to an organization where the avenues for advancement are not open or do not exist.

On the basis of the above arguments, we theorize that there would be positive correlations between organizational commitment and each of the following vari-

Figure 11.6
Schematic diagram of the theoretical framework.

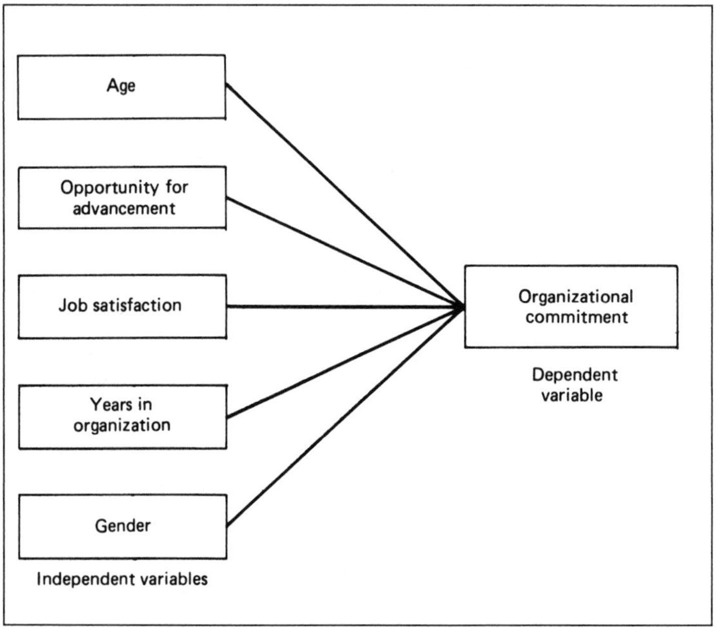

ables: age, opportunities for advancement, job satisfaction, the number of years in the organization, and the gender of the employees, with women being more committed than men.

The theoretical framework is depicted in Figure 1.

Hypotheses

From the theoretical framework discussed above, seven hypotheses were developed for this research. They are as follows:

H_A 1. The older an employee is, the greater will be the individual's level of commitment to the organization.

H_A 2. If an opportunity for advancement is perceived by the employee, then there will be a greater degree of organizational commitment.

H_A 3. There will be a positive correlation between organizational commitment and the number of years served in the organization.

H_A 4. Females will have greater organizational commitment than males.

H_A 5. The perceived opportunities for promotion will be greater among male employees than among female employees.

H_A 6. There will be a positive correlation between job satisfaction and organizational commitment.

H_A 7. The five independent variables will significantly explain a high percentage of the variance in the organizational commitment of employees at Natural Supermarket.

The Research Design Details

Type of Study

The purpose of this research project was to establish the relationships between the independent variables of age, gender, opportunity for advancement, job satisfaction, and number of years served in the organization, and the dependent variable of organizational commitment; thus, this project was a correlational rather than a causal study.

Nature of Study

Because this research project attempted to analyze the relationships between the dependent and independent variables, this study was analytical in nature.

Study Setting

This is a field study because it examined attitudes and behaviors of people in their natural work environment. Variables were neither controlled nor manipulated, and no artificial setting was created for the study.

Time Horizon

The data for this research were collected over a two-month period. Because no previous research had been done by the team on this organization, nor was any subsequent extension of the research contemplated, the study is cross-sectional in nature.

Unit of Analysis

Because the researchers were interested in ascertaining the degree of organizational commitment of Natural employees, the unit of analysis for this project was each individual employee.

METHOD SECTION

Population and Sample

The population for the study comprised employees in the various departments within the Rollinghills, Illinois, Natural Supermarket store. Natural currently has a workforce of 80 employees. Unstructured and structured interviews were conducted using a convenience sample of 15 employees each time, to surface potential areas for investigation. A questionnaire consisting of 29 items was later administered to a representative sample of 40 employees selected through a simple random sampling procedure.

Data-Collection Methods

The questionnaires were administered on the premises on a Thursday evening and a Saturday afternoon, because practically all the employees report to work on these two days. Our research team assured the employees that their responses would be anonymous and confidential, and the respondents completed the questionnaires in the back room within 10 to 15 minutes.

Sample Characteristics

The sample comprised 53 percent women and 47 percent men. The mean age of the respondents was 26. Fifty-five percent of the respondents were not married. The mean pay of the respondents was between $9.00 and $12.00 per hour, and the mean length of service of the employees in the organization was two to four years. All had at least a high school education, 10 percent had a bachelor's degree, and 20 percent were in college.

Variables and Measures

The 29-item questionnaire tapped nine personal information items: age, gender, education, marital status, number of children, tenure, number of other organizations worked for, job status, and pay. These were measured by single items. Opportunity for advancement, job satisfaction, and organizational commitment were measured through multiple items on a five-point Likert-type scale as described below.

Opportunity for Advancement

This variable was tapped through five items that measured employees' perceived scope for advancement, management's willingness to promote efficient workers, and general overall norms for promotion in the organization. A sample item is "The opportunities to get promoted in this organization are very good." The Cronbach's alpha for these items was .84. The items had factorial validity.

Job Satisfaction

In an attempt to operationalize the definition of job satisfaction, the concept was divided into three related dimensions: satisfaction with work, satisfaction with supervision, and satisfaction with co-workers. These three dimensions were each tapped through two questions. The six questions that measured job satisfaction had Cronbach's alpha of .76. All of the items appeared to have face validity.

Organizational Commitment

Steers and Spencer (1977) have defined organizational commitment as the individual's degree of identification with the employing organization. Buchanan (1974) defined commitment as an individual's attachment to an organization's goals and ideals. Because the reliability and validity of the measure used in these reports has been established, eight items were randomly drawn from the two sources in order to measure the concept for this research project. The Cronbach's alpha of these eight items was .89 for this sample.

Data-Analysis Methods

Frequency distributions, correlations, and means, standard deviations, and other statistics were obtained by the Frequencies, Pearson Corr, and Condescriptive commands. The hypotheses were tested through the correlations obtained, *t*-Tests, and simple multiple regression analysis.

RESULTS

Feel for the Data

The mean, standard deviation, and the variance of the three variables of organizational commitment, job satisfaction, and perceived opportunity for advancement are as in Table 1. As can be seen from the table, all three variables are a little to the left on the five-point scale, denoting average commitment, satisfaction, and opportunity for advancement. All three have very little variance. However, the maximum and minimum on each of the variables are such that there is sufficient indication that the responses ranged through all points on the scales.

The Pearson correlation matrix of the eight variables investigated in this study is shown in Table 2. As can be seen, two of the variables are correlated over .59. The intercorrelations among organizational commitment, job satisfaction, and opportunities for advancement were greater than .5.

Table 1

Means, Standard Deviations, and Variances of the Three Multiple-Item Variables in the Natural Supermarket Sample[a]

Variable[b]	Mean	Standard Deviation	Variance
Organizational commitment	2.88	.64	.41
Satisfaction	2.69	.64	.41
Opportunity for advancement	2.77	.78	.62

[a]$n = 40$.
[b]The means for the three variables rest on a five-point scale, with 1 denoting very high, and 5 denoting very low on the variables.

Table 2
Pearson Correlation Matrix for the Natural Supermarket Sample ($n = 40$)

	Organizational Commitment	Job Satisfaction	Opportunities for Advancement	Tenure	Pay	Age	Sex	Education
Organizational commitment	1.0							
Job satisfaction	.56[b]	1.0						
Opportunities for advancement	.60[b]	.51[b]	1.0					
Tenure	−.17	.09	.15	1.0				
Pay	−.35[b]	−.12	−.04	.73[b]	1.0			
Age	−.31[c]	−.21	−.20	.55[b]	.48[b]			
Gender[a]	−.19	−.13	−.39[b]	.06	.04	−.20	1.0	
Education	.01	.11	.05	.22	.18	.07	−.10	1.0

[a]Females, 1; males, 2.
[b]$p \le .01$.
[c]$p \le .05$.

Hypotheses Testing

Hypothesis 1

H_O: There is no relationship between age and organizational commitment.

H_A: The greater the age of an employee, the greater will be the level of commitment to the organization.

The Pearson correlation results showed a correlation coefficient of −.31, significant at the $p = .04$ level. Remembering that 1 on the five-point scale meant high commitment and 5 signified low commitment, we find that, as hypothesized, age and organizational commitment are significantly correlated. Thus, this hypothesis was substantiated.

Hypothesis 2

H_O: There is no relationship between perceived opportunity for advancement and the extent of organizational commitment of employees.

H_A: If a good opportunity for advancement is perceived, then there will be a greater degree of organizational commitment.

A significant correlation of .60 was found at the $p = .0001$ level (see Pearson correlation matrix). Thus the null hypothesis was rejected and the alternate hypothesis accepted.

Hypothesis 3

H_O: There is no relationship between tenure and organizational commitment.

H_A: There will be a positive correlation between organizational commitment and the number of years served by employees in the organization.

The correlation between tenure and organizational commitment, though in the hypothesized direction, was not significant ($r = -.17; p = .14$). Thus the alternate hypothesis was not substantiated.

Hypothesis 4

H_O: There will be no gender differences in the organizational commitment felt by the employees.

H_A: Females will have greater organizational commitment than males.

No significant mean differences in the organizational commitment of men and women were found through the use of a t-test analysis ($t = .37; p = .25$). Thus this hypothesis was also not substantiated.

Hypothesis 5

H_O: There will be no mean differences in the perceived opportunities for promotion among male and female employees in the organization.

H_A: The opportunities for promotion will be perceived to be greater by the male employees.

A t-Test showed significant differences between the mean score of 2.5 for males and that for females of 3.7 ($t = 3.6; p = .001$). Thus this hypothesis was substantiated. Women perceived themselves as having fewer opportunities for advancement in the organization. (A higher score indicates fewer opportunities.)

Hypothesis 6

H_O: There will be no relationship between job satisfaction and organizational commitment.

H_A: There will be a positive correlation between job satisfaction and organizational commitment.

The correlation between job satisfaction and organizational commitment is significant ($r = .56; p = .0001$), as can be seen from the Pearson correlation matrix. Thus the null hypothesis was rejected and the alternate hypothesis accepted.

Table 3
Results of the Multiple Regression Analysis Regressing
the Five Independent Variables Against
Organizational Commitment

Predictors	Beta	*F*
Age	.09	.32
Tenure	.08	.27
Gender	.07	.25
Job satisfaction	.38	18.2[a]
Opportunities for advancement	.57	27.4[a]

$$R^2 = .402$$
$$F = 29.86^a$$
$$DF = 5,34$$

[a]$p < .001$.

Hypothesis 7

H_O: The five independent variables in the theoretical framework will not significantly explain the variance in the organizational commitment of the employees.

H_A: The five independent variables of age, tenure, gender, job satisfaction, and opportunities for advancement will significantly explain the variance in the organizational commitment of the employees.

The results of the multiple regression analysis, regressing the five independent variables against organizational commitment, is shown in Table 3. As can be seen, the five variables together significantly explained 40 percent of the variance in organizational commitment ($R^2 = .402$; $F = 29.86$; $p = .0001$). The beta values of both job satisfaction and opportunities for advancement were significant. Thus, the hypothesis that the five predictors would significantly explain the variance in organizational commitment was substantiated.

In sum, five of the seven hypotheses were substantiated and two were not. The results indicated that older employees were more committed to the organization; employees who perceived greater opportunities for advancement were more committed; men perceived more opportunities for advancement than females; those who experienced higher levels of job satisfaction were more committed; and the five independent variables in the theoretical framework did significantly explain 40 percent of the variance in organizational commitment. There were no gender differences in organizational commitment, and tenure was not significantly correlated to commitment, for this sample at least.

DISCUSSION, CONCLUSION, AND RECOMMENDATION

This study was undertaken to provide some recommendations to the manager of Natural Supermarket on how the organizational commitment of the employees can be enhanced. The results of the study clearly indicate that older employees are more committed, probably because they cannot easily find other jobs. It makes sense that perceived opportunities for advancement would increase the commitment of the employees to stay with the organization. However, it is perturbing to note that women, who formed 53 percent of the sample, perceived fewer opportunities for advancement than men. If their perceptions are incorrect, the facts must be made clear to them; if they are correct, the manager should reassess the situation as to why this is so.

The reason why tenure might not be related to organizational commitment could be due to the fact that not many long-term employees were in the sample (the mean tenure of the employees in the sample was between two and four years).

In terms of practical suggestions to enhance commitment, while perceived advancement opportunities might enhance organizational commitment, there are not many higher level jobs for employees to advance to in the supermarket. Most employees, who are baggers or working on the cash registers, might perforce have to be in deadend jobs—a reality over which the manager might have no control. There is also a limit to the number of managers and assistant managers in the produce, meat, and other departments. Thus, the manager of Natural Supermarket may not have much option to enhance the opportunities for promotion of his employees. However, the results show that employees who are more job satisfied are also more committed. This information might be useful to increase the organizational commitment of employees.

Job satisfaction, as shown in many studies, is a function of giving employees the freedom to plan and organize their activities in the manner that best suits them, ensuring congenial superior–subordinate relationships and friendly co-worker interactions at the workplace, and recognizing the good work done by employees through praise, having an "employee of the month award," and such. These can be relatively easily implemented or achieved without much financial costs by the manager, creating a conducive climate within the supermarket, as discussed later.

Possible Courses of Action and Recommendation

Recruitment of Older Employees

Since older employees seem to be more committed, the manager could plan on hiring more mature employees in the future. However, this might be construed as discriminatory, and adverse consequences might follow. Hence, this is not recommended. In any case, for the more responsible positions such as managers of the various departments, only the more experienced and older members are hired. Since it is relatively easy to train baggers and cash register operators, turnover among them due to lack of organizational commitment should not be of too much concern.

Enhancing Job Satisfaction

As discussed earlier, organizational commitment can be increased by enhancing the job satisfaction of employees. Several strategies to increase job satisfaction were also mentioned. These are further discussed below.

Increasing Autonomy.   While there may not be very much that can be done to expand the job scope or responsibilities for personnel doing routine jobs such as that of the baggers and cash counter employees, the purchasers, staff of the various departments including the managers, and the cashiers and accountants can be given a lot of freedom to plan and organize their work themselves. During the interviews, several of these individuals indicated that they were closely supervised and had very little autonomy. By giving these individuals more responsibility to handle their work, job satisfaction can be considerably increased.

Superior–Subordinate Relationships.   It might be recalled that during the interviews, several complained that the relationships among the employees—whether between superiors and subordinates or among co-workers—were not very congenial. The respondents used such terms as "rivalry," "backstabbing," and such. Operating in such a hostile environment will be detrimental to the job satisfaction and commitment of the employees. Measures have to be taken to improve the climate within each department and in the supermarket as a whole, as detailed later.

Recognition of Good Work.   The manager can boost the morale of employees at all levels by paying attention to them. By taking rounds at various times of the day, Mr. Begee can talk to several employees to show his friendliness, compliment personnel when things are proceeding smoothly, offer "employee of the month" awards based on some prespecified criteria of performance, and so on. Though monetary incentives help, nonfinancial strategies such as the ones specified above also work just as effectively. All it takes is some time on the part of superiors and the manager, Mr. Begee himself.

IMPLEMENTATION

Changing the culture of a system takes time and considerable effort. Manager Begee should obtain the help of a consultant who can start the process of facilitating change in the system. The consultant can assist Mr. Begee in (1) building more autonomy into the jobs of all the managers, supervisors, purchasers, and other staff; (2) having training sessions for all those who supervise others in effective interpersonal relationships; (3) developing processes by which cooperative rather than competitive interactions are encouraged among all employees; (4) developing criteria for recognizing and rewarding employees with superior performance; and (5) evaluating the effectiveness of these changes several months after the changes are initiated.

Costs and Benefits of Implementing the Recommendations

The costs of hiring a good consultant for about three months to work with the system and bring about organizationwide changes will be around $40,000. There might be an additional cost of about $5,000 to $7,000 for subsequent evaluation of the success of the changes initiated, say after another six months. This cost of about $50,000 may be too much for the Natural Supermarket to bear. However, as part of its community service, the College of Business at Southern helps businesses in the vicinity with their expertise. Professors Susan McHose and Harold Bailey from the Management Department have facilitated such organization development and change processes at other institutions. It may be useful for Mr. Begee to approach the Dean of the College of Business for help in this matter.

In summary, the organizational commitment of the employees can be enhanced by enhancing their job satisfaction. Several simple strategies as discussed above can achieve this goal. It is suggested that Mr. Larry Begee contact the Dean of the School of Business to obtain help in implementing the recommendations made in this report.

A FINAL NOTE TO THE STUDENT

Research is a part of organizational reality that helps businesses to continuously improve, as is evident from the discussions in this book. Though you may not have become an *expert* researcher after one semester of coursework, I am sure you have gained a good appreciation for business research—a great asset in dealing effectively with consultants. Being able to discriminate between the *good* and the *not so good* research will also be invaluable to you in sifting the materials you will be reading in the practitioner and academic journals in your professional life as managers.

If you have satisfactorily met the following objectives, you can be confident that you have one of the primary requisites to becoming an effective manager.

1. Developing a sensitivity for, and being able to identify, important variables operating in a particular situation.
2. Being able to gather information quickly by asking the appropriate questions, of appropriate sources of information, and in an unbiased manner.
3. Locating and being able to extract relevant information from published sources.
4. Being able to conceptualize clearly the logical relationships among variables in any given situation.
5. Becoming sensitive to sources of biases in both published articles and project reports given to you by consultants and researchers, and thus becoming more discriminating and sophisticated consumers of research.

I wish you success in your academic and professional career!

Uma Sekaran

GLOSSARY OF TERMS

Alternate Hypothesis The educated conjecture that sets the parameters that one expects to find. This alternate hypothesis is tested to see if the null is to be rejected or not.

Ambiguous Questions Questions that are not clearly worded and that respondents may interpret in different ways.

Analytical Study A study that tries to explain why or how certain variables influence the dependent variable of interest to the researcher.

ANOVA Stands for Analysis of Variance, which tests for significant mean differences in variables among multiple groups.

Applied Research Research conducted in a particular setting with the specific intention of solving an existing problem in the situation.

Area Sampling Cluster sampling within a specified area or region; a probability sampling design.

Attitudinal Factors People's feelings, dispositions, and reactions toward the organization and to factors in the work environment such as the work itself, the co-workers, or supervision.

Basic Research Research conducted to generate knowledge and understanding of phenomena (in the work setting) that would add to the existing body of knowledge (about organizations and management theory).

Behavioral Factors Actual behaviors exhibited by employees on the job such as being late, working hard, remaining absent, or quitting work.

Bias Any error that creeps into the data. Biases can be introduced by the researcher, the respondent, the measuring instrument, the sample, etc.

Bibliography A systematic alphabetical listing of authors, referencing the titles of their works that are of relevance to the study, indicating where they can be located.

Broad Problem Area A situation where one senses a possible need for research and problem solving, even though the specific problem is not clear.

Causal Analysis Analysis done to detect cause → effect relationships between two or more variables.

Causal Study A research study conducted to establish cause → effect relationships among variables.

Chi-square Test A nonparametric test that establishes the independence or otherwise between two nominal variables.

Classification Data Personal information or demographic details of the respondents such as age, marital status, and educational level.

Closed Questions Questions with a clearly delineated set of alternatives that confine the respondents' choice to selecting from among the given alternatives.

Cluster Sampling A probability sampling design in which the sample comprises groups or chunks of elements with intragroup heterogeneity and intergroup homogeneity.

Comparative Study A study conducted by collecting data from several settings or organizations.

Complex Probability Sampling Several probability sampling designs (such as systematic and stratified random), which offer an alternative to the cumbersome, simple random sampling design.

Concurrent Validity Relates to criterion-related validity, which is established at the same time that the test is administered.

Confidence The probability estimate of how much reliance we can place on the findings. The accepted level of confidence in social science research is usually 95 percent.

Construct Validity Testifies to how well the results obtained from the use of the measure fit the theories around which the test was designed.

Content Validity Establishes the representative sampling of a whole set of items that measures a concept, and reflects how well the dimensions and elements of the concept have been delineated.

Contextual Factors Factors relating to the organization being studied such as the background and environment of the organization, including the origin and purpose of the company, size, resources, financial position, and the like.

Contrived Setting An artificially created or "lab" environment in which research is conducted.

Control Group The group that is not exposed to any treatment in an experiment.

Controlled Variable Any exogenous or extraneous variable that could contaminate the cause → effect relationship, but the effects of which can be controlled by the researcher in an experiment through the process either of matching or of randomization.

Convenience Sampling A nonprobability sampling design in which information or data for the research are gathered from members of the population who are conveniently accessible to the researcher.

Convergent Validity is established when the scores obtained by two different instruments measuring the same concept, or the scores obtained by measuring the concept by two different methods, are highly correlated.

Correlational Analysis Analysis done to trace the mutual influence of variables on one another.

Correlational Study A research study conducted to identify the important factors associated with the variables of interest.

Criterion-Related Validity This is established when the measure differentiates individuals on a criterion that it is expected to predict.

Criterion Variable The main variable that poses the problem for a study (i.e., the variable of primary interest to the researcher—the dependent variable).

Cross-Sectional Study A research study for which data are gathered just once (maybe stretching over a period of days, weeks, or months) to answer the research question.

Deduction The process of arriving at conclusions based on the interpretation of the meaning of the results of data analysis.

Dependent Variable *See* Criterion Variable.

Descriptive Statistics Statistics such as frequencies and the mean and standard deviation, which describe the data that have been gathered.

Descriptive Study A research study that describes the variables in a situation that are of interest to the researcher.

Directional Hypothesis An educated conjecture as to the direction of the relationship between two variables; the relationship could be positive or negative, or differences could be more or less.

Discriminant Validity This is established when, based on theory, two variables are predicted to be uncorrelated, and the scores obtained by measuring them are indeed empirically found to be so.

Disproportionate Stratified Random Sampling A probability sampling design that involves a procedure in which the number of sample subjects chosen from various strata is not directly proportionate to the total number of elements in the respective strata.

Double-Barreled Question Refers to the improper framing of a single question that should be posed as two or more separate questions, so that the respondent can give clear and unambiguous answers.

Double Sampling A probability sampling design that involves the process of collecting information from a set of subjects twice (such as using a sample to collect preliminary information, and later using a subsample of the primary sample for more information).

Dynamic Panels Consist of a changing composition of members who serve as the sample subjects for a research study conducted over an extended period of time.

Editing Data The process of going over the data and ensuring that they are complete and acceptable for data analysis.

Efficiency in Sampling Attained when the sampling design chosen either results in a cost reduction to the researcher or offers greater precision in terms of sample size.

Element A single member of the population.

Experimental Design A study design in which the researcher imposes some artificial constraints in the setting, manipulates the independent variable to establish cause $\rightarrow$ effect relationships, or both.

Experimental Group The group that is exposed to a treatment in an experimental design.

Exploratory Study A research study in areas where very little prior knowledge or information is available on the subject under investigation.

External Consultants Research experts outside the organization who are hired to research specific problems and find solutions.

External Validity The extent of generalizability of the results of a causal study to other field settings.

Face-to-Face Interview The information-gathering situation in which the interviewer asks the interviewee the information needed for the research when both meet in person for the purpose.

Face Validity An aspect of content validity examining whether the test item, on the face of it, reads as if it is measuring what it is supposed to measure.

Factorial Validity Indicates, through the use of factor-analytic techniques, whether a test is a pure measure of some specific factor or dimension.

Field Experiment An experiment done to detect cause → effect relationships in the natural environment in which events normally occur.

Field Study A study conducted in the natural environment of the organizational setting, with a minimal amount of researcher interference with the flow of events in the situation.

Fundamental Research *See* Basic Research.

Funneling Technique The questioning technique that consists of initially asking general and broad questions of respondents, and gradually narrowing the focus until the questions center on more specific themes.

Generalizability The extent of applicability of the research findings in one setting to other settings.

Graphic Rating Scale. A scale where the respondent indicates the response by placing a mark at the appropriate point on a line, which serves as a guide in locating the rating, rather than provides any discrete categories of responses.

History Effects Factors that might unexpectedly occur while the experiment is in progress that would contaminate the cause → effect relationships and thus threaten the internal validity of the experimental results.

Hypothesis An educated conjecture about the logically developed relationship between two or more variables, expressed in the form of testable statements.

Hypothetico-Deductive Method of Research The seven-step process of observing, preliminary data gathering, theorizing, hypothesizing, further more-focused data collection, data analysis, and interpreting the meaning of results to arrive at conclusions.

Independent Variable A variable that influences the dependent or criterion variable and accounts for (or explains) the variance in the dependent variable.

Inferential Statistics Statistics that help to establish relationships among variables, from which conclusions can be drawn.

Instrumentation Effects The threat to internal validity in experimental designs caused by changes in the measuring instrument between the pretest and the posttest.

Interitem Consistency Reliability A test of the consistency of responses to all the items of a measure, thus establishing the fact that all the items measuring the concept hang together as a set.

Internal Consistency Homogeneity of the items in the measure that tap a construct.

Internal Consultants Research experts within the organization who are utilized to investigate and find solutions to the organization's problems.

Internal Validity of Experiments The extent of precision and confidence in establishing cause → effect relationships in experimental designs.

Interrater Reliability The consistency of the judgment of several raters on how they see a phenomenon or interpret the responses of subjects.

Interval Scale A multipoint scale that taps the differences, the order, and the equality of the magnitude of the differences in the responses on the scale.

Intervening Variable A variable that surfaces as a function of the independent variable, and helps in conceptualizing and explaining the influence of the independent variable on the dependent variable.

Interviewing A data-collection method in which the researcher asks for information verbally from the respondents.

Itemized Rating Scale A scale that offers several categories of responses, out of which the respondent picks the one that is most relevant for answering the question.

Judgment Sampling A purposive, nonprobability sampling design in which the sample subject is chosen on the basis of the individual's ability to provide the type of special information needed by the researcher.

Lab Experiment An experimental design set up in an artificially contrived setting where controls and manipulations are introduced to establish cause → effect relationships among variables of interest to the researcher.

Leading Questions Questions phrased in such a manner as to lead the respondent to give the responses that the researcher would like to obtain.

Likert Scale An interval scale that specifically uses the five anchors of Strongly Disagree, Disagree, Neither Disagree Nor Agree, Agree, and Strongly Agree.

Literature Review The documentation of a comprehensive review of the published work from secondary sources of data in the areas of specific interest to the researcher.

Literature Survey *See* Literature Review.

Loaded Questions Questions that would elicit highly biased, emotional responses from the subjects.

Longitudinal Study A research study for which data are gathered at several points in time to answer a research question.

Manipulation The way the researcher exposes the independent variable to the subjects, to determine cause → effect relationships in experimental designs.

Matching A method for controlling contaminating variables in experimental studies. The experimental and control groups are "matched" or evenly spread with respect to the variables that are expected to confound the cause → effect relationships investigated by the researcher. Matching deliberately spreads the contaminating factors equally across all groups.

Maturation Effects A threat to internal validity that is a function of the biological, psychological, and other processes operating within the respondents as a result of the passage of time.

Moderating Variable A variable on which the relationship between two other variables is contingent. That is, if the moderating variable is present (or absent), the theorized relationship between two variables will hold good—not otherwise.

Mortality The loss of research subjects as experiments are in progress, which confounds the cause → effect relationships.

Motivational Research A particular data-gathering technique directed toward surfacing information, ideas, and thoughts that are not easily verbalized, or that remain at the unconscious level in the respondents.

Multiple Regression Analysis A statistical technique to predict the variance in the dependent variable by regressing the independent variables against the dependent variable.

Multistage Cluster Sampling A probability sampling design that could be described as a stratified sampling of clusters.

Nominal Scale A scale that categorizes individuals or objects into mutually exclusive and collectively exhaustive groups, and offers basic, categorical information on the variable of interest.

Noncontrived Setting Research conducted in the natural environment where events normally occur (i.e., the field setting).

Nondirectional Hypothesis An educated conjecture of a relationship between two variables, the directionality of which cannot be guessed.

Nonparticipant-Observer A researcher who collects observational data without becoming an integral part of the system.

Nonprobability Sampling A sampling design in which the elements in the population do not have a known or predetermined chance of being selected as sample subjects.

Nuisance Variable A variable that contaminates the cause → effect relationship.

Null Hypothesis The conjecture that postulates no differences or no relationship between or among variables.

Objectivity Interpreting the results on the basis of the facts emanating from the data analysis, as opposed to subjective or emotional interpretations.

Observational Survey The gathering of data by observing people or events either in the lab setting or in the natural environment and recording the information.

One-Shot-Study *See* Cross-Sectional Study.

Open-Ended Questions Questions that enable the respondent to give answers in a free-flowing format without restricting the range of choices to a set of specific alternatives suggested by the researcher.

Operational Definition Defining a construct in measurable terms by reducing it from its level of abstraction by delineating the dimensions and elements.

Ordinal Scale A scale that not only categorizes the qualitative differences in the variable of interest, but also allows for the rank ordering of these categories in some meaningful way.

Panel Studies Studies conducted over a period of time to determine the effects of certain changes made in a situation by using a panel or group of subjects as the sample base.

Parallel-Form Reliability Reliability that is established when responses to two comparable sets of measures tapping the same construct are highly correlated.

Parsimony This is gained by efficiently explaining the variance in the dependent variable of interest through the use of a smaller, rather than a larger number of independent variables.

Participant-Observer A researcher who collects observational data by becoming a member of the system from which data are collected.

Population The entire group of people, events, or things that the researcher desires to investigate.

Population Frame A listing of all the elements in the population from which the sample is drawn.

Posttest A test given to the subjects to measure the dependent variable of interest to the researcher, after exposing them to a treatment.

Precision The closeness of the estimated sample characteristics to the population characteristics; determined by the extent of the variability of the sampling distribution of the sample mean.

Predictive Study A study that enables the prediction of the relationships among the variables in a particular situation.

Predictive Validity This is the ability of the measure to differentiate among individuals as to a future criterion.

Predictor Variable *See* Independent Variable.

Pretest A test given to the subjects to measure the dependent variable of interest to the researcher before exposing them to a treatment.

Primary Data Data collected from the problem situation firsthand, in order to analyze them and find solutions to the problem being researched.

Probability Sampling The sampling design in which the elements in the population have some known chance or probability of being selected as sample subjects.

Problem Definition A precise, succinct statement of the question or issue that is to be investigated, with the objective of finding answers and solutions to the problem.

Problem Statement *See* Problem Definition.

Projective Methods Ways of eliciting responses through such means as word association, sentence completion, thematic apperception tests, and the like, which would otherwise be difficult to gauge.

Proportionate Stratified Random Sampling A probability sampling design in which the number of sample subjects drawn from each stratum is proportionate to the total number of elements in the respective strata.

Purposiveness in Research The situation in which research is focused on solving a well-identified and defined problem, rather than aimlessly looking for answers to vague questions.

Purposive Sampling A nonprobability sampling design in which the required information is gathered from special or specific targets or groups of people on some rational basis.

Qualitative Data Data that are not immediately quantifiable unless they are coded and categorized in some way.

Questionnaire A preformulated written set of questions to which the respondent records the answers, usually within rather closely delineated alternatives.

Quota Sampling A form of purposive sampling in which a predetermined proportion of people is sampled from different subgroups of interest to the researcher.

Randomization The process of controlling for the nuisance variables by randomly assigning members among the various experimental and control groups, such that the confounding variables are randomly distributed across all groups.

Ratio Scale A scale that has an absolute zero origin, and hence indicates not only the magnitude of the differences but also the proportion of the differences.

Recall-Dependent Questions Questions that elicit from the respondents information that involves recalling experiences from the past that may be hazy in their memory.

Reliability This indicates the extent of consistency and stability of the measuring instrument.

Replicability The extent to which similar results can be obtained when identical research is conducted at different times or in different organizational settings.

Representativeness of the Sample The extent to which the sample that is selected possesses the same characteristics as the population from which it is taken.

Research An organized, systematic, data-based, critical, scientific inquiry or investigation into a specific problem, undertaken with the objective of finding answers or solutions to it.

Restricted Probability Designs *See* Complex Probability Sampling.

Rigor The theoretical and methodological precision adhered to in conducting research.

Sample A subset or subgroup of the population.

Sample Size The actual number of subjects chosen as a sample to represent the population characteristics.

Sampling The process of selecting items from the population so that the sample characteristics can be generalized to the population. Sampling involves both design choice and sample size decisions.

Scale A tool or mechanism by which individuals, events, or objects are distinguished on the variables of interest in some meaningful way.

Scientific Investigation A step-by-step, logical, organized and rigorous effort to solve problems.

Secondary Data Data that have already been gathered by researchers, data published in statistical and other journals, and information available from any published or unpublished source available either within or outside the organization—all of which the researcher might find useful.

Selection Effects The threat to internal validity that is a function of improper or unmatched selection of subjects for the experimental and control groups.

Semantic Differential Usually a seven-point scale with bipolar attributes indicated at its extremes.

Simple Random Sampling A probability sampling design in which every single element in the population has a known and equal chance of being selected as a subject.

Simulation A model-building technique for assessing the possible effects of changes that might be introduced in a system.

Social Desirability The respondents' need to give socially or culturally acceptable responses to the questions posed by the researcher even if they are not true.

Solomon Four-Group Design The experimental design that sets up two experimental groups and two control groups, giving one experimental group and one control group both the pretest and the posttest, and giving the other experimental group and control group only the posttest.

Split-Half Reliability The correlation coefficient between one half of the items measuring a concept and the other half of the items measuring the same concept.

Stability of a Measure The ability of the measure to repeat the same results over time with low vulnerability to changes in the situation.

Static Panels Consist of the same group of people serving as the sample subjects over an extended period of time for a research study.

Statistical Regression The threat to internal validity that results when various groups in the study have been selected on the basis of their extreme (very high or very low) scores on some important variables.

Stratified Random Sampling A probability sampling design that first divides the population into meaningful, nonoverlapping subsets, and then randomly chooses the subjects from each subset.

Structural Variables Factors related to the form and design of the organization such as the roles and positions, communication channels, control systems, reward systems, and span of control.

Structured Interviews Interviews conducted by the researcher with a predetermined list of questions to be asked of the interviewer.

Structured Observational Studies Studies in which the researcher observes and notes down specific activities and behaviors that have been clearly delineated as important factors to the research before the commencement of the study.

Subject A single member of the sample.

Synopsis A brief summary of the research study.

Systematic Sampling A probability sampling design that involves the choosing of every nth element in the population for the sample.

t-**Test** A statistical test that establishes a significant mean difference in a variable between two groups.

Telephone Interview The information-gathering method by which the interviewer asks the interviewee over the telephone for the information needed for the research, instead of during a personal meeting.

Test–Retest Reliability A way of establishing the stability of the measuring instrument by correlating the scores obtained by administering the instrument to the same set of respondents at two different points in time.

Testability The ability to subject the data collected to appropriate statistical tests in order to substantiate or reject the hypotheses developed in the research study.

Testing Effects The distorting effects on the experimental results (the posttest scores) caused by the respondents having been sensitized to the posttest through the pretest.

Theoretical Framework A logically developed, described, and elaborated network of associations among variables of interest to the research study.

Treatment The manipulation of the independent variable in experimental designs so as to determine its effects on some dependent variable of interest to the researcher.

Unbiased Questions Questions posed in a way that elicits the least bias in the response. This can be ensured by following the principles of wording and measurement, and by taking care not to emphasize certain key words, not making inappropriate suggestions to the interviewee, not inflecting the voice, and so on.

Unit of Analysis The level of aggregation of the data that are collected for analysis, in order to answer the research question.

Unobtrusive Measures Measures obtained not through the cooperation of the subjects themselves, but through the gathering of data from sources other than people, such as examining birth and death records or counting the number of cigarette butts in the ashtray.

Unrestricted Probability Sampling *See* Simple Random Sampling.

Unstructured Interviews Interviews conducted with the primary purpose of surfacing some important preliminary issues relevant to the problem situation, without the researcher having a planned or predetermined sequence of questions.

Unstructured Observational Studies Studies in which the researcher observes and makes notes of almost all of the activities and behaviors that occur in the situation without predetermining what particular variables will be of specific interest to the study.

Validity Evidence that the instrument, technique, or process used to measure a concept does indeed measure the intended concept.

Variable Anything that can take on differing or varying values.

ANSWERS TO EXERCISES

Exercise 3.1   The dependent variable is *organizational commitment* because it is the primary variable of interest to the applied researcher, who wants to increase the commitment of the members in the bank.

Exercise 3.2   The dependent variable is *communication* because the production manager is interested in knowing why workers are reluctant to communicate with him.

Exercise 3.3

Variable	Label	Reason
Production	Dependent variable	Main variable of interest
Supervision	Independent variable ⎫	⎧ Help to explain the variance
Training	Independent variable ⎭	⎩ in production

Explanation

Production is the dependent variable because the manager seems to be interested in raising the level of production of workers. That is, the manager wants to explain the variance in production levels through the two variables according to her initial hunches. Supervision and training are the two independent variables, which, in the manager's opinion, are likely to explain the variance in the production level that is the dependent variable.

Diagram

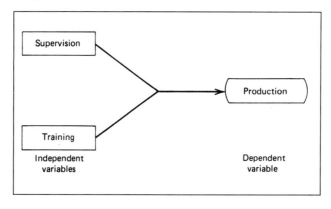

Exercise 3.4

Variable	Label	Reason
Job satisfaction	Dependent variable	Variable of primary interest
Pay	Independent variable ⎱	⎰ Influence job satisfaction and explain
Fringe Benefits	Independent variable ⎰	⎱ the variance in it

Explanation

Job satisfaction, the dependent variable, is of primary interest to the consultant, who speculates that the variables of pay and fringe benefits actually decrease it. Pay and fringe benefits are the independent variables because they are, in this case, expected to influence job satisfaction in a negative way. That it, as pay and fringe benefits go up, job satisfaction is expected to go down. The variance in job satisfaction would thus be explained by pay and fringe benefits.

Diagram

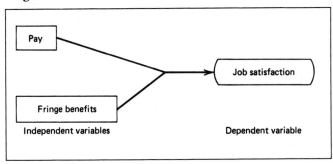

Exercise 3.5

Variable	Label
Productivity	Dependent variable
Off-the-job classroom training	Independent variable
Age	Moderating variable

Explanation

The main variable of interest to the manager is productivity—the dependent variable—the variance in which is expected to be explained by the independent variable, off-the-job classroom training. The more off-the-job training given to the workers, the greater the productivity. However, only those who are under fifty years of age would increase their productivity with increased off-the-job training. This will not be true for those who are over fifty years of age. Thus age is the moderating variable.

Diagram

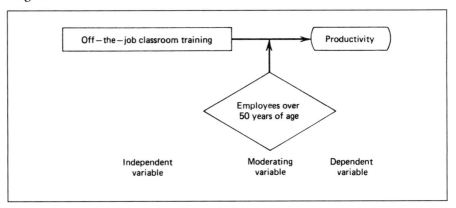

Off–the–job classroom training → Productivity

Employees over 50 years of age

Independent
variable

Moderating
variable

Dependent
variable

Exercise 3.6

Variable	Label
Pub visits	Dependent variable
Interaction	Independent variable
Gender	Moderating variable

Explanation

The dependent variable is visits to the pub, the variance in which can be accounted for by the independent variable, interaction among the workers. The more job-related interactions of the workers, the more their inclination to stay together after the work hours and go to the pub for a drink. However, this relationship between interaction and visits to the pub does not hold true for *all* the workers; it is true only for male workers. The female workers, no matter how much they interact—and they interact just as much as the men do—do not tend to stay after work and join the men for a drink at the local pub. Thus gender moderates the relationship between interaction and going to the pub for a drink.

Diagram

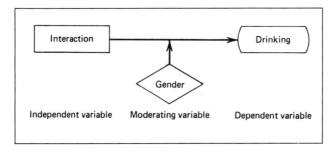

Interaction → Drinking

Gender

Independent variable   Moderating variable   Dependent variable

Exercise 3.7   Situation 1
Motivation to Work as an *Independent* Variable

The performance of employees is influenced by their motivation to work.

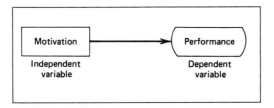

Situation 2

Motivation to Work as an *Intervening* Variable

Employees perform better when they are given challenging jobs, because such jobs tend to motivate them to work.

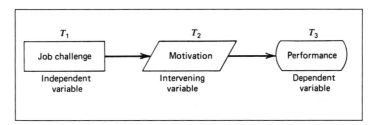

Situation 3

Motivation to Work as a *Moderating* Variable

The performance of employees with low levels of motivation to work will not improve despite increases in job challenge.

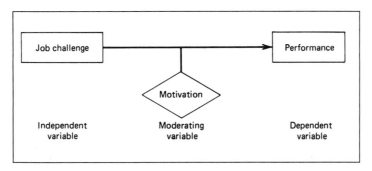

Exercise 3.8

Variable	Label
Life satisfaction	Dependent variable
Multiple roles	Independent variable
Stress	Intervening variable
Self-concept	Moderating variable

Explanation

Life satisfaction is the dependent variable, which is of primary interest, and attempts are made to explain the variance in life satisfaction through several factors. Life satisfaction is directly influenced by multiple roles, the independent variable. The greater the number of roles taken on by dual-career family members, the lesser their experienced satisfactions in life. This relationship is clarified by noting that stress is experienced because dual-career family members take on multiple roles, which, in turn, lowers the levels of satisfaction in their lives. In other words, stress is a function of taking on the multiple roles, and this intervening variable helps us to see how multiple roles influence life satisfaction. Although this relationship among multiple roles, stress, and life satisfaction generally holds true, it is not true for *all* dual-career family members. Those who have a high self-concept do not derive lower levels of satisfaction, even though they take on multiple roles, and may even feel stressed by it. Only those who do not have a high self-concept experience lower levels of life satisfaction when they take on multiple roles, and feel stressed because of it.

Diagram

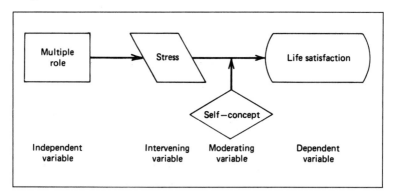

Exercise 3.9

Variable	Label
Morale	Dependent variable
Working conditions	Independent variable
Pay scale	Independent variable
Vacation benefits	Independent variable
Side income	Moderating variable
Happiness	Intervening variable

Explanation

The independent variables of improved working conditions, better pay, and vacation benefits influence the dependent variable of morale. When these three independent variables are high in a work situation, then morale is also high. However, increased pay will not increase the morale of all workers. Only those who do not have good side incomes will experience greater happiness (the intervening variable) when their pay is increased, and consequently also higher morale. For others, the relationships between pay and morale will not hold good. The intervening variable, happiness, is a function of high pay (for those without side incomes). It clarifies the relationship between pay and morale.

Diagram

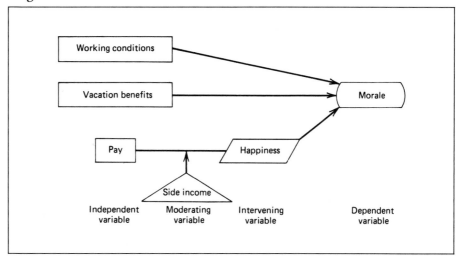

Problem Statement

Will improving the working conditions and increasing pay scales and vacation benefits improve the morale of all employees?

Exercise 3.10

Problem Statement

How can the job satisfaction and family satisfaction of both spouses in dual-career families be increased?

Theoretical Framework

The family counselor is interested in finding ways to increase both the job satisfaction and family satisfaction of dual-career family members. Therefore, both job satisfaction and family satisfaction are dependent variables. There are four independent variables in this situation, two of them influencing job satisfaction and two influencing family satisfaction. The two independent variables that help explain the variance in job satisfaction are job involvement and discretionary time spent on job-related activities. This relationship between the two independent variables and job satisfaction is, however, moderated by the gender of the spouse. In other words, only male members in dual-career families (i.e., husbands) derive greater job satisfaction when their job involvement increases and they spend more of their discretionary time in job-related matters. The reason for this may be that because men are the traditional breadwinners, their identity is tied to the work setting; thus the more ego-involved they become in their jobs, the more satisfactions they derive from the job setting. Likewise, the more discretionary time they spend on job-related activities, the more job satisfaction they derive, because they identify so closely with their role of careerpersons and breadwinners. It also seems logical that the more time they spend on job-related activities, the more they are going to be ego-involved in their jobs, and the more the job involvement, the greater the probability of their spending more time on job-related activities. Thus there is a relationship between the two independent variables themselves, each influencing the other.

This relationship between the two independent variables and the dependent variable, however, does not hold true for wives in dual-career families. This is because wives have traditionally been homemakers, and their taking on the career roles does not absolve them of their family responsibilities and domestic work. This dual role and responsibility might restrict the satisfactions they derive from the job, and even when they get more job-involved and invest more discretionary time in job-related matters, their job satisfaction may not be enhanced. Thus, the relationship among job involvement, discretionary time, and job satisfaction might hold good for men but not for women.

The dependent variable of family satisfaction is influenced by the two independent variables of couples: (1) spending more time in each other's company, and (2) helping each other in planning family activities. This is understandable, because any satisfaction derived in the family situation or setting is a function of the harmonious and meaningful interactions among the family members. The more time spent together, and the more the joint and harmonious planning of family activities, the greater will be the family satisfactions enjoyed by both spouses in dual-career families.

Diagram

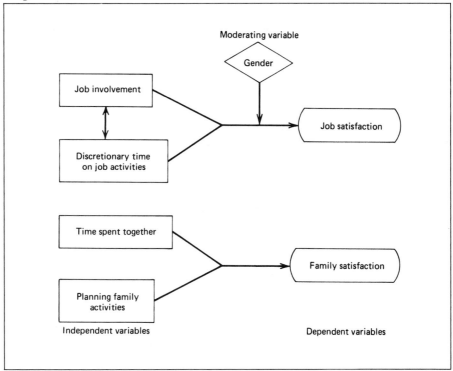

Exercise 3.11

1. H_O: There is no relationship between working conditions and the morale of employees.

   H_A: If working conditions are improved, then the morale of the employees will also improve.

2. H_O: There is no relationship between vacation benefits and employees' morale.

   H_A: Better vacation benefits will improve employee's morale.

3. H_O: There is no difference in the relationship between pay and happiness among those who have side incomes and those who do not.

   H_A: Only those who do not have side incomes will become happier if their pay is increased.

4. H_O: There is no relationship between happiness and morale.

   H_A: Happiness and morale are positively correlated.

5. H_O: Working conditions, vacation benefits, and pay have no influence on the morale of employees.

   H_A: Working conditions, vacation benefits, and pay all have positive influences on morale.

Exercise 4.1

1. This would be a *causal study* because the operator wants to prove to the supervisor that the fumes are causing operators to be low in their efficiency. In other words, the machine tool operator is trying to establish the fact that fumes *cause* low efficiency in workers.

2. This is an *analytical study* because the machine tool operator wants to establish that fumes cause low efficiency and convince her workshop supervisor through such analysis.

3. This would be a *field experiment* because though it would be designed in the natural environment where the work naturally is done, the amount of fumes will have to be manipulated while other factors such as atmospheric pressure may have to be controlled. Because the experimental design would be set up in the natural environment of the workers, this will be a *field experiment.*

4. The unit of analysis would be the *individual operators.* The data will be collected with respect to each operator and then the conclusion will be made as to whether the operators are less efficient because of the fumes emitted in the workshop.

5. This would be a *longitudinal* study because data will be gathered at more than one point in time. First, the efficiency of the operators would be assessed at a given rate of fume emission. Then the fumes emitted would be manipulated to varying degrees, and at each manipulation the efficiency of the workers would again be assessed to confirm that the high rate of fume emission causes a drop in operators' efficiency.

Exercise 6.1   Ten questions that would measure stress are as follows:

1. To what extent do you feel anxious and nervous?
2. How often do you feel unduly pressured by the events that are happening in your life?
3. How often are you confused by the situation surrounding you?
4. How frequently have you had headaches and/or stomach upsets during the past four weeks?
5. How often do you feel that the demands on you are overwhelming?
6. How often has your blood pressure shot up during the past six months?
7. How well do you sleep at night?
8. Do you ever feel that you are going to have a nervous breakdown?
9. Are you troubled by your hands sweating so that you feel damp and clammy?
10. Do you wake up rested in the morning?

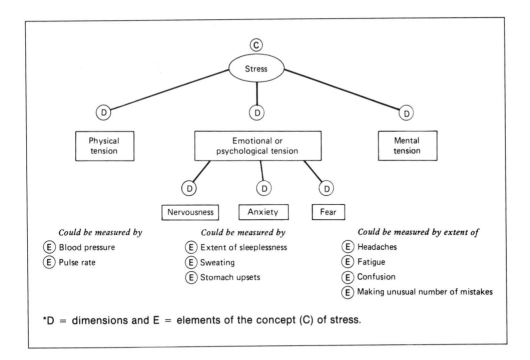

*D = dimensions and E = elements of the concept (C) of stress.

Exercise 6.2   Twelve items to measure the concept of enriched jobs are as follows:

1. To what extent do you find your job challenging?
2. To what extent does your job use all the skills and knowledge you possess?
3. To what extent does your job permit you to do a task from beginning to end instead of only doing fragmented pieces of the task?
4. How repetitious are your duties?
5. How much opportunity do you have to do a job from beginning to end?
6. To what extent do you find out how well you are doing on the job as you are working?
7. How meaningful is the work you do in the sense of it making a contribution to society?
8. To what extent do you feel you are doing something worthwhile on your job?
9. How good do you feel about the challenges that your job offers?
10. How much are you left on your own to do your work?
11. How much opportunity do you have to do a number of different things?
12. How significant to others is the work you do?

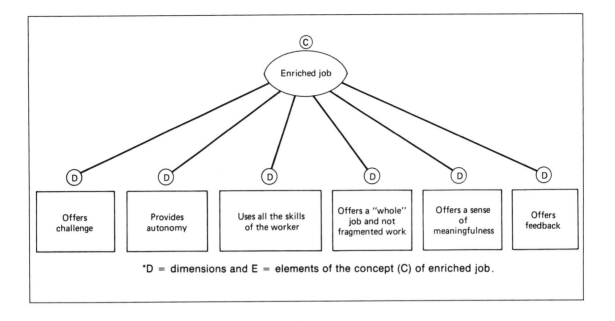

*D = dimensions and E = elements of the concept (C) of enriched job.

Exercise 6.3   Two variables that lend themselves to nominal scaling, along with mutually exclusive and collectively exhaustive categories, are as follows:

Types of Employees in a Computer Firm

☐ Accounts clerk   ☐ Systems analyst

☐ Machine operator   ☐ Supervisor

☐ Mechanic   ☐ Manager

☐ Other (specify)

Types of Departments in a Research Laboratory

☐ Mathematics department

☐ Physics department

☐ Chemistry department

☐ Statistics department

☐ Computer sciences department

☐ Operations research department

☐ Other (specify)

Exercise 6.4   The following is an ordinal scale for consumer preferences for different brands of beer.

> Rank the following brands of beer in the order of your preference. In the boxes provided next to each brand name, write the number that denotes your ranking. That is, write 1 next to your favorite brand, 2 next to the next favorite one, and so on, until each brand name has a number. If you do not drink beer at all, put a check mark (√) in the last box.

    ☐ Budweiser   ☐ Olympia
    ☐ Coors   ☐ Pabst
    ☐ Michelob   ☐ Strohs
    ☐ Miller   ☐ Do not drink beer at all

Exercise 6.5   Three variables that could be tapped on an interval scale are morale, enthusiasm, and level of activity.

Exercise 6.6

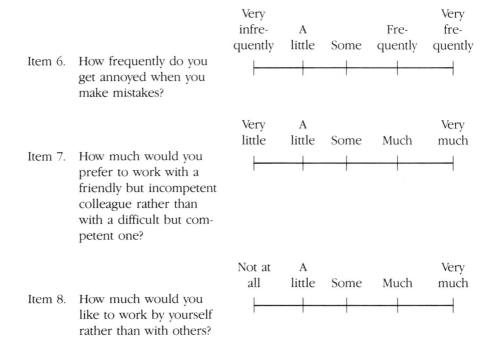

Item 9.   To what extent would you prefer a job that is difficult but challenging to one that is easy and routine?

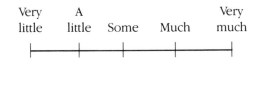

Item 14. How often do you get frustrated when people do not give you feed-back on how you are performing or progress-ing?

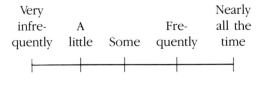

Exercise 6.7

Scale	Variable and Explanation
Nominal	Buyers of a product can be nominally grouped under three categories: those who like the product and buy, those who are indifferent to the product and buy, and those who do not like the product, yet buy it anyway.
Ordinal	Customer rank ordering of preferences for various name brands of jeans.
Interval	Extent of appeal of a particular advertisement to customers on a five point scale ranging from very little to very much. Here customers are split into five groups; they are ranked from those who like very little to those who like very much; there is also an assessment of the *extent* of the appeal; and we know that the difference between two adjacent points in the scale have the same magnitude of difference.
Ratio	Percentage of sales increase of a product. There is an absolute zero origin (when there is no additional sale made at all during a particular year, the sales increase is zero), and a 10 percent increase in sales is twice as much as a 5 percent increase. Thus this scale has both a zero origin and a measure of proportion. Hence, it is a ratio scale.

Exercise 7.1   Before we can design a questionnaire, we need to list the variables to be tapped and operationally define the more abstract concepts. The following variables are mentioned in the study:

1. Involvement (or the other end of the continuum, alienation).
2. Satisfaction with work life (i.e., satisfaction at the workplace).

The following demographic variables might be of interest to the study:

3. Gender.
4. Tenure (number of years in organization).
5. Job level.
6. Age.
7. Education.

These demographic variables are chosen because they might have an influence on the involvement (or alienation) of the employees, their level of satisfaction, and the relationship between the two.

Operational Definition of Involvement

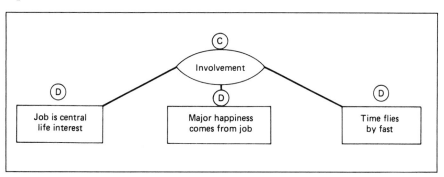

Low involvement can be considered as alienation. Items that measure involvement are as follows:

1. The major happiness of my life comes from my job.
2. Time at work flies by quickly.
3. Working here is a drag.
4. Most things in life are more important than work.
5. I live, eat, and breathe my job.
6. My work is not the most important part of my life.

Operational Definition of Satisfaction

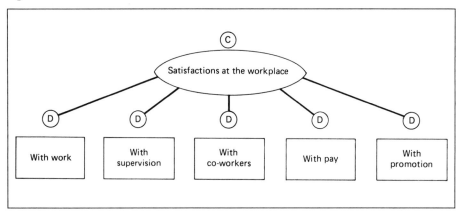

Questions that tap satisfaction at the workplace are as follows:
To what extent would you agree with the following statements?

1. My work is fascinating.
2. My work gives me a sense of accomplishment.
3. My supervisor praises good work.
4. My supervisor is not very capable.
5. My co-workers are very stimulating.
6. I get a lot of cooperation at the workplace.
7. My pay is barely adequate to take care of my expenses.
8. People can live comfortably with their pay in this organization.
9. The opportunities for advancement are very good here.
10. The promotion policies here are very unfair.

Note: In the questionnaire, items 7 and 8, and items 9 and 10, will *not* be placed consecutively as they appear above.

Questionnaire

Serakan Company, Inc.

1606 E. Mars
Osio, IL 67160
December 4, 1991

Dear Employee,
    As the president of your company, I am interested in conducting a minisurvey on your reactions to working in this organization. The responses you give, might give

me an indication of any changes that may be necessary for offering you a better quality of worklife. Your honest and straightforward answers will help me to help you. I do not need your names—only your truthful answers. Any suggestions from you will be most welcome.

Thank you for your cooperation.

Yours truly,

(Sd)

Anita Krish, President

Personal Data

Department in which you are working: _____

> Please check the boxes most appropriate for the items below.

Age (years)	**Education**	**Sex**
☐ Under 25	☐ High school	☐ M
☐ 25–35	☐ Some college	☐ F
☐ 36–45	☐ Bachelor's degree	
☐ 46–55	☐ Master's degree	
☐ Over 55	☐ Doctoral degree	

Job Level	**Number of Years in this Organization**
☐ Manager	☐ Less than 1
☐ Supervisor	☐ 1–3
☐ Clerk	☐ 4–8
☐ Secretary	☐ 9–15
☐ Technician	☐ Over 15
☐ Other (specify)	

> Here are some questions that ask you to tell us how you experience your worklife in general. Please circle the appropriate number on the scales below.

To what extent would you agree with the following statements, on a scale of 1 to 7, 1 denoting very low agreement and 7 denoting very high agreement.

	Very Low						Very High
1. The major happiness of my life comes from my job.	1	2	3	4	5	6	7
2. Time at work flies by quickly.	1	2	3	4	5	6	7
3. I live, eat, and breathe my job.	1	2	3	4	5	6	7
4. My work is fascinating.	1	2	3	4	5	6	7
5. My work gives me a sense of accomplishment.	1	2	3	4	5	6	7
6. My supervisor praises good work.	1	2	3	4	5	6	7
7. The opportunities for advancement are very good here.	1	2	3	4	5	6	7
8. My co-workers are very stimulating.	1	2	3	4	5	6	7
9. People can live comfortably with their pay in this organization.	1	2	3	4	5	6	7
10. I get a lot of cooperation at the workplace.	1	2	3	4	5	6	7
11. My supervisor is not very capable.	1	2	3	4	5	6	7
12. Most things in life are more important than work.	1	2	3	4	5	6	7
13. Working here is a drag.	1	2	3	4	5	6	7
14. The promotion policies here are very unfair.	1	2	3	4	5	6	7
15. My pay is barely adequate to take care of my expenses.	1	2	3	4	5	6	7
16. My work is not the most important part of my life.	1	2	3	4	5	6	7

In the space provided below, please make any comments that you like regarding any aspect of the work or organization. Your suggestions for improvement will be very much appreciated.

Thank you!

Exercise 8.1   The population of interest to the study is the 80 hospitals in the four regions of New York City.

The sampling plan could be either area sampling or a stratified (proportionate) random sampling plan, depending on whether there are known wide variabilities in the number of cancer cases in each of the regions.

Assuming no high variability, an *area sampling* plan would be appropriate. First, of the four regions, any two can be chosen at random. Then, since we know that each region has about 20 hospitals, we can choose two clusters at random. That is, select four hospitals in close proximity to each other in each of the two clusters. Thus, 8 of the 20 hospitals in each of the two regions, or a total of 16 hospitals, can be surveyed. Costs and time will be less here because of less distance traveled.

If, on the other hand, there is a known great variability, then a *stratified (proportionate) random sampling* plan should be used. Each of the regions would be treated as a stratum, and four hospitals from each of these four strata can be chosen using a simple random sampling procedure. Thus, 16 hospitals out of the total 80 hospitals can again be studied. However, here the costs will be more since there is more travel involved across regions and within each region since the hospitals chosen may not fall within close proximity.

If there is no information known on the variability, the stratified random sample would be useful for purposes of greater confidence in generalizability.

Exercise 8.2   The population for the survey should, strictly speaking, be the entire campus, but in this case, it would be just the people in the Women's Caucus Meeting.

Since the idea just occurred to the Director of UWPA as she was sitting in the meeting that it would be great to get the opinions of the members, it can be presumed that all that the Director would expect to get out of the survey is to have *some idea* of how UWPA is perceived. It may not be very important to the Director that she obtain extremely reliable data. In this case a *convenience sampling* is what the Director would (and can) resort to.

The Director can stand at the door outside and get hold of whomever she can, as people walk out of the door. She can then ask them some quick questions. Even if she polls the opinions of about 15 individuals, she would get some idea of how they feel about UWPA's accomplishment.

Exercise 8.3   The population will be all the patients who walk into the doctor's office with flu during that flu season. Unfortunately, the population frame will not be available before the survey starts since there is no way of generating, ahead of time, a list of all the people who will walk in during the entire flu season.

Since the doctor seems to have a steady clientele, it is highly probable that she would be treating many patients who walk in with flu on a daily basis. Under the circumstances, the doctor can administer the drug to every tenth person she diagnoses as having flu, until she has administered the new drug to 50 patients. This means the doctor has to keep a careful count of the number of patients who walk in with the flu. She would also need to keep a careful record of the patients who received the drug so as to test the efficacy of the drug (however she might want to measure this). This sampling design would be a nontraditional (because no population frame is available) *systematic sampling* plan, and it can be expected that all the variations in the contributory factors curing the flu, such as drinking more water, resting, and so on, will be evenly distributed among these 50 patients.

Exercise 8.4   The population of interest seems to be international women, and particularly the Indian and Malaysian students.

A *quota sample* would be the most appropriate here. Martha can survey about 10 Indian and 30 Malaysian women students (in proportion to the population). There need be no probability sampling plan involved here. In addition, Martha can talk to five other international students from countries other than India and Malaysia. Talking to these 45 individuals will give her an idea of the demand that might exist for her services.

Exercise 8.5   The population will be all the vacuum cleaners in the stock room.

A *simple random sampling* plan can be used to select the 50 items that should be inspected. Since each item has a serial number on it, a random numbers table would help pick the 50 items at random. Thereafter the appropriate decision criteria would help determine whether a lot can be released for sale, or if every item in the lot has to be inspected before it is sent out, or whatever other policy is formulated.

Exercise 8.6   The population frame here is all the 285 original respondents.

In this case, it is most useful to resort to *double sampling*. That is, 30 of the 285 respondents can be chosen through a systematic sampling design and interviewed to find out how they interpreted the two items.

REFERENCES

Abbott, C. C. (1966). *Basic research in finance: Needs and prospects.* Charlottesville, VA: University Press.

Abdel-khalik, A. R., & Ajinkya, B. B. (1979). *Empirical research in accounting: A methodological viewpoint.* Sarasota, FL: American Accounting Association.

American Psychological Association Publication Manual (3rd ed.). (1983). Washington, D.C.: American Psychological Association.

Angell, R. C., & Freedman. R. (1966). The use of documents, records, census materials, and indices. In L. Festinger & D. Katz (Eds.), *Research methods in the behavioral sciences.* New York: Holt, Rinehart and Winston.

Baker, R. L., & Schutz, R. E. (Eds.). (1972). *Instructional product research.* New York: Van Nostrand.

Balsley, H. L., & Clover, V. T. (1988). *Research for business decisions: Business research methods* (4th ed.). Columbus, OH: Publishing Horizons.

Bendig, A. W. (1954). Transmitted information and the length of rating scales. *Journal of Experimental Psychology, 47,* 303–308.

Billings, R. S., & Wroten, S. P. (1978). Use of path analysis in industrial/organizational psychology: Criticisms and suggestions. *Journal of Applied Psychology, 63*(6), 677–688.

Blank, G. (1989, March 14). Finding the right statistic with statistical navigator. *PC Magazine,* p. 97.

Boot, J. C. G., & Cox, E. B. (1970). *Statistical analysis for managerial decisions.* New York: McGraw Hill.

Bordens, K. S., & Abbott, B. B. (1988). *Research design and methods: A process approach.* Mountain View, CA: Mayfield Publishing.

Brown, L. D., & Vasarhelyi, M. A. (1985). *Accounting research directory: The database of accounting literature.* New York: Markus Wiener Publishing.

Bruner, G. C., & Hensel, P. J. *Multi-term scales for marketing research.* (Forthcoming).

Campbell, A. A., & Katona, G. (1966). The sample survey: A technique for social science research. In L. Festinger & D. Katz (Eds.), *Research methods in the behavioral sciences.* New York: Holt, Rinehart and Winston.

Campbell, D. T. (1976). Psychometric theory. In M. D. Dunnette (Ed.), *Handbook of industrial and organizational psychology.* Chicago: Rand McNally.

Campbell, D. T., & Fiske, D. W. (1959). Convergent and discriminant validation by the multitrait–multi-method matrix. *Psychological Bulletin, 56,* 1, 81–105.

Campbell, D. T., & Stanley, J. C. (1966). *Experimental and quasi-experimental designs for research.* Chicago: Rand-McNally.

Cannell, C. F., & Kahn, R. L. (1966). The collection of data by interviewing. In L. Festinger & D. Katz (Eds.), *Research methods in behavioral sciences.* New York: Holt, Rinehart and Winston.

Carlsmith, J. M., Ellsworth, P. C., & Aronson, E. (1976). *Methods of research in social psychology.* Reading, MA: Addison-Wesley.

Cattell, R. B. (1966). The scree test for the number of factors. *Multivariate Behavioral Research, 1,* 245–276.

Chein, I. (1959). An introduction to sampling. In C. Selltiz, M. Jahoda, M., Deutsch, & S. W. Cook (Eds.), *Research methods in social relations.* New York: Holt, Rinehart and Winston.

Churchill, G. A. (1987). *Marketing research: Methodological foundations.* Chicago: Dryden Press.

Cohen, J. (1969). *Statistical power analysis for the behavioral sciences.* New York: Academic Press.

Cohen, J. (1990, December). Things I have learned (so far). *American Psychologist,* pp. 1304–1312.

Cook, T. D., & Campbell, D. T. (1979). *Quasi-experimentation: Design and analysis issues for field settings.* Boston: Houghton-Mifflin.

Cook, T. D., & Campbell, D. T. (1979). Four kinds of validity. In R. T. Mowday & R. M. Steers (Eds.), *Research in organizations: Issues and controversies.* Santa Monica, CA: Goodyear Publishing.

Coombs, C. H. (1966). Theory and methods of social measurement. In L. Festinger & D. Katz (Eds.), *Research methods in the behavioral sciences.* New York: Holt, Rinehart and Winston.

Cronbach, L. J. (1946). Response sets and test validating. *Educational and Psychological Measurement, 6,* 475–494.

Cronbach, L. J. (1990). *Essentials of psychological testing* (5th ed.). New York: Harper and Row.

Crowne, D. P., & Marlowe, D. (1980). *The approval motive: Studies in evaluative dependence.* Westport, CT: Greenwood Press.

Davies, G. R., & Yoder, D. (1937). *Business statistics.* New York: John Wiley.

Davis, D., & Cosenza, R. M. (1988). *Business research for decision making* (2nd ed.). Boston: PWS-Kent Publishing.

Drenkow, G. (1987, April). Data acquisition software that adapts to your needs. *Research and Development,* pp. 84–87.

Edwards, A. L. (1957). *Manual for the Edwards personal preference schedule.* New York: Psychological Corporation.

Elmore, P. E., & Beggs, D. L. (1975). Salience of concepts and commitment to extreme judgements in response pattern of teachers. *Education, 95*(4), 325–334.

Emory, C. W. (1985). *Business research methods* (3rd ed.). Homewood, IL: Richard D. Irwin.

Ferris, K. R. (1988). *Behavioral accounting research: A critical analysis.* Columbus, OH: Century VII Publishing.

Festinger, L. (1966). Laboratory experiments. In L. Festinger & D. Katz (Eds.), *Research methods in the behavioral sciences.* New York: Holt, Rinehart and Winston.

Festinger, L., & Katz, D. (1966). *Research methods in the behavioral sciences.* New York: Holt, Rinehart and Winston.

Fiedler, F. (1967). *A theory of leadership effectiveness.* New York: McGraw-Hill.

Fishbein, M. (1967). *Readings in attitude theory and measurement.* New York: John Wiley.

French, J. R. P. (1966). Experiments in field settings. In L. Festinger & D. Katz (Eds.), *Research methods in the behavioral sciences.* New York: Holt, Rinehart and Winston.

Gaski, J. F., & Etzel, M. J. (1986, July). The index of consumer sentiment toward marketing. *Journal of Marketing, 50,* 71–81.

Glaser, B. G., & Strauss,ʾA. L. (1967). *The discovery of grounded theory.* Chicago: Aldine.

Gorsuch, R. L. (1974). *Factor analysis.* Philadelphia: Saunders.

Gorsuch, R. L. (1983). *Factor analysis* (2nd ed.). Philadelphia: Saunders.

Green, P. E., Kedia, P. K., & Nikhil, R. S. (1985). *Electronic questionnaire design and analysis with CAPPA*. Palo Alto, CA: The Scientific Press.

Hoel, P. G., & Jessen, R. J. (1971). *Basic statistics for business and economics*. New York: John Wiley.

Horst, P. (1968). *Personality: Measurement of dimensions*. San Francisco: Jossey-Bass.

Kanuk, L., & Berenson, C. (1975). Mail surveys and response rates: A literature review. *Journal of Marketing Research, 12,* 440–453.

Kaplan, A. (1979). *The conduct of inquiry: Methodology for behavioral science*. New York: Harper & Row.

Katz, D. (1966). *Research methods in the behavioral sciences*. New York: Holt, Rinehart and Winston.

Kelly, F. J., Beggs, D. L., McNeil, K. A., Eichelberger, T., & Lyon, J. (1969). *Research design in the behavioral sciences: Multiple regression approach*. Carbondale, IL: Southern Illinois University Press.

Kerlinger, F. N. (1986). *Foundations of behavioral research* (3rd ed.). New York: Holt, Rinehart and Winston.

Kidder, L. H., & Judd, C. H. (1986). *Research methods in social relations*. New York: Holt, Rinehart and Winston.

Kirk, R. E. (1982). *Experimental design: Procedures for the behavioral sciences*. Belmont, CA: Brooks/Cole.

Kish, L. (1965). *Survey sampling*. New York: John Wiley.

Kish, L. (1966). Selection of the sample. In L. Festinger & D. Katz (Eds.), *Research methods in the behavioral sciences*. New York: Holt, Rinehart and Winston.

Knechel, W. R. (1986). A simulation study of the relative effectiveness of alternative analytical review procedures. *Decision Sciences, 17*(3), 376–394.

Kornhauser, A., & Sheatsley, P. B. (1959). Questionnaire construction and interview procedure. In C. Sellitz, M. Jahoda, M. Deutsch, & S. W. Cook (Eds.), *Research methods in social relations*. New York: Holt, Rinehart and Winston.

Krejcie, R., & Morgan, D. (1970). Determining sample size for research activities. *Educational and Psychological Measurement, 30,* 607–610.

Kuder, G. F., & Richardson, M. W. (1937). The theory of the estimation of test reliability. *Psychometrika, 2,* 151–160.

Labaw, P. (1980). *Advanced questionnaire design*. Cambridge, Mass: Abt Books.

Lazarsfeld, P. F. (1935). The art of asking why. *National Marketing Research, 1,* 26–38.

Leedy, P. D. (1985). *Practical research: Planning and design* (3rd ed.). New York: Macmillan Publishing.

Likert, R. (1932). A technique for the measurement of attitudes. *Archives of Psychology,* No. 140.

Lombardo, M. L., McCall, M., & DeVries, D. L. (1983). *Looking glass*. Glenview, IL: Scott Foresman, Co.

Luconi, F. L., Malone, T. W., & Scott Morton, M. S. (1986). Expert systems: The next challenge for managers. *Sloan Management Review, 27*(4), 3–14.

A Manual of Style. (1969). Chicago: Chicago University Press.

Marascuilo, L. A., & McSweeney, M. (1977). *Nonparametric and distribution-free methods for the social sciences*. Monterey, CA: Brooks/Cole.

McClave, J. T., & Benson, P. G. (1988). *Statistics for business and economics* (4th ed.). San Francisco: Dellen Publishing Co.

McNeil, K. A., Kelly, F. J., & McNeil, J. T. (1975). *Testing research hypotheses using multiple linear regression.* Carbondale, IL: Southern Illinois University Press.

Merton, R. K., & Kendall, P. L. (1955). The focused interview. In P. F. Lazarsfeld & M. Rosenberg (Eds.), *The language of social research.* New York: The Free Press.

Muehling, D. D. (1987). An investigation of factors underlying attitude-toward-advertising-in-general. *Journal of Advertising, 16*(1), 32–40.

Murdick, R. G., & Cooper, D. R. (1982). *Business research: Concepts and guides.* Columbus, OH: Grid Publishing.

Namboodiri, N. K., Carter, L. F., & Blalock, H. M. (1975). *Applied multivariate analysis and experimental designs.* New York: McGraw-Hill.

Nocks, E. C., & Einstein, G. O. (1986). *Learning to use the SPSS batch system.* Englewood Cliffs, NJ: Prentice Hall.

Norusis, M. J. (1988). *SPSS/PC + Studentware.* Chicago, IL: SPSS Inc.

Oppenheim, A. N. (1986). *Questionnaire design and attitude measurement.* Great Britain: Gower Publishing.

Osborn, R. N., & Vicars, W. M. (1976). Sex stereotypes: An artifact in leader behavior and subordinate satisfaction analysis? *Academy of Management Journal, 19,* 439–449.

Payne, S. L. (1951). *The art of asking questions.* Princeton, NJ: Princeton University Press.

Peak, H. (1966). Problems of objective observation. In L. Festinger & D. Katz (Eds.), *Research methods in the behavioral sciences.* New York: Holt, Rinehart and Winston.

Pedhazur, E. J. (1982). *Multiple regression in behavioral research: Explanation and prediction* (2nd ed.). New York: CBS College Publishing.

Perrier, C., & Kalwarski, G. (1989, October 30). Stimulating simulations: Technique shows relationship between risk, funding. *Pensions and Investment Age,* pp. 41–43.

Price, J. L. (1972). *Handbook of organizational measurement.* Lexington, Mass: D. C. Heath.

Rao, C. R. (1973). *Linear statistical inference and its applications* (2nd ed.). New York: John Wiley.

Resta, P. A. (1972). *The research report.* New York: American Book Co.

Riley, M. W., & Nelson, E. E. (1974). *Sociological observation: A strategy for new social knowledge.* New York: Basic Books.

Rizzo, J. R., House, R. J., & Lirtzman, S. I. (1970). Role conflict and role ambiguity in complex organizations. *Administrative Science Quarterly, 15,* 150–163.

Roscoe, J. T. (1975). *Fundamental research statistics for the behavioral sciences* (2nd ed.). New York: Holt, Rinehart and Winston.

Runkel, P. J., & McGrath, J. E. (1972). *Research on human behavior: A systematic guide to method.* New York: Holt, Rinehart and Winston.

Salvia, A. A. (1990). *Introduction to statistics.* Philadelphia: Saunders.

SAS User's Guide. (1985). Raleigh, NC: SAS Institute Inc.

Schmitt, N. W., & Klimoski, R. J. (1991). *Research methods in human resources management.* Cincinnati, OH: South-Western Publishing.

Selltiz, C., Jahoda, M., Deutsch, M., & Cook, S. W. (1959). *Research methods in social relations.* (rev. ed.) New York: Holt, Rinehart, and Winston.

Selltiz, C., Wrightsman, L. S., & Cook, S. W. (1981). *Research methods in social relations* (4th ed.). New York: Holt, Rinehart and Winston.

Shurter, R. L., Williamson, J. P., & Broehl, W. G., Jr. (1965). *Business research and report writing.* New York: McGraw-Hill.

Smith, C. B. (1981). *A guide to business research: Developing, conducting, and writing research projects.* Chicago, IL: Nelson-Hall.

Smith, P. C., Kendall, L., & Hulin, C. (1969). *The measurement of satisfaction in work and retirement.* Chicago: Rand McNally, pp. 79–84.

SPSSX User's Guide: Basics (5th ed.). (1988). Chicago, IL: SPSS Inc.

SPSSX User's Guide: Statistics. (1988). Chicago, IL: SPSS Inc.

Steufert, S., Pogash, R., & Piasecki, M. (1988). Simulation-based assessment of managerial competence: Reliability and validity. *Personnel Psychology, 41*(3), 537–557.

Stone, E. (1978). *Research methods in organizational behavior.* Santa Monica, CA: Goodyear Publishing.

Webb, E. J., Campbell, D. T., Schwartz, R. D., & Sechrest, L. (1966). *Unobtrusive measures: Non-reactive research in the social sciences.* Chicago, IL: Rand-McNally.

White, J. K., & Ruh, R. A. (1973). Effects of personal values on the relationship between participation and job attitudes. *Administrative Science Quarterly, 18*(4), 506–514.

Williams, C. T., & Wolfe, G. K. (1979). *Elements of research: A guide for writers.* Sherman Oaks, CA: Alfred Publishing.

Williams, J. (1990). Visual Decision Support: Choice of representation form by managers. Unpublished paper, Department of Management, Southern Illinois University, Carbondale.

Zetterberg, H. (1955). On axiomatic theories in sociology. In P. F. Lazarsfeld & M. Rosenberg (Eds.), *The language of social research.* New York: The Free Press.

SUPPLEMENTARY READINGS

CHAPTER 1: INTRODUCTION TO RESEARCH

Topic	Reference	Chapter	Pages
Definition of research	Balsley & Clover (1988)	1	2
	Emory (1985)	1	3–17
	Leedy (1985)	1	3–10
Applied and basic research	Balsley & Clover (1988)	1	2
	Bordens & Abbott (1988)	1	18–19
	Murdick & Cooper (1982)	3	44–51
	Selltiz, Wrightsman, & Cook (1981)	5	83
Scientific investigation	Balsley & Clover (1988)	2	23–45
	Bordens & Abbott (1988)	1	13–17
	Kerlinger (1986)	1	3–14
	Murdick & Cooper (1982)	2	15–31
	Roscoe (1975)	1	1–9
Hypothetico-deductive method	Balsley & Clover (1988)	3	47–67
	Emory (1985)	2	32–39
	Kaplan (1979)	1	9–11
	Selltiz, Wrightsman, & Cook (1981)	6	102–103
Managers and research	Balsley & Clover (1988)	1	4–12
	Davis & Cosenza (1988)	5	123–124
	Emory (1985)	1	14–16

CHAPTER 2: THE RESEARCH PROCESS: STEPS 1 TO 3

Topic	Reference	Chapter	Pages
Problem area and problem definition	Balsley & Clover (1988)	3	47–54
	Davis & Cosenza (1988)	3	54–57
	Murdick & Cooper (1982)	6	83–104
	Selltiz, Jahoda, Deutsch, & Cook (1959)	2	28–35
Primary and secondary sources of data	Balsley & Clover (1988)	4	76–90
	Bordens & Abbott (1988)	2	32–33
	Davis & Cosenza (1988)	9–10	241–288
	Emory (1985)	6–7	135–183
	Williams & Wolfe (1979)	3	

CHAPTER 3: THE RESEARCH PROCESS: STEPS 4 AND 5

Topic	Reference	Chapter	Pages
The research process	Balsley & Clover (1988)	2	23–45
	Bordens & Abbott (1988)	1	21–23
	Emory (1985)	2	18–40
	Murdick & Cooper (1982)	2	23–24
	Selltiz, Wrightsman, & Cook (1981)	1,2	4–41
	Stone (1978)	2	15–34
Types of variables	Bordens & Abbott (1988)	1	19–20
	Davis & Cosenza (1988)	5	104–106
	Emory (1985)	3	72–74
	Kerlinger (1986)	3	26–41
	Selltiz, Wrightsman, & Cook (1981)	2	26–27
	Stone (1978)	2	22–32
Theory and theoretical framework	Bordens & Abbott (1988)	16	473–500
	Davis & Cosenza (1988)	2	26–32
	Emory (1985)	2	30–40
	Kaplan (1979)	8	294–326
	Selltiz, Jahoda, Deutsch, & Cook (1959)	14	480–499
	Selltiz, Wrightsman, & Cook (1981)	1	9–13
Hypotheses development	Bordens & Abbott (1988)	1	13–16
	Kerlinger (1986)	2	15–25
	Murdick & Cooper (1982)	3	48–49
	Roscoe (1975)	1	7–9
	Selltiz, Jahoda, Deutsch, & Cook (1959)	2	3–40
	Zetterberg (1955)		533–540

CHAPTER 4: THE RESEARCH PROCESS: Step 6

Topic	Reference	Chapter	Pages
Research design	Bordens & Abbott (1988)	3	57–78
	Davis & Cosenza (1988)	5	104–114
	Emory (1985)	3	57–81
	Katz (1966)	2	56–97
	Murdick & Cooper (1982)	8	127–136
	Selltiz, Jahoda, Deutsch, & Cook (1959)	10	153–178
	Selltiz, Jahoda, Deutsch, & Cook (1959)	3	49–78

CHAPTER 5: EXPERIMENTAL DESIGN

Topic	Reference	Chapter	Pages
Experimental designs	Balsley & Clover (1988)	6	137–151
	Campbell & Stanley (1966)	The entire book offers an excellent treatment covering all subtopics.	
	Carlsmith, Ellsworth, & Aronson (1976)	1	8–52
	Davis & Cosenza (1988)	5	111–114
	Emory (1985)	3	74–78
	Kirk (1982)	Entire book	
	Selltiz, Wrightsman, & Cook (1981)	2	28–38
Exogenous and endogenous, and controlled and uncontrolled variables	Emory (1985)	3	72–74
Matching and randomization	Bordens & Abbott (1988)	8	205–215
	Carlsmith, Ellsworth, & Aronson (1976)	5	134–169
	Emory (1985)	3	76
		11	343–346
	Kerlinger (1986)	20	319–328
Lab experiments and field experiments	Bordens & Abbott (1988)	3	67–71
	Carlsmith, Ellsworth, & Aronson (1976)	7	220
	Davis & Cosenza (1988)	5	108–109
	Festinger (1966)	4	136–172
	French (1966)	3	98–135
	Kerlinger (1986)	23	364–376

CHAPTER 5 (CONTINUED)

Topic	Reference	Chapter	Pages
Lab experiments and field experiments (con-tinued)	Runkel & McGrath (1972)	4	103–107
	Selltiz, Wrightsman, & Cook (1981)	2	22–26
	Stone (1978)	7	116–128
Internal and external validity	Bordens & Abbott (1988)	3	64–67
	Davis & Cosenza (1988)	5	114–116
	Emory (1985)	5	115–119
	Selltiz, Wrightsman, & Cook (1981)	1	7–8
	Stone (1978)	6	108–110
Quasi-experimental design	Bordens & Abbott (1988)	6	160–165
	Davis & Cosenza (1988)	5	120–123
	Emory (1985)	5	126–130
	Selltiz, Wrightsman, & Cook (1981)	3	47–57
	Stone (1978)	6	100–104
Simulation	Bordens & Abbott (1988)	3	68–70
	Davis & Cosenza (1988)	11	325–326
	Runkel & McGrath (1972)	4	96–99
	Stone (1978)	7	120–124

CHAPTER 6: MEASUREMENT OF VARIABLES

Topic	Reference	Chapter	Pages
Measurement of vari-ables	Bordens & Abbott (1988)	4	83–95
	Coombs (1966)	11	471–535
	Selltiz, Jahoda, Deutsch, & Cook (1959)	5	146–198
Operational definition	Bordens & Abbott (1988)	2	29–30
	Davis & Cosenza (1988)	6	142–143
	Emory (1985)	2	25–26
	Runkel & McGrath (1972)	6	150–152
	Selltiz, Jahoda, Deutsch, & Cook (1959)	2	41–44
	Selltiz, Wrightsman, & Cook (1981)	7	122–126
Scales and scaling	Bendig (1954)	(journal article)	
	Bordens & Abbott (1988)	4	86–89
	Davis & Cosenza (1988)	6–7	145–149
			181–183

(*continued*)

CHAPTER 6 (CONTINUED)

Topic	Reference	Chapter	Pages
Scales and scaling (continued)	Emory (1985)	4	86–92
			256–289
	Likert (excerpted in Fishbein, 1967)	9	90–95
	Selltiz, Jahoda, Deutsch, & Cook (1959)	10	343–384
	Selltiz, Wrightsman, & Cook (1981)	9	199–227
Reliability and validity	Bordens & Abbott (1988)	4	85
	Cook & Campbell (1979)	6	77–101
	Davis & Cosenza (1988)	6	149–158
	Emory (1985)	4	94–100
	Kerlinger (1986)	26, 27	404–434
	Selltiz, Jahoda, Deutsch, & Cook (1959)	5	154–186
	Selltiz, Wrightsman, & Cook (1981)	7	122–133
	Stone (1978)	3	43–60

CHAPTER 7: DATA-COLLECTION METHODS

Topic	Reference	Chapter	Pages
Data collection methods	Balsley & Clover (1988)	7	164–184
Interviewing	Bordens & Abbott (1988)	7	184–185
	Cannell & Kahn (1966)	8	327–380
	Davis & Cosenza (1988)	10	271–276
	Emory (1985)	7	160–169
	Kornhauser & Sheatsley (1959)	Appendix C	205–223
	Merton & Kendall (1955)		476–491
	Selltiz, Wrightsman, & Cook (1981)	8	178–187
Motivational research	Balsley & Clover (1988)	7	172–175
	Kerlinger (1986)	30	468–485
	Selltiz, Jahoda, Deutsch, & Cook (1959)	8	280–311
Observational studies	Bordens & Abbott (1988)	6	143–155
	Davis & Cosenza (1988)	10	268–270
	Emory (1985)	7	176–183
	Peak (1966)	6	243–299

CHAPTER 7 (CONTINUED)

Topic	Reference	Chapter	Pages
Observational Studies (continued)	Riley & Nelson (1974)	Part III	117–120
	Selltiz, Wrightsman, & Cook (1981)	11	263–290
Panel studies	Balsley & Clover (1988)	7	175–182
	Davis & Cosenza (1988)	10	286–287
	Selltiz, Wrightsman, & Cook (1981)	4	63–64
Unobtrusive measures	Angell & Freedman (1966)	7	300–326
	Emory (1985)	7	182–183
	Webb, Campbell, Schwartz, & Sechrest (1966)	A good reference book	
Questionnaire design	Balsley & Clover (1988)	8	197–223
	Bordens & Abbott (1988)	7	170–179
	Davis & Cosenza (1988)	7	186–187
	Kornhauser & Sheatsley in Selltiz, Jahoda, Deutsch, & Cook (1959)	Appendix C	546–574
	Selltiz, Wrightsman, & Cook (1981)	8	159–178

CHAPTER 8: SAMPLING

Topic	Reference	Chapter	Pages
Sampling	Balsley & Clover (1988)	5	95–121
	Bordens & Abbott (1988)	7	186–192
	Campbell & Katona (1966)	2	15–55
	Chein (1959)	Appendix B	509–545
	Davis & Cosenza (1988)	8	203–207
	Emory (1985)	10	275–301
	Kish (1965)		316
	Kish (1966)	5	175–240
	Selltiz, Wrightsman, & Cook (1981)	4	78–80
	Stone (1978)	5	77–86
Representativeness of sample	Balsley & Clover (1988)	5	95–105
	Bordens & Abbott (1988)	7	185–186
	Davis & Cosenza (1988)	8	207–209
	Emory (1985)	10	277–278
	Selltiz, Wrightsman, & Cook (1981)	2	38–40

(*continued*)

CHAPTER 8 (CONTINUED)

Topic	Reference	Chapter	Pages
Sample size	Balsley & Clover (1988)	12	299–321
	Bordens & Abbott (1988)	7	192–194
	Davis & Cosenza (1988)	8	206
	Emory (1985)	10	288–301
	Roscoe (1975)	20	182–186
Selection of the sample	Davis & Cosenza (1988)	8	207
	Kish (1966)	5	175–239

CHAPTER 9: A REFRESHER ON SOME STATISTICAL TERMS AND TESTS

The following books will be useful for clarifications/explanations:

Boot & Cox (1970)

Davies & Yoder (1937)

Hoel & Jessen (1971)

McClave & Benson (1988)

Roscoe (1975)

Salvia (1990)

CHAPTER 10: DATA ANALYSIS AND INTERPRETATION

Topic	Reference	Chapter	Pages
Editing data	Balsley & Clover (1988)	9	244–246
	Davis & Cosenza (1988)	12	332–334
	Emory (1985)	11	319–320
	Selltiz, Wrightsman, & Cook (1981)	8	163
Handling blank and Don't Know responses	Balsley & Clover (1988)	5	104–105
	Bordens & Abbott (1988)	7	179
	Davis & Cosenza (1988)	10	278–280
	Emory (1985)	11	325–327
Statistical analysis of data	Davis & Cosenza (1988)	12	332–369
	Emory (1985)	12	385–410
	Selltiz, Wrightsman, & Cook (1981)	4	66–78

CHAPTER 10 (CONTINUED)

Topic	Reference	Chapter	Pages
Hypotheses testing	Davis & Cosenza (1988)	12	346–351
	Emory (1985)	12	350–384
	Kerlinger (1986)	12	186–200
	Roscoe (1975)	19, 20	170–186
	Selltiz, Wrightsman, & Cook (1981)	13	333–341
Correlations	Balsley & Clover (1988)	14	351–356
	Bordens & Abbott (1988)	11	315–319
	Roscoe (1975)	31	264–269
Chi-square tests	Balsley & Clover (1988)	13	323–342
	Bordens & Abbott (1988)	12	349–352
	Davis & Cosenza (1988)	12	361–364
	Roscoe (1975)	28–30	242–262
t-Test	Balsley & Clover (1988)	10	272–276
	Bordens & Abbott (1988)	12	336–338
	Davis & Cosenza (1988)	12	365–368
	Roscoe (1975)	23–25	210–229
	Selltiz, Wrightsman, & Cook (1981)	13	337–341
ANOVA	Balsley & Clover (1988)	11	281–297
	Bordens & Abbott	12	338–349
	Davis & Cosenza (1988)	13	384–402
	Kerlinger (1986)	13	203–224
	Roscoe (1975)	36–41	292–361
Multiple regression analysis	Balsley & Clover (1988)	14	363–372
	Bordens & Abbott (1988)	15	452–456
	Davis & Cosenza (1988)	13	413–420
	Kelly, Beggs, McNeil, Eichelberger, & Lyon (1969)	Entire Book	
	Kerlinger (1986)	35, 36	569–617
	McNeil, Kelly, & McNeil (1975)		
	Pedhazur (1982)	Exhaustive discussion in book	
	Roscoe (1975)	42–46	362–408
Factor analysis	Bordens & Abbott (1988)	15	446–450
	Cattell (1966)		
	Davis & Cosenza (1988)	14	442–447
	Gorsuch (1983)		
	Rao (1973)		

(*continued*)

CHAPTER 10 (CONTINUED)

Topic	Reference	Chapter	Pages
Nonparametric methods	Davis & Cosenza (1988) Marascuilo & McSweeney (1977)	13	420–422 Entire Book
Statistical terms and tests	Boot & Cox (1970) Salvia (1990)		Entire Book
Statistical programs	*SPSS User's Guide* *SAS User's Guide* Norusis (1988) CAPPA		

CHAPTER 11: RESEARCH REPORT

Topic	Reference	Chapter	Pages
Report writing	Leedy (1985) Resta (1972) Shurter, Williamson, & Broehl (1965) Smith (1981)		Entire Book

APPENDIX

STATISTICAL TABLES

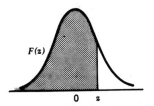

Table I
Cumulative Normal Probabilities

z	$F(z)$	z	$F(z)$	z	$F(z)$
.00	.5000000	.30	.6179114	.60	.7257469
.01	.5039894	.31	.6217195	.61	.7290691
.02	.5079783	.32	.6255158	.62	.7323711
.03	.5119665	.33	.6293000	.63	.7356527
.04	.5159534	.34	.6330717	.64	.7389137
.05	.5199388	.35	.6368307	.65	.7421539
.06	.5239222	.36	.6405764	.66	.7453731
.07	.5279032	.37	.6443088	.67	.7485711
.08	.5318814	.38	.6480273	.68	.7517478
.09	.5358564	.39	.6517317	.69	.7549029
.10	.5398278	.40	.6554217	.70	.7580363
.11	.5437953	.41	.6590970	.71	.7611479
.12	.5477584	.42	.6627573	.72	.7642375
.13	.5517168	.43	.6664022	.73	.7673049
.14	.5556700	.44	.6700314	.74	.7703500
.15	.5596177	.45	.6736448	.75	.7733726
.16	.5635595	.46	.6772419	.76	.7763727
.17	.5674949	.47	.6808225	.77	.7793501
.18	.5714237	.48	.6843863	.78	.7823046
.19	.5753454	.49	.6879331	.79	.7852361
.20	.5792597	.50	.6914625	.80	.7881446
.21	.5831662	.51	.6949743	.81	.7910299
.22	.5870604	.52	.6984682	.82	.7938919
.23	.5909541	.53	.7019440	.83	.7967306
.24	.5948349	.54	.7054015	.84	.7995458
.25	.5987063	.55	.7088403	.85	.8023375
.26	.6025681	.56	.7122603	.86	.8051055
.27	.6064199	.57	.7156612	.87	.8078498
.28	.6102612	.58	.7190427	.88	.8105703
.29	.6140919	.59	.7224047	.89	.8132671

(continued)

Table I (*Continued*)

z	$F(z)$	z	$F(z)$	z	$F(z)$
.90	.8159399	1.37	.9146565	1.84	.9671159
.91	.8185887	1.38	.9162067	1.85	.9678432
.92	.8212136	1.39	.9177356	1.86	.9685572
.93	.8238145	1.40	.9192433	1.87	.9692581
.94	.8263912	1.41	.9207302	1.88	.9699460
.95	.8289439	1.42	.9221962	1.89	.9706210
.96	.8314724	1.43	.9236415	1.90	.9712834
.97	.8339768	1.44	.9250663	1.91	.9719334
.98	.8364569	1.45	.9264707	1.92	.9725711
.99	.8389129	1.46	.9278550	1.93	.9731966
1.00	.8413447	1.47	.9292191	1.94	.9738102
1.01	.8437524	1.48	.9305634	1.95	.9744119
1.02	.8461358	1.49	.9318879	1.96	.9750021
1.03	.8484950	1.50	.9331928	1.97	.9755808
1.04	.8508300	1.51	.9344783	1.98	.9761482
1.05	.8531409	1.52	.9357445	1.99	.9767045
1.06	.8554277	1.53	.9369916	2.00	.9772499
1.07	.8576903	1.54	.9382198	2.01	.9777844
1.08	.8599289	1.55	.9394292	2.02	.9783083
1.09	.8621434	1.56	.9406201	2.03	.9788217
1.10	.8643339	1.57	.9417924	2.04	.9793248
1.11	.8665005	1.58	.9429466	2.05	.9798178
1.12	.8686431	1.59	.9440826	2.06	.9803007
1.13	.8707619	1.60	.9452007	2.07	.9807738
1.14	.8728568	1.61	.9463011	2.08	.9812372
1.15	.8749281	1.62	.9473839	2.09	.9816911
1.16	.8769756	1.63	.9484493	2.10	.9821356
1.17	.8789995	1.64	.9494974	2.11	.9825708
1.18	.8809999	1.65	.9505285	2.12	.9829970
1.19	.8829768	1.66	.9515428	2.13	.9834142
1.20	.8849303	1.67	.9525403	2.14	.9838226
1.21	.8868606	1.68	.9535213	2.15	.9842224
1.22	.8887676	1.69	.9544860	2.16	.9846137
1.23	.8906514	1.70	.9554345	2.17	.9849966
1.24	.8925123	1.71	.9563671	2.18	.9853713
1.25	.8943502	1.72	.9572838	2.19	.9857379
1.26	.8961653	1.73	.9581849	2.20	.9860966
1.27	.8979577	1.74	.9590705	2.21	.9864474
1.28	.8997274	1.75	.9599408	2.22	.9867906
1.29	.9014747	1.76	.9607961	2.23	.9871263
1.30	.9031995	1.77	.9616364	2.24	.9874545
1.31	.9049021	1.78	.9624620	2.25	.9877755
1.32	.9065825	1.79	.9632730	2.26	.9880894
1.33	.9082409	1.80	.9640697	2.27	.9883962
1.34	.9098773	1.81	.9648521	2.28	.9886962
1.35	.9114920	1.82	.9656205	2.29	.9889893
1.36	.9130850	1.83	.9663750	2.30	.9892759

Table I (*Continued*)

z	F(z)	z	F(z)	z	F(z)
2.31	.9895559	2.45	.9928572	2.59	.9952012
2.32	.9898296	2.46	.9930531	2.60	.9953388
2.33	.9900969	2.47	.9932443	2.70	.9965330
2.34	.9903581	2.48	.9934309	2.80	.9974449
2.35	.9906133	2.49	.9936128	2.90	.9981342
2.36	.9908625	2.50	.9937903	3.00	.9986501
2.37	.9911060	2.51	.9939634	3.20	.9993129
2.38	.9913437	2.52	.9941323	3.40	.9996631
2.39	.9915758	2.53	.9942969	3.60	.9998409
2.40	.9918025	2.54	.9944574	3.80	.9999277
2.41	.9920237	2.55	.9946139	4.00	.9999683
2.42	.9922397	2.56	.9947664	4.50	.9999966
2.43	.9924506	2.57	.9949151	5.00	.9999997
2.44	.9926564	2.58	.9950600	5.50	.9999999

This table is condensed from Table 1 of the *Biometrika Tables for Statisticians*, Vol. 1 (1st ed.), edited by E. S. Pearson and H. O. Hartley. Reproduced with the kind permission of E. S. Pearson and the trustees of *Biometrika*.

Table II

Upper Percentage Points of the t Distribution

v	$Q = 0.4$ $2Q = 0.8$	0.25 0.5	0.1 0.2	0.05 0.1	0.025 0.05	0.01 0.02	0.005 0.01	0.001 0.002
1	0.325	1.000	3.078	6.314	12.706	31.821	63.657	318.31
2	.289	0.816	1.886	2.920	4.303	6.965	9.925	22.326
3	.277	.765	1.638	2.353	3.182	4.541	5.841	10.213
4	.271	.741	1.533	2.132	2.776	3.747	4.604	7.173
5	0.267	0.727	1.476	2.015	2.571	3.365	4.032	5.893
6	.265	.718	1.440	1.943	2.447	3.143	3.707	5.208
7	.263	.711	1.415	1.895	2.365	2.998	3.499	4.785
8	.262	.706	1.397	1.860	2.306	2.896	3.355	4.501
9	.261	.703	1.383	1.833	2.262	2.821	3.250	4.297
10	0.260	0.700	1.372	1.812	2.228	2.764	3.169	4.144
11	.260	.697	1.363	1.796	2.201	2.718	3.106	4.025
12	.259	.695	1.356	1.782	2.179	2.681	3.055	3.930
13	.259	.694	1.350	1.771	2.160	2.650	3.012	3.852
14	.258	.692	1.345	1.761	2.145	2.624	2.977	3.787
15	0.258	0.691	1.341	1.753	2.131	2.602	2.947	3.733
16	.258	.690	1.337	1.746	2.120	2.583	2.921	3.686
17	.257	.689	1.333	1.740	2.110	2.567	2.898	3.646
18	.257	.688	1.330	1.734	2.101	2.552	2.878	3.610
19	.257	.688	1.328	1.729	2.093	2.539	2.861	3.579
20	0.257	0.687	1.325	1.725	2.086	2.528	2.845	3.552
21	.257	.686	1.323	1.721	2.080	2.518	2.831	3.527
22	.256	.686	1.321	1.717	2.074	2.508	2.819	3.505
23	.256	.685	1.319	1.714	2.069	2.500	2.807	3.485
24	.256	.685	1.318	1.711	2.064	2.492	2.797	3.467
25	0.256	0.684	1.316	1.708	2.060	2.485	2.787	3.450
26	.256	.684	1.315	1.706	2.056	2.479	2.779	3.435
27	.256	.684	1.314	1.703	2.052	2.473	2.771	3.421
28	.256	.683	1.313	1.701	2.048	2.467	2.763	3.408
29	.256	.683	1.311	1.699	2.045	2.462	2.756	3.396
30	0.256	0.683	1.310	1.697	2.042	2.457	2.750	3.385
40	.255	.681	1.303	1.684	2.021	2.423	2.704	3.307
60	.254	.679	1.296	1.671	2.000	2.390	2.660	3.232
120	.254	.677	1.289	1.658	1.980	2.358	2.617	3.160
∞	.253	.674	1.282	1.645	1.960	2.326	2.576	3.090

This table is condensed from Table 12 of the *Biometrika Tables for Statisticians*, Vol. 1 (1st ed.), edited by E. S. Pearson and H. O. Hartley. Reproduced with the kind permission of E. S. Pearson and the trustees of *Biometrika*.

Table III
Upper Percentage Points of the χ^2 Distribution

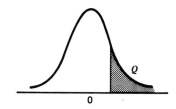

Q v	0.995	0.990	0.975	0.950	0.900	0.750	0.500
1	$392704 \cdot 10^{-10}$	$157088 \cdot 10^{-9}$	$982069 \cdot 10^{-9}$	$393214 \cdot 10^{-8}$	0.0157908	0.1015308	0.454937
2	0.0100251	0.0201007	0.0506356	0.102587	0.210720	0.575364	1.38629
3	0.0717212	0.114832	0.215795	0.351846	0.584375	1.212534	2.36597
4	0.206990	0.297110	0.484419	0.710721	1.063623	1.92255	3.35670
5	0.411740	0.554300	0.831211	1.145476	1.61031	2.67460	4.35146
6	0.675727	0.872085	1.237347	1.63539	2.20413	3.45460	5.34812
7	0.989265	1.239043	1.68987	2.16735	2.83311	4.25485	6.34581
8	1.344419	1.646482	2.17973	2.73264	3.48954	5.07064	7.34412
9	1.734926	2.087912	2.70039	3.32511	4.16816	5.89883	8.34283
10	2.15585	2.55821	3.24697	3.94030	4.86518	6.73720	9.34182
11	2.60321	3.05347	3.81575	4.57481	5.57779	7.58412	10.3410
12	3.07382	3.57056	4.40379	5.22603	6.30380	8.43842	11.3403
13	3.56503	4.10691	5.00874	5.89186	7.04150	9.29906	12.3398
14	4.07468	4.66043	5.62872	6.57063	7.78953	10.1653	13.3393
15	4.60094	5.22935	6.26214	7.26094	8.54675	11.0365	14.3389
16	5.14224	5.81221	6.90766	7.96164	9.31223	11.9122	15.3385
17	5.69724	6.40776	7.56418	8.67176	10.0852	12.7919	16.3381
18	6.26481	7.01491	8.23075	9.39046	10.8649	13.6753	17.3379
19	6.84398	7.63273	8.90655	10.1170	11.6509	14.5620	18.3376
20	7.43386	8.26040	9.59083	10.8508	12.4426	15.4518	19.3374
21	8.03366	8.89720	10.28293	11.5913	13.2396	16.3444	20.3372
22	8.64272	9.54249	10.9823	12.3380	14.0415	17.2396	21.3370
23	9.26042	10.19567	11.6885	13.0905	14.8479	18.1373	22.3369
24	9.88623	10.8564	12.4011	13.8484	15.6587	19.0372	23.3367
25	10.5197	11.5240	13.1197	14.6114	16.4734	19.9393	24.3366
26	11.1603	12.1981	13.8439	15.3791	17.2919	20.8434	25.3364
27	11.8076	12.8786	14.5733	16.1513	18.1138	21.7494	26.3363
28	12.4613	13.5648	15.3079	16.9279	18.9392	22.6572	27.3363
29	13.1211	14.2565	16.0471	17.7083	19.7677	23.5666	28.3362
30	13.7867	14.9535	16.7908	18.4926	20.5992	24.4776	29.3360
40	20.7065	22.1643	24.4331	26.5093	29.0505	33.6603	39.3354
50	27.9907	29.7067	32.3574	34.7642	37.6886	42.9421	49.3349
60	35.5346	37.4848	40.4817	43.1879	46.4589	52.2938	59.3347
70	43.2752	45.4418	48.7576	51.7393	55.3290	61.6983	69.3344
80	51.1720	53.5400	57.1532	60.3915	64.2778	71.1445	79.3343
90	59.1963	61.7541	65.6466	69.1260	73.2912	80.6247	89.3342
100	67.3276	70.0648	74.2219	77.9295	82.3581	90.1332	99.3341
z_Q	−2.5758	−2.3263	−1.9600	−1.6449	−1.2816	−0.6745	0.0000

(*continued*)

Table III   continued

Q v	0.250	0.100	0.050	0.025	0.010	0.005	0.001
1	1.32330	2.70554	3.84146	5.02389	6.63490	7.87944	10.828
2	2.77259	4.60517	5.99147	7.37776	9.21034	10.5966	13.816
3	4.10835	6.25139	7.81473	9.34840	11.3449	12.8381	16.266
4	5.38527	7.77944	9.48773	11.1433	13.2767	14.8602	18.467
5	6.62568	9.23635	11.0705	12.8325	15.0863	16.7496	20.515
6	7.84080	10.6446	12.5916	14.4494	16.8119	18.5476	22.458
7	9.03715	12.0170	14.0671	16.0128	18.4753	20.2777	24.322
8	10.2188	13.3616	15.5073	17.5346	20.0902	21.9550	26.125
9	11.3887	14.6837	16.9190	19.0228	21.6660	23.5893	27.877
10	12.5489	15.9871	18.3070	20.4831	23.2093	25.1882	29.588
11	13.7007	17.2750	19.6751	21.9200	24.7250	26.7569	31.264
12	14.8454	18.5494	21.0261	23.3367	26.2170	28.2995	32.909
13	15.9839	19.8119	22.3621	24.7356	27.6883	29.8194	34.528
14	17.1170	21.0642	23.6848	26.1190	29.1413	31.3193	36.123
15	18.2451	22.3072	24.9958	27.4884	30.5779	32.8013	37.697
16	19.3688	23.5418	26.2962	28.8454	31.9999	34.2672	39.252
17	20.4887	24.7690	27.5871	30.1910	33.4087	35.7185	40.790
18	21.6049	25.9894	28.8693	31.5264	34.8053	37.1564	42.312
19	22.71578	27.2036	30.1435	32.8523	36.1908	38.5822	43.820
20	23.8277	28.4120	31.4104	34.1696	37.5662	39.9968	45.315
21	24.9348	29.6151	32.6705	35.4789	38.9321	41.4010	46.797
22	26.0393	30.8133	33.9244	36.7807	40.2894	42.7956	48.268
23	27.1413	32.0069	35.1725	38.0757	41.6384	44.1813	49.728
24	28.2412	33.1963	36.4151	39.3641	42.9798	45.5585	51.179
25	29.3389	34.3816	37.6525	40.6465	44.3141	46.9278	52.620
26	30.4345	35.5631	38.8852	41.9232	45.6417	48.2899	54.052
27	31.5284	36.7412	40.1133	43.1944	46.9630	49.6449	55.476
28	32.6205	37.9159	41.3372	44.4607	48.2782	50.9933	56.892
29	33.7109	39.0875	42.5569	45.7222	49.5879	52.3356	58.302
30	34.7998	40.2560	43.7729	46.9792	50.8922	53.6720	59.703
40	45.6160	51.8050	55.7585	59.3417	63.6907	66.7659	73.402
50	56.3336	63.1671	67.5048	71.4202	76.1539	79.4900	86.661
60	66.9814	74.3970	79.0819	83.2976	88.3794	91.9517	99.607
70	77.5766	85.5271	90.5312	95.0231	100.425	104.215	112.317
80	88.1303	96.5782	101.879	106.629	112.329	116.321	124.839
90	98.6499	107.565	113.145	118.136	124.116	128.299	137.208
100	109.141	118.498	124.342	129.561	135.807	140.169	149.449
z_Q	+0.6745	+1.2816	+1.6449	+1.9600	+2.3263	+2.5758	+3.0902

This table is taken from Table 8 of the *Biometrika Tables for Statisticians*, Vol. 1 (1st ed.), edited by E. S. Pearson and H. O. Hartley. Reproduced with the kind permission of E. S. Pearson and the trustees of *Biometrika*.

Table IV

Percentage Points of the *F* Distribution: Upper 5% Points

v_2 \ v_1	1	2	3	4	5	6	7	8	9	10	12	15	20	24	30	40	60	120	∞
1	161.4	199.5	215.7	224.6	230.2	234.0	236.8	238.9	240.5	241.9	243.9	245.9	248.0	249.1	250.1	251.1	252.2	253.3	243.3
2	18.51	19.00	19.16	19.25	19.30	19.33	19.35	19.37	19.38	19.40	19.41	19.43	19.45	19.45	19.46	19.47	19.48	19.49	19.50
3	10.13	9.55	9.28	9.12	9.01	8.94	8.89	8.85	8.81	8.79	8.74	8.70	8.66	8.64	8.62	8.59	8.57	8.55	8.53
4	7.71	6.94	6.59	6.39	6.26	6.16	6.09	6.04	6.00	5.96	5.91	5.86	5.80	5.77	5.75	5.72	5.69	5.66	5.63
5	6.61	5.79	5.41	5.19	5.05	4.95	4.88	4.82	4.77	4.74	4.68	4.62	4.56	4.53	4.50	4.46	4.43	4.40	4.36
6	5.99	5.14	4.76	4.53	4.39	4.28	4.21	4.15	4.10	4.06	4.00	3.94	3.87	3.84	3.81	3.77	3.74	3.70	3.67
7	5.59	4.74	4.35	4.12	3.97	3.87	3.79	3.73	3.68	3.64	3.57	3.51	3.44	3.41	3.38	3.34	3.30	3.27	3.23
8	5.32	4.46	4.07	3.84	3.69	3.58	3.50	3.44	3.39	3.35	3.28	3.22	3.15	3.12	3.08	3.04	3.01	2.97	2.93
9	5.12	4.26	3.86	3.63	3.48	3.37	3.29	3.23	3.18	3.14	3.07	3.01	2.94	2.90	2.86	2.83	2.79	2.75	2.71
10	4.96	4.10	3.71	3.48	3.33	3.22	3.14	3.07	3.02	2.98	2.91	2.85	2.77	2.74	2.70	2.66	2.62	2.58	2.54
11	4.84	3.98	3.59	3.36	3.20	3.09	3.01	2.95	2.90	2.85	2.79	2.72	2.65	2.61	2.57	2.53	2.49	2.45	2.40
12	4.75	3.89	3.49	3.26	3.11	3.00	2.91	2.85	2.80	2.75	2.69	2.62	2.54	2.51	2.47	2.43	2.38	2.34	2.30
13	4.67	3.81	3.41	3.18	3.03	2.92	2.83	2.77	2.71	2.67	2.60	2.53	2.46	2.42	2.38	2.34	2.30	2.25	2.21
14	4.60	3.74	3.34	3.11	2.96	2.85	2.76	2.70	2.65	2.60	2.53	2.46	2.39	2.35	2.31	2.27	2.22	2.18	2.13
15	4.54	3.68	3.29	3.06	2.90	2.79	2.71	2.64	2.59	2.54	2.48	2.40	2.33	2.29	2.25	2.20	2.16	2.11	2.07
16	4.49	3.63	3.24	3.01	2.85	2.74	2.66	2.59	2.54	2.49	2.42	2.35	2.28	2.24	2.19	2.15	2.11	2.06	2.01
17	4.45	3.59	3.20	2.96	2.81	2.70	2.61	2.55	2.49	2.45	2.38	2.31	2.23	2.19	2.15	2.10	2.06	2.01	1.96
18	4.41	3.55	3.16	2.93	2.77	2.66	2.58	2.51	2.46	2.41	2.34	2.27	2.19	2.15	2.11	2.06	2.02	1.97	1.92
19	4.38	3.52	3.13	2.90	2.74	2.63	2.54	2.48	2.42	2.38	2.31	2.23	2.16	2.11	2.07	2.03	1.98	1.93	1.88
20	4.35	3.49	3.10	2.87	2.71	2.60	2.51	2.45	2.39	2.35	2.28	2.20	2.12	2.08	2.04	1.99	1.95	1.90	1.84
21	4.32	3.47	3.07	2.84	2.68	2.57	2.49	2.42	2.37	2.32	2.25	2.18	2.10	2.05	2.01	1.96	1.92	1.87	1.81
22	4.30	3.44	3.05	2.82	2.66	2.55	2.46	2.40	2.34	2.30	2.23	2.15	2.07	2.03	1.98	1.94	1.89	1.84	1.78
23	4.28	3.42	3.03	2.80	2.64	2.53	2.44	2.37	2.32	2.27	2.20	2.13	2.05	2.01	1.96	1.91	1.86	1.81	1.76
24	4.26	3.40	3.01	2.78	2.62	2.51	2.42	2.36	2.30	2.25	2.18	2.11	2.03	1.98	1.94	1.89	1.84	1.79	1.73
25	4.24	3.39	2.99	2.76	2.60	2.49	2.40	2.34	2.28	2.24	2.16	2.09	2.01	1.96	1.92	1.87	1.82	1.77	1.71
26	4.23	3.37	2.98	2.74	2.59	2.47	2.39	2.32	2.27	2.22	2.15	2.07	1.99	1.95	1.90	1.85	1.80	1.75	1.69
27	4.21	3.35	2.96	2.73	2.57	2.46	2.37	2.31	2.25	2.20	2.13	2.06	1.97	1.93	1.88	1.84	1.79	1.73	1.67
28	4.20	3.34	2.95	2.71	2.56	2.45	2.36	2.29	2.24	2.19	2.12	2.04	1.96	1.91	1.87	1.82	1.77	1.71	1.65
29	4.18	3.33	2.93	2.70	2.55	2.43	2.35	2.28	2.22	2.18	2.10	2.03	1.94	1.90	1.85	1.81	1.75	1.70	1.64
30	4.17	3.32	2.92	2.69	2.53	2.42	2.33	2.27	2.21	2.16	2.09	2.01	1.93	1.89	1.84	1.79	1.74	1.68	1.62
40	4.08	3.23	2.84	2.61	2.45	2.34	2.25	2.18	2.12	2.08	2.00	1.92	1.84	1.79	1.74	1.69	1.64	1.58	1.51
60	4.00	3.15	2.76	2.53	2.37	2.25	2.17	2.10	2.03	1.99	1.92	1.84	1.75	1.70	1.65	1.59	1.53	1.47	1.39
120	3.92	3.07	2.68	2.45	2.29	2.17	2.09	2.02	1.96	1.91	1.83	1.75	1.66	1.61	1.55	1.50	1.43	1.35	1.25
∞	3.84	3.00	2.60	2.37	2.21	2.10	2.01	1.94	1.88	1.83	1.75	1.67	1.57	1.52	1.46	1.39	1.32	1.22	1.00

(continued)

413

Table IV (*continued*)
Upper 2.5% Points

v_2 \ v_1	1	2	3	4	5	6	7	8	9	10	12	15	20	24	30	40	60	120	∞
1	647.8	799.5	864.2	899.6	921.8	937.1	948.2	956.7	963.3	968.6	976.7	984.9	993.1	997.2	1001	1006	1010	1014	1018
2	38.51	39.00	39.17	39.25	39.30	39.33	39.36	39.37	39.39	39.40	39.41	39.43	39.45	39.46	39.46	39.47	39.48	39.49	39.50
3	17.44	16.04	15.44	15.10	14.88	14.73	14.62	14.54	14.47	14.42	14.34	14.25	14.17	14.12	14.08	14.04	13.99	13.95	13.90
4	12.22	10.65	9.98	9.60	9.36	9.20	9.07	8.98	8.90	8.84	8.75	8.66	8.56	8.51	8.46	8.41	8.36	8.31	8.26
5	10.01	8.43	7.76	7.39	7.15	6.98	6.85	6.76	6.68	6.62	6.52	6.43	6.33	6.28	6.23	6.18	6.12	6.07	6.02
6	8.81	7.26	6.60	6.23	5.99	5.82	5.70	5.60	5.52	5.46	5.37	5.27	5.17	5.12	5.07	5.01	4.96	4.90	4.85
7	8.07	6.54	5.89	5.52	5.29	5.21	4.99	4.90	4.82	4.76	4.67	4.57	4.47	4.42	4.36	4.31	4.25	4.20	4.14
8	7.57	6.06	5.42	5.05	4.82	4.65	4.53	4.43	4.36	4.30	4.20	4.10	4.00	3.95	3.89	3.84	3.78	3.73	3.67
9	7.21	5.71	5.08	4.72	4.48	4.32	4.20	4.10	4.03	3.96	3.87	3.77	3.67	3.61	3.56	3.51	3.45	3.39	3.33
10	6.94	5.46	4.83	4.47	4.24	4.07	3.95	3.85	3.78	3.72	3.62	3.52	3.42	3.37	3.31	3.26	3.20	3.14	3.08
11	6.72	5.26	4.63	4.28	4.04	3.88	3.76	3.66	3.59	3.53	3.43	3.33	3.23	3.17	3.12	3.06	3.00	2.94	2.88
12	6.55	5.10	4.47	4.12	3.89	3.73	3.61	3.51	3.44	3.37	3.28	3.18	3.07	3.02	2.96	2.91	2.85	2.79	2.72
13	6.41	4.97	4.35	4.00	3.77	3.60	3.48	3.39	3.31	3.25	3.15	3.05	2.95	2.89	2.84	2.78	2.72	2.66	2.60
14	6.30	4.86	4.24	3.89	3.66	3.50	3.38	3.29	3.21	3.15	3.05	2.95	2.84	2.79	2.73	2.67	2.61	2.55	2.49
15	6.20	4.77	4.15	3.80	3.58	3.41	3.29	3.20	3.12	3.06	2.96	2.86	2.76	2.70	2.64	2.59	2.52	2.46	2.40
16	6.12	4.69	4.08	3.73	3.50	3.34	3.22	3.12	3.05	2.99	2.89	2.79	2.68	2.63	2.57	2.51	2.45	2.38	2.32
17	6.04	4.62	4.01	3.66	3.44	3.28	3.16	3.06	2.98	2.92	2.82	2.72	2.62	2.56	2.50	2.44	2.38	2.32	2.25
18	5.98	4.56	3.95	3.61	3.38	3.22	3.10	3.01	2.93	2.87	2.77	2.67	2.56	2.50	2.44	2.38	2.32	2.26	2.19
19	5.92	4.51	3.90	3.56	3.33	3.17	3.05	2.96	2.88	2.82	2.72	2.62	2.51	2.45	2.39	2.33	2.27	2.20	2.13
20	5.87	4.46	3.86	3.51	3.29	3.13	3.01	2.91	2.84	2.77	2.68	2.57	2.46	2.41	2.35	2.29	2.22	2.16	2.09
21	5.83	4.42	3.82	3.48	3.25	3.09	2.97	2.87	2.80	2.73	2.64	2.53	2.42	2.37	2.31	2.25	2.18	2.11	2.04
22	5.79	4.38	3.78	3.44	3.22	3.05	2.93	2.84	2.76	2.70	2.60	2.50	2.39	2.33	2.27	2.21	2.14	2.08	2.00
23	5.75	4.35	3.75	3.41	3.18	3.02	2.90	2.81	2.73	2.67	2.57	2.47	2.36	2.30	2.24	2.18	2.11	2.04	1.97
24	5.72	4.32	3.72	3.38	3.15	2.99	2.87	2.78	2.70	2.64	2.54	2.44	2.33	2.27	2.21	2.15	2.08	2.01	1.94
25	5.69	4.29	3.69	3.35	3.13	2.97	2.85	2.75	2.68	2.61	2.51	2.41	2.30	2.24	2.18	2.12	2.05	1.98	1.91
26	5.66	4.27	3.67	3.33	3.10	2.94	2.82	2.73	2.65	2.59	2.49	2.39	2.28	2.22	2.16	2.09	2.03	1.95	1.88
27	5.63	4.24	3.65	3.31	3.08	2.92	2.80	2.71	2.63	2.57	2.47	2.36	2.25	2.19	2.13	2.07	2.00	1.93	1.85
28	5.61	4.22	3.63	3.29	3.06	2.90	2.78	2.69	2.61	2.55	2.45	2.34	2.23	2.17	2.11	2.05	1.98	1.91	1.83
29	5.59	4.20	3.61	3.27	3.04	2.88	2.76	2.67	2.59	2.53	2.43	2.32	2.21	2.15	2.09	2.03	1.96	1.89	1.81
30	5.57	4.18	3.59	3.25	3.03	2.87	2.75	2.65	2.57	2.51	2.41	2.31	2.20	2.14	2.07	2.01	1.94	1.87	1.79
40	5.42	4.05	3.46	3.13	2.90	2.74	2.62	2.53	2.45	2.39	2.29	2.18	2.07	2.01	1.94	1.88	1.80	1.72	1.64
60	5.29	3.93	3.34	3.01	2.79	2.63	2.51	2.41	2.33	2.27	2.17	2.06	1.94	1.88	1.82	1.74	1.67	1.58	1.48
120	5.15	3.80	3.23	2.89	2.67	2.52	2.39	2.30	2.22	2.16	2.05	1.94	1.82	1.76	1.69	1.61	1.53	1.43	1.31
∞	5.02	3.69	3.12	2.79	2.57	2.41	2.29	2.19	2.11	2.05	1.94	1.83	1.71	1.64	1.57	1.48	1.39	1.27	1.00

Upper 1% Points

$\nu_2 \backslash \nu_1$	1	2	3	4	5	6	7	8	9	10	12	15	20	24	30	40	60	120	∞
1	4052	4999.5	5403	5625	5764	5859	5928	5982	6022	6056	6106	6157	6209	6235	6261	6287	6313	6339	6366
2	98.50	99.00	99.17	99.25	99.30	99.33	99.36	99.37	99.39	99.40	99.42	99.43	99.45	99.46	99.47	99.47	99.48	99.49	99.50
3	34.12	30.82	29.46	28.71	28.24	27.91	27.67	27.49	27.35	27.23	27.05	26.87	26.69	26.60	26.50	26.41	26.32	26.22	26.13
4	21.20	18.00	16.69	15.98	15.52	15.21	14.98	14.80	14.66	14.55	14.37	14.20	14.02	13.93	13.84	13.75	13.65	13.56	13.46
5	16.26	13.27	12.06	11.39	10.97	10.67	10.46	10.29	10.16	10.05	9.89	9.72	9.55	9.47	9.38	9.29	9.20	9.11	9.02
6	13.75	10.92	9.78	9.15	8.75	8.47	8.26	8.10	7.98	7.87	7.72	7.56	7.40	7.31	7.23	7.14	7.06	6.97	6.88
7	12.25	9.55	8.45	7.85	7.46	7.19	6.99	6.84	6.72	6.62	6.47	6.31	6.16	6.07	5.99	5.91	5.82	5.74	5.65
8	11.26	8.65	7.59	7.01	6.63	6.37	6.18	6.03	5.91	5.81	5.67	5.52	5.36	5.28	5.20	5.12	5.03	4.95	4.86
9	10.56	8.02	6.99	6.42	6.06	5.80	5.61	5.47	5.35	5.26	5.11	4.96	4.81	4.73	4.65	4.57	4.48	4.40	4.31
10	10.04	7.56	6.55	5.99	5.64	5.39	5.20	5.06	4.94	4.85	4.71	4.56	4.41	4.33	4.25	4.17	4.08	4.00	3.91
11	9.65	7.21	6.22	5.67	5.32	5.07	4.89	4.74	4.63	4.54	4.40	4.25	4.10	4.02	3.94	3.86	3.78	3.69	3.60
12	9.33	6.93	5.95	5.41	5.06	4.82	4.64	4.50	4.39	4.30	4.16	4.01	3.86	3.78	3.70	3.62	3.54	3.45	3.36
13	9.07	6.70	5.74	5.21	4.86	4.62	4.44	4.30	4.19	4.10	3.96	3.82	3.66	3.59	3.51	3.43	3.34	3.25	3.17
14	8.86	6.51	5.56	5.04	4.69	4.46	4.28	4.14	4.03	3.94	3.80	3.66	3.51	3.43	3.35	3.27	3.18	3.09	3.00
15	8.68	6.36	5.42	4.89	4.56	4.32	4.14	4.00	3.89	3.80	3.67	3.52	3.37	3.29	3.21	3.13	3.05	2.96	2.87
16	8.53	6.23	5.29	4.77	4.44	4.20	4.03	3.89	3.78	3.69	3.55	3.41	3.26	3.18	3.10	3.02	2.93	2.84	2.75
17	8.40	6.11	5.18	4.67	4.34	4.10	3.93	3.79	3.68	3.59	3.46	3.31	3.16	3.08	3.00	2.92	2.83	2.75	2.65
18	8.29	6.01	5.09	4.58	4.25	4.01	3.84	3.71	3.60	3.51	3.37	3.23	3.08	3.00	2.92	2.84	2.75	2.66	2.57
19	8.18	5.93	5.01	4.50	4.17	3.94	3.77	3.63	3.52	3.43	3.30	3.15	3.00	2.92	2.84	2.76	2.67	2.58	2.49
20	8.10	5.85	4.94	4.43	4.10	3.87	3.70	3.56	3.46	3.37	3.23	3.09	2.94	2.86	2.78	2.69	2.61	2.52	2.42
21	8.02	5.78	4.87	4.37	4.04	3.81	3.64	3.51	3.40	3.31	3.17	3.03	2.88	2.80	2.72	2.64	2.55	2.46	2.36
22	7.95	5.72	4.82	4.31	3.99	3.76	3.59	3.45	3.35	3.26	3.12	2.98	2.83	2.75	2.67	2.58	2.50	2.40	2.31
23	7.88	5.66	4.76	4.26	3.94	3.71	3.54	3.41	3.30	3.21	3.07	2.93	2.78	2.70	2.62	2.54	2.45	2.35	2.26
24	7.82	5.61	4.72	4.22	3.90	3.67	3.50	3.36	3.26	3.17	3.03	2.89	2.74	2.66	2.58	2.49	2.40	2.31	2.21
25	7.77	5.57	4.68	4.18	3.85	3.63	3.46	3.32	3.22	3.13	2.99	2.85	2.70	2.62	2.54	2.45	2.36	2.27	2.17
26	7.72	5.53	4.64	4.14	3.82	3.59	3.42	3.29	3.18	3.09	2.96	2.81	2.66	2.58	2.50	2.42	2.33	2.23	2.13
27	7.68	5.49	4.60	4.11	3.78	3.56	3.39	3.26	3.15	3.06	2.93	2.78	2.63	2.55	2.47	2.38	2.29	2.20	2.10
28	7.64	5.45	4.57	4.07	3.75	3.53	3.36	3.23	3.12	3.03	2.90	2.75	2.60	2.52	2.44	2.35	2.26	2.17	2.06
29	7.60	5.42	4.54	4.04	3.73	3.50	3.33	3.20	3.09	3.00	2.87	2.73	2.57	2.49	2.41	2.33	2.23	2.14	2.03
30	7.56	5.39	4.51	4.02	3.70	3.47	3.30	3.17	3.07	2.98	2.84	2.70	2.55	2.47	2.39	2.30	2.21	2.11	2.01
40	7.31	5.18	4.31	3.83	3.51	3.29	3.12	2.99	2.89	2.80	2.66	2.52	2.37	2.29	2.20	2.11	2.02	1.92	1.80
60	7.08	4.98	4.13	3.65	3.34	3.12	2.95	2.82	2.72	2.63	2.50	2.35	2.20	2.12	2.03	1.94	1.84	1.73	1.60
120	6.85	4.79	3.95	3.48	3.17	2.96	2.79	2.66	2.56	2.47	2.34	2.19	2.03	1.95	1.86	1.76	1.66	1.53	1.38
∞	6.63	4.61	3.78	3.32	3.02	2.80	2.64	2.51	2.41	2.32	2.18	2.04	1.88	1.79	1.70	1.59	1.47	1.32	1.00

This table is abridged from Table 18 of the *Biometrika Tables for Statisticians*, Vol. 1 (1st ed.), edited by E. S. Pearson and H. O. Hartley. Reproduced with the kind permission of E. S. Pearson and the trustees of *Biometrika*.

INDEX